St. Maximilian ------

The Collected Essays of Peter Damian Fehlner, OFM Conv.

Volume 1:
Marian Metaphysics

Volume 2:
Systematic Mariology

Volume 3:
Franciscan Mariology—Francis, Clare, and Bonaventure

Volume 4:
Bonaventure, John Duns Scotus, and the Franciscan Tradition

Volume 5:
Ecclesiology and the Franciscan Charism

Volume 6:
St. Maximilian Kolbe

Volume 7:
Theology of Creation

Volume 8:
Studies Systematic and Critical

St. Maximilian Kolbe

The Collected Essays of Peter Damian Fehlner, OFM Conv:
Volume 6

Peter Damian Fehlner,
OFM Conv.

EDITED BY
J. Isaac Goff

INTRODUCTION BY
Louis Maximilian Smith,
OFM Conv.

WIPF & STOCK · Eugene, Oregon

ST. MAXIMILIAN KOLBE
Collected Essays of Peter Damian Fehlner, OFM Conv: Volume 6

Wipf & Stock
An Imprint of Wipf and Stock Publishers
199 W. 8th Ave., Suite 3
Eugene, OR 97401

www.wipfandstock.com

PAPERBACK ISBN: 978-1-5326-6392-5
HARDCOVER ISBN: 978-1-5326-6393-2
EBOOK ISBN: 978-1-5326-6394-9

10/11/23

Contents

Permissions

The publisher and editor wish to thank the following for permission to reuse previously published material:

Chapter 1: "Total Consecration, Baptism and the Franciscan Ideal," originally appeared as "Consacrazione totale, battesimo e ideale francescano," in *Miles Immaculatae* (1982) 60–92.

Chapter 2: "A Thesis of St. Maximilian Concerning St. Francis and the Immaculate in the Light of Recent Research," originally appeared as "Una tesi di S. Massimiliano su S. Francesco e l'Immacolata alla luce della ricerca recente," in *Miles Immaculatae* 20 (1984) 165–86.

Chapter 3: The Immaculate and the Mystery of the Trinity in the Thought of St. Maximilian Kolbe," originally appeared in *Miscellanea Francescana* 85 (1985) 382–416.

Chapter 4: "Complementum Ss. Trinitatis," originally appeared in *Miles Immaculatae* 21 (1985) 177–204.

Chapter 5: "Niepokalanów in the Counsels of the Immaculate," originally appeared in *Miles Immaculatae* 21 (1985) 309–81.

Chapter 6: "*Vertex Creationis*: St. Maximilian and Evolution," originally appeared in *Miles Immaculatae* 21 (1985) 236–59.

Chapter 8: "The Immaculate and the Extraordinary Synod," originally appeared in *Miles Immaculatae* (1985) 1–4.

Chapter 9: "Mother of the Redeemer and *Redemptoris Mater*," originally appeared as "Madre del Redentore i Redemptoris Mater," in *Miles Immaculatae* 23 (1987) 223–8.

Chapter 10: "A Proposal," originally appeared in *Miles Immaculatae* 24 (1988) 16–18.

Chapter 11: "Marian Geography of Faith: The Kolbean Perspective," originally appeared as "Geografia mariana della fide prospettive Kolbiane," in *Miles Immaculatae* 24 (1988) 259–63.

Chapter 12: "Marian Slavery: Slavery of Love," originally appeared in *Miles Immaculatae* 24 (1988) 10–15.

Chapter 13: "The Other Page," originally appeared in *Miles Immaculatae* 24 (1988) 512–31.

Chapter 14: The Immaculate Conception: "Outer Limits of Love," originally appeared in *Miles Immaculatae* 25 (1989) 537–48.

Chapter 15: "Mulieres Dignitatem," originally appeared in *Miles Immaculatae* 25 (1989) 1–9.

Chapter 16: "Marian Doctrine and Devotion: A Kolbean Perspective," originally appeared in *De cultu mariano saeculis XIX–XX*, 303–21(Rome: Pontificia Academia Mariana Internationalis, 1991).

Abbreviations

1, 2 Cel.   Thomas of Celano. *S. Francisci Assisiensis Vita et Miracula.* Edited by Eduardus Alenconiensis. Rome: Desclée, Lefebvre, 1906.

AAS   *Acta Apostolicae Sedis*

Brev.   Bonaventure. *Breviloquium.* In vol. 5 of Opera Omnia, 201–91. Florence: Ad Claras Aquas, 1891.

Chr. mag.   Bonaventure. *Christus unus omnium magister.* In vol. 5 of Opera Omnia, 567–79. Florence: Ad Claras Aquas, 1891.

Comm. Luc.   Bonaventure. *Commentarius in evangelium S. Lucae.* Vol. 7 of Opera Omnia. Florence: Ad Claras Aquas, 1895.

De don. Spir.   Bonaventure. *Collationes de septem donis Spiritus Sancti.* In vol. 5 of Opera Omnia, 457–503. Florence: Ad Claras Aquas, 1891.

DH   Heinrich Denzinger, Peter Hünnermann, and Robert Fastiggi, eds. *Compendium of Creeds, Definitions, and Declarations on Matters of Faith and Morals.* San Francisco: Ignatius, 2012.

Hex.   Bonaventure. *Collationes in Hexaëmeron.* In vol. 5 of Opera Omnia, 329–454. Florence: Ad Claras Aquas, 1891.

I, II, III, IV Sent.   Bonaventure. *Commentarius in IV libros Sententiarum.* In vols. 1–4 of Opera Omnia. Florence: Ad Claras Aquas, 1882–89.

Itin.   Bonaventure. *Itinerarium mentis in Deum.* In vol. 5 of Opera Omnia, 295–313. Florence: Ad Claras Aquas, 1891.

Leg. maj.	Bonaventure. *Legenda maior.* In vol. 8 of Opera Omnia, 504–564. Florence: Ad Claras Aquas, 1898.
Ord. I, II, III, IV.	John Duns Scotus. *Doctoris Subtilis et Mariani Ioannis Duns Scoti Ordinis Fratrum Minorum opera omnia,* 14 vols. Edited by Charles Balic, Barnaba Hechich, et al. Rome: Typis Vaticanis, 1950–2013.
ST	Thomas Aquinas. *Summa Theologiae.* Opera Omnia. Vols. 4–12. Rome: Typographia Polyglotta S.C. de Propaganda Fide, 1888–1903.
WK	Maximilian Kolbe. *The Writings of St. Maximilian Maria Kolbe,* 2 vols. Florence: Nerbini International, 2016.

Abbreviations for Distinctions in Individual Texts

a.	articulus	fm.	fundamentum
ad	ad oppositum	n.	numerus
au.	articulus unicus	opp.	oppositum
c.	capitulum	prol.	prologus
col.	collatio	prooem.	prooemium
con.	contra	q.	quaestio
d.	distinctio	resp.	respondeo

Introduction

Fr. Peter Damian Fehlner: A Contemporary Prophet in the Footsteps of St. Maximilian M. Kolbe

FR. LOUIS MAXIMILIAN SMITH, OFMCONV.

Introduction

ANY QUEST TO UNDERSTAND the significance of the Kolbean thought of Fr. Peter Damian Fehlner, OFM Conventual, presents a daunting challenge to the scholar and practitioner alike. One must not suppose that the majority of Fehlner's Kolbean contributions extend mostly over about a ten-year period, the time span covered by most of the articles republished in this volume. Nor do these contents come anywhere close to comprising a majority of the material.

First, we have to take into account the fact that Fehlner prepared two major book-length studies on Kolbe, which expands the source material considerably. Next, when we increase our range of study to consider Kolbean-related themes treated in his other writings, we are talking about the addition of an enormous volume of other material covering four decades. Finally, if we seek to better understand the origins of what I call Fehlner's "Kolbean doctrine," we'll need to broaden our horizons even more. Our cause would be greatly helped if we delve more deeply into the theology and metaphysics of St. Bonaventure and Bl. John Duns Scotus, the two towering figures in the Franciscan intellectual tradition, because they are the ones upon whom Fehlner and Kolbe greatly depend. It will go even better for us if we come to the realization that these two great figures do not oppose one another in their thought, as even many Franciscan scholars have supposed.

There is, of course, much need for such serious and accurate study—which, however, the Franciscan masters remind us, needs to be carried out in a spirit of prayer and devotion. Fehlner and Kolbe would ask us: Why not go to the feet of the Virgin Mary, mother and teacher of the apostles, of theologians, and of all who sincerely wish to become true disciples of her Son, Jesus Christ? That is what they did. Or, better, Our Lady looked upon them with love, and they decided to receive what she wanted to give them and to follow her plan.

She is the one who imparted the treasures of wisdom to St. Maximilian Kolbe, Martyr of Charity, and to Fr. Peter Damian Fehlner, who was the destined recipient of this tradition. Our Lady did this not only for their sake, but for ours as well—indeed for the whole church. She is the one who will help us understand what she is trying to tell us through them. And, if we believe what St. Maximilian Kolbe and Fr. Peter Damian Fehlner have to say, we need to sit up and pay close attention. Our Lady is looking upon us with love, and she has a plan for us as well—a Marian itinerary in this "age of Mary and the Holy Spirit" that leads to God. "It is not so much a question of what place Mary has in our lives," Fehlner states succinctly, "as what place we occupy in hers that is the starting point of any discussion."[1]

There is no doubt that Fehlner is to be ranked among the foremost of Kolbean scholars who have so far appeared on the scene. As lengthy as this introductory essay is, we can only begin to scratch the surface regarding his contribution and encourage the interested reader to explore further what Fehlner has to offer. Because Fehlner's Kolbean teaching involves an itinerary which is our common heritage, I have felt it necessary to include a lengthy exposition, in part one of this essay, on the significance of that Marian itinerary for Fehlner. Then we will be in a better position, in part two, to expound Fehlner's Kolbean doctrine.

Part One: Peter Damian Fehlner's Marian Itinerary: The "Golden Thread"

The Kolbean Inspiration

Few Catholic saints have left such a striking impression on the modern mind, Catholic and non-Catholic alike, as St. Maximilian M. Kolbe, the famed Martyr of Charity who, in 1941, in an act of heroic charity, offered his life in place of a condemned prisoner, Franciszek Gajowniczek, in the concentration camp at Auschwitz. Kolbe's heroic virtue was definitively affirmed not long afterward when Pope St. Paul VI beatified him in 1971, declaring him

---

1. Fehlner, "Mary in the Franciscan" *CE* 3, chapter 5.

a confessor of the faith. Eleven years later, in 1982, when he was canonized a saint, Pope John Paul II additionally declared him a martyr.

This twofold declaration of St. Maximilian's sanctity corresponds to the two crowns, one white and the other red, the Virgin Mary offered him in the celebrated vision of his childhood. As is well documented, the life of Kolbe from that point forward bore this ineffaceable Marian stamp. St. Maximilian has been ranked alongside St. Louis Grignion de Montfort as among the greatest Marian saints of our times. As the two Cities of the Immaculate, the Militia of the Immaculate (M.I.) he co-founded with six other Conventual Franciscan friars in 1917, and the extraordinary mass media apostolate he founded and directed in the 1920s and 1930s all illustrate, perhaps no one spent himself more completely in this life in service of the Mother of God.

Paul VI affirmed the prophetic character of Kolbe's life and spirituality on the occasion of his beatification:

> The original quality of Blessed Kolbe's devotion, of his "hyperdulia" to Mary, is the importance he attributes to it with regard to the present needs of the church, the efficacy of her prophecy about the glory of the Lord and the vindication of the humble, the power of her intercession, the splendor of her exemplariness, the presence of her maternal charity. The Council confirmed us in these certainties, and now from heaven Father Kolbe is teaching us and helping us to meditate upon them and live them.[2]

Despite such affirmations by Paul VI and John Paul II, the status of Kolbe as a contemporary prophet and especially as a theologian of the highest caliber remains largely unfathomed. Part of the reason is attributable to the fact that Kolbe did not leave behind a completed systematic work either of a devotional or of a speculative nature. It was in his mind to write a Mariology which would be a "dogmatic theology, but [written] in popular style, animated, vivacious."[3] This project of his was interrupted by his arrest and subsequent martyrdom. What has survived is a series of his dictations intended as material for such a projected book, as well as various correspondence, articles, conferences and other notes of his.[4] It is from these sources that the diligent

2. Paul VI, "Homily of Beatification," October 17, 1971.

3. These were the words of St. Maximilian's brother, Fr. Alphonse, who, like St. Maximilian, had become a Conventual Franciscan friar. Reported by Domanski, "La genesi," 255.

4. The collected works of St. Maximilian Kolbe are available in English in two volumes, *The Writings*. My citations of Kolbe's writings in this introduction are taken from this work; the reference format is the prefix *WK* followed by the number of the writing in the volume.

researcher must apprehend the Marian theology and spirituality of St. Maximilian. One finds therein, however, a unified and coherent vision, which on one occasion the saint summed up in this way when describing the M.I.: "a global vision of Catholic life in a new form, consisting in the bond with the Immaculata, our universal mediatrix before Jesus."[5]

Perusing the various Kolbean fonts, one encounters a number of striking phrases the saint employed to describe the special relationship of Mary with the Holy Trinity, on the one hand, and with the community of believers comprising the mystical body of Christ, on the other. The ramifications for the fields of Trinitarian theology and ecclesiology—indeed, all of theology—are not few. The saint's insights, however, have not been received with universal approbation, and indeed many have refused to regard the Martyr of Charity as a theologian in any real sense.[6] Moreover, as is well documented, the saint himself, though always supported by his superiors, faced serious opposition to the practical expression of this vision as contained in the original statutes of the M.I. and as put into action in the Cities of the Immaculate. As we shall see, Fehlner's voice has been among the foremost to uphold the theological and prophetic character of St. Maximilian's thought.

Among the first scholars to recognize and promote the significance of St. Maximilian's insights was one who knew St. Maximilian personally. Fr. Jerzy Domanski took his first steps as a Conventual Franciscan friar in the community of Niepokalanów, the City of the Immaculate in Poland, in the 1930s, when St. Maximilian was guardian (superior) of the community. Fr. Domanski went on to himself become guardian of the same community some years after the saint's martyrdom. He also edited the Polish language publication, *Rycerz Niepokalanej* ("Knight of the Immaculate"), which St. Maximilian founded and which was widely circulated in Poland, and *Miles Immaculatae*, a periodical for clergy also founded by St. Maximilian which is still being published today. From the 1950s onward, Domanski published a number of useful studies on Kolbean thought, including a 1984 Italian language study which is foundational for understanding the principles underlying the saint's Mariology, especially as it is situated within the Franciscan tradition.[7]

Fehlner, who entered the Conventual Franciscan friars in the United States in the 1940s, later crossed paths with Domanski and came to know him well; he was assistant editor of *Miles Immaculatae* under Domanski in

5. *WK* 1220.

6. See Fehlner, *Theologian of Auschwitz*, 23–7; Fehlner, *Kolbe . . . Pneumatologist*, 13–21.

7. Domanski, "La genesi," 246–76.

1983 and 1984, before succeeding him as editor from 1985 through 1989. In this way, Fehlner was accorded direct access to the Kolbean patrimony of which Domanski was the blessed recipient.

Origins of Fehlner's Kolbean Vision: Charity at the Heart of the Church

Endowed with a uniquely gifted intellect, during his years of formation as a religious and of higher studies, Fehlner acquired a remarkable breadth, depth and subtlety of knowledge that spanned and plumbed the depths of the church's various theological and philosophical traditions, from the patristic era all the way up to modernity. This singular grasp of the church's intellectual patrimony permitted Fehlner to accurately assess the various currents of thought which arose in modernity and to perceive how the Holy Spirit has been at work in the church before, during and after the Second Vatican Council. It also enabled him to recognize the unique gifts St. Maximilian possessed as a theologian and spiritual master, and later to authoritatively respond to the various criticisms leveled against Kolbean thought.

What can be said about Fehlner's mastery of the church's spiritual and theological patrimony as a whole is even more true with regard to the Franciscan tradition. Completing his higher studies at the Seraphicum in Rome in the 1950s, Fr. Peter Damian walked the same hallowed grounds as his predecessor, St. Maximilian, did four decades earlier, breathing in the same Franciscan spirit. "A modern heir to the Franciscan intellectual tradition," Fehlner "embodies what the Seraphic and Subtle Doctors [St. Bonaventure and Bl. John Duns Scotus] proffered." Perhaps no contemporary scholar "memorized and stored the Bonaventurian opus as profoundly as Fr. Peter Damian."[8]

St. Bonaventure is the one who, having inherited the seraphic mantle from St. Francis of Assisi, employed the full weight of his considerable mystical and speculative gifts to ponder the meaning of the vocation of St. Francis for the church.[9] It is epitomized by two of the Seraphic Father's encounters with the crucified Christ: (1) in the Church of San Damiano in 1206: "Francis, go and repair my house which, as you see, is all being destroyed";[10] and (2) at La Verna, eighteen years later, in 1224, when he received the stigmata,

8. McCurry, "Homage, xii.

9. The Seraphic Doctor himself describes how, during a celebrated retreat in 1259, he received enlightenment concerning the mystical experience of St. Francis at La Verna in 1224, when he received the stigmata. See Bonaventure, *Itin.*, prologue.

10. Bonaventure, *Leg. mag.*, c. 2, *Francis of Assisi*, 536.

an exterior seal confirming his interior conformity to our crucified Savior. For Bonaventure, the "repairing" is, first of all, interior, involving the human heart; but it has a fundamentally ecclesial character, at the heart of which is charity—the very charity originating in the Trinity which is extended into creation through the mediation of Jesus Christ.

This deep Bonaventurian imprint is evident in Fehlner's doctoral dissertation, *The Role of Charity in the Ecclesiology of St. Bonaventure*, which he defended in 1959 and published in 1965. Already in this work, Fehlner demonstrates his ability to draw out and build upon a theme not systematized but certainly evident and consistently expressed throughout Bonaventure's writings.[11]

The tenor of Fehlner's dissertation reflects his deep interest, "from his first studies in philosophy and theology," in questions regarding the mystery "of the Holy Spirit and of that Spirit in the economy of salvation."[12] Above all, as he explained in the preface of his dissertation, he was driven by "a deeply rooted, but as yet unarticulated conviction of the significance of the Franciscan spirit for theology and of the possibilities for renewal and progress in theology in our days through a study and application of the Franciscan theological approach in its chief representatives—St. Bonaventure and John Duns Scotus. . . ."[13] In a word, after the manner of Bonaventure, he was seeking to understand the meaning and implications of the command the Lord gave to St. Francis—"rebuild my church"—for the present age.

Among the themes present in the dissertation to which Fehlner would frequently return are the following: (1) the extension of the divine communion of love to creation, in the form of an *exitus-reditus*, realized in the heart of Church; (2) the Bonaventurian exemplary causality; (3) the complementarity of the missions of the Son and the Holy Spirit; (4) the union of creature and Creator through conformity of wills; (5) the unique relationship between the Virgin Mary and the Holy Trinity, which is "fundamentally a union of charity";[14] and (6) the maternal mediation of Mary in regard to the work of the Holy Spirit in the church.[15] Also

---

11. Time and again Fehlner demonstrated this rarefied ability to recognize patterns of thought escaping the attention of most other theologians. This gift is evident especially in his ability to recognize parallels of thought between Bl. John Duns Scotus and St. John Henry Newman, and—more importantly for the present volume—the Franciscan theological and metaphysical underpinnings of Kolbean thought.

12. Fehlner, "Marian Charismatic Contemplation," *CE* 5, chapter 14.

13. Fehlner, *Role of Charity*, *CE* 3, part 3.

14. Fehlner, *Role of Charity*, *CE* 3, part 3.

15. In the original dissertation, the Virgin Mary's mediatorial role is mentioned specifically in reference to her exercise "in an altogether unique manner over men

present is the Bonaventurian doctrine of appropriation in reference to the Holy Spirit, who is "the bond of the everlasting communion of the Three [divine Persons], wherever they might be acting or dwelling," and where the outpouring of this divine goodness "is likened to and manifests the mode of procession of the Holy Spirit."[16]

Although Fehlner does not explicitly address Kolbean thought in the original dissertation, the fundamental ideas presented therein remained a constant theme in his later writings, ideas later refined over time by elements of Scotistic thought and given expression through a Kolbean lens.[17] Fehlner's classic Franciscan formation, culminating in the publication of his dissertation, "set the table" for the "Marian plan" which would later enter the scene and definitively serve as his spiritual guide.

The "Marian Plan" Revealed to Fehlner: The "Golden Thread"

This "Marian plan" did not explicitly make an appearance in his writings until 1978 onward, when *ex abrupto* Fehlner composed a series of articles and essays in which he argued that the key to the renewal of Catholic theology and praxis is necessarily rooted in Marian mediation which, in turn, finds its basis in the mystery of the Immaculate Conception. This conviction of his seems to have appeared as a bolt out of the blue. While already present in his dissertation years earlier, the doctrine of Marian mediation (and, with it, the dogma of the Immaculate Conception) had suddenly become the *necessary principle* upon which such a renewal must be based.

This striking shift in his approach is introduced in his first essay dating from this period, "Mary and Theology: Scotus Revisited," written in 1978.[18] For Fr. Edward J. Ondrako, OFM Conventual, "Mary and

---

and angels" of "purifying, illuminating and perfecting." *Role of Charity, CE,* 3, part 3, chapter 3. Marian mediation enjoys a prominent place in the theology of Bonaventure, encapsulated in his expression: "(Maria) Mediatrix est inter nos et Christum, sicut Christus inter nos et Deum," *III Sent.*, d. 3, p. 1, a. 1, q. 2. In his later works, Fr. Peter Damian frequently made reference to the presence of Marian mediation in the works of Bonaventure in his own development of the theme.

16. Fehlner, *Role of Charity, CE* 3, part 3, chapter 3. See Bonaventure, *III Sent.*, d. 4, a.1, q. 1.

17. Shortly before his death, Fehlner made revisions to his original dissertation which drew out how themes present in the dissertation find their expression in Kolbean theology.

18. It was written in 1978 for delivery at the 1979 meeting of the Mariological Society of America. However, it was never published in their journal, *Marian Studies*. It was published privately at the time and then republished in Ondrako, ed., *Newman Scotus*

Theology: Scotus Revisited" is Fehlner's "mystical experience in writing as the *Itinerarium* is for Bonaventure."[19] Ondrako further notes that this essay was the immediate fruit of a month-long retreat taken by Fehlner, which Ondrako views as parallel to the experience of Bonaventure at La Verna in 1259.[20] Fehlner himself alludes to a personal "charismatic conversion experience" in 1978, from which he emerged with a "newly found realization that living and thinking the mystery of the Spirit is inseparable from living and thinking the mystery of Mary Mediatrix, that is, the mystery of the Immaculate Conception created and uncreated," finding expression in "Mary and Theology: Scotus Revisited."[21]

Whatever may have transpired in Fr. Peter Damian's soul, it is hard to avoid the conclusion that Our Lady herself directly intervened at this critical juncture of his life, at a time when he was in the midst of a profound spiritual crisis.[22] The parallel to St. Maximilian's own spiritual itinerary then becomes very compelling, for in the saint's life, too, there are the telltale signs of the hand of Our Lady discreetly but surely guiding him.

In "Mary and Theology: Scotus Revisited," for the first time Fehlner recommends "unconditional devotion or consecration to Mary Immaculate, along the lines of St. Maximilian."[23] In virtue of the Immaculate Conception, Mary is the primary term of the mission of the Holy Spirit, making her not only mother but teacher in the Spirit. "To know her as the Immaculate is to know clearly and distinctly the Spirit as well."[24] Consequently:

> Since Mary . . . is not simply a subordinate or incidental peda-
> gogue, but a primary exponent of the Sacred Page, for the
> church as well as for the Christian, it is the nature of theology
> to be Marian in character, with the tendency of sound theo-
> logical thought to reflect her personal influence as teacher, the
> more it progresses.[25]

Reader, 111–74. Appears in *CE* 1, chapter 1.

19. Private email correspondence with the author, 18 November 2020. Reproduced here with permission.

20. Ondrako, *Rebuild my Church*, c. 1. It was Bonaventure's retreat and mystical experience in 1259 that preceded the production of the *Itinerarium Mentis in Deum*. Placed in this light, "Mary and Theology" may be seen as this journey described by Bonaventure, placed in its Marian context.

21. Fehlner, "Marian Charismatic Contemplation," *CE* 5, chapter 14.

22. Fehlner makes mention of this crisis in another essay, "Marian and Charismatic Movements," *CE* 5, chapter 13.

23. Fehlner, "Mary and Theology," *CE* 1, chapter 1.

24. Fehlner, "Mary and Theology," *CE* 1, chapter 1.

25. Fehlner, "Mary and Theology," *CE* 1, chapter 1. St. Maximilian clearly enunciates

Hence, the basic principle of theology and Christian living is this: *de Maria numquam satis*.[26] To support this thesis, key elements of Scotistic theology and metaphysics, especially univocity of being, the pure perfections, and the doctrine of the absolute primacy of Christ, are incorporated as refinements to the Bonaventurian system of thought. Fehlner neatly summed up his thesis in this way:

> Indeed, the key insight of St. Maximilian's Mariology, the correlation between the procession of the Holy Spirit and the Immaculate Conception, is no more than an explication of a basic dimension of Bonaventure's theology by way of Scotus' theology of the Immaculate Conception, which clarifies both the mediation of Mary and that of the church. The present thesis is but a particular application, on which a great many probabilities converge.[27]

From the standpoint of its application, he would later give a similarly succinct description:

> We may say that the role of charity in the church animating every other dimension of the mystical Body is to make real in all the members the personality of the Immaculate, that is, to make them her property and possession. Without this the Franciscan ideal of "repairing the church" is impossible of attainment.[28]

Fehlner thus retained the same convictions expressed in his dissertation, but his thinking was now recalibrated along the lines of Kolbe, revolving around the principle of the Immaculate Conception.

Just as St. Maximilian viewed the mystery of the Immaculate Conception as the "golden thread" of the Franciscan Order and tradition[29]—a thesis which Fehlner clearly embraced—so I view the same mystery as the "golden thread" constantly present and guiding Fehlner's spiritual and theological itinerary. His whole life up to 1978 is, as it were, a "preparation"; and the period from 1978 onward was an "incorporation," reflected in a life ever more intensely dedicated to the "cause of the Immaculate" and in the vast collection of his Marian writings dating from this period forward.[30]

---

this point in *WK* 1306.

26. Fehlner, "Mary and Theology," *CE* 1, chapter 1.

27. Fehlner, "Mary and Theology," *CE* 1, chapter 1.

28. Fehlner, *Kolbe . . . Pneumatologist*, 153–54.

29. See Kolbe, *WK* 21, *WK* 99, *WK* 486; Fehlner, "Two Testaments," *CE* 6, chapter 18; Fehlner, *Theologian of Auschwitz*, 4, 98.

30. Far from proposing an alternative view to Fr. Ondrako's tripartite division of

The *Hereditas Kolbiana* (Kolbean Heritage)

Fehlner's now total dedication to the "cause of the Immaculate," in the footsteps of Kolbe, was borne out by the steady stream of essays, articles and presentations which began to flow forth from his hand soon after the 1978 essay and continued through 1992. To the articles republished in this volume which date from this period must be added the set of essays dedicated to the place of the Immaculate Conception in the vocation of St. Francis and in the Franciscan Order, because by them Fehlner intended to demonstrate the thesis of St. Maximilian "that St. Francis not only knew and honored the Immaculate as such, but also had consciously and deliberately assigned to his Order as its principal concern Her Cause."[31] Not to be forgotten either is Fehlner's 1986 essay on St. Francis Anthony Fasani (1685–1742), whose Mariology, centered on the mystery of the Immaculate Conception, provides one of the most vivid illustrations of how this immaculatist Fransciscan tradition was handed on and developed over time, down to the day of St. Maximilian.[32]

Some of these writings were of a more speculative character (e.g., "The Immaculate in the Mystery of the Trinity"), others more practical (e.g., his proposal at the 1986 General Chapter of the Conventual Franciscan Friars to wholeheartedly embrace the *Hereditas Kolbiana*). The main vehicles for transmission of these works were *Civitas Immaculatae*, a publication internal to the United States Province of the Conventual Franciscans to which Fehlner belonged in the 1980s; *Miles Immaculatae*, the aforementioned international Kolbean publication, and the international scholarly journal of Franciscan theology, *Miscellanea Francescana*.

On October 1, 1982, the eve of the canonization of St. Maximilian (October 10), there appeared in the *National Catholic Reporter* an article by Peter Hebblethwaite assailing Kolbe's "doubtful" and "unsound"

Fehlner's religious itinerary, which he details in chapter 1 of *Rebuild My Church*, I am suggesting that this golden thread sheds further light on his excellent analysis of what at first sight appears to be a rather complex itinerary, during which Fehlner departed from the Conventual Franciscan Friars in 1993 to become a member of the post-Vatican II religious institute of the Franciscan Friars of the Immaculate, only to return to the Conventual Franciscans shortly before his death in 2016. During this entire period, operating under religious obedience, his Marian output continued unabated, and his core convictions remained unshaken. It is not difficult to discern along the entire way the presence of the steady, guiding hand of Our Lady, whom he, as Kolbe, acknowledged under the banner of the Immaculate Conception.

31. Fehlner, "Thesis of St. Maximilian," *CE* 6, chapter 2.

32. Fehlner, "St. Francis Anthony Fasani," *CE* 3, chapter 8. For an in-depth analysis of this work and its significance, see Ondrako, *Rebuild My Church*, c. 6.

spirituality—in a word, heterodox. He was not the first "doubter" to appear on the scene; Fr. Domanski notes that reservations were expressed by scholars as early as 1953,[33] and many more "doubters" were documented by the time of the First International Congress on the Mariology of St. Maximilian Kolbe in 1984.[34] This particular article served as somewhat of a spur to Fehlner's production during this period. These negative assessments are one reason why his Kolbean writings sometimes exhibit a quasi-apologetic character, which reflects his efforts to defend Kolbe and his theology against what he regarded as baseless or ill-informed criticisms.

Aside from this consideration, we may identify six primary goals Fehlner aimed to realize through dissemination of these works: (1) foster a greater general knowledge of the Kolbean patrimony; (2) illustrate the theological-metaphysical principles, above all Franciscan, upon which Kolbean terminology depends; (3) encourage a deeper study of the same theology and metaphysics; (4) demonstrate the applicability of the Kolbean "global vision of Catholic life" to the present day; (5) insist on this "Marian principle" as the key to realizing a proper sanctification of the intellect in a spirit of prayer and devotion; and (6) advocate for a greater willingness among his Conventual Franciscan confreres to embrace the *Hereditas Kolbiana* as key to renewal of the Franciscan Order.

As Fr. Angelo (Timothy) Geiger has noted, Fr. Peter Damian's "Kolbean apostolate" among his Conventual confreres assumed an increasingly urgent tone during this period. At a 1979 inter-province conference of the Conventuals, holding up Kolbe as an example of the fruit of an authentic renewal of religious life, Fehlner observes that the saint's interpretation of the Franciscan intellectual and theological tradition by way of his program of total consecration and service to the Immaculate "may well provide the providential starting point" for assessing the role of Conventual Franciscanism in modernity.[35] But with time, he arrived at "an ever more explicit conclusion that the Kolbean heritage was both the solution to the renewal of Franciscan religious life in obedience to the Council and the recovery of the greatest features of the Conventual tradition."[36] By the time of his 1986 address to the Extraordinary General Chapter of the Conventual Franciscan Friars,[37] it had become his unshakeable conviction that the "cause of

33. Domanski, "La genesi," 259.

34. Fehlner, *Kolbe . . . Pneumatologist*, 23–24. See Piacentini, "Analisi degli scritti," 327–81.

35. Fehlner, "Community, Prayer and Apostolates," *CE* 5, chapter 8.

36. Geiger, "'Counsels of the Immaculate,'" 66.

37. Fehlner, "Hereditas Kolbiana," *CE* 6, chapter 7. His essay, "Two Testaments," published the previous year, in some ways lays the groundwork for his address to the

the Immaculate," as Kolbe describes it, defines the very *raison d'être* of the
Franciscan Order, is its patrimony, and is the only sound basis upon which
a true renewal of the Order can be effected.

Fehlner's 1986 address is his clarion call. The Immaculate Conception
"historically and spiritually is the 'Franciscan thesis.'"[38] St. Francis knew Our
Lady under the banner of the Immaculate Conception, if not in name, then
in fact. In 1719, the Conventual Franciscan Order had officially recognized
the existence of this unique tradition dating back to its origin, i.e., St. Francis, and as such had affirmed the identification of the Order with the "cause
of the Immaculate."[39] "The heart of Franciscan spirituality and missionary
zeal is the mystery of the Immaculate Conception." The goal of the order, for
which reason it was called into existence by Our Lady, is "the realization of
her cause in the church," which, in our day, as Kolbe explained, means "incorporation of the mystery into life."[40] It forms the heart and gives meaning
to every apostolic endeavor and aspect of Franciscan spirituality.

> Naturally it is possible to theorize about a central goal of the
> order other than that of the cause of the Immaculate, for the
> simple reason that the Order is not necessary to the plans of
> the Immaculate, and is not compelled to agree to these plans.
> Whether one can argue that the acceptance of these plans by
> the order is not necessary for the order to be genuinely and fully
> Franciscan, or whether failure to support these plans with any-
> thing less than full cooperation could be anything but tragic for
> the order in every way, is quite another matter . . . The existence
> of the order can indeed be construed apart from the mystery
> of the Immaculate; but it is no more likely to come alive in fact
> than the theology and devotion of the order can flower apart
> from the mystery of the Immaculate.[41]

St. Maximilian's is the prophetic voice showing the way for what that
means in our day. The form is indicated by the M.I., the essential element
of which is "total consecration as the possession and property of the Immaculate," given concrete expression by Niepokalanów in St. Maximilian's
day. What is needed at this critical juncture is for the Order to reaffirm this
tradition by embracing the Kolbean heritage bequeathed to it, allowing itself

---

Extraordinary General Chapter.

    38. Fehlner, "Hereditas Kolbiana," *CE* 6, chapter 7.

    39. See Kolbe, *WK* 1184 for the text of the decree, ratified by the General Chapter
in 1719 and confirmed by Pope Clement XI the following year.

    40. Fehlner, "Hereditas Kolbiana," *CE* 6, chapter 7.

    41. Fehlner, "Hereditas Kolbiana," *CE* 6, chapter 7.

to be guided by the principles of the M.I., and thus permit a "relaunching" of the rightful Marian influence in the Franciscan order, which is the envisioned response to the Lord's command to "rebuild my church."[42]

In an unpublished essay written in the following year, Fehlner did not hide his disappointment that the 1986 Chapter chose not to adopt his recommendation: "It cannot be said . . . that this chapter in any way filled the lacuna of the Constitutions in regard to a more precise and workable explanation of the conventual charism, or in any essential way modified the overall relation between the M.I. and the Constitutions as described above. . . . The validity of the conventual charism as an integral aspect of franciscan life with a still unrealized potential for the future ultimately rests on the service 'conventualism' renders to the cause of the Immaculate."[43]

Mariae Advocatae Causa: Fehlner's Prophetic Message for the Church

A new chapter in in Fr. Peter Damian's Kolbean itinerary opened up with his co-founding, along with Fr. James McCurry, OFM Conventual, of the Marian publishing house known as the Academy of the Immaculate in 1992.

"If the Immaculata wishes," St. Maximilian once wrote, "we will organize a Marian Academy to study, teach and publish all over the world what the Immaculata is. Perhaps an academy with a doctorate in Mariology. Thus, it is still a relatively unknown field and yet so necessary for practical life,

---

42. "Fr. Bede Hess' [Minister General of the Conventual Franciscans] May 1942 Circular Letter to the entire Order on the Militia of the Immaculate and the Marian character of the Franciscan Order from its beginning, together with his statute later in the year for the entire Order to be consecrated to the Immaculate Heart each year on December 8, a consecration to include not only a ritual, but also a personal and spiritual commitment of each friar, are official actions (never rescinded) proving the correctness of St. Maximilian on the essence of the Franciscan Order." *Theologian of Auschwitz*, 125; see also 127n39.

43. Fehlner, "Conventual Charism," *CE* 5, chapter 10. It was Fehlner's dying hope that at least an abridged form of his final work, *Theologian of Auschwitz*, would be made available to the capitulars participating in the Extraordinary General Chapter of the Conventuals in 2018, which oversaw another revision of the Constitutions. Fehlner's hope went unrealized, however, as the work was not published until after the Chapter. The revised Constitutions, subsequently approved by the Holy See, do acknowledge the Kolbean heritage and the "golden thread" of the Immaculate Conception; therefore, they leave room for future realization of the goals outlined in Fehlner's 1986 address. But it is probable that, if he were still alive at the time of the writing of this Introduction, Fr. Peter Damian would still hold to the conviction that, to a great extent, this work remains to be undertaken.

for the conversion and sanctification of souls."[44] He wished in particular "to explore more critically the relationship of our Father St. Francis, of his followers, and of the Order to the Blessed Virgin Mary, particularly with regard to her privilege of Immaculate Conception."[45] The saint's aspirations have been partially realized through the Academy of the Immaculate.

An in-depth analysis of Fehlner's nearly twenty-five-year involvement in the Academy's operation would itself comprise a whole study. We could reference many indices to gauge his spectacular industry at the service of the Academy; one impressive index is the symposia on Marian coredemption held yearly from 2000 to 2009, which Fr. Peter Damian organized, and of whose proceedings of well over four thousand pages combined he oversaw the editing and preparation for publication. To echo the thought of Fr. Angelo Geiger, "it is fair to say that no one has done more to fulfill St. Maximilian's desire in this regard than Father Peter Damian."[46]

The Academy started up not long after Fehlner's departure as editor of *Miles Immaculatae* and just before his transfer to the Franciscan Friars of the Immaculate. Although the circumstances surrounding his transfer make for a complex narrative, [47] at least in regard to Fehlner's Kolbean itinerary this development may be seen as providential, as his presence for a time with the Friars of the Immaculate gave him a free hand to organize the work of the Academy and, in my view, provided an extra stimulus (also in a negative way) for the production of his later Kolbean contributions. Especially in light of the well-publicized negative (though non-magisterial) judgment of the Czestochowa Commission in 1996 regarding the definability of Marian coredemption as a dogma,[48] it seems unlikely that he would otherwise have been in the position to make such an enormous contribution on this doctrine, which rests on the mystery of the Immaculate Conception.

An important development during this period concerns Fr. Peter Damian's 2002 essay, "Martyr of Charity—Man of the Millennium: St. Maximilian Mary Kolbe." In this essay, Fehlner, considering the reflections of the Holy Father on the dawn of a new millennium and the role of Our Lady in its preparation and celebration, reprises Bonaventure's theology of

44. Kolbe, *WK* 508.

45. Letter to Fr. Ephrem Longpré, OFM, *WK* 564.

46. Cf. Geiger, "Tribute to Fr. Peter," 23.

47. See Fr. Ondrako's analysis in *Rebuild My Church,* c. 1.

48. Regarding the controversy surrounding the Czestochowa Commission, see Miravalle, "Continued Dialogue," 359–97.

history, as contained in his *Collationes in Hexaemeron*, considered in light of the witness of St. Maximilian.[49]

All of history is ordered to the incarnation, and, as such, ultimately rests on a metaphysical (being-unchanging) principle rather than being simply event-driven (becoming). The merit of St. Maximilian is that he brings this universal principle into sharp focus: the principle of the *Immaculate Conception*. It is opposed to what we might call the "anti-principle" of secularism. Failure to accept, or better, conscious rejection of the former inexorably leads one down the path toward an embrace of the latter, involving a secularization rather than sanctification of the intellect.[50] St. Maximilian is the "man of the millennium," because:

> [H]istory is now entering that period when until the final coming its most prominent feature will be the Marian, the Immaculatist, that of total consecration to and total possession by the Immaculate of all who belong to the body of Christ. As the Virgin Mother is the great sign of the fullness of time, the incarnation, so the city of the Immaculate, "Niepokalanów," is the great sign of that fullness for the church. . . .[51]

Although a more universal outlook (i.e., beyond the confines of the Franciscan Order and Franciscan spirituality) is already evident in Fehlner's Kolbean writings from the 1980s, now it has assumed a much greater prominence. Moreover, the same tone of urgency which permeates his 1986 address to the Conventuals now finds its way into various other conferences of this period. For this reason, I believe that this essay should be considered together with three other conferences Fehlner delivered during this period: (1) His 2004 conference, "*Virgo Ecclesia Facta*: The Immaculate Conception, St. Francis of Assisi, and the Renewal of the Church"; (2) "*Mariae Advocatae Causa*: The Marian Issue in the Church Today," a conference he delivered at

---

49. Bonaventure's theology of history has been the subject of much interest, most famously by Josef Ratzinger, who made this the subject of his doctoral research. In Fehlner's view, Ratzinger is to be enumerated among those who "tend to read the Seraphic Doctor 'existentially,' rather than 'essentially' (as in this conference), in explaining his theology of history, and so find more links with Joachim of Fiore than I believe can be justified" ("Martyr of Charity," *CE* 6, chapter 17). Others, in misinterpreting the thought of Bonaventure on this subject, have accused him of a fideistic pietism.

50. Fehlner, "Martyr of Charity," *CE* 6, chapter 17. Regarding the danger of prioritizing experience over metaphysics, see Fehlner, "Neo-Patripassianism," *CE* 8, chapter 5. This error lies at the heart of much contemporary thought, especially in its Kantian and Hegelian forms—an error, however, which can be traced back to Joachim of Fiore.

51. Fehlner, "Martyr of Charity," *CE* 6, chapter 17.

Fatima, Portugal, in 2005;[52] and (3) a popular conference on "The Marian Issue in the Church," delivered at Greenwood, Indiana in 2007—a conference for which he received a standing ovation from the many participants.[53]

Thus, speaking about the incorporation of the mystery of the Immaculate Conception into the life of the church and the world, of which St. Maximilian speaks,[54] Fr. Peter Damian affirms: "It was precisely the failure before the [Second Vatican] Council to accomplish this incorporation, viz., to marianize every aspect of the life of faith, including theology and philosophy, which made the Council necessary, but which also made the results of the Council so far inconclusive at best."[55] Therefore, "there can be no resolution of the crisis of faith affecting all mankind, and not merely Catholics, unless all particular programs, good in themselves, rest on this most basic means of renewal [total consecration to the Immaculate]."[56] His stance is even more categorical in his 2005 Fatima conference, in reference to Marian coredemption, which must "be seen as the basis for living total consecration of the Church and of every soul to the Immaculate Heart."[57] "Either solemnly confess the *Theotokos* is Coredemptrix for the same reason she is virginal Mother of God, because the Immaculate, or get ready for total enslavement to sin. Secularism . . . can only be overcome by publicly and solemnly affirming the *Theotokos* to be the *Coredemptrix*, both titles based on her being the *Immaculate Conception*. . . ."[58] He further proposes the cre-

---

52. Fehlner, "*Mariae Advocatae Causa*," CE 2, chapter 4. The contributions to this symposium on Marian coredemption were delivered in various languages, but that of Fehlner was in English. As many of the contributors were cardinals of the church, of all Fehlner's conferences, this one was directed toward perhaps the most distinguished audience.

53. For an edited transcription of this conference, see Fehlner, "Marian Issue," 24–31.

54. Kolbe, *WK* 486.

55. Fehlner, "*Virgo Ecclesia Facta*," CE 3, chapter 6. Fehlner advances the thesis that the failure of the Council of Trent to solemnly (i.e., dogmatically) affirm the Immaculate Conception is correlated to a delay of the fruits reaped from that Council and a solidification of the Protestant Reformation that paved the way to the secularist Enlightenment that followed. He draws a parallel between Trent and Vatican II insofar as, while Vatican II did re-present the teaching on Mary's universal mediation (a theme developed by Pope St. John II, especially in his 1987 Encyclical, *Redemptoris Mater*), it declined to dogmatically formulate this Church teaching. It is in this reticence, Fehlner argues, that one can find the source for a delay in the hoped-for renewal. Hence, the importance of Kolbe's program for the incorporation of the Immaculate Conception into the life of the Church.

56. Fehlner, "*Virgo Ecclesia Facta*," CE 3, chapter 6.

57. Fehlner, "*Mariae Advocatae Causa*," CE 2, chapter 4.

58. Fehlner, "*Mariae Advocatae Causa*," CE 2, chapter 4.

ation of a pontifical commission to further study the definability of Marian coredemption, following consultation with the bishops of the world.[59] This theme is reechoed in the 2007 Greenwood conference, with Fehlner pointing to the miracle of the sun at Fatima in 1917 as a sign that Our Lady is the one given to us by God to save us from present dangers, on the condition that we explicitly honor her, as God wishes.[60]

As Fr. Ondrako sagely observes,[61] it was never Fehlner's intention in any of this to "force the hand of the Church," as it were, or in any other way to act out of step with the church or advocate that anyone else do so. Rather, what we see is how well Fehlner had inherited the prophetic mantle of Kolbe, while contributing his own insights as he interpreted the signs of the times.

Marian Metaphysics and a Marianized Theology

Gradually over time, beginning in the early 2000s, Fehlner devoted himself to a deeper reflection and exposition of the metaphysical and theological foundations of Kolbe's thought. He reasoned that such would be not only the most useful, but also the most necessary contribution he could offer to ensure the continued development and vitality of the Franciscan-Kolbean heritage.

At first, this work overlapped with the other initiatives described above. However, especially after more serious difficulties arose within the community of the Franciscan Friars of the Immaculate later in the same decade, he dedicated himself ever more exclusively to this metaphysical-theological project for the remainder of his scholarly career. Fehlner's most complete Kolbean contributions came during this period, in the form of two books: *St. Maximilian M. Kolbe, Martyr of Charity: Pneumatologist*, published in 2004; and *The Theologian of Auschwitz: St. Maximilian M. Kolbe on the Immaculate Conception in the Life of the Church*, completed shortly before his death and published posthumously in 2019.[62] Those who wish to gain a complete picture of Fehlner's Kolbean doctrine must be sure to add these two books to their reading lists, the contents of which comprise a substantial addition to the material republished in this volume.

---

59. Fehlner, "*Mariae Advocatae Causa*," *CE* 2, chapter 4.

60. See Fehlner, "Marian Issue," 27–29.

61. See Ondrako, *Rebuild My Church*, c. 1.

62. It is highly significant that, aside from his dissertation and these two works, Fehlner neither projected nor wrote any other books during his long scholarly career, however much one might be forgiven for thinking that a number of his essays and articles are books in themselves!

In 2001, Fehlner wrote three detailed essays on Marian metaphysics according to the mind of St. Bonaventure. These essays were published in the Italian scholarly journal of the Franciscan Friars of the Immaculate, *Immaculata Mediatrix*. In these three essays Fehlner reiterates that, because of Mary's unique participation in Christ's one mediation in virtue of the Immaculate Conception and the Divine Maternity, she is our Mother and Teacher. As such, by her "interior teaching" she is capable of bringing about "a spiritual conception of the Word . . . in the minds and hearts of those who become her children."[63]

This (and all) mediatory activity, hierarchical in character and reflective of the processions of the Son and the Holy Spirit within the Trinity, involves what Bonaventure terms "exemplary causality," which, in the first place, entails personal action and cannot simply be reduced to the classic fourfold physical causality as defined by Aristotle and distinctive of Thomistic-based systems of thought.[64] "It is this mysterious 'self-initiation' of the created person, when properly subordinated to the Creator-Savior, which permits the created person to participate in the mediation of Christ."[65]

> Because of the Immaculate Conception [Mary] constitutes, in the words of Bonaventure a hierarchical order by herself, above all creatures, that is, she enters as Mother of God (Divine Mother) into the order of the hypostatic union and economy of salvation resting on it. For that reason, her maternal mediation touches not only the descent of the Word from heaven to become flesh, but also the transformation of the created person so as to live and die no longer for himself, but for Jesus. What St. Maximilian calls "transubstantiation" into the Immaculate is but a recognition of the manner in which with the divine persons she too terminates as Daughter, Mother and Spouse the triple power of the soul in coming to remember, know and love as do divine persons.[66]

This personal influence of Our Lady is decisive in the sanctification of the intellect and the will, whereby the intellect, according to the Franciscan tradition, is oriented toward wisdom, and knowledge is "totally transfused by the *praxis* of charity."[67] Failure to let oneself be guided in this way leads either to secularism (a scientific agnosticism) or to a pietistic

63. Fehlner, "Mater et Magistra Apostolorum," *CE* 1, chapter 2.

64. See Fehlner, "Metaphysica mariana quaedam," *CE* 1, chapter 3.

65. Fehlner, "Metaphysica mariana quaedam," *CE* 1, chapter 3.

66. Fehlner, "Metaphysica mariana quaedam," *CE* 1, chapter 3.

67. Fehlner, "Scientia et Pietas," *CE* 1, chapter 4.

fideism. Though seemingly at the opposite ends of the spectrum, these two errors "are agreed on one central point: the intellect has nothing to do with piety, being radically autonomous."[68] The so-called "critical question," the resolution of which seems to have been at the heart of Fehlner's spiritual crisis in the 1970s, "concerns not a claimed *a priori* dubious character of the correspondence between mental and extra-mental in the first concept of being [à la Immanuel Kant], but rather the fullness of the resolution of intellectual activity into wisdom."[69] The mysteries of the Immaculate Conception and of the coredemption "make the difference between an intellect totally sanctified, without doubt about the Truth of Christ and one totally destabilized," and they render "possible both the cooperation of created persons in the work of sanctification and salvation and constitute the nature of that holiness in charity once achieved."[70]

Then, in *St. Maximilian M. Kolbe, Martyr of Charity: Pneumatologist*, Fehlner deepens his reflections on the originality of St. Maximilian's theology of the Holy Spirit as revealed in his terminology, once again using the Bonaventurian system of thought as his base. Mary is "a created *quasi-part* of the Trinity . . . because *Complement of the Trinity* . . . Complement because *Spouse of the Holy Spirit*, Spouse because *Created Immaculate Conception*, a name shared uniquely with the Holy Spirit."[71] Fehlner thus neatly shows the relationship of these Kolbean terms, with which we may include St. Maximilian's expression of Mary as the Holy Spirit "quasi-incarnate." The Bonaventurian doctrine of appropriation reappears here as he explains the careful differentiation St. Maximilian makes between the union of Mary and the Holy Spirit, consisting in a union of wills (a theme reprised especially from Fehlner's two 1985 studies republished in this volume), and the hypostatic union, which involves a union of natures. This natural-voluntary distinction reflects the distinct but complementary processions of the Son and the Holy Spirit in the Trinity.

The singular genial insight of St. Maximilian concerns his use of the name "Immaculate Conception" to denote both Our Lady (Created) and the Holy Spirit (Uncreated). Fehlner notes Bonaventure's use of the word "conception" in describing the person (as well as the procession) and mission of the Holy Spirit,[72] but then adds that St. Maximilian's reflection goes far beyond what is indicated by the Seraphic Doctor.

68. Fehlner, "Scientia et Pietas," *CE* 1, chapter 4.

69. Fehlner, "Scientia et Pietas," *CE* 1, chapter 4.

70. Fehlner, "Scientia et Pietas," *CE* 1, chapter 4.

71. Fehlner, *Kolbe . . . Pneumatologist*, 71.

72. See Fehlner, *Kolbe . . . Pneumatologist*, 112.

Immaculate Conception, then, is the point where *exitus* and
reditus, reductio, creative action and created action, meet and
mutually penetrate. . . . Thus, the circle of Trinitarian love in
eternity is expanded so as to include the created order . . . and
the nature of love, which excludes all sin, is made clear, not
only essentially, but personally. It is the Holy Spirit or Uncreated Immaculate Conception, fruit of the love of Father and
Son from eternity; it is the Virgin Mother, fruit of the love of
Father and Word Incarnate in time, because She also is the Immaculate Conception, the vertex of love.[73]

Kolbe's insights are perfectly valid and orthodox, because they maintain
the true unity of the triune Godhead in eternity and the absolute centrality
of the Word Incarnate in the so-called "economic Trinity."[74] Thus, the key
to Mary's maternal mediation as a unique sharing in the one mediation of
Christ "is the coordination of the two processions in eternity and missions in
time of Son and Spirit. The point of juncture indicated by St. Maximilian is
the Immaculate Conception where the ultimate in pure divine charity permeates the ultimate in created to extend as it were the Trinity into the church, an
authentically Scotistic exposition of the primacy of charity."[75]

Finally, Kolbe's use of the term "transubstantiation into the Immaculate" to denote the Marian mode of our transformation in Christ, as
analogous to Eucharistic transubstantiation, is also qualified in terms of
charity, i.e., a union of wills, and is therefore likewise shown to be perfectly
admissible.[76]

The Contribution of the Thought
of St. John Henry Newman

Around 2008, Fehlner, thanks to his reconnection with Fr. Ondrako, a
former student of his, and now a Newman scholar, embarked on a major
project, bringing Duns Scotus and John Henry Newman into dialog. As
in the case of the church fathers, medieval scholars, and other theological

---

73. Fehlner, *Kolbe . . . Pneumatologist*, 113–14; see *WK* 1310, 1318.

74. See Fehlner, *Kolbe . . . Pneumatologist*, 86.

75. Fehlner, *Kolbe . . . Pneumatologist*, 134.

76. See Fehlner, *Kolbe . . . Pneumatologist*, 147–48. The term, "transubstantiation,"
was employed in a similar way by Russian Orthodox scholars in the earlier twentieth
century; and it is probable, in Fehlner's opinion, that St. Maximilian was acquainted
with their works. See *Theologian of Auschwitz*, 97, 103n55, 278–79.

and spiritual masters, Fehlner had acquired a deep understanding and love of the thought of Cardinal Newman.

Already in 1978, in his essay, "Mary and Theology: Scotus Revisited," Fehlner's grasp of the subject is readily apparent. Of more importance for this volume is that, by this time, he had already recognized affinities linking Newman with Bonaventure and Scotus, finding in his writings certain principles validating or in accordance with Kolbean thought.[77] This research reached its apex in 2010, with the production of a true masterpiece of Fehlnerian thought: "Scotus and Newman in Dialogue."[78] In this book-length essay are the results of a groundbreaking study that uncovers an overwhelming number of points of contact between the two great thinkers. The study is "built upon an exercise of apologetics which is neither metaphysics nor dogmatic theology, but presupposes both, where they meet the life of any believer or potential believer in Christ."[79]

The table found in this essay, illustrating the parallel thought patterns in Bonaventure, Scotus and Newman, supported by more than one hundred pages of documentation, is really the first of its kind, showing Fehlner's extraordinary subtilty in discerning these patterns. Of maximal interest is that Fehlner's method, made possible only by a unique laser-like penetration of Bonaventurian and Scotistic metaphysics and theology, and their affinities, is later reprised in a similarly groundbreaking (in my view) analysis of the affinities of thought patterns between Scotus and Kolbe later on, in *The Theologian of Auschwitz*.

Newman's development of doctrine finds a correspondence in Kolbe's "fixed idea." But whereas for Newman the idea has a more abstract character, for St. Maximilian it is resolved in the person of the Immaculate (and, therefore, personal and very concrete).[80] Thus, for St. Newman the Immaculate Conception is an eminent example of doctrinal development, but for Kolbe *it is the very principle which governs doctrinal development,* his famous "golden thread," because that principle is a person—Our Lady—who is guiding history.[81] The significance of this development cannot be overstated, yet it maintains perfect continuity between the thought of the two, because, for Newman, as for the great Franciscan masters, Mary is the

77. There is no evidence indicating that St. Maximilian was familiar with any of Newman's writings.

78. Fehlner, "Scotus and Newman," *CE* 8, chapter 9. He delivered this presentation in three parts at the Newman-Scotus Symposium, held in Washington, D.C., on October 22–24, 2010.

79. Ondrako, *Rebuild My Church*, c. 7.

80. See Fehlner, *Theologian of Auschwitz*, 41–42.

81. See Fehlner, "Niepokalanów in the Counsels," *CE* 6, chapter 5.

one who "clarifies" the truth of her Son par excellence (thus, he accepts her as the primary term of the mission of the Holy Spirit).

> For Newman, even the most explicit truths of Scripture concerning Christ are impervious to understanding, if one attempts to understand them apart from the influence of Mary. We can unravel the logic of doctrinal development, not by relating this solely to the laws of logic, or comparing this to the life of something it is not, but by relating it to the personal influence of Mary Immaculate on each believer in the church and on the church itself.[82]

An important point of contact between Newman and Scotus, which had implications for further development of Fehlner's Kolbean doctrine, regards the existence and resolution of the critical question, which for both (as well as for Bonaventure) entails entering into one's heart. They approach it "on the same basis: the primacy of the will and the person," following upon the distinction of natural vs. voluntary action.[83] Failure to do so leaves one hard-pressed to explain the personal character of intellectual life; or else, in the case of Kant and his disciples, one is led down the path to a radical skepticism and an arbitrary voluntarism. For Newman, what is involved is an exercise of what he calls the "illative sense" in the attainment of a personal act of faith which gives a certainty that is otherwise unattainable:

> Carried on in union with Mary, every effort to understand more clearly, however metaphysical, will always be an assent tending on the real [reference to Cardinal Newman] because, in this case, the metaphysical style is what it is intended to be: an ascesis of the intellect, a purification that enables one to perceive more clearly, and a preparation for the ecstatic joy of contemplation.[84]

Space limitations do not permit a fuller presentation of Newman's affinities to Scotus here, and the reader is referred to Fehlner's original study for more. To cite just one example, Fehlner notes a compelling convergence of thought between the two in Newman's brief *Memorandum on the Immaculate Conception*, of relevance for this volume on Kolbe. The Immaculate Conception is not in view of original sin, Newman affirms, but rather sin is subordinated to grace. Hence,

---

82. Fehlner, "Mary and Theology," *CE* 1, chapter 1.

83. Fehlner, "Scotus and Newman," *CE* 8, chapter 9.

84. Fehlner, "Mary and Theology," *CE* 1, chapter 1. See Newman, *Grammar of Assent*, c. 4.

[O]riginal sin is to be understood and explained in relation to
the logically prior mystery of the Immaculate Conception and
preservative redemption in the divine counsels of salvation.
This is simply the Marian mode of Scotus's position: the incarnation is not for the sake of either redemption or creation; but
creation and redemption are for the sake of the incarnation
and divine Maternity.[85]

Highly significant also is Fehlner's analysis of Newman's *Oxford University Sermon* 15, on Mary's faith being the pattern of ours. Here he sees

Newman's linking of the Virgin Mary both with his theory of
doctrinal development . . . and with the positions taken by him
in the *Grammar of Assent*. Inspiration for the *Development of
Doctrine* is not Hegel and that for the *Grammar of Assent* is not
Kant, but is for both Our Lady. Not only Scotus, but Newman
may be described as *Doctor Marianus*.[86]

In sum, we may say that the personalist vision already present in the
theology and metaphysics of Scotus and evident in the thought of St. John
Henry Newman finds its full expression in Kolbe, which Fehlner then ap-
propriates and situates within the present climate of modernity.

Last Will and Testament:
The Theologian of Auschwitz

From about 2008 onward, controversies regarding the governance of the
Franciscan Friars of the Immaculate prompted within Fehlner a rethinking
of his religious vocation which eventually led to his return to the Conventual Franciscan Friars in 2016. I see in this prolonged period of intense suffering of Fr. Peter Damian the hand of Our Lady guiding him along the way
of perfection in the final stages of his spiritual itinerary.

Already by the time of these events, and perhaps even as soon as the
2004 publication of his first book on St. Maximilian, Fehlner began laying the groundwork for the compilation of this book, which was completed
only shortly before his death in 2018. This final book, *The Theologian of
Auschwitz*, is Fehlner's "Last Will and Testament," a fitting culmination
and capstone of the "Marian plan" laid out in his 1978 study and which

85. Fehlner, "Scotus and Newman," *CE* 8, chapter 9. Newman explicitly embraces
this Scotistic view in two letters to Frederick William Faber, dated 9 and 14 December
1849.

86. Fehlner, "Scotus and Newman," *CE* 8, chapter 9.

developed with great fruitfulness over the forty years that followed. In this volume, Fehlner neatly brought together all the threads that ran through his multifaceted research. The one thread that tied them all together was, of course, the "golden thread": the Immaculate Conception.

The stated purpose of his final volume is to demonstrate that St. Maximilian is a genuine theologian by illustrating how his theology is firmly grounded in the Franciscan and ecclesial theological tradition, through the examination in particular of the materials Kolbe had compiled for a book on the Immaculate,[87] a project cut short by his arrest and death. An "assessment of the significance of St. Maximilian's work, both for Mariology and for the whole of theology . . . explains how, in the ecclesial life envisioned by Vatican II, it could well provide the key to a total renewal of theology as well as of spirituality in terms of the mission of the Holy Spirit."[88]

Referring to Bonaventure's consideration of theology under the three modes of *symbolic, proper,* and *mystical-contemplative,* Fehlner considers Kolbe to be a genuine theologian in regard to all three modes,[89] but above all he excelled as a contemplative-mystical theologian, and as a superior theologian in the Franciscan tradition.[90] A close examination of the principles informing his theology reveals St. Maximilian "not only [to be] a genuine theologian, but one to be ranked among the more important theologians of our times."[91]

> A first-time presentation and promotion of a "global vision of Catholic life in a new form" postulates a theologian, not only genuinely such, but unique. Kolbe is the only such theologian in sight.[92]

"In a sense," Fr. Peter Damian affirms, St. Maximilian "seems to resemble in the second page of the Order's history what is often said of the theological work of St. Bonaventure during the first page: the second founder of the [Franciscan] Order," because he was "capable of recognizing and correctly interpreting the Marian character of the Franciscan Order as founded by St. Francis." He correctly interpreted the Immaculate Conception as the "golden thread" guaranteeing "the unchangeable unity of the Order" which permitted its proper development; recognized the Order's fundamental activity,

---

87. Kolbe, *WK* 1304–34.

88. Fehlner, *Theologian of Auschwitz,* 6.

89. Fehlner, *Theologian of Auschwitz,* 32.

90. See Fehlner, *Theologian of Auschwitz,* 51–76.

91. Fehlner, *Theologian of Auschwitz,* 24.

92. Fehlner, *Theologian of Auschwitz,* 25.

namely, service of the cause of the Immaculate for the good of the church; and demonstrated through his own life, death and apostolate, that the work of Marianization of everything is the fundamental activity to be undertaken at the present time.[93] That work of Marianization is to be extended to the whole church, the blueprint of which is contained in the original statutes of the M.I., and the model of which is Niepokalanów.

Perhaps the most distinguished contribution of Fehlner in this volume is his brilliant analysis of consistently Scotistic patterns of thought in Kolbe's writings and conferences. Aside from a specific recommendation to study Scotus and his thesis of the absolute primacy of Christ (and Mary),[94] Kolbe's Scotistic influences are harder to recognize than those of Bonaventure; they consist, in Fehlner's words, of a "coloration" or "nuancing" of Bonaventurian thought. But the heart of St. Maximilian's Marian metaphysics "is precisely the heart of the metaphysic of Scotus: the absolute primacy of Christ . . . univocity of being and disjunctive transcendentals in re the divine infinity, the hypostatic union, the Immaculate Conception and the *perfectiones simplicer simplices* or pure perfections as the basis for an 'infinity secundum quid' of those creatures capable of divinization—not ontologically, but in the order of blessedness."[95] Two particular footprints scattered throughout Kolbe's writings, Fehlner notes, are his preference of the use of the term "man-God" rather than "God-man" when referring to Christ, and his theory of the will which hearkens back to Scotus' view of the will as a *perfectio simpliciter simplex* in God and man.

Using a method similar to that employed in "Scotus and Newman in Dialogue," Fehlner does a painstaking analysis of various texts and conferences of the saint to uncover his Scotistic mindset.[96] Only someone with a precise knowledge of Scotus could succeed, as Fehlner does, in this endeavor. Throughout this entire exercise, Fehlner demonstrates the continuity rather than contrast in thought between Bonaventure and Scotus. Regarding this last point, Fehlner has performed an incalculable service by rendering the Franciscan tradition, finding its consummation in Marian mode in Kolbe, more broadly accessible to future generations of scholars and practitioners.

For this reason, *The Theologian of Auschwitz* is a prophetic reminder of the privileged place Franciscan theology and metaphysics holds in the

93. See Fehlner, *Theologian of Auschwitz*, 311–12.

94. Kolbe, Roman Conference V, 1937, *Roman Conferences*, 38.

95. Fehlner, *Theologian of Auschwitz*, 159–60.

96. Much of this work is found in chapters 7 and 9 of Fehlner, *Theologian of Auschwitz*.

church, confirmed for all time by the proclamation of the dogma of the Immaculate Conception in 1854. This prominent place has never been denied, but in my view, it has been obscured in recent times, not so much by the proliferation of neo-Thomism and other contemporary theological currents, but by the failure of too many Franciscans to properly under- stand and embrace their own intellectual and spiritual heritage.[97] There is, therefore, an urgent need for Franciscans to reclaim what is already theirs, and St. Maximilian clearly shows the way.

> In a fully Marianized church, including a Marianized theology based on the Immaculate Conception, a theology which, in St. Maximilian Kolbe, takes the form of a Scotistic pneumatology, with its practical import for the maternal mediation of the Vir- gin as memory of the church, there is not the slightest doubt that the theological metaphysics of Scotus will not only find a new lease on life, but become one of the most important features of the thought and culture, characteristic of Catholic life.[98]

As Fehlner notes, "Kolbe has integrated three sections of theology in terms of the Immaculate Conception and the City of the Immaculate: the Christological, the pneumatological and ecclesiological."[99] In this way, he did indeed anticipate the Second Vatican Council and its presentation of "the Blessed Virgin Mary, Mother of God, in the Mystery of Christ and in the Church" (the title of chapter 8 of the Constitution on the Church, *Lumen Gentium*), for "the mystery of the Immaculate or spousal union with the Holy Spirit (communion) is a key not only to the unity of the church, but also to the fruitfulness of her sacramental system and missionary effort."[100]

For the same reason, especially evident in his insight on the created and uncreated Immaculate Conception, Kolbe has shed fresh light on the mystery of the Trinity, expounded by Fehlner at great length especially in Bonaventurian terms. Finally, the Immaculate Mediatrix is the one who is at the center of the correct formulation and resolution of the "critical

---

97. This is a strong statement, but I believe a correct assessment of the present situ- ation. This is one reason why I think Fehlner was drawn to the Franciscan Friars of the Immaculate for a period of time. Whatever the underlying motivations, the disman- tling of the library of over 100,000 books Fehlner had amassed up through the 1980s is, in my view, symbolic of the neglect by too many Franciscans of their own intellectual tradition, so vital to the Franciscan charism and to the entire Church. Could Fehlner's study help usher in a renewed interest and revival among Franciscans in our day?

98. Fehlner, "Sources of Scotus' Mariology," *CE* 4, chapter 9.

99. Fehlner, *Theologian of Auschwitz*, 270.

100. Fehlner, *Theologian of Auschwitz*, 182.

question," for she mediates this grace as well, as I believe Fehlner personally experienced at a crucial point in his spiritual itinerary.

The Theologian of Auschwitz represents the culmination of Fehlner's spiritual itinerary. Present at all stages of this itinerary is the "golden thread," the Immaculate Conception—in preparatory mode during the first three decades of his religious life, and in "incorporative" mode during the last three decades. As St. Maximilian Kolbe, so Fr. Peter Damian is a sign for what "incorporation of the Immaculate into life," what "Marianization" means for individuals, for the Franciscan Order, and for the church in this "age of Mary and the Holy Spirit."

Part Two: The Kolbean Doctrine of Fehlner

Having analyzed the trajectory of the "Marian plan" of Fehlner's life, let us now turn our attention to the contours of Fehlner's Kolbean thought. First, I will give a brief overview of the articles presented in this volume of Fehlner's collected works. Then, I will highlight some of the major themes presented both in these articles and in his two books on St. Maximilian.

If Fr. Peter Damian is correct about the relevance of Kolbe's "global vision" for the Franciscan Order and the church in this "age of Mary and the Holy Spirit,"[101] then Fehlner's studies, considered in their breadth, depth and originality, constitute an important point of reference when considering, both from a theoretical and practical standpoint, the question of what form the "incorporation of the mystery of the Immaculate Conception" takes for this age, especially in the aftermath of the Council.

Overview of Fehlner's Kolbean Works in This Volume

We may group the Kolbean works of Fehlner contained in this volume into four broad categories: (1) studies of Kolbean theology and Kolbe's theological method; (2) essays and conferences illustrating the place of the Kolbean vision within the Franciscan tradition; (3) essays and conferences exploring the relevance of Kolbean themes in an ecclesial context; and (4) essays treating of applications of Kolbean doctrine. It is possible to fit some of the articles into more than one of these categories.

1. Fehlner's most significant contribution on Kolbean theology during this period is the conference, "The Immaculate and the Mystery of the

---

101. See Fehlner, "Martyr of Charity," *CE* 6, chapter 17; Fehlner, *Theologian of Auschwitz*, 131, 270.

Trinity in the Thought of St. Maximilian Kolbe." Beginning with a reflection on the mystery of the Trinity rooted in Bonaventure and expanded by Kolbe, Fehlner proceeds to demonstrate how this mystery is revealed to us through the mystery of the Immaculate Conception, and how the Immaculate herself, Spouse of the Holy Spirit and Mother of the Word Incarnate, is the focal point where the "Trinitarian circle" is widened to encompass creation. The terminology employed by Kolbe rests upon this Bonaventurian theology, completed by the insights of Bl. John Duns Scotus.

Several other articles of Fehlner, in one way or another, illustrate the unique theological insight of Kolbe, who repeatedly builds upon valid theological expressions of others to better illustrate the mystery of the Immaculate in relation to the other mysteries of the faith. Thus, for example, the Immaculate as Spouse of the Holy Spirit is also *Complement of the Trinity*, the one, as the "vertex of love," in whom is found all the love of the Trinity. He recasts reflections on the Thomistic quasi-infinite dignity of the Divine Maternity and the divine omnipotence to illustrate the incomparable dignity of the Immaculate Conception ("The Immaculate Conception: Outer Limits of Love"). And he develops a theme first presented by a nineteenth-century Conventual Franciscan friar into the celebrated "golden thread" as a theology of history of the Franciscan Order and, by extension, the church ("The Other Page").

Finally, in "Marian Doctrine and Devotion: A Kolbean Perspective," Fehlner affirms how the Kolbean program of Marianization realizes a felicitous harmonization of doctrine and devotion, assured by the primacy of charity at the heart of the Franciscan School. Thus, Kolbe's "Mariocentric" view (meant in a derogatory way by his critics) is none other than the Christocentrism at the heart of the Franciscan charism and the church.

2. A second collection of essays concerns the Kolbean vision situated within the Franciscan charism. Among these works are included "Total Consecration, Baptism and the Franciscan Ideal," "Thesis of St. Maximilian. . ." "Niepokalanów in the Counsels of the Immaculate," "Two Testaments," and the 1986 *Hereditas Kolbiana*. To these should be added the related works of the same period documenting the presence of the Immaculate Conception in the spirituality of St. Francis.

In these works, Fehlner documents modern research regarding St. Maximilian's affirmation of the Immaculate Conception guiding the Franciscan tradition from its origins, affirms the role of Niepokalanów in that tradition, and highlights the significance of the Kolbean "global vision" for the contemporary Catholic movement. This culminates with his signature contribution, the *Hereditas Kolbiana*, his Kolbean blueprint for the renewal of the Franciscan Order, which I have described above in part one. There is a certain catechetical and apologetic tone present in most of these works, as Fehlner evidently directs his attention in the first place toward his own Conventual Franciscan confreres. And in the *Hereditas Kolbiana*, that tone becomes one of an exhortation or even a plea to his own to embrace what is already theirs as a gift from the Immaculate.

3. Fehlner devotes another series of mostly short essays to the ecclesial dimension of Kolbean thought, particularly as confirmed by Pope St. John Paul II. This echo is evident especially in the 1987 encyclical letter, *Redemptoris Mater*, through which the pope reproposes the Marian teaching of Vatican II, devoting much attention to the Immaculate Conception, Our Lady's maternal mediation, and the relation between these two mysteries, so much at the heart of the Kolbean synthesis. Other short articles bring out additional aspects of this same encyclical related to Kolbean thought ("Marian Geography of Faith") or relate further notable interventions of the Holy Father around the same time ("The Immaculate and the Extraordinary Synod 1985," "Marian Slavery: Slavery of Love").[102] Because "St. Maximilian with the Militia of the Immaculate, as then Card. Wojtyla noted in his press conference of Oct. 14, 1971, anticipated the teaching of Vatican II,"[103] particularly in regard to Marian mediation, Fehlner's "proposal" is for St. Maximilian to be considered for the title "Doctor of the Church."

Fehlner's 2002 conference, "Man of the Millennium," is situated in the context of John Paul II's 1994 Apostolic Letter, *Tertio millennio adveniente*, issued in preparation for the celebration of the Jubilee Year, 2000. The focus here is on the prophetic nature of the person and program of St. Maximilian Kolbe who, Fehlner advocates, anticipates the teaching of the pope in characterizing the present age as one distinctly Marian.

4. In the final category are two essays. In one of them, *"Mulieres Dignitatem,"* Fehlner reiterates the position of John Paul II that the dignity of woman "passes through the mystery of Mary to reach the mystery of the incarnation, in the light of which only does the eternal truth about man made in the image and likeness of God, male and female, find full understanding."[104] A most suitable means for upholding the dignity of women is the promotion of the M.I. In the other essay, "Vertex Creationis: St. Maximilian and Evolution," Fehlner reiterates Kolbe's wholesale rejection of any form of material evolutionism as diametrically opposed to the

102. A full analysis of the points of contact between the Kolbean vision and the magisterium of Pope St. John Paul II would comprise volumes and entail multiple advanced research projects. The fruit of one such project is the work of Calkins, *Totus Tuus.*

103. Fehlner, "A Proposal," *CE* 6, chapter 10.

104. Fehlner, *"Mulieres Dignitatem," CE* 6, chapter 15.

order of grace extended into creation through the mediation of Christ, in whom all things are recapitulated through the Immaculate.

Elements of Kolbe's Franciscan Metaphysical and Theological Foundation

As Frs. Fehlner and Domanski have noted, St. Maximilian was the beneficiary of the Franciscan intellectual tradition, which survived only with difficulty in the late nineteenth and early twentieth centuries, but was carried forward at the Seraphicum at Rome, where the saint pursued his higher studies in the 1910s.[105]

Fehlner sees in the foundations of Kolbe's theological expositions the Bonaventurian notion of theology: *Theologia est speculationis gratia, ut boni fiamus, et principaliter ut boni fiamus.*[106] Thus, an emphasis is placed on the practical character of theology, which is to be done in the spirit of prayer and devotion. It follows that the highest mode of theology is what Bonaventure terms contemplative or mystical theology, pointing to the primacy of charity. It is especially from this perspective that Kolbe's theological contributions can receive their just appraisal.

For Fehlner, St. Maximilian's writings and conferences clearly reflect the Franciscan intellectual and spiritual tradition dating back to the origins of the Order. In the case of the Seraphic Doctor, "the amazing number of coincidences between the thought of Bonaventure and of Maximilian, especially on Our Lady, must suggest that, at the very least, the mind of Maximilian is that of an *anima theologica naturaliter seraphica.*"[107]

The Bonaventurian Trinitarian theology is well represented in Kolbean thought, especially regarding the complementarity of the processions *ad intra* and of the missions *ad extra* of the Son and the Holy Spirit, the mediation of the Son as "middle person" of the Trinity, and the universal mediation of Mary, also in the intellectual order as *Magistra theologiae et theologorum.*[108]

---

105. See Domanski, "La genesi," 250; Fehlner, "Sources of Scotus' Mariology," *CE* 4, chapter 9.

106. "Theology is for the sake of speculation that we become good, and principally that we become good." Bonaventure, *I Sent.*, Proemium, q. 3.

107. Fehlner, *Theologian of Auschwitz*, 61. To give a couple of examples, he cites (1) the parallel between *WK* 1306 and Bonaventure, *Itin.*, prol., n. 4; and (2) the correspondence between *WK* 1318, "division is always in view of unification, which is creative," and Bonaventure, *Myst. Trin.*, q. 8.

108. See Fehlner, *Theologian of Auschwitz*, 160.

The hierarchical structure present within the Trinity is reflected in various degrees in creation, and the work of mediation *ad extra* is "the typically supernatural action by which the lowest grades of being are through the action of the relatively higher or absolutely highest grade of being recapitulated and so reduced to the Father and the communion of the divine persons."[109] This participation in or entry into the one mediation of Christ finds its culmination in his mother, an order or hierarchy unto herself.[110] Closely related is the doctrine of exemplary causality, which in Scotus translates to personal act. As exemplar with and under Christ, Our Lady exercises a mediatorial influence on her spiritual children in their growth in faith and holiness which cannot be reduced to the fourfold physical causality of the Aristotelian system—involving what in the Franciscan school is termed voluntary causality as distinguished from natural causality.

The Bonaventurian doctrine of appropriation comes into play when distinguishing the union of Mary and the Holy Spirit (St. Maximilian: "two persons and two natures") from the hypostatic union ("one person and two natures"). Mary is properly the mother of her Son, Jesus, but her union of love with God is appropriated to the Holy Spirit. From Fehlner's perspective, this doctrine is crucial in distinguishing the mission of the Holy Spirit from that of the Son; inadequate reflection or explanation risks either substituting the mission of the Holy Spirit in place of the Son, or of obscuring the nature of the Son's mission.[111]

The uncovering of the Scotistic origins in Kolbe's writings and conferences presents more of a challenge; but Fehlner was up to the challenge. I consider his study on the Kolbe-Scotus connection in *The Theologian of Auschwitz* to be a first-class example of his intellectual gifts put fully to work.[112] Fehlner sees plenty of evidence in Kolbe's writings pointing to a dependence on the Scotistic absolute primacy of Christ, around which his whole system of metaphysics and theology revolves. The freely bestowed love of God in creation is nowhere demonstrated more perfectly than in the Immaculate Conception, the "perfect fruit of a perfect Redemption by a perfect Redeemer."

It is in view of the incarnation, where finite and infinite meet, that Scotistic univocity of being, the disjunctive transcendentals and the pure perfections come into play. Kolbe's comparison of the divine *I am* (Exod 3:14; John

109. Fehlner, "Mater et Magistra Apostolorum," *CE* 1, chapter 2.

110. See Fehlner, "Complementum Ss. Trinitatis," *CE* 6, chapter 4.

111. See Fehlner, "Immaculate . . . Mystery of the Trinity," *CE* 6, chapter 3.

112. Fehlner, *Theologian of Auschwitz*, especially chapters 7 and 9. I compare the method he uses here to that which he employed to expose the Newman-Scotus connection in "Scotus and Newman."

8:58) with Our Lady's *I am the Immaculate Conception* is placed "in relation to the 'univocal' point of juncture between infinite and finite: the vertex of love."[113] The finite and infinite "touch" in the union of natures in the person of the Word, and it is possible for a creature to be elevated to an infinite mode of knowing and loving, through a union of wills, a union entailing a divinization or spiritualization, but without the loss of personal distinction. This Scotistic metaphysics of being is, for Fehlner, crucial for correctly understanding such Kolbean terminology as "transubstantiation" into the Immaculate, and Our Lady as the Holy Spirit "quasi-incarnate."

The Kolbean "Method"

St. Maximilian's "Marianized theology" is but a drawing out and development of the Franciscan tradition upon which he depends, perfectly in accord with Newman's theory of the development of doctrine, evident especially in Kolbe's striking terminology, revelatory of "theology 'in a new form': that reflecting the Immaculate Mediatrix."[114]

> Whether or not St. Maximilian was acquainted with the work of Newman on spiritual development in the area of dogma, he surely shared Newman's view of the "idea." Moreover, Kolbe went beyond Newman by framing his theory of development, what is commonly referred to as the historical-evolutionary dimension of anything in time, in terms of a metaphysical-Marian basis.[115]

The Kolbean *coloratio*, as Fehlner terms it, of the metaphysics and theology of Bonaventure and Scotus, consists in drawing out its Marian dimension or mode. It entails a view of the Immaculate Conception not merely from a "negative" perspective (preservation from original sin), but from a "positive" one as well—fullness of grace, or fullness of the love of God. Thus, we see in Our Lady the personification of the Holy Spirit, by virtue of a union of wills, making possible our sanctification as well. Such development is frequently encountered in the thought of St. Maximilian, whether in his terminology or in his other theological insights:

> Even a superficial reading of those passages of St. Maximilian's writings where thoughts encountered by him in the works of others are reflected is sufficient to demonstrate that he neither

113. Fehlner, *Theologian of Auschwitz*, 177.
114. Fehlner, *Theologian of Auschwitz*, 5.
115. Fehlner, *Theologian of Auschwitz*, 158.

simply repeated nor commented on these. Rather he habitually recast and deepened them in associating them with or incorporating them into a line of thought his own. In these instances it is not what he was reading which suggested the line of thought; rather the line of thought he was pursuing—under the influence of the Immaculate—enabled him to perceive an aspect of the truth about our Lady suggested by the content of his reading.[116]

Thus, for example, he applies a phrase he attributes to St. Bonaventure (the source, instead, of which is Conrad of Saxony) to illustrate more plainly the dignity of Mary in terms of the Immaculate Conception.[117] Fehlner illustrates that while St. Maximilian retains the principles in the statements of the medieval and modern theologians upon which he appears to rely, he proceeds to recast their reflections in light of the Immaculate Conception to illustrate in a more profound way what the original authors were conveying. "In summary St. Maximilian has borrowed reflections on the 'infinity' of the Mother God, originally set forth in contexts dealing with the omnipotence or the excellence of the divine maternity, to illustrate the grandeur of the Immaculate."[118]

A second characteristic of St. Maximilian's method is his employment of concepts from other realms such as empirical science as an aid in his enunciation of certain theological principles. Thus, from classic Newtonian mechanics he makes a repeated application of the law of action and reaction:

> [T]o complete and illustrate the analysis of St. Bonaventure by focusing on the mission of the Holy Spirit in the person of the Immaculate, and to pinpoint the practical character of the mystery of the Trinity in our theology, just where the outer limits of divine creative love meet an equal and contrary response in the outer limits created love, namely the vertex of love which is the Immaculate, the point at which the return to the Father is begun through the mediation of the Son of God. . . .[119]

While resting on the complementarity of the processions within the Trinity, reflected in the missions *ad extra*, Kolbe's application also "has interesting ramifications, both in respect to contemporary philosophy of science

---

116. Fehlner, "Outer Limits of Love," *CE* 6, chapter 14.

117. "God—as St. Bonaventure says—can create a greater and more perfect world, but cannot elevate any other creature to a dignity higher than the one to which he elevated Mary." Kolbe, *WK* 1232. The original thought appears to be rooted in St. Anselm.

118. Fehlner, "Outer Limits of Love," *CE* 6, chapter 14.

119. Fehlner, "Immaculate . . . Mystery," *CE* 6, chapter 3.

and as a counter-weight to currently popular and often abused 'psychological' and 'sociological' analogies in Trinitarian theology."[120]

A third characteristic of Kolbe's method is the terminology itself,
expressing above all the union of Our Lady with the Holy Spirit and our
sanctification (or divinization) in terms of this union.[121] For example,
when St. Maximilian refers to Our Lady as the complement of the Trinity, he means to describe "a unique closeness of one created person to the
divine person, based on a spousal union, a union of love, so perfect as to
effect an enlargement of the divine circle, without in any way violating
the divine transcendence. . . ."[122] Just as, within the Holy Trinity, the Holy
Spirit is the consummation of the love of the Father and the Son, so also
"*ad extra* the Immaculate by that fact of being the repository of the total
love of Father and Son consummates that love."[123]

Such terminology, the culmination of which is "created and uncreated
Immaculate Conception," reveals the depth of St. Maximilian's mystical
insights,[124] as well as his deftness in employing the principle of analogy to
plumb the depths of these mysteries. "The study of these phrases [Kolbe's
terminology] can contribute to the renewal of theology and of apologetics,
an integral aspect of our theology as practical, and ultimately to a deeper
appreciation of the relation of theology to the Seat of Wisdom and 'Interemptrix omnium haeresum' [destroyer of all heresies]."[125]

The Critical Question and Sanctification of the Intellect

Fr. Peter Damian devotes attention to the issue of the so-called "critical
question" which involves a harmonization of the tension between cultivation of the intellect and a desire for God, an entering into the heart. At stake
is the sanctification of the soul or its secularization, depending on a humble
submission to the divine light or refusal to place such an act:

"The love of learning so connatural to the created person is rooted in
the desire for God," Fehlner writes, in the footsteps of St. Bonaventure, "a

120. Fehlner, "Immaculate . . . Mystery," *CE* 6, chapter 3.

121. For a useful summary, see Miravalle, "Mary and Divinization," 88–96. Fehlner
gives a detailed analysis especially in *Kolbe . . . Pneumatologist*.

122. Fehlner, "Complementum Ss. Trinitatis," *CE* 6, chapter 4.

123. Fehlner, "Complementum Ss. Trinitatis," *CE* 6, chapter 4.

124. "Only a charismatic gift of a very high order could have permitted Bl. Maximilian to have discovered among these mysteries of faith the analogy explained by him in
his writings." Van Asseldonk and Pyfferoen, "Maria Santissima," 438, cited by Fehlner,
"A Thesis," *CE* 6, chapter 2.

125. Fehlner, "Complementum Ss. Trinitatis," *CE* 6, chapter 4.

desire which cannot reach fulfillment except via sanctification of the intellect in the Word of God made flesh."[126] Failure to sanctify the intellect "is to
leave the intellect prone to agnosticism and atheism, even if that unnatural
condition first appears under the guise of false devotion."[127]

For St. Maximilian, resolution is achieved through Marianization,
because Mary is not only the one in whom human thought and human
love is perfected by grace, i.e., the intellect and will are perfectly harmo-
nized and sanctified, but she is the one who mediates that perfection in
us. They are Marianized because they tend toward that perfection realized
in Mary. Thus, "a genuine intellectual life reaches its apex only when fully
marianized, i.e., integrated fully with devotion to the Immaculate."[128] Ultimately, then, the interior acceptance of this Marian principle is opposed
to and effectively counters what Fehlner terms the "principle of private
judgment,"[129] the basis of secularism:

> For Kolbe, apart from the guidance of Mary, the critical ques-
> tion can be incorrectly understood in terms of an impersonal
> or essentialist character, revealing itself as a form of fideism
> (putatively deriving from Bonaventure) or rationalism (tribu-
> tary from Scotus), two misconceptions at the root of Kantian
> agnosticism. Kolbe denies this and shows why his position is
> correct, because it is grounded in an affirmation of the Immacu-
> late Conception capable of mediating our return to the Father,
> through the Son in the unity of the Holy Spirit.[130]

The program of Marianization proposed by Kolbe and exercised in
concrete form in Niepokalanów does not lead to a narrow pietism, as some
of his critics have alleged, because his approach is that of Bonaventure with
the refinements of Scotus. As Kolbe makes clear, a program of Marianization entails not a neglect of study, but an intensified study—provided, however, that it is done in the spirit of prayer and devotion, and provided that
one accepts Mary not only as mother but teacher:

> The choice [with] which the M.I. confronts us is not that be-
> tween the intellectual life of the independent thinker and that
> of the pious, but uncritical believer (in practice "credulous"),
> but between the conduct of the intellectual life on one's own

126. Fehlner, "Introduction," *Triple Way*, 52.

127. Fehlner, "Marian Doctrine and Devotion," *CE* 6, chapter 16.

128. Fehlner, "Marian Doctrine and Devotion," *CE* 6, chapter 16.

129. See Fehlner, "Total Consecration, Baptism," *CE* 6, chapter 1; Fehlner, "Niepokalanów in the Counsels," *CE* 6, chapter 5.

130. Fehlner, *Theologian of Auschwitz*, 67–8.

terms (radically unnatural and culpably blinding, as our Lord observed in the case of the Pharisees), or on those of the Creator-Savior, "unus omnium Magister," whose "cathedra" is the Blessed Virgin Mary.[131]

A Metaphysics of Will

The Kolbean program of Marianization, preoccupied with conformity to the divine will via conformity of one's will with the will of the Immaculate, is highly dependent on the Franciscan tradition regarding the primacy of charity and the absolute primacy of Christ, with the related metaphysics of univocity of being, the disjunctive transcendentals, the pure perfections (*perfectiones simpliciter simplices*), a conception of will as freely choosing to love the good, voluntary causality as personal act and the formal distinction *a parte rei*.

Over and over, St. Maximilian stresses that the essence of holiness or divinization consists "only in *fulfilling the Will of God* in every moment of our lives and surrendering completely to such will."[132] He encapsulates it in Conferences III and IV of his Roman Conferences, in his well-known mathematical-type formulae, $V + v = S$, and $S: V = v$:

> How does one persevere? Very simply: by annihilating one's own will to do the will of God. In this consists sanctity, for the simple reason that God loves us, and whatever he wills, he wills for our good. $S: v = V$. S signifies sanctity; one reaches sanctity when the creature's will [Latin: *voluntas*], the tiny v, equals and is united to the will of God, the big V.[133]

Commenting on this passage, Fehlner writes:

> One cannot speak of "annihilation" except in the context of a theory of will, not as intellectual appetite, but a formally distinct mode of action, the ultimate term of all intellectual activity and so formal essence of beatitude, *actus purus*. In the Scotistic theory of hypostatic union we see a particular application of this, in so far as the natural personal independence of the human nature assumed becomes personal dependence on the Person of the Word via termination of the human nature assumed in the order of subsistence. This mode of human

131. Fehlner, "Marian Doctrine and Devotion," *CE* 6, chapter 16.
132. Kolbe, *WK* 643.
133. Kolbe, Roman Conference III, *Roman Conferences*, 14.

existence is a purely personal act enabling the Man-God to enjoy divine life in an infinite mode, *secundum quid*, a mode extended via transubstantiation into the Holy Spirit in the sons of God by the grace of adoption. The key here is perfect obedience as the mode of transformation and elevation of the created will to a supernatural level of divine complacence. This underlies the distinction of *voluntas complacens* or *affectus justitiae*, and *voluntas accedens* or *affectus commodi*, and the very different modes of the *voluntas antecedens*,[134] moral or personal causality as basis of physical causality. All this postulates a metaphysic of being based on univocity, out of which arises a notion of the supernatural order of grace involving infinity and intrinsic necessity *secundum quid* as the basis for personhood in creatures in the two modes—of the hypostatic union and of transubstantiation into the Immaculate.[135]

In short, for the finite creature there is a certain "opening upon" the infinite through a union of wills, by the exercise of obedience to the divine will, though remaining a finite creature. "The created person as person, independent *secundum quid*," Fehlner writes, "is capable of personal union without ceasing to be a creature—capable via a union of wills to become conformed to Christ and, therefore, an adopted son of the Father. The Scotistic solution is not [the Bonaventurian] distinction of image and vestige, but *perfectio simpliciter simplex* with disjunctive transcendentals: infinite and finite personality or personhood. Here, the created person is finite in the natural order, infinite in the supernatural order. . . ."[136]

This mysterious union of love is made possible through the "supernatural order of grace" which is extended to creatures by way of the incarnation. However, the incarnation, whereby God lowers himself to us, and our return to God, are accomplished only by way of "that final rung in the ladder of creation by which heaven descends to earth, and earth rises to heaven . . . the Immaculate, the apex of creation and . . . a ship across infinity. . . ."[137] It is because only in her, the Immaculate Conception, do we find "that conformity [to the divine will] is perfect by grace."[138]

---

134. Regarding the *voluntas acceptans et complacens*, the *voluntas accedens*, and *voluntas antecedens* as distinct modes of willing at the heart of personal act, see "Metaphysica mariana quaedam," 17–18. See also Goff, *Caritas in Primo*, 270–72, 277–80.

135. Fehlner, *Theologian of Auschwitz*, 173–74.

136. Fehlner, *Theologian of Auschwitz*, 278.

137. Fehlner, "Immaculate . . . Mystery," *CE* 6, chapter 3. See also Kolbe, *WK* 1291.

138. Fehlner, "Immaculate . . . Mystery," *CE* 6, chapter 3.

For St. Maximilian, then, we can correctly speak of doing the will of the Immaculate as doing the will of God—as he does repeatedly[139]—and of our becoming perfectly conformed to the divine will through "transubstantiation into the Immaculate," whereby the Immaculate purifies our love (act of the will), and Jesus, the Word Incarnate, "divinizes" or "infinitizes" that love:[140] *Divinisatio hominis usque ad Deum-hominem per Dei-hominis Matrem:*[141]

> She herself is the Immaculate Conception. As a result, she is such in us as well and transforms us into herself as immaculate beings. . . . She is the Mother of God, and also the Mother of God within us . . . and makes us gods and mothers of God, who generate Jesus Christ in the souls of men. . . . How sublime! . . .[142]

This mystical insight of the saint exquisitely expresses the Bonaventurian metaphysics of Marian mediation, incorporating Scotistic insights, complementing and completing them. Therefore, it is absolutely correct to say that "perfection consists in fulfilling the will of the Immaculate; when the Immaculate lives and works in us (in-existence), perfection is attained."[143] For this reason, at the heart of the program is total consecration to the Immaculate, because it, "engages the will at its most essential, viz., in that which makes the will a distinctive power to love at the heart of personal existence."[144] In other words, because it engages our will in a relation to the will of the Immaculate, total consecration to the Immaculate constitutes the program of our proportionate "reaction" to the "action" of divine love, of our return to God.

139. See, for example, Kolbe, *WK* 140; 380; 1334.

140. Fehlner, "Immaculate . . . Mystery," *CE* 6, chapter 3; Kolbe, *WK* 1224. The employment of the language of "transubstantiation," in the analogical sense, appears to reflect Bonaventure's view of sanctifying grace as involving a certain substantial (and not merely accidental) transformation of the soul, in view of "partaking of the divine nature" (cf. 2 Pet 1:4), of loving as God loves. See Fehlner, *Kolbe . . . Pneumatologist,* 63–64n133; Miravalle, "Mary and Divinization," 91–92.

141. Kolbe, *WK* 508.

142. Kolbe, *WK* 486.

143. Fehlner, *Theologian of Auschwitz,* 250.

144. Fehlner, "Total Consecration," *CE* 6, chapter 1.

Pneumatology, Trinitarian Theology
and Christocentrism

Much of the theological terminology of St. Maximilian touches on the mystery of the Holy Spirit in one way or another, whether it concerns the mystery of the Trinity and the nature of the person and procession of the Holy Spirit, or whether we are speaking of the so-called economy of salvation and the mission of the Holy Spirit. In both cases, there is an accentuation of the close association of the Holy Spirit with charity: in Bonaventurian terms, within the Trinity, the procession is the consummation of the unity of the Father and the Son, reflected in the mission of the Holy Spirit as a mission of charity.[145]

"The core of Catholic pneumatology," Fehlner writes, is "to reveal the nature of divine charity in living the love of the Father and Son in the Immaculate Conception, uncreated and created."[146] The Immaculate Conception is the special "unveiling," or revelation, of Trinitarian love, standing "in the same relation to Father and Son in the economic Trinity as the Holy Spirit in eternity. The fulness of their love in the Holy Spirit is in her in time."[147]

St. Maximilian keys in on the Immaculate Conception as the "vertex of love," the one who is "woven into the love of the Most Blessed Trinity. . . . In the union of the Holy Spirit with her, not only does love unite these two beings, but the first one of them is all the love of the most holy Trinity, while the second is all the love of creation. Thus, in this union heaven meets earth, all of heaven with all of the earth, all uncreated love with all created love."[148] So united are the Immaculate and the Holy Spirit in love that they share the name *Immaculate Conception*:

> In bringing the dogma of the Immaculate Conception into intimate relation with the procession and mission of the Holy Spirit St Maximilian has brought to theology considerable depth and freshness. Both the Holy Spirit and the Mother of God can say: I am the Immaculate Conception, because in each is the totality of love of the Father and Son, in the first by nature, in the second by grace; hence they are different persons.[149]

---

145. Fehlner, *Role of Charity*, 92.

146. Fehlner, *Kolbe . . . Pneumatologist*, 180.

147. Fehlner, "Complementum Ss. Trinitatis," *CE* 6, chapter 4.

148. Kolbe, *WK* 1318.

149. Fehlner, "Immaculate . . . Mystery," *CE* 6, chapter 3.

The very name, *Immaculate Conception*, then, is that of spousal love. Therefore, Mary herself, though remaining a creature, reveals the person and mission of the of the Holy Spirit, and "by venerating the Immaculata, we venerate in a very special way the Holy Spirit."[150] Because theirs is a union of love, the union of Mary with the Holy Spirit is clearly differentiated from the hypostatic union: "The Immaculate is not united to the Holy Spirit hypostatically, but in a spousal union so intimate that the obedient humility of the Immaculate reveals the Holy Spirit as the eternal [receptacle] of the total love of Father and Son."[151]

By his stupendous insight, St. Maximilian highlights what is already plain in the theology of Bonaventure and Scotus (and in the church): the differentiation of the processions and missions of the Son and the Holy Spirit. The complementarity of their missions is clarified by the distinction of their mediatorial roles, as clarified in Mary Immaculate: "The mediation of the Savior-Redeemer is distinctively that of the Son; but the mediation whereby the work of the incarnation is sanctified (viz., whereby a true man is literally truly a divine person) and that work becomes sanctificatory of others through redemptive sacrifice, involves what is distinctive of mediation of the Spirit. In the economy of salvation this mediation is distinctively Marian and maternal."[152]

This mediation is revelatory and clarifying in character, unveiling the mystery of the mediation of the Son also in eternity. These complementary missions of the Son and the Holy Spirit in the economy of salvation is reflective of their processions within the Holy Trinity—the Son by generation, the Holy Spirit by spiration-conception. The Immaculate Conception further sheds light on how this mysterious "unfolding" and "enfolding" of divine love at the heart of the Trinity, as Fehlner describes it, is enlarged into creation, explained by St. Maximilian with the Newtonian "action-reaction" analogy to describe the "sending forth" of divine love from the God and the return to him, the culmination of which is found in the "vertex of love," the starting point of that proportionate return.

Contrary to what some critics have claimed, Fehlner reiterates that acceptance of Kolbe's insights into the Immaculate Conception is a safeguard against falling into a false "pentecostalism" that would exalt the mystery of the Holy Spirit at the expense of the incarnation and true Christocentrism, for it decisively upholds the centrality of the incarnation (in Franciscan terms: the absolute primacy of Christ). At the same time, it prevents relegation of

---

150. Kolbe, *WK* 634.

151. Fehlner, "Immaculate . . . Mystery," *CE* 6, chapter 3.

152. Fehlner, *Kolbe . . . Pneumatologist*, 130.

the person and mission of the Holy Spirit to obscurity, for without the presence of the Holy Spirit in union with Our Lady, "the mediatory character of the Son in his divinity, and hence the mediatory work accomplished in his humanity, [would] remain for us impenetrable mysteries."[153]

It is the mystery of the Immaculate Conception that brings these mysteries and their interrelation into sharp focus: "the fecundity of the Holy Spirit is for the sake of the incarnation and Redemption; the mediation of the Holy Spirit is for the sake of our incorporation into Christ as his members. In virtue of the first the created Immaculate Conception is Mother of God and coredemptrix; in virtue of the second Mother of the Church."[154] A sound pneumatology and a sound Christology are informed and guided by this "Marian principle."

The fecundity of the Holy Spirit, the fruit of which is the Word Incarnate, is not realized apart from her; and the mediation of the Holy Spirit is not exercised apart from her. Therefore, this Marian principle upholds true Christocentrism, which in turn sheds light on the mystery of the church.

> Not all 'christocentrism' is authentic, and not all authentic christocentrism is Marian in the same way. Not 'Christus solus' [Christ alone], but 'Christus cum Maria et per Mariam et in Maria' [Christ with Mary and in Mary and through Mary] defines authentic christocentrism; and Franciscan christocentrism is defined in relation to the Immaculate Conception. . . .[155]

A denial or neglect of the mystery of the Immaculate Conception as lying at the heart and nexus of these branches of theology leads inevitably to a "colonization" of these fields of study, which raises the risk of veiling these mysteries, above all the mystery of the Holy Trinity. "It is the great merit of St. Maximilian, in illustrating theologically the Trinitarian character of the mystery of the Immaculate, also to have shown how and why total consecration to the Immaculate, without restriction, is the only basis for a thoroughly Christocentric spirituality."[156]

Ecclesiology

We may sum up Fehlner's ecclesiological approach in this one phrase, borne out by his 1965 dissertation: "charity at the heart of the church." It is

153. Fehlner, "Immaculate . . . Mystery," *CE* 6, chapter 3.
154. Fehlner, "Immaculate . . . Mystery," *CE* 6, chapter 3.
155. Fehlner, "Mary and Franciscanism," *CE* 3, chapter 1.
156. Fehlner, "Immaculate . . . Mystery," *CE* 6, chapter 3.

a charity which is the bond of the unity of the church, carries the enduring presence of Christ in the most holy Eucharist and in his mystical members, and points to the mystery of the Holy Trinity. The church is none other than:

> an outpouring of divine grace that in one way or another includes every other particular grace, and to be a manifestation of that dynamic, communicative, disinterested divine charity which motivated every work of God *ad extra*, and which lies at the very heart of the Trinity itself. The return of men to the Father from whom they came cannot be anything but ecclesiological, through the church and in the church, as the means and actualization of that pilgrimage.[157]

This divine charity flows through the veins of the church, as it were, through the maternal mediation of the Virgin Mary, as spouse of God through her supereminent relationship of charity with the persons of the holy Trinity, and as Mother of God and Mother of the Church. By constantly drawing from the wellsprings of charity in her time of pilgrimage, the church is progressing toward that perfection already realized in Our Lady. This is the meaning behind the expression, *Virgo Ecclesia facta* ("Virgin made Church"), addressed by St. Francis to Our Lady, which zeroes in on the ecclesiological import of the mystery of the Immaculate Conception: "What is fully realized in Mary as the 'created Immaculate Conception' since Pentecost has been in the process of being fully realized in the church."[158]

Notably, when he revised his dissertation near the end of his life, Fehlner added this title of Our Lady to the existing title of his revised dissertation, in a tip of the hat to this Marian principle pervading St. Bonaventure's ecclesiology: *Virgo Ecclesia Facta: The Role of Charity in the Ecclesiology of St. Bonaventure*. Thus, for Fehlner, the title, *Virgo Ecclesia facta*, "does neatly synthesize his [Bonaventure's] teaching on the role of charity in the unity of the church: a unity found first in the Virgin Mother via the indwelling of the Spirit in her soul and body and then extended through the maternal mediation of Mary to the church."[159]

> In a very unique way the personal relation of the Holy Spirit and Mary Immaculate, whereby the mystery of the incarnation and all aspects of that mystery are Marian in mode, guarantees the Christological character of ecclesiology as so also the Trinitarian via the hierarchization of the church as the "Trinitas œconomica." In our times this central role of the Holy Spirit and the

---

157. Fehlner, *Role of Charity*, CE 3, part 3.

158. Fehlner, *Role of Charity*, CE 3, part 3.

159. Fehlner, *Role of Charity*, CE 3, part 3.

Virgin Mary in realizing in the church that mysterious charity which is its unity has been set forth as that of the uncreated and created Immaculate Conception.[160]

The import of this observation of Fehlner cannot be overstated. In drawing out the ecclesiological implications of St. Maximilian's mystical insight, based on a sound Christology and Trinitarian theology, Fehlner opens up a whole new realm of reflection on the theological patrimony of the saint. This is why, for Fehlner, this age of the Immaculate and of the Holy Spirit is also the *age of the church*.[161] The dogmatic clarification of the Immaculate Conception marked "the beginning of a profounder, more explicit grasp of the mystery of the church itself."[162] By contemplation of this mystery, the church arrives at a deeper understanding of her true identity, because it is through the prism of the Immaculate Conception that "the church grasps the mystery of grace . . . without which that created communion which is the church would not and could not be. It is through this prism as well that the church comes to grasp the nature of her mission for men in the contemporary world."[163]

The close link between and integration of ecclesiology, Christology and Trinitarian theology (as well as pneumatology) can be perceived through the lens of the primacy of charity, and in light of the mystery of the Immaculate Conception, reflected in the presentation of "the Blessed Virgin Mary, Mother of God, in the Mystery of Christ and in the church," in chapter 8 of the Vatican II Constitution, *Lumen Gentium*. It is particularly in this sense that St. Maximilian can be said to have anticipated the Second Vatican Council, and why the work of Fr. Peter Damian breathes the true spirit of the Council, even by way of anticipation in his dissertation, and even before his writings explicitly reflected the priority of the Marian principle. The latter point, namely, the priority of the Marian principle in the church, even with

---

160. Fehlner, *Role of Charity*, CE 3, part 3.

161. See Fehlner, "Mary and Franciscanism," *CE* 3, chapter 1; Fehlner, "Immaculate . . . Extraordinary Synod 1985," *CE* 6, chapter 8; Fehlner, "Complementum Ss. Trinitatis," *CE* 6, chapter 4; Fehlner, "Niepokalanów in the Counsels," *CE* 6, chapter 5; Fehlner, "Marian Doctrine and Devotion," *CE* 6, chapter 16; Fehlner, "Martyr of Charity," *CE* 6, chapter 17; Fehlner, "Opening Address," *CE* 4, chapter 9; Fehlner, *Theologian of Auschwitz*, 8n24, 97–98, 131–32, 143, 176, 183, 269–70; see Kolbe, *WK* 664, 1242, 1248; see also Fehlner, "Two Testaments," *CE* 6, chapter 18, and the conference of St. Maximilian, June 13, 1933.

162. Fehlner, "Mary and Theology," *CE* 1, chapter 1.

163. Fehlner, "Immaculate . . . Extraordinary Synod 1985," *CE* 6, chapter 8.

respect to the Petrine and apostolic principles, has been explicitly confirmed by the post-Vatican II papal magisterium.[164]

This brings us to Fehlner's consideration of Mary in the exercise of her maternal mediation as "memory of the church," in light of the confirmation of this title by St. John Paul II. Her presence at the heart of the church is a living memory of her Son, and a reminder of the presence of the Holy Spirit.[165] Fehlner observes: "The apostolic hierarchy continues to teach as an extension of Christ here and now, but only in dependence on Mary as memory, just as understanding follows upon and from remembering, and terminates in love of God":[166]

> The church herself recognizes this maternal mediation not as a substitute for the authoritative teaching and work of the Apostles and their successors, but as its premise. . . . By making Mary's faith her own, the church remains faithful to her head and Savior.[167]

The maternal mediation of Mary as "memory of the church" is also crucial for theologians and their work for the church, for she guides theologians in understanding and embracing the church's various theological traditions.[168]

As far as what the practice of total consecration on the ecclesial level looks like, that is, what the incorporation of the mystery of the Immaculate into the life of the church means, the community of Niepokalanów of St. Maximilian's day serves as the type, the *ecclesiola*. As was the case at Niepokalanów, so as more and more members of the church enter into this mystery, the "Marian personality" of the church is placed in greater relief through a sort of "corporate transubstantiation into the Immaculate."[169] Thus, while the program of total consecration to the Immaculate and "incorporation of the mystery of the Immaculate" is something that is to be put in practice by individuals, it has a fundamentally ecclesial orientation and finds its highest expression as an ecclesial act.[170] It follows that any

164. Fehlner, "Marian Slavery," *CE* 6, chapter 12. In recent papal teachings: John Paul II, Speech, December 22, 1987; Benedict XVI, Homily, March 25, 2006.

165. See John Paul II, Homily, January 1, 1987; Benedict XVI, Regina Caeli, May 9, 2010.

166. Fehlner, "Sources of Scotus' Mariology," *CE* 4, chapter 9.

167. Fehlner, "*Redemptoris Mater*," *CE* 6, chapter 9.

168. See Fehlner, "Sources of Scotus' Mariology," *CE* 4, chapter 9.

169. See Fehlner, *Kolbe . . . Pneumatologist*, 151.

170. This is precisely the nature of the numerous papal consecrations to the Immaculate Heart of Mary over the last century.

practice of "Marian consecration" that would lead to a sectarianism is at variance with what St. Maximilian describes, to the degree that it obscures the ecclesial unity which manifests the charity of the uncreated and created Immaculate Conception.

This, in turn, has implications for the question of ecumenism, because if the charity at the heart of the church is the bond of unity, it is also the source of reunification with our separated brothers and sisters. Thus, the Immaculate Conception is the principle and basis for true ecumenism, contrary to the desire in many Catholic circles to eliminate Our Lady from the question (which results, not in reunification, but a spiritual condition risking loss of Catholic faith). A Marianized or "immaculatized" approach to theology integrates what is true among different approaches into a "higher synthesis." In such a setting, unlimited consecration to the Immaculate is "a corollary of valid sacramental baptism and the gift of faith (at the ontological level) at the empirical or conscious level of theology and spirituality for all: Catholics and separated brethren in good faith."[171]

The "Golden Thread" of the Immaculate Conception: A Theology of History

"It is clear," Fehlner writes, that St. Maximilian "held as certain (and not merely as a working hypothesis) that St. Francis knew the Immaculate and had made Her Cause that of his Order. For him, it is not sufficient to say that St. Francis had some way anticipated the doctrinal development."[172] It is a legacy Our Lady herself conferred as a gift to St. Francis and, through him, to the Franciscan Order and the church.[173] This legacy was publicly ratified by the Conventual Franciscans in 1719 and confirmed universally by the dogmatic definition of the mystery in 1854. The legacy is not only to be embraced but developed to its fullest implications for the greatest glory of God; hence, the "cause of the Immaculate" is still a central concern both for the Franciscan Order and for the church.

---

171. Fehlner, "Redemption, Metaphysics," *CE* 4, chapter 6.

172. Fehlner, "A Thesis," *CE* 6, chapter 2. For Fehlner, the title, "Spouse of the Holy Spirit," a title first given to Our Lady by St. Francis, and the *Salute to the Virgin*, are two primary sources in St. Francis' own writings for recognizing *de facto* what is otherwise explicitly missing: the title, "Immaculate Conception." See "Mary in the Franciscan," *CE* 3, chapter 5; "Saint Francis and Mary," *CE* 3, chapter 3.

173. This legacy is reflected and—we may even say—enshrined in chapter 8 of the Vatican II Constitution on the Church, *Lumen Gentium*. See Ondrako, *Rebuild My Church*, c. 6.

The thesis of Kolbe concerning the Marian (immaculatist) character of the Franciscan Order appears to find its proximate basis in a well-
known nineteenth-century work by Fr. Filippo Rossi, who saw in the 1854
dogmatic definition of the Immaculate Conception a counterpart to the
founding of the Order of Friars Minor in 1209. His main thesis: The Immaculate Conception "stands at the very center of the plan of salvation and
the life of the church."[174] Through his image of the "golden thread," Kolbe
builds upon the thesis of Fr. Rossi to affirm a "second page" inaugurated
after the dogmatic definition, which involves "incorporation" of the mystery into the life of the Franciscan Order and the church. In this second
page, "the former theological-metaphysical cultural tradition of the Franciscan Order is not lost or abandoned, but restored in being recapitulated
in this fuller setting, whose heart is total consecration to the Immaculate,
the conscious and definitive realization in a communal and institutional
form of the radical Marian dimensions of poverty, chastity and obedience
envisioned in the Rule of St. Francis."[175] By way of the golden thread, following upon the dogmatic definition of the Immaculate Conception, Our
Lady guides the Franciscan charism to the fullness of its development, a
"newness within institutional continuity."[176]

The mystery of the Immaculate Conception, then, is the focal point
for understanding not only the *nature*, but the *history* of the Franciscan
Order, for she "stands at the point where dogma, metaphysics and history
meet."[177] Fehlner, like Kolbe, goes further in affirming that the influence
of this mystery (1) has a *universal* extension, touching the history of the
church, of the world, and of each individual soul; and (2) is *active* and *dynamic*, because it is *personal*, in light of her universal maternal mediation
which rests on this mystery, itself intimately connected with the absolute
primacy of Christ: "The Virgin Mother is the 'Mediatrix' par excellence
of all history and of every history, because she conceived not a human
person, but a divine [person]."[178]

---

174. Fehlner, "Other Page," *CE* 6, chapter 13.

175. Fehlner, "Mary and Franciscanism," *CE* 3, chapter 1.

176. Fehlner, *Theologian of Auschwitz*, 119.

177. Fehlner, "Marian Geography of Faith," *CE* 6, chapter 11.

178. Fehlner, "Marian Geography of Faith," *CE* 6, chapter 11. This insight is marvelously confirmed by St. John Paul II in his Encyclical Letter, *Redemptoris Mater*, 25, who
speaks of the presence of Mary in the history of souls. Fehlner reflects: "That faith [of
Mary] defining the history of her interior life is the pattern for the church's history, for
the history of every soul, and so affects the whole of history." Fehlner, "*Redemptoris
Mater*," *CE* 6, chapter 9.

Thus, the Immaculate Conception is the basis of a *theology of history* and the principle of the intelligibility of history, pointing to the recapitulation of all things in Christ and their return to the Father. It is a principle which is valid for all times, places and peoples:

> The entire structure of the M.I. and of the spirituality of total consecration and "transubstantiation" into the Immaculate is predicated on the mystery of the Immaculate Conception and the implications of her universal mediation for the theology of history. In a word there is nothing dated about it, for it is the practical coefficient of the basic dogmatic-metaphysical principle governing the theology of history. At the heart of that principle is the charity of Christ, whose noblest fruit is the Immaculate.[179]

In the history of souls there occurs at both the personal and societal level what St. Maximilian describes as "spiritual evolution," which he articulates clearly in his 1933 letter to the seminarians of the Conventual Franciscan Order.[180] This spiritual evolution entails not a "change of species" at the material level—which Kolbe flatly rejects[181]—but a spiritual perfection of the creature, a divination or sanctification via "transubstantiation into the Immaculate." In the "second page," this perfection assumes an ever-greater profile in the history of individuals, as well as in the history of the church and the world. Regarding the Franciscan Order, it means for Kolbe that the goal of the Order is not simply to attain or reclaim the seraphic ideal of St. Francis, but to develop that ideal, surpassing the holiness of the Seraphic Father. For the church, this spiritual evolution, characterized by a progressive realization of the "global vision of Catholic life in a new form," leads to "the glorification of the church begun at Pentecost, to be consummated at the second coming of Jesus, to claim the church, his bride, without spot or wrinkle, immaculatized like Mary and by her."[182]

In this regard, Fehlner draws a parallel between St. Maximilian's thesis and the somewhat enigmatic theology of history outlined by St. Bonaventure in his *Collationes in Hexaemeron*, in particular collations 20–23. Bonaventure characterizes the life of the Order founded by St. Francis as "cherubic," whereas the higher "seraphic" spirituality of St. Francis would seem to find

179. Fehlner, "Martyr of Charity," *CE* 6, chapter 17.

180. Kolbe, *WK* 486.

181. See in particular Kolbe, *WK* 1169, *Non credo*, "I Do Not Believe." Kolbe's rejection of any sort of material evolution is the subject of Fehlner's essay, "Vertex Creationis," *CE* 6, chapter 6.

182. Fehlner, *Theologian of Auschwitz*, 92.

expression in a form of life perhaps not yet concrete in Bonaventure's day. In 2002, Fehlner suggests in "Martyr of Charity" that this form of life corresponds "to that which St. Maximilian cultivated, based on total consecration, the primary (or fourth) Marian vow and 'transubstantiation' into the Immaculate as the highest form of perfect conformity to the Crucified."[183] Later on (in 2012), he presses this reflection further:

> Could this community be a Franciscan institute which by way of the Marian vow of St. Maximilian expressly lives the Marian mystery at the center of Francis' charism, and fully illustrates the mystery of charity and contemplation so central to the *Triple Way*, a mystery which is also that of the created Immaculate Conception...?[184]

In his last work (completed in 2017), *The Theologian of Auschwitz*, Fehlner clarifies that "St. Bonaventure notes a certain gap between the Marian character of St. Francis' vocation and the rebuilding [of] the *domus Domini*. This leads to either another new order of St. Francis or to exactly what St. Maximilian was proposing as the desire of Mary Immaculate for the perfection of the original Order founded by St. Francis."[185] He states further:

> A careful reading of St. Bonaventure's *Collationes in Hexaemeron* ... suggests that St. Maximilian's two pages correspond to the sixth and seventh stages or ages of the church in which Bonaventure places St. Francis and his Order. More concretely, that which brings about the full Franciscan character of the Order is the cause of the Immaculate centered on total consecration of its members to the Immaculate Heart and incorporation of the mystery of the Immaculate Conception into the Order at its very center. ... Kolbe's focus, in particular, is upon religious orders and, above all, the Franciscan Order, in inaugurating in the church, via incorporation of the mystery of the Immaculate Conception, its divinization or spiritualization of the church.[186]

Hence, whereas, at one point, Fehlner appears to raise the possibility of the emergence of a new juridical entity within the church reflecting the Kolbean vision, he ultimately interprets the "global vision" proposed by St. Maximilian in terms of the Order founded by St. Francis and of the M.I.,

183. Fehlner, "Martyr of Charity," *CE* 6, chapter 17. Further on in this introduction, I discuss Fehlner's views of the Marian vow in more detail.

184. Bonaventure, *Triple Way*, 191n163. In Ratzinger, *Theology of the History*, Ratzinger also suggests a juridical form within the church of such a "seraphic order."

185. Fehlner, *Theologian of Auschwitz*, 87.

186. Fehlner, *Theologian of Auschwitz*, 132–33. See Bonaventure, *Hex.*, col. 22.

and posits the "inauguration" of his vision in the church on that basis. In the view of Kolbe and Fehlner, Our Lady has given the gift to the church in this manner, and the community of Niepokalanów founded by St. Maximilian is the enduring sign.[187]

In Niepokalanów, the *ecclesiola*, we see the concrete expression for what it means in the "second page" to "incorporate the mystery of the Immaculate Conception" into the lives of individuals, of the Franciscan Order, of the church, and of the world. Such is possible only through a total and exclusive dedication to the "cause of the Immaculate," i.e., the practice of unlimited consecration at all levels. For the Franciscan Order, this means that "the Order exists only for the sake of a service to Mary in rebuilding the church . . . Marian theology and devotion is not a secondary or marginal aspect of Franciscan life, but its very foundation."[188]

For this reason, in his day St. Maximilian strenuously defended the life and distinct program of formation of Niepokalanów against efforts, even well-meaning, that would undermine the community. Evidently, it requires a serious quest for personal holiness—with emphasis on sanctification of the intellect in a spirit of prayer and devotion—a sincere intention to live out the program of Marian consecration with its demand of a radical disposal of one's entire self to Our Lady, and an acceptance of the underlying Franciscan theology and metaphysics.[189]

It is important to underscore the purpose for which Niepokalanów was established: the service of the Immaculate, not the reform of the Order. In fact, however, the renewal of franciscan life in the perfect observance of

187. See Fehlner, "Niepokalanów in the Counsels," *CE* 6, chapter 5; Fehlner, "*Hereditas Kolbiana*," *CE* 6, chapter 7.

188. Fehlner, *Theologian of Auschwitz*, 105.

189. Fehlner treats at length the various objections raised against Niepokalanów or proposals for "reform" and St. Maximilian's response. See, in particular, Fehlner, "Niepokalanów in the Counsels," *CE* 6, chapter 5; Fehlner, *Theologian of Auschwitz*, 105–27. Among the classes of objections raised were: (1) the supposed incompatibility of life at Niepokalanów with the *Constitutions* of the Franciscan Order; (2) difficulties with adjustment to the heroic form of life with its missionary orientation; (3) the risk of a voluntaristic exercise of authority stemming from a defective notion of religious obedience; (4) the supposed "divergence" of the form of observance and discipline from the received Franciscan traditions; (5) the placement of an explicitly Marian goal for the observance of discipline; and (6) objections concerning practical observance of such a Marian program. With the support of his superiors, St. Maximilian responded that such objections did not touch upon the essence of the life. Regarding the risk of voluntarism, however, which is manifested in a distortion in the understanding and/or practice of obedience, Fehlner does note that "the possibility of voluntarism as a philosophy of authority and obedience being present in cities of the Immaculate and how to deal with it is a problem still to be fully analyzed": Fehlner, *Theologian of Auschwitz*, 110.

the *Rule* and *Constitutions* naturally followed upon this, because without a heroic observance of the *Rule*, Niepokalanów would not be itself the possession of the Immaculate, completely at her disposition, and its members would not be living fully their total consecration.[190]

It follows that one is not to seek out unlimited consecration or belonging to the Immaculate *in order to effect* renewal of the Order. Rather, consecration is in view of the "cause of the Immaculate"; but if it is sincerely and perseveringly practiced, it will yield the fruit of renewal, because it is God, through the Immaculate, who makes all things new (cf. Rev 21:5).

The Marian Vow

As far as I can tell, the first reference Fr. Peter Damian makes to the Marian vow made privately by St. Maximilian and some of his fellow religious is in his 1982 essay, "Total Consecration, Baptism and the Franciscan Ideal." That vow consisted of a "special promise" to obey the command of one's legitimate superiors to be sent to the missions. This special promise pertains to the M.I. and the City of the Immaculate insofar as it regards the unlimitedness of consecration to the Immaculate, which in Kolbe's mind is directly correlated to unlimited availability for the missions. The friar who makes the vow freely binds himself to this availability in accordance with the command of the superiors—the condition of which is specified in chapter 12 of the *Rule* of St. Francis. The motivation for making the vow, in St. Maximilian's view, is to give the Immaculate unlimited freedom to dispose of her subjects in view of her universal mission of saving souls. Such a vow presupposes not only the consecration, but, at least at the most intense level of that consecration, the form of life characterizing the City of the Immaculate:

> This special promise, his fourth vow, St. Maximilian identifies with total consecration in the third degree. And inasmuch as St. Francis deeply desired this kind of martyrdom in and for the missions as the crown of his calling, and was granted it in his stigmatization, and inasmuch as Francis always asserted the Marian inspiration and guidance of all facets of his vocation, the Kolbean interpretation and application of chapter twelve of the Rule under the aegis of the Immaculate is an insight fully in accord with the mind of his Father Francis.
>
> Within chapter 12 of the *Regula Bullata* St. Francis juxtaposes three aspects of his vocation that have subsequently been recognized on all sides as distinctive of the Franciscan spirit:

190. Fehlner, "Niepokalanów in the Counsels," *CE* 6, chapter 5.

zeal for the missions, obedience to the pope and exact observance of the Gospel, living humbly and in poverty. A part of
the genius of St. Maximilian has been to make clear the reason
for this linkage: perfect obedience through total consecration
to the Immaculate.[191]

Although Fehlner does not otherwise explicitly mention the vow in his
writings during this period, he does make a number of other references to
the removal of the restriction of chapter 12 of the Rule for the reason of total
service in the cause of the Immaculate.[192]

After his transfer to the Franciscan Friars of the Immaculate, Fehlner
makes reference to this vow in the context of the Marian vow taken within
that religious institute. He writes that "Franciscan life lived in a spirit of
total consecration to the Immaculate [is] ultimately realized in the Marian
vow of total consecration, or of transubstantiation into the Immaculate."[193]
He further states:

> Placed at the foundation core of the evangelical counsels, total
> consecration to the Immaculate, in particular in the form of the
> Marian vow, radicalizes poverty, chastity and obedience, and
> so does not merely remove restrictions on their observance[194]
> found in the Rule or dispensations therefrom in view of the
> characteristic feature of the Franciscan Order during the first
> page of its history. More importantly, it provides the key to the
> realization of their full import as a form of life for the "repair" or
> upbuilding of the church as immaculate bride of Christ, without
> spot or wrinkle, because transubstantiated into the Immaculate.

We see in the above statements a number of specifications of his earlier thought. The first is that the vow is associated with the Kolbean ideal of
"transubstantiation into the Immaculate," although it is important to make
the distinction that the "transubstantiation" does not pertain to the content
of the vow *in itself*; rather, the vow is the efficacious means for the disposal
of oneself in this regard. Second, while not supplying for any supposed "lacuna" in the evangelical counsels, the Marian vow nonetheless makes plain
that at their base is what we might call a "Marian principle" which, when so

191. Fehlner, "Total Consecration," *CE* 6, chapter 1. St. Maximilian outlines his
views of this vow in the following letters of his writings: *WK* 395, 398, 399, 402, 409,
412, 419, 492, 588, 653.

192. See Fehlner, "Niepokalanów in the Counsels," *CE* 6, chapter 5; Fehlner, "Conventual Charism," *CE* 5, chapter 10; Fehlner, "*Hereditas Kolbiana*," *CE* 6, chapter 7.

193. Fehlner, "Mary and Franciscanism," *CE* 3, chapter 1.

194. Fehlner, "Mary and Franciscanism," *CE* 3, chapter 1.

acknowledged and consciously put into practice in the context of religious life, leads to a perfection in the observance of the counsels—a perfection already present in the Blessed Virgin who, as Spouse of the Holy Spirit, stands, as it were, at the origin of all forms of religious life. Third, the Marian consecration expressed in the form of the vow is placed in direct relation to the command the Lord gave St. Francis to "rebuild my church." Not only is Marian consecration and the vow in accord with the Franciscan charism, they give full expression to that charism, insofar as they are directly correlated to the Marian character of the vocation of the Seraphic Father.

The most extensive reflections Fehlner has to offer on the subject are in his final work, *The Theologian of Auschwitz*, completed after his return to the Conventual Friars. The observations he makes here may be summarized as follows:

- The Marian vow rests upon the consecration, and not vice versa.

- The vow is placed in relation to the Statue of the M.I., insofar as it pertains to its effectiveness.

- The core of Marian consecration and the object of the vow "is possession by the Immaculate of the consecrated person, precisely as an extension of the Immaculate Mediatrix in and for the church."[195]

- The vow pertains not to the nature of the evangelical counsels, but to the degree of perfection of their observance. In no way must the vow be seen as a substitute for or replacement of the three religious vows, in whole or in part.[196]

- Therefore, the vow "does not constitute a different species of consecrated life, more perfect than religious life generally."[197]

- However, the vow is indeed the basis for structuring the common life of prayer and mission.[198]

- One must distinguish *intensive* from *extensive* unlimitedness of Marian consecration. Intensively there are no limits, but extensively unlimitedness will be qualified by circumstances such as one's daily duties and state of life. In the case of religious life, there will always be juridical limitations.

---

195. Fehlner, *Theologian of Auschwitz*, 119.

196. See Fehlner, *Theologian of Auschwitz*, 93–95, 98.

197. Fehlner, *Theologian of Auschwitz*, 119.

198. Fehlner, *Theologian of Auschwitz*, 106.

- The effectiveness and envisioned fruits of observance of the vow, and the prevention or correction of abuses stemming from deformities in its implementation, require its observance to be verified just as much (or even more) in religious superiors as in their subjects.

Fehlner drew out some of the implications of Kolbe's thought and contributed his own observations based on his experiences of living among the Conventual Franciscan Friars and the Franciscan Friars of the Immaculate. As with the M.I., we can indeed envision the Marian vow as destined for the whole church, something which is its common patrimony and, therefore, ultimately subject to its oversight and juridical regulation.[199]

Mariology and the Marian Principle

Is it apparent that what in modern theology comprises the discipline of Mariology pervades the whole of Kolbean thought and the whole corpus of Fehlner's Kolbean reflections as well. At the heart of Kolbe's Marian program is a Mariology that finds its source in the theology of Bonaventure and Duns Scotus, builds upon that and finds its eminent expression in the relation between the Holy Spirit and Mary as the uncreated and created Immaculate Conception. This insight sheds light on the rest of theology, showing that what Kolbe was expounding, far from being restricted to the enrichment of Mariology, was the basis for the renewal of all of theology by way of its *Marianization* or *immaculatization*—part of his "global vision of Catholic life in a new form." Fehlner elaborates this Marian principle for the renewal of theology in his 1978 "Mary and Theology: Scotus Revisited." That essay is the "Marian plan," the starting point for understanding the prophetic character of the Fehlner-Kolbe program of renewal. For Fehlner, "Marianization of our faith means not simply additional devotional exercises, or additional study of Marian dogmas, but a total marianization of the structures of Christian existence, personal and communal."[200]

Fehlner was, of course, deeply invested in the development of Mariology as a discipline in its own right, demonstrated above all by his enormous contribution on the subject of Marian coredemption—a contribution that, in terms of sheer volume of output, has perhaps never been equaled. He taught Mariology as a seminary professor, and he had in mind the compilation of a dogmatic treatise on Mariology organized around the Immaculate

199. The observance and promotion (albeit discreetly) of the Marian vow as a private vow, as practiced by St. Maximilian and his confreres, were known and approved by his religious superiors: Geiger, "Marian Vow," Unpublished manuscript.

200. Fehlner, "*Virgo Ecclesia Facta*," *CE* 3, chapter 6.

Conception as its "first principle."[201] A Mariology so presented would follow historical contours, because it is organized with respect to "the order of execution of the divine plan," which "presupposes the order of intention."[202]

But the focus of Kolbe and Fehlner transcends Mariology strictly speaking and considers the Marian principle, centered on the mystery of the Immaculate Conception, as the basis for the renewal of all of theology. The Marian principle may be considered under the characteristics of *clarifying*, *unifying*, and *harmonizing*.

The Marian principle is *clarifying* insofar as it directs us to a more precise understanding of the mysteries of the Faith and their proper interrelation. Resting on the absolute primacy of Christ, it is the basis of a sound Christocentrism, "which places Christ between Father and Holy Spirit within the Trinity; and without places him between the Father and the Immaculate, and the Immaculate between us and him."[203] Thus accepted, it serves as a safeguard against all forms of spirituality and theological exposition which are based upon a distortion of these mysteries:

> The mystery of the Immaculate in the Kolbean approach guarantees the exclusion of any excess in spirituality or practical pneumatology, whether the extreme be that of devotionalism, Pentecostalism, joachimism, or that of "liberation theology." It does so, because the mystery of the Immaculate is not the kingdom, but the necessary mode of that one kingdom ruled by Christ, Son of God and of Mary: necessary because so willed by the Father as the mode of that absolute kingship, absolute because realized in a Marian way. A spirituality or a Mariology not centered in Christ is impossible in an immaculatist context.[204]

Conscious rejection of the Marian principle leads to confusion regarding the mystery of Christ, as the Christological controversies in the early part of the first millennium illustrate.[205] "It is the great merit of St.

---

201. Fehlner began but never completed this project. It remains for someone else so inspired to fulfill it.

202. Fehlner, *Theologian of Auschwitz*, 285. "Mary is Immaculate," Fehlner writes, "to be the Mother of God and Mother of God because Immaculate. This formula expresses the relation between person (Immaculate Conception) and nature-role (divine and spiritual maternity) and, therefore, in a sense it is the resolution of the debate over whether the first principle of Mariology is the Immaculate Conception or the Divine Maternity." Fehlner, *Theologian of Auschwitz*, 289.

203. Fehlner, "Immaculate . . . Mystery," *CE* 6, chapter 3.

204. Fehlner, *Kolbe . . . Pneumatologist*, 122–23.

205. In his discourse, "The Glories of Mary," St. John Henry Newman makes the same point.

Maximilian in illustrating theologically the Trinitarian character of the mystery of the Immaculate, also to have shown how and why total consecration to the Immaculate, without restriction, is the only basis for a thoroughly Christocentric spirituality."[206]

The Marian principle is *unifying* because, clarifying the relationship between the various mysteries of the faith, it is the source of integration of the various fields of theological study. It calls for a fresh look at these mysteries in light of their relationship to the mystery of the Immaculate, in view of this integration. Thus, for example:

> [T]he old controversy between christotypology and ecclesio-typology can in a certain sense be rethought and resolved in terms of the mystery of the Immaculate Conception *ad mentem S. Maximiliani*. St. Maximilian's thought is not governed by a *Christus solus* approach to the mystery of the incarnation and Redemption, precisely because he follows the Seraphic Doctor in affirming Mary as the mode of the incarnation, and the subtle Doctor, Bl. John Duns Scotus, in affirming the Immaculate Conception as the proof of the absolute primacy of Christ.[207]

This mindset is reflected in Vatican II's situation of the mystery of Mary in the context of Christ and the church. So considered, the Marian principle is unifying because, as *Mater unitatis*, Mary is the source of unity for all Christians and for all members of the church. Such a position has found recent magisterial support in St. Paul VI's solemn proclamation of Mary as Mother of the Church on November 21, 1964, and the church's 2018 inscription of a memorial honoring Our Lady under this title in its universal liturgical calendar.

The Marian principle is *harmonizing* because, as mother and teacher, Our Lady guides the soul toward the all-important sanctification of the intellect. The absence (or rejection) of this guidance runs the risk of an "imbalance," leading either to a secularization of the intellect, characteristic of all forms of modern rationalism, or a devolution into an irrational pietism which, when present in a religious community, can open the door toward authoritarianism and infantilization.[208] The flourishing of a community

206. Fehlner, "Immaculate . . . Mystery," *CE* 6, chapter 3.

207. Fehlner, *Kolbe . . . Pneumatologist*, 125–26.

208. Oftentimes in an ecclesial setting, I believe this "imbalance" of either form manifests itself as a distorted perception of the proper relationship between the hierarchical and charismatic dimensions of the church, essential to understanding the mystery of ecclesial communion. For this reason, I consider the 2016 intervention of the Congregation for the Doctrine of the Faith, *Iuvenescit Ecclesia*, which examines just this relationship, to be a timely one.

such as Niepokalanów not only presupposes a docility to the influence of the Immaculate in carrying out this delicate work of sanctification, but also a certain progress along the way: "A person has free will and there lies all the risk, for unless that person honestly wishes to get to work on himself, then even the work that others do on him will come to nothing."[209]

The Triumph of the Immaculate Heart

As is well-documented, the proximate occasion for the founding of the M.I. on October 16, 1917, was the violent demonstrations of the freemasons. Here is Fehlner's narrative: "Less than four days after the miracle of the sun in Fatima (October 13), on the feast of St. Margaret Mary Alacoque, and just two weeks before the enemy of the Woman made a counter move during the Russian revolution of 1917 on the feast day of All Saints, Mary organized her own spiritual militia and so was prepared to deal with the establishment of the Communists' worldwide headquarters in the Cathedral of the Assumption in the Moscow Kremlin."[210]

In Fehlner's mind, the temporal convergence of these events is no coincidence, but reflective of the apocalyptic struggle of the Woman and the devil (Rev 12) which precedes the ultimate triumph of the Woman and her offspring. The sign of the triumph is the "victorious establishment of the 'City of the Immaculate,'" a decision which "had already been taken by Christ and Mary. Its implementation would be the triumph of the Immaculate Heart and reign of the Sacred Heart of Jesus as revealed at Fatima, and the organization of its work would be set in motion by the establishment of the Militia of Mary Immaculate."[211]

With the establishment of the M.I. is accentuated active participation in the mission of the Immaculate Mediatrix, with the goal of bringing all men and women under the influence of Our Lady's universal queenship, that is, hastening the triumph of the Immaculate Heart predicted by Our Lady at Fatima. St. Maximilian repeated on occasion the prophecy of St. Catherine Labouré that "the Immaculata will become the Queen of the

---

209. Kolbe, *WK* 339. See Domanski, *Il pensiero mariano*, 91n416.

210. Fehlner, *Theologian of Auschwitz*, 83. Related to and preceding the Russian revolution is the beginning of the Protestant revolt four centuries earlier, in 1517, and the establishment of freemasonry two centuries earlier, in 1717. Fehlner brings these events in relation to one another to illustrate that the Immaculate is the one who is guiding history; the enemy of souls has only as much power to act in the world as she permits. See Fehlner, "Niepokalanów in the Counsels," *CE* 6, chapter 5.

211. Fehlner, *Theologian of Auschwitz*, 83.

whole world and every single soul" and identified the mission of the M.I. with this prophecy.[212]

The triumph is progressively realized to the degree that the mystery of the Immaculate Conception is incorporated into the lives of individuals and the life of the church. In a sense, the triumph is realized by way of anticipation or by sign in the community of Niepokalanów:

> History is now entering that period when until the final coming its most prominent feature will be the Marian, the Immaculatist, that of total consecration to and total possession by the Immaculate of all who belong to the body of Christ. As the Virgin Mother is the great sign of the fullness of time, the incarnation, so the city of the Immaculate, "Niepokalanów," is the great sign of that fullness for the church. . . .[213]

If the triumph of the Immaculate Heart is of relevance to the church and the whole world, how much more so for the Order she brought into existence through her humble servant, St. Francis? In this regard, Fehlner makes this observation about Our Lady's guidance of the history of the Franciscan Order:

> The relative failures and imperfections of the friars, the compromises within the Rule for whatever reasons, the narrow pietism, the scandalous quarrels in the name either of reform or adaptation of the past, found a certain limit beyond which they were not permitted to impede in any definitive way the steady advancement toward the attainment of the first and central aim of Mary Immaculate in the founding of the Franciscan Order, viz., the dogmatic acceptance by the church of her Immaculate Conception. The queenly hand of Mary in the Order effectively defines that limit. And once defined the truth of that mystery becomes the starting point for affirming and achieving in the church a fuller realization of Christ's absolute primacy in and over all, just as once defined the divine maternity of the ever-Virgin Mary secured the confession of her Son's divinity.[214]

There is the suggestion here that, just as the "queenly hand of Mary defines the limit" of disorder and division within the Franciscan Order in the "first page," so her hand will continue to operate in this way in the Order in the "second page," in "affirming and achieving in the church a fuller realization

212. See Kolbe, *WK* 341, 382, 1090,

213. Fehlner, "Martyr of Charity," *CE* 6, chapter 17.

214. Fehlner, "Mary and Franciscanism," *CE* 3, chapter 1.

of Christ's absolute primacy in and over all." Such would be consistent with the thought of Kolbe, outlined in his 1933 letter to the seminarians of the Order.[215] He prophesied the reunification of the various branches of the Franciscan Order "under the banner of the Immaculata," because "the Immaculata is common to us all."[216] Will there be a triumph of the Immaculate Heart also in the Franciscan Order? It is in Our Lady's hands. As Mary is the memory of the church, so also she is the memory of the Seraphic Order.

Other Ecclesial and Theological Considerations

In the 1980s, Fehlner made a number of relatively brief contributions concerning the echo of the Kolbean vision in the magisterium of St. John Paul II, the most ardent supporter of Kolbe yet to ascend to the papal throne. A particular reflection of Kolbean thought is found in the Encyclical Letter, *Redemptoris Mater*, in which "the Holy Father shows how the exemption of Our Lady from original sin in her Immaculate Conception is the basis of a life of faith, of obedience, of humility on which the mystery of the incarnation and of our redemption depends, and which therefore is the divinely willed means of our life of faith."[217] For Fehlner, the Franciscan-Marian connection is clear:

> To seek to make converts and to live for their sanctification is to 'beget' Christ in one's neighbor. Is not this the essence of "repairing" the church? And how else can such repair be effected, except by a life of faith, of prayer, of penance? Thus it is no surprise that the Franciscan thesis: the maternal mediation of the Immaculate based on her unique election in Christ to be his Mother and her unique participation in the work of redemption because preserved free of the stain of original sin, should find such dear confirmation in the first and second parts of the encyclical where the predestination of the Virgin as the Immaculate in Christ and her place in the church are treated.[218]

In his Apostolic Letter, *Mulieres Dignitatem*, John Paul II proposes the Virgin Mary as "the new principle of the dignity and vocation of the woman,

---

215. Kolbe, *WK* 486.

216. Kolbe, *WK* 324. See also *WK* 480 and 485, where he conditions this envisioned reunification on the spirit of the M.I. coming to be reflected in the Constitutions of the Conventual Friars, i.e., the Immaculate becoming the "soul of the Constitutions."

217. Fehlner, "*Redemptoris Mater*," *CE* 6, chapter 9.

218. Fehlner, "*Redemptoris Mater*," *CE* 6, chapter 9.

of all and of each."[219] The struggle of every woman to realize her true femininity is akin to the victorious struggle of the Virgin Mary against the evil one, through the merits of her Son. Each woman realizes victory in her turn, to the degree that she "strives to find in the Immaculate Virgin Mother her Advocate and Ideal," a striving that is "crucial to the salvation of souls, to the welfare of the human family on earth and the final triumph of Christ's kingdom." The blueprint for victory and the key to the attainment of dignity is found in the program of St. Maximilian. [220]

In his article, "Vertex Creationis," Fr. Peter Damian analyzes St. Maximilian's negative stance with regard to material evolution. Kolbe stakes his unequivocal opposition on the grounds of (1) the absolute primacy of Christ, (2) the doctrine of recapitulation and recirculation, and (3) the hierarchical structure of participation in the mediation of Christ, culminating in the Immaculate Virgin.

All mediatory activity is in view of the fact that creation not only comes forth from the hand of God, but is made to return to God—something not accounted for in the various theories of material evolution. But that return or "reaction" is not perfect, Kolbe notes, except in the *vertex creationis*, the Immaculate, giving rise to the need for mediation. "Progress does not effect," Fehlner writes, "but presupposes the differentiated grades of being. The less perfect can never be the [principal] cause of the more perfect. This is why an evolutionary mode of conceiving the world and its development and one based on a hierarchical system of graduated mediation at whose vertex is the Mother of God, the Immaculate, mediatrix of all graces, are naturally incompatible."[221]

> That [mediatory] action on her part is not the result of our progress at any level, but its premise. That is why the mystery of the Immaculate Mediarix of all graces precludes an evolutionary explanation of the origin of the species, of the grades of perfection in the world. Such a theory is radically pelagian in its tendency to deny the need of grace, viz., the need of mediation in approaching God as our last end. In a kolbian perspective, then, theistic evolution fails to take account of the order, of grace, because though recognizing the origin of the world in a creative act of God, it fails to note the term of that act is not, without further intervention of God as Mediator, capable of a reaction

219. Fehlner, "*Mulieres Dignitatem*," *CE* 6, chapter 15.
220. Fehlner, "*Mulieres Dignitatem*," *CE* 6, chapter 15.
221. Fehlner, "Vertex Creationis," *CE* 6, chapter 6.

equal and contrary that of the divine action, or of autonomously
advancing in perfection so as to be capable of such.[222]

All mediatory activity reveals the centrality of the incarnation, and
its various grades of participation point to its perfection in the mystery
of the Immaculate Conception. "The difference between the physical and
the spiritual, the natural and the voluntary, of which true love is the finest
form the mediatory role which that difference implies in the 'reaction' of
creation to the love of the Creator, and the consequent anti-evolutionary
stand of St. Maximilian are but logical complements to his profound appreciation of the mystery of the Immaculate."[223]

Conclusion: Significance of Fehlner's Kolbean Contribution for the Church

"Since her entry into salvation history," Vatican II proclaims, Mary "unites
in herself and re-echoes the greatest teachings of the faith as she is proclaimed and venerated, [calling] the faithful to her Son and his sacrifice and
to the love of the Father."[224] In Mary, the "vertex of love," we perceive that
it is divine charity, God himself, from which all history originates, toward
whom all history is oriented, and who guides all of history. That charity
has been poured forth from the heart of the Mother into the heart of the
church. It is the Immaculate who guides the church along on her pilgrim
journey to the fullness of that charity revealed in the sacrifice of her Son,
who laid down his life for his bride—the fullness of which she already possesses, for she "brought forth the price [of our salvation]; she paid it; and
she possessed it."[225] She is this, and she did this, because she is the Immaculate Conception, a name she shares with the Holy Spirit.

Fr. Peter Damian Fehlner studied and taught this "theology of charity" which is the quintessence of the Franciscan theological tradition, resolving in what I have termed the Marian principle or, more precisely, the
principle of the Immaculate Conception. Fehlner was certainly aware of
this principle even in the early years of his theological career, but it was
not until well into his career, in the late 1970s, that he came to *consciously
embrace* this principle as the guiding principle in his own life. Allowing
himself to be so guided by Our Lady, this "theologian of charity" became,

222. Fehlner, "Vertex Creationis," *CE* 6, chapter 6.
223. Fehlner, "Vertex Creationis," *CE* 6, chapter 6.
224. *Lumen Gentium*, 65.
225. Bonaventure, *Seven Gifts*, col. 6, 124.

in the footsteps of Kolbe, "Our Lady's torchbearer" to proclaim this prophetic message to the present-day Church.

Having become well versed in the dizzying array of theological currents comprising modernity, Fehlner was not afraid to engage them, but ultimately in view of shining the light of this Marian principle directly on them. He thus showed how the renewal called for by Vatican II is to be accomplished, and how it is that St. Maximilian and his "global vision" anticipated such a renewal, applying it to the present needs of the church as she navigates the troubled waters of a deep theological and practical crisis.

Remarkable is the parallel, Fr. Ondrako has noted, between the life of Fehlner and that of Cardinal Joseph Ratzinger. The latter, too, underwent a certain "Marian enlightenment" after the council, and the result is reflected in his magnificent Marian magisterium after ascending the papal throne as Benedict XVI. "If Mary no longer finds a place in many theologies and ecclesiologies," Cardinal Ratzinger once said, "the reason is obvious: they have reduced faith to an abstraction. And an abstraction does not need a Mother."[226] The Franciscan tradition zeroes in on that "something" concrete which makes all the difference, or rather, that "someone"—the Word Incarnate, *quem amor humanavit*[227]—revealed by the Immaculate Mother. He is the one who has commanded Francis and his sons to "rebuild my church." Kolbe, and Fehlner after him, have made clear the condition for that rebuilding or renewal to be effected: the establishment of the throne of the Immaculate Mother in the hearts of her children; that is, the incorporation of the mystery of the Immaculate Conception into the life of the church and the lives of her members.

Substantial is the role of Fehlner in laying the groundwork for this renewal.[228] Here I will briefly summarize what I consider to be his most outstanding contributions from the standpoint of his Kolbean doctrine.

1. The Theological-Metaphysical Framework of Kolbean Thought

Fehlner has illustrated how the Kolbean "global vision" is deeply rooted in the Franciscan theological-metaphysical tradition dating back all the way to the Seraphic Father, a tradition that is one and that has been ratified definitively

226. Ratzinger, *Ratzinger Report*, 108.

227. "Whom Love made man." See *Legend of Saint Clare*, III, 5, in *Clare of Assisi*, 284.

228. Fr. Ondrako's volume, *Rebuild My Church*, addresses this exact subject in great detail.

by the church with the dogmatic definition of the Immaculate Conception in 1854. In that tradition can be discerned the notes of the development of doctrine, as specified by St. John Henry Newman. Newman's own theological reflections, as Fehlner has shown, independently demonstrate how extraordinarily relevant this tradition is today. One of the great merits of Fehlner is to painstakingly demonstrate how and why Kolbe is to be regarded as one of the great theologians of our times, and why his theological vision does indeed constitute the basis for the renewal called for by the Second Vatican Council. By way of his subtle analysis of the theological and metaphysical foundations of Kolbean thought, Fehlner has laid the groundwork for a revitalization of the Franciscan intellectual tradition.

2. Renewal of Franciscanism

In a particular way, Fehlner fixed his sights on what the Kolbean vision means for the renewal of the Franciscan Order. That the Order is in need of renewal Fehlner had no doubts; such a conviction was corroborated by the Vatican II Decree on the Adaptation and Renewal of Religious Life, *Perfectae Caritatis*, which advocated a "return to the sources" and a holding in honor of all "sound traditions." Fehlner laid out his blueprint for renewal in his presentation to the Extraordinary General Chapter of the Conventual Franciscans in 1986. A sober reading of this document, in conjunction with his other writings on the subject, shows him not the least bit interested in "turning back the clock" as sort of a knee-jerk reactionary response to modernity. He was well aware of the need to consider legitimate adaptation of the Kolbean ideal in the light of Conventual tradition and ecclesial oversight. But renewal in continuity will only happen, Fehlner insisted, to the degree that the direct relationship between the Lord's command to "rebuild my church" and what St. Maximilian's terms the "cause of the Immaculate" is recognized and put into practice. Our Lady is the one who is guiding the history of the Order as it sets out on the "second page," and she awaits the cooperation of her chosen ones in bringing the Order to its glorious consummation in Christ. It means that the Franciscan Order has by no means run its course, but rather that a new day, inaugurated by the Immaculate, is dawning.

3. Ecclesiological Vision

This new day is situated within the age of the Immaculate and the Holy Spirit, which is the age of the church. The interchangeability of these terms is neatly summarized by two titles St. Francis gave Our Lady: *Spouse of the Holy Spirit*, and *Virgin Made Church* (*Virgo Ecclesia facta*). At the heart of the church is that same spousal love, reflecting the communion of love in the Holy Trinity, in which the mystery of the incarnation is enveloped. Seen in this light, the command the Lord gave St. Francis to "rebuild my Church" may be understood as having been placed at the request of Our Lady herself. The fulfillment of that command, then, consists in doing what St. John the Apostle did, namely, welcoming Our Lady into the homes of our hearts (John 19:27). This "incorporation of the mystery of the Immaculate" described by St. Maximilian means none other than for the church to be renewed in that divine charity which is the church's heritage. The seal of this heritage is the Immaculate Conception. Fehlner grasped this lofty vision of the church already in his dissertation, which he perceived in the ecclesiology of St. Bonaventure. Over time he expounded this ecclesiological vision in light of the great Kolbean insight of the uncreated and created Immaculate Conception. Such an ecclesiology is radically Marian, fully in accord with the theological vision of the Second Vatican Council, and fully responsive to the needs of the present day. As "memory of the church," the Immaculate Virgin is instrumental in that ecclesial exercise of "remembering forward"[229] as the church proceeds along her pilgrimage toward the fullness of charity she contemplates in the Blessed Virgin.

4. Mariological Contributions

Although the title is not explicitly given in Fehlner's original dissertation, the presence of the *Virgo Ecclesia facta* pervades Fr. Peter Damian's doctoral dissertation, where he brought in the Bonaventurian theology of Marian mediation and Mary's unique relationship with the Holy Trinity into his analysis of the role of charity in Bonaventure's ecclesiology. The *Virgo Ecclesia facta* is, in a sense, the starting point for scaling the breadth, depth and height of his Mariological contributions. It is also the key to understanding how his subsequent Mariological trajectory along overtly Kolbean lines is part of one and the same Marian itinerary. We have mentioned his noteworthy contributions on the subject of the relationship of Mary and the holy Trinity, Marian metaphysics and Marian coredemption. His Marian program for the renewal of theology set forth in "Mary and Theology: Scotus Revisited" is based on the principle, *de Maria numquam satis*, carried out under the universal influence of Mary as Mother and Teacher. As *Mater*

---

229. I borrow this happy phrase from Fr. Ondrako, which captures the ever-unfolding renewal in continuity, in charity, at work in the church.

unitatis, Fehlner saw in Mary the one in whom we find the key to the integration of the various branches of theology, and the principle of unity of all Christians of good faith. In recognition of these stupendous contributions, the Mariological Society of America awarded Fr. Peter Damian its prestigious Cardinal John J. Wright Award in 2015.

5. Application of the "Global Vision" to Modernity: The Priority of the Golden Thread

Fehlner's prophetic voice found its range in confronting the complexities of modernity. Key to finding that range was the assimilation of the thought of St. John Henry Newman, who already in his day was in the midst of modernity's onslaught. Fehlner recognized parallels between Newman's response to modernity, with its emphasis on the role of conscience, the distinction between natural and revealed religion, practical epistemology, personalism, and a phenomenological approach, and the scholastic approach of the Franciscan masters which anticipated the complexities of modernity. Newman saw in the definition of the Immaculate Conception a preeminent example of doctrinal development giving wonderful confirmation of the Scotistic thesis; in Kolbe the Immaculate Conception became the principle. With this we are struck with the inscrutable ways of divine wisdom, for modernity finds itself placed in relation to the "golden thread" of the Immaculate Conception, and not the other way around. That thread has passed through Bonaventure, Scotus, Fasani, Newman, Kolbe and, now, Fehlner. Modernity cannot escape the grasp of the golden thread![230]

6. Fehlner's Prophetic "Marian Program"

If the "first page" described by St. Maximilian culminates in the 1854 definition of the Immaculate Conception, then the "second page" will reach its conclusion "when Christ finally comes to consummate his kingdom."[231] Consequently, the golden thread passing through Bonaventure, Scotus, Fasani, Newman, Kolbe and Fehlner has not yet reached its end. In many respects we still find ourselves at the dawn of the second page. In what manner does Our Lady wish to continue to weave this thread in the second page? St. Maximilian Kolbe laid the foundations, and Fr. Peter

---

230. The apparitions of Lourdes demonstrated in a powerful way the priority of the golden thread. That St. Maximilian realized the connection is clearly reflected in a number of his writings, especially the articles he published in *Rycerz Niepokalanej*.

231. Fehlner, "Other Page," *CE* 6, chapter 13.

Damian Fehlner, with his "middle-voice,"[232] has "touched up" this Kolbean blueprint and presented it as the "Marian plan" for this age of the church. The general outline of this program is especially evident in "Mary and Theology: Scotus Revisited," the *Hereditas Kolbiana*, and *The Theologian of Auschwitz*, complemented by the Marian metaphysics he expounded, and crowned by the testimony of his life completely spent in service of Our Lady. But it was in Fr. Peter Damian's mind not so much to specify the details of the program as to clarify its principles and to lay stress on its fundamentally ecclesial orientation.

Ultimately, it is not a question of material reduplication of Niepokalanów and of the conditions that existed in St. Maximilian's day, but rather of an organic development of this Marian ideal on the largest scale possible, suitable for our own day—just as St. Maximilian understood the life at Niepokalanów to be an organic development within the Franciscan tradition.[233] The "global vision of Catholic life in a new form" is to be realized in the midst of modernity, not in some imaginary space as if modernity did not exist, and in these post-council years Fehlner has given us the road map by "remembering forward." Remembering forward is remembering the eternal, the fruit of pondering divine charity with the heart of Our Lady, the created Immaculate Conception.

"When you start to read something on the Immaculata," St. Maximilian once said, "do not forget that at that moment you come into contact with a living being, who loves you, who is pure, without any stain . . . Acknowledge that she alone must enlighten you more and more. She alone must draw your heart toward herself with love."[234]

May this guidance of the Immaculate, originating in the wellsprings of divine charity flowing through her heart into the church, which led St. Maximilian Kolbe to his martyrdom of charity and Fr. Peter Damian Fehlner to consume his life out of love for her, be as a brightly shining light to illuminate the history of our souls to their perfection in that same charity.

Ave Maria!

232. Ondrako, *Rebuild My Church*, c. 2.

233. "One day, a visiting priest stopped before one of the imposing rotary presses in the printing plant [at Niepokalanów] and asked Father Maximilian, 'If the Poverello (St. Francis) were alive today, what would he say about all these expensive printing machines?' Father Maximilian responded without a minute's hesitation: 'Why, he would roll up his sleeves like these good brothers and turn the presses at full speed using this modern means of spreading the glory of God and the Immaculata.'" Kalvelage, ed., *Saint of the Immaculata*, 70.

234. Kolbe, *WK* 1306.

1

Total Consecration, Baptism, and
the Franciscan Ideal

THE FOUNDING OF THE Militia of Mary Immaculate in 1917 represents
the beginning of a major contribution of the contemporary Marian movement to Catholic spirituality, a contribution consummated in the heroic
martyrdom of its founder in 1941, and publicly acknowledged by the
church and by Christ speaking through the church in the canonization of
St. Maximilian Kolbe. The essence of Catholic spirituality is charity, whose
fundamental criterion is obedience. If you love me, says the Lord, keep
my commandments. And his commandment is that we love one another
as he has loved us. No greater love, he observes, has any man than that he
give his life for another, as Christ did, for that reason he was born of the
Immaculate Virgin to die on the cross for the salvation of men. And in
order that we might love in this, the only genuine way, our Savior dying
on the cross entrusted all his disciples to the care of the Woman conceived
without sin, whose love inspired his.

The life and death of St. Maximilian is an efficacious illustration of
how such loving obedience is to be realized: by *total consecration* to the
Immaculate who told the servants at Cana to do whatever he would tell
them to do, who herself inspired her Son and Savior to the obedience of his
Father's command to die on the cross, because he was so totally dedicated
to her whose will of all creatures was so totally one with that of her Creator
for the salvation of souls.[1]

---

1. *WK* 1289–90. These two passages in which St. Maximilian mentions together the
Johannine passages dealing with Mary in the work of salvation, when read in view of
the theology of total consecration, take on particular importance in locating the scriptural bases for his views on the role of the Immaculate as Coredemptrix and mediatrix.
Cf. Also *WK* 1295, when St. Maximilian discusses the action of the Father in entrusting
his Son to the Immaculate in the incarnation, and the parallel action of the Son from
the Cross in entrusting believers in him to the Immaculate.

The importance of total consecration to the Immaculate as the key to participation in the life of the Savior rests on the unique and all-pervasive role of the Immaculate qua Immaculate in the realization of the plan of salvation. Because that role as mediatrix of all graces, touching even the grace of the incarnation granted only after her "fiat," is so basic, the quality of obedience entailed in total consecration *eo ipso* involves the one making it in a Militia, i.e., in the struggle between the Prince of Peace and the prince of this world, the Woman and the serpent, under the headship of the King of kings and the guidance of the Queen of Heaven. Total consecration means total obedience, an active disposition to implement whatever commands the Immaculate makes known via the system of authority pre-arranged in the church by her Son. To speak of the Militia and of total consecration is to speak simply of two inseparable elements of that one spirituality at the heart of the gospel life, viz., the following of Christ as his true disciples.

It would be an unfortunate misrepresentation of the distinct contribution of St. Maximilian to imagine that his was the first or only major contribution to Marian-Catholic spirituality. From the beginning of the church, as John Henry Newman notes,[2] the principle so clearly expounded by St. Maximilian in word and deed, has been operative, and under the guidance of Mary and the church the nature of that principle has been gradually and providentially clarified to meet the needs of the church and souls. In more recent times, and it is St. Maximilian who calls our attention to this,[3] the concept of total consecration was prophetically expounded by St. Louis Grignon de Montfort, while the Legion of Mary, founded but a few years after the Militia of Mary Immaculate and based on the spirituality of Montfort provides a very striking and successful illustration of the apostolic dimension of Catholic life under the guidance of the mediatrix of all graces.[4]

Nonetheless, the Militia is not a duplication of the contributions of other leaders and groups within the Marian movement today. Rather than duplication or rivalry, all these contributions, particularly those pointing to the Immaculate as such, complement one another, because they have one common source in the activities of the Queen of Heaven on behalf

2. Newman, "Letter to E. B. Pusey." See especially 68–76, on her intercessory power.

3. *WK* 1129. Cf. also Louis de Montfort, *True Devotion*, 76–77. The introduction of Fr. Faber, written in 1862, also refers to the providential discovery of this marvelous work some twenty years earlier as a negation of the efforts of Satan to oppose this practice by hiding its explanation. Perhaps there is a parallel with the canonization of St. Maximilian inasmuch as this event undoes the efforts of Satan to prevent the universal spread of this devotion in the form of the Militia by confusing it with pietism and ridiculing its practice as fanaticism.

4. *WK* 865a. Cf. Domanski, *Il Pensiero Mariano*, 99–100.

of the church and of souls. To appreciate the distinctiveness of each is to acquire a deeper understanding of holiness, and to progress in virtue and the service of the Lord.

According to a number of commentators,[5] and as it seems St. Maximilian as well,[6] there are a number of distinctive features in his explanation of the nature of total consecration, features directly related to the manner in which total consecration is the effective means of achieving a kind of mass movement among Catholics directed not only to the revival of their faith received at baptism, but to the conversion of the non-believer, the heretic and in particular those infected by the vice of private judgment and indifferentism symbolized by the anti-clericalism of freemasons in modern times. Such an approach makes clear in the practical order the common roots of Marian and Catholic piety in baptism.

At the center of this movement, and as it were serving as a mirror for the whole, is that achievement most distinctively Kolbean, viz., the City of the Immaculate. That achievement, so thoroughly Franciscan in its inspiration and implementation, fully manifests this meaning and purpose of the distinctive features of total consecration to the Immaculate as taught by St. Maximilian. Such is the character of that achievement that any appreciation of these features should reflect their Franciscan background, and conversely why any understanding of the central purpose of the Franciscan ideal today eventually leads to a study of the common life and apostolate in a City of the Immaculate. The exposition of the distinctive features of total consecration according to St. Maximilian in terms of its Franciscan backdrop is also a commentary on the saint's interpretation of Franciscan history in terms of its central scope: to secure the primacy or reign of the Sacred Heart by forming a way of life and community at the service of and reflecting the mystery of the Immaculate as such.[7] Thus the history of the Order falls into two major periods: first the one in which the mystery of the Immaculate Conception was elaborated theologically so as to be ready for dogmatic definition; the second during which the practical implications of the mystery of the Immaculate for the fullest realization of Christ's kingdom

---

5. Blasucci, *Il Celeste Pegno*, 78ff; Domanski, *Il Pensiero Mariano*, 76ff.

6. *WK* 1329.

7. *WK* 33, 339, 637 (proposed formula of consecration of the Order to the Immaculate), 1298 (where St. Maximilian discusses the influence or power of the Immaculate on the Sacred Heart). The love of the Immaculate for the Sacred Heart is the measure of the perfection of our love and praise for God. Where there is perfect identity with hers as in total consecration, there the praise is greatest.

are being systematically realized, viz., via total consecration to the Immaculate and thereby participation in her Militia.[8]

Total Consecration: Its Distinctive Features

Though relatively brief, and at first glance merely of an occasional and practical character, the writings of St. Maximilian on further consideration show themselves to possess an amazing theological depth, precision, and distinctiveness. This is certainly the case with his explanation of the nature of total consecration to the Immaculate. It is not only a description of a pious exercise, but before all else a statement, theologically valid and eminently practical, of an act basic to the pursuit of holiness.

It is first of all an act of the will of the one making such a consecration.[9] As such it is the most fundamental response that the creature can make to the love of God. Thus, it engages the will at its most essential, viz., in that which makes the will a distinctive power to love at the heart of personal existence, or to borrow the term of Scotus in that which makes it a "*perfectio simpliciter simplex*," that is, which of its very form and concept entails no necessary limitation in existing. There are many ways of responding by the created person to God's love. Some of these are good, but limited; some are sinful. Total consecration is distinctive as an act of the will in that it transcends the limits of one and of the other. It is, therefore, the most pleasing and acceptable love that anyone can offer to the Father, Son, and Holy Spirit.[10]

As an act of the will, St. Maximilian states, it requires no set formulation. Nonetheless, he is quick to point out, it is an act, neither vague or indeliberate. Total consecration to the Immaculate is a quite distinct, deliberate, reasonable act, intimately and inseparably related to an assent, at least implicit, to the truth. In this sense it tends when practiced to express itself conceptually and verbally in a distinctive manner. St. Maximilian has identified four elements normally reflected in such an act of love.[11]

(1) Invocation of the Immaculate as such. All proponents of total consecration begin their explanations of this act with some invocation of Our Lady as mediatrix of all grace. In this invocation St. Maximilian insists repeatedly on invoking Mary precisely under her title as the Immaculate, especially in respect to the grace of total consecration. This distinctiveness surely reflects St. Maximilian's Franciscan antecedents, not only the privilege

8. *WK* 486.
9. *WK* 1354.
10. *WK* 1330.
11. *WK* 1329–1330.

of Mary central to the traditional Marian piety of the Order, but the manner in which the theology of the Immaculate contributed and contributes to the sanctification of the intellect in the spirit of prayer and devotion. More exactly, the theological contribution which St. Maximilian brings to the subject of total consecration provides a sound basis for distinguishing it from that pietism and fideism with which it is so frequently confused, and on the basis of which so many objections are raised against it. His thought further illustrates in a strikingly practical way the wisdom of Catholic teaching on actual grace and our cooperation therewith; the more complete our surrender to the initiative of the Immaculate in making her desires and commands rather than our own the basis of a willing and responsible action, the more perfectly the inner nature of our freedom and love is perfected. And the gratuity of grace, especially actual grace, i.e., why it cannot be presumed, is nowhere so apparent than in the fact that it stems initially from the free "fiat" or intercession of the Mother of God, without which it is not given. That the stimulus which her action provides to all whom she loves can and does provoke that "equal and contrary reaction" rests on the fact that she is the Immaculate, Spouse of the Holy Spirit.[12]

(2) Total consecration is unlimited and unconditional. St. Maximilian's contribution to the subject of total consecration is not only theological, providing grounds for an appreciation of the profound reasonableness of so paradoxical a practice and thus for achieving a harmonious integration of faith and piety, but affective as well. The final reason for insisting on the invocation of the Immaculate as such is to be found not only in her role as mediatrix of this grace, but the nature of this grace which makes so perfect a response to the saving love of God possible. The response is unlimited, precisely because total consecration to the Immaculate achieves a complete identification in the subject with the will of the Immaculate. The degree of our consecration to her is the measure of our response or reaction to God's prior love for us, and when that identification with her total consecration to God, i.e., with her as the Immaculate Conception, is total on our part, then our charity is perfect as it can be.[13] In obtaining

12. *WK* 597. A good example is provided here of the application of St. Maximilian's thought on the need for grace, more concretely the intercession of our Lady to obtain that grace, to sanctify the intellect. His views on the role of our Lady as mediatrix of all graces are consistent with the traditional belief of the church in the contingency of the created order (*WK* 1118, 1207); and the more specific Trinitarian dimensions of that contingency he presents in his discussion of the love of the Holy Spirit as the inspiration for the divine creative act (*WK* 1024, 1310, 1329) and the love of the Immaculate, Spouse of the Holy Spirit, as the concrete realization of that inspiration in the created order (*WK* 1284, 1286).

13. *WK* 1354.

this grace for us, her total consecration, i.e., her reaction-surrender qua Immaculate to the love of Father and Son for her as the most perfect fruit of a perfect redemption becomes in turn an "action" provoking an "equal and contrary reaction" in each believer to the love of the Father and the Incarnate Word, her Son.[14] Or to phrase this scotistically: her perfect preservation from all stain of sin is what makes possible, theoretically and practically, our perfect liberation from all sin.

(3) Obedience. Total consecration as identification with the will of the Immaculate is not merely an affective identification, but a thoroughly effective, practical love, that is to say total obedience to the Immaculate, a willingness and a readiness to do whatever she asks one to do.

At two points St. Maximilian makes what may aptly be called distinctive observations on the common view of the obedience entailed in total consecration. First: to the objection, does not total consecration establish a dual system of allegiance for the believer, one to Christ and the other to Mary, thus in practice, if not in theory, so to maximalize Mary as to detract from Christ, St. Maximilian indicates the essential answer in defining the Immaculate as Spouse of the Holy Spirit. Just as the procession of the Spirit in eternity and his mission in time do not detract from the sufficiency and uniqueness of the procession and mission of the Son, but are their complement and response, so also the mediation of Mary Immaculate in the church and in souls, far from detracting from Christ is the complement of Christ's work of atonement, and within the economy of salvation the key to the implementation of that work in our lives, as her "fiat" was the key to the incarnation of the work in her womb. To define the Immaculate qua Immaculate as Spouse of the Holy Spirit is to link the work of each so as to make them inseparable.[15] No one is possessed by the Spirit of truth, unless Mary Immaculate possesses that soul totally. Total obedience to Mary Immaculate, best described as possession by her, is the means to implement the commands of Christ in the fullest manner, not a substitute for these, for his commands in regard to our salvation are what she assented to in her "fiat," and the commands Christ gives us are exactly those she intercedes for.

The obedience entailed in total consecration on our part places us in a relationship to Our Lady exactly parallel to that of her Son's. As her reaction to his salvific love was the inspiration for his obedience to his Father's command to die on the cross to establish the order of salvation, viz., the church, so it is for us the stimulus to the perfect implementation of Christ's

---

14. *WK* 1283, where a simple but clear outline of the key position of the Immaculate vis-à-vis the Trinity in the return of all creatures to God.

15. *WK* 1229.

commands and instructions for our salvation in the church, and thus in practice animates the system of obedience to a sacerdotal hierarchy established
by Christ in the church for the salvation of souls. Through the influence and
power of the mediatrix of all graces the saving will of God is made immediate
and actual in the life of each member of the church.[16]

The prosperity of the church and the salvation of souls is then in the
hands of the Woman. The importance of total consecration to the Immaculate as such as the distinctive goal of the movement launched by St. Maximilian is grossly underestimated by large numbers, precisely because they
do not grasp that there is no substitute for the work of the Immaculate Mediatrix of all graces in charge of the "order of mercy"; that when it is said that
the incarnation depended on the free consent of the Immaculate, exactly
that is meant; and that when it is said that the extension of that mercy won
by Christ on the cross depends initially in each instance on the Immaculate,
exactly that is meant, such is her power to move her Son to act. Without her
"fiat," and without her unconditional identification with that "fiat," the only
alternative is a terrible judgment. Her will is concerned with mercy and
salvation, not with the judgment of condemnation reserved by the Father to
his Son, to be meted out on all those who refuse mercy, i.e., the ministration
of the Virgin Mary (and by extension the church), without whom no mercy
is dispensed. Where her love is accepted, first on the cross by her Son, and
then in the church by the faithful who keep his laws, the work accomplished
is a work of atoning justice and obedience crowned by glory. Refusal of her
love is followed by another kind of just judgment that punishes the refusal
to heed the Spouse of the Holy Spirit parallel to that judgment, passed by the
Savior on the sin against the Spirit of truth.[17]

Second: the term possession by Mary Immaculate to describe the
state of the soul totally consecrated to her is one particularly stressed by St.
Maximilian.[18] He notes that this state has also been described as a kind of
childhood and as a kind of slavery. He acknowledges the validity of both
descriptions, but adds that the term possession precludes misunderstandings easily attached to both, viz., that the one making such a consecration

16. St. Maximilian's views on obedience, particularly on the manner in which the
Immaculate makes her will known through the church, are easily found by consulting
the index to his writings under the entry "Obedience." Perhaps the best synthesis he
has left is his letter to his brother, Fr. Alphonse, *WK* 25, most of which appears as
the second reading for the Office of his feast. For further references cf. Domanski, *Il
Pensiero Mariano*, 78ff.

17. *WK* 1339. It is not possible to gain the goal of salvation without some identity
of will with that of the Immaculate in matters of salvation and all opposed to it, a point
repeatedly stressed by St. Maximilian. Cf. *WK* 1160, 1212, 1292, 1329, 1332, 1354.

18. *WK* 1329.

obtains some special rights with Our Lady, or in some way acts under compulsion, whereas in fact total consecration places one totally at the disposition of the Immaculate in a quite willing fashion. He does not mean to deny that Mary has a motherly care for each one of us in accord with our Lord's request of the cross that she should be our Mother. But she exercises this responsibility, even if we have not made total consecration to her. Rather the focus of total consecration and the obedience it implies is the formation of an instrument, a true militia perfected by an effective obedience, whereby the Immaculate may obtain those ends proper to her as the Woman who crushes the head of the serpent, the father of lies.

The preference for the term possession by the Immaculate to describe this state suggests an underlying scriptural-liturgical parallel: we are only fully free of the influence or possession of Satan, when we are fully possessed by Mary Immaculate. Personal independence, in the intellectual order the principle of private judgment, so well symbolized by the ethos of freemasonry, is a gross deception, making a basic slavery to the prince of this world. Total humility is the only sure way to freedom. Between these two choices there is no third ground on which to stand.

The term is, finally, interesting for its Franciscan overtones, present whether intended by St. Maximilian or not. The use of this term by St. Maximilian constitutes a useful commentary on St. Francis' analogy of the corpse to describe the condition of one who obeys perfectly, in a supernatural manner.[19] Further, the use of this term recalls St. Francis' love of the Portiuncula—the little portion of possession of Mary Queen of the Angels. One might be inclined to see in this the possession of Mary by Francis, and this is true. But it is true, only because Mary possessed Francis and his brethren in a special way. The reality of total consecration is strongly suggested in his love for the Portiuncula.[20]

(4) Scope. In general the scope of total consecration is to know, love and serve the Immaculate as much as possible, and to make her known, loved and served in the same way as others, especially through her commands to pray and to do penance for the conversion of sinners and the triumph of the sacred heart of her Son: in a word to make her aims totally one's own. In this the views of Maximilian coincide with those of other leaders of contemporary Marian spirituality, because they reflect their common source in the Blessed Mother.

---

19. *2 Cel.*, 112.

20. Cf. Fehlner, "Mary in the Franciscan," *CE* 3, chapter 5; Fehlner, "Saint Francis and Mary Immaculate," *CE* 3, chapter 3.

Total consecration, however, as expounded by St. Maximilian, results in the formation of a Militia for the Immaculate and under her complete direction as Queen of heaven, as her chosen instrument for the achievement of this goal.[21] Herein is made evident the specific goal of those distinctive features that St. Maximilian's life, work and death have brought to the practice of total consecration. The notion of a Marian militia is neither original nor exclusive to him. But with his insistent emphasis on the place of the Immaculate as such in total consecration he gives to this practice a centrality, universality and precision in scope hitherto neither explicit nor actual.

(a) Centrality: The purpose of the three divine persons in creating and redeeming us, viz., to share their life with us, and our goal as creatures made in the image and likeness of God to participate in that life through conformity to the incarnate-crucified Son of God, the perfect image of the Father, converge in the Immaculate as Spouse of the Holy Spirit.[22] That this convergence in this life should take the form of a militia arises immediately from the nature of the triumphant struggle of the Woman preserved free of original sin in breaking our bondage to Satan and in reversing the consequences of the fall.

(b) Universality: Such a militia as the most basic, concrete form of Marian spirituality in the church is not a social form superimposed upon or added to that of the church, but as Catholic as the church herself. The militia of Mary Immaculate is not so much an organization in the first instance as a movement to render conscious and deliberate the spirit of the mystery made real in each member of the church through baptism, viz., conformity to the crucified Savior and apostolate with him to make all men his disciples, i.e., members of his Church, children of his mother.[23]

(c) Precision: The occasion of the founding of the Militia in 1917 was the anti-clerical hatred and violence of the freemasons, particularly as this

---

21. *WK* 1330. It is important to observe the stress placed by St. Maximilian on two texts: one from Genesis (3:15) dealing with the total and irrevocable enmity between the Woman into whose hands has been entrusted our salvation and the father of lies; the other from the liturgy—*Dignare me laudare te, Virgo Sacrata; da mihi virtutem contra hostes tuos*, where enemies are first of all understood as enemies of faith, viz., heretics, and in a particular way the quintessence of all heresy, the exercise of self-will in principle in the use of the intellect, called by St. Francis the poison of self-will (Admonition six), and otherwise known as the principle of private judgment, symbolized by the ethos of freemasonry. Cf. also *WK* 1293, 1305. Newman makes essentially the same point, "Letter to E. B. Pusey," 76, with the same texts. The focal point of the battle and its outcome is expressed well in this text, often cited by St. Maximilian: *tu interemisti omnes haereses in universo mundo.*

22. *WK* 1293, 1326.

23. *WK* 1210, 1211.

was directed at the successor of St. Peter as Vicar of Christ, the great high priest.[24] Ever after in expounding the missionary thrust of the Militia of the Immaculate St. Maximilian placed an emphasis on the conversion of heretics and schismatics, especially freemasons.[25] This is no mere coincidence. The distinct character and goal of the Militia and total consecration to the Immaculate is intimately linked with questions of faith as that forms the basis for the life of the church and of Catholics, and with the very potent attack on that faith as found in the heresy, or rather the essence of all heresy symbolized by the ethos of freemasonry, the principle of private judgment, i.e., the refusal on principle to give unconditional obedience to the word of God and his teaching as this is expounded by his sacerdotal vicars.

Herein is the precise task which total consecration in the Militia of the Immaculate is designed to accomplish throughout the church under the aegis of the Queen of Heaven: to oppose to this principle so fundamental to the success of the stratagems of the father of lies in seeking to undermine the faith of the church and of Christians, its exact contrary, i.e., heroic obedience to the desires of the Mother of Truth, the Immaculate.[26] The humility of true obedience will always unmask the slavery of false freedom; and in any conflict between the methods of Satan and those of the Woman the latter will always triumph over the former, because in the Immaculate and in those consecrated to her is revealed the beauty and goodness of divine love won for us by Mary's Son on the cross. No greater love has anyone than that he give his life for his friend. So did the Son of Mary; so did St. Maximilian. There is the root of that irresistible fascination that he exercises over the multitude, in his union with the one who is all fair, in whom there is no stain of sin, whom God himself could not resist.

The Theology of Total Consecration

In no other area perhaps is the distinctively Kolbean contribution to total consecration so evident than in the theology he has as it were incorporated into its practice. That theology reflects his Franciscan origins, a concern that the intellect should be sanctified, not ignored or repressed in the quest for holiness, and that all understanding of the truth should be in some way the guide and connatural antecedent of the love of the one who is all

24. *WK* 1328.

25. *WK* 865a. This letter contains an interesting insight into the hardly innocuous character of the indifferentism masked by the relatively mild conduct of American freemasonry.

26. *WK* 1210.

Good and in whom is every good because he is Truth itself. St. Maximilian finds the center of this concern in the intellectual-theological efforts of the Franciscan Order to promote the dogma of the Immaculate Conception as the prelude for the realization of the highest degree of spiritual perfection in being conformed to the crucified.[27]

The formula chosen by St. Maximilian to synthesize this theology, viz., every action provokes an equal and contrary reaction,[28] reflects the typically scientific interests of the contemporary mind,[29] and possesses in his thought a role exactly parallel to the formula reflecting the logical interests of the medievals employed by St. Bonaventure in his theology to express the Trinitarian character of the economy of salvation, viz., the emanation of all things from God and their reduction to him are correlatives, centered on the Word Incarnate. In neither saint's thought is the formula a proof of the Trinity, but an illustration facilitating our appreciation of the mystery at the heart of all Catholic practice, the Trinity, an illustration validated by a metaphysics of exemplarism.

A review of St. Bonaventure's position will clarify the theological background of St. Maximilian and make it easier to grasp what some have found to be the most difficult point of his thought: the Immaculate as Spouse of the Holy Spirit.

St. Bonaventure's theology of the Trinity begins with a reflection of God's name as Good.[30] The Father in whom that fontal plenitude of goodness essentially one is found originally would be neither the greatest good, if he could not totally share that goodness with another, nor the most loving good, if he could but did not. And since that sharing would not be divine unless eternal and infinite, the Father begets a co-equal and co-eternal Son. Further, the Son being a perfect image of the Father loves him with a co-equal love. That mutual love they share with another in the procession of the Holy Spirit. To the question: how is it possible that there be a creation, or something other than God, and how is it possible that this creation once brought forth by God out of nothing return to God from whom it came, the answer is the same—because antecedently to and independently of that creation (*emanatio*) and return (*reductio*) the Father has begotten a co-equal Son, through whom he creates all, and by his incarnation and atoning love access is provided us to the Father through the Holy Spirit.[31] The formula

27. *WK* 486.

28. *WK* 1286.

29. *WK* 1386; cf. Domanski, *Il Pensiero Mariano*, 7–9.

30. *Brev.*, p. 1, c. 2; *Myst. Trin.*, q. 1, a. 2.

31. *Myst. Trin.*, q. 8, a. un., ad 7; q. 1, a. 2, ad 13.

neatly illustrates the basis of Franciscan Christocentrism in the mystery of the Trinity, and in one way or another has pervaded every genuine Franciscan theology since—including St. Maximilian's.

When however our attention is drawn not to the "how" or "what" of holiness, viz., through Jesus Christ and in conformity to him, but to the "why" of holiness, i.e., to the question of why God creates and redeems us so that we might be conformed to the image of his only-begotten Son, and why in the first instance we are moved to do what God wants us to do, then the formula of St. Maximilian becomes the connatural complement to that of St. Bonaventure in turning our attention to the procession and mission of the Holy Spirit.

To the question: why in eternity should the Father share his goodness in begetting a Son and the Son love him equally from eternity, St. Maximilian replies that their mutual love is an action provoking an equal and contrary reaction in the Holy Spirit. The procession of the Holy Spirit. The procession of the Holy Spirit then is the perfect or purest crown of the mutual love of Father and Son, alone eternally worthy of it, and for which the loving action of Father and Son in "conceiving" the Spirit as the fruit of their love is alone sufficient. In this sense the procession of the Spirit is a conception-fructification distinct from the generation of the Son, and its final motivation or reason.[32] But not only is this so in eternity; on the hypothesis of a creation and redemption that "reaction" to the love of the Father and Son in creating and in redeeming us is the only motive worthy of that love, as their creative and redemptive action is the only one sufficient to "conceive" such love.[33]

The application of the adage within the economy of salvation follows logically. The crown and purest fruit of the creative-redemptive love Father in sending his Son to be incarnate and die for us, is Mary, the Immaculate. This is her name, because preserved free of original sin in virtue of the merits of her Son, she is Spouse of the Holy Spirit, in time the purest fruit of the mutual love of Father and Incarnate Word as in eternity the Spirit is the purest fruit of the love of Father and Son. Outside the Trinity she and she alone is the Immaculate, is the worthy "motive" or final "reason" for the incarnation, through whom and for whom all things were made; and only the redemptive love of her Son is the sufficient "action" for producing so pure a "fruit." Thus, in the economy of salvation the love of the Immaculate, Spouse of the Holy Spirit, and therefore inseparably from that Spirit, is the

---

32. WK 1285–86. Cf. *Brev.*, p. 1, c. 3, n. 2.

33. WK 1224, 1310, 1329.

complement of the work of the incarnate Son, as the procession of the Spirit in eternity is the necessary complement of that of the Son.[34]

So it comes about that the love of the Immaculate, her "reaction" to the love of her Son and his Father, i.e., her faith, her intentions, her prayers are in practice the primary stimulus for the incarnation and Redemption, and then for the implementation of the fruits of the Savior's work in the church. Her activity as Mother of God and as Mother of the Church and of believers is the starting point as it were of a chain "reaction" culminating in total consecration to her as the Immaculate and under her direction forming a militia. Her name, the Immaculate, is the exact expression of the perfect response in time to the name of God, goodness itself. This theological contribution of St. Maximilian, so clearly reflecting the Franciscan theological tradition, echoes the salute of St. Francis to the Virgin Mary wherein he calls her the one full of grace, unique among woman, in whom is every good.[35] And in making clear the bearing of Mary's name, the Immaculate, on her role as mediatrix of all graces and on total consecration St. Maximilian gives to that practice a form as Catholic and distinctive as the Poverello of Assisi.

The Form of Total Consecration

As the response to the Immaculate's love is the inspiration of her Son to be born of her and to die for our sins, so it is also the inspiration of our rebirth and renewal and desire to die for love of his love who didst deign to die for love of our love.[36] The perfection of that life of divine love in us is directly proportionate to the degree of perfection of our consecration to the Immaculate and of our membership in her Militia. That our "reaction" to her initiative should take the form of a Militia (or that her Militia should possess a certain distinctiveness) rests on two considerations: one general—the nature of baptism by which we are reborn; and one particular—Franciscan profession, in both of which she makes known her will to dispense mercy, and when her will finds a response in total consecration it is successfully accomplished.

---

34. WK 1295.

35. WK 1291, 1292, 1317, 1318.

36. Cf. the prayer "absorbeat," often attributed to St. Francis, and the prayer found in the "Little Flowers of St. Francis," third Consideration on the Stigmata.

1. Baptism

That consecration to the Immaculate should take a social form, and specifically that of a militia stems from the role of the Immaculate in baptism whereby we are initially snatched from the power of Satan through the forgiveness of our sins and infusion of sanctifying grace, are conformed to Christ and made members of his Church. In the first section of an interesting discussion of the scope of the Militia, part of the materials for a book on the Immaculate,[37] St. Maximilian recapitulates the foregoing theology and concludes with a very significant observation: alone of all creatures on earth the human "reaction" to divine love is neither equal to or worthy of it, with one exception, that of the Immaculate, untouched by the fall of our first parents, because chosen antecedently to that fall, i.e., absolutely, to be the Mother of the Incarnate Word. This apparent exception is in fact an integral part of the primitive plan of God, for the Immaculate is the ultimate inspiration for a creation centering on the incarnation, and the key to its salvation in the event of the fall.

Thus, in the second section of this discussion St. Maximilian states that our response to the love of the Father and crucified Lord begins in principle to be equal to theirs in baptism because of the action of the Immaculate therein. The waters of baptism, he says, remind us of the purity of her who effectively acts on us in that sacrament as mediatrix of all grace. This is not at all the novel and startling view of baptism and of the sacramental system that it might seem, putting as it were Mary in the place of Christ. Rather St. Maximilian draws out what is implicit in the traditional view assigning to the faith and intention of the church a part in the efficacy of the sacraments, especially baptism, not in competition with or in substitution of that of Christ and his vicars, but as the complement and inspiration thereof, first in the administration of the sacraments, and then in their fruitfulness. What St. Maximilian has done is suggest a parallel between the role of the church in complementing that of Christ in the sacramental order and that of the Immaculate as mediatrix of all grace, the first presupposing and dependent on the latter, and both rooted in the character of the mission of the Spirit in the church, centered on the one who is his spouse.[38]

Consecration to the Immaculate, then, as a response to the mediatory action of the Immaculate (and the church) in baptism, has a scope as basic and as Catholic as the sanctifying grace by which our sins are forgiven,

37. *WK* 1329.

38. A careful consideration of the study of Scarfia, "The Role," and of that of DiFonzo, *Doctrina S. Bonaventurae*, in the light of St. Maximilian's insight will be most effective and serve as a commentary on the phrase of St. Francis: "Virgin made Church."

we are conformed to the image of the Son of God and of Mary, in a word transferred from the realms of darkness into the kingdom of light. It is a response rooted in the fact that by baptism a believer is made a temple of the Holy Spirit and a member of the church, Christ's body, one which recognizes that such is the fact because to be a temple of the Spirit and member of Christ is to be the possession of the Immaculate, to belong to her who being Spouse of the Spirit is full of grace and mediatrix of all grace. Total consecration is but the perfect, conscious, deliberate response to the mother of believers, and thus is but the measure of the perfect animation of the life of faith that performs the works of charity by doing what the Savior of the church "tells us to do," as Mary indicated to the servants at Cana. And because in virtue of baptism one cannot belong to the Immaculate without belonging to the church, total consecration is the measure of the animation of the life of faith in the church, especially of the hierarchical-sacerdotal system of obedience established therein by Christ, whereby he shepherds souls and guides the evangelization of the nations.

What the church is, the immaculate bride of Christ, and what the church can and does accomplish is linked to the name of her who is her premier member, the Immaculate, Spouse of the Spirit, Virgin made church, and her universal mediation in the church.[39] Were she the only member, the church would still be real, and Catholic and effective. And where and when the other members of the church practice total consecration to the Immaculate, there the church's involvement in the struggle of the Woman to rescue souls from the power of Satan and transfer them into the kingdom of her Son is that much more efficacious and fruitful. Hence, the ultimate goal in practice of the Militia of the Immaculate is to gain as many believers as possible as adherents of the Militia and practitioners of total consecration, i.e., to sanctify themselves as fully Catholic by sharing as much as they can in the sufferings of Christ and in so sharing seek to bring others to know and love him. Such is possible and in fact occurs because Mary's preservation from all sin is the basis of our liberation from all sin.

2. Franciscan Profession

St. Maximilian distinguishes three degrees in the practice of total consecration.[40] The first, which is essential and the one to be practiced by all

---

39. The two titles, Spouse of the Holy Spirit, and Virgin made Church, were dear to St. Francis. For additional references, cf. Van Asseldonk., "Maria, Sposa"; Fehlner, "Saint Francis and Mary," CE 3, chapter 3.

40. WK 1330.

Catholics in virtue of their baptism, consists in making the consecration, enrolling in the Militia, and then according to the circumstances of one's life living it out, striving wherever possible to make the Immaculate better known and loved. A second degree is subordinate to this and consists in joining other Militia members in an organized unit, to serve as a means for promoting more effectively the spread of the Militia and above all the spirit of the Immaculate. However useful and important, St. Maximilian always taught that this organizational aspect of the movement was a means to the end and not the essence.[41]

In addition, however, there is a third degree requiring a special grace— hence only for those chosen by the Immaculate for this—consisting in the promise to do all that the Immaculate might desire done for the cause of her Son, no matter how dangerous and humanly speaking impossible the assignment given. Such a promise entails the willingness to sacrifice all other forms of life and work legitimate for Catholicism, and indeed religious, for the sake of that which the Immaculate commands, in a word to surrender without reserve to the Immaculate every aspect of one's freedom. This is a commitment not only to live the kind of obedience postulated by the baptismal promises for all Catholics, but to a kind of heroic obedience transcending the obligations normally entailed by the religious vow of obedience.

The founding of the Militia by St. Maximilian led, then, not only to the establishment of a pious union, but also of the City of the Immaculate, whose members all make the total consecration in this form, wherein the essential is the living of a life of heroic obedience to Christ in prayer and penitential poverty under the aegis of the Immaculate, while the subordinate work and organization is directed to the promotion of the Immaculate and her plans for the triumph of the sacred heart of her Son. The original realization of the Marian dimensions of baptism is in fact a distinctive form of religious life, implementing in the highest degree the obedience of faith by sharing in the suffering obedience of the Savior on the cross, i.e., in the form of a penitential life in atonement for sin.

In this the City of the Immaculate bears a special relation to the Franciscan background of the saint chosen by the Immaculate to found it and in founding it to prepare himself for the white and red crowns she promised him and with which her work in that City would be confirmed and recommended to all. Even if all Franciscans to be good Franciscans need not make total consecration in this manner,[42] nonetheless the Franciscan

41. Cf. Domanski, *Il Pensiero Mariano*, 91ff; WK 1226.

42. WK 299, 300. It is important to observe the basis on which St. Maximilian differentiates between Franciscan life in a City of the Immaculate and in other friaries. That difference is not (except incidentally) one between strict observance and lax

ideal and that of the Immaculate's City sustain one another, the City being the heart of the Franciscan ideal today and total consecration in the third degree the manner of observing the Rule of St. Francis most perfectly, while the Franciscan way of life provides the connatural background and source of that feature essential to the City of the Immaculate, heroic obedience to the Immaculate as she makes known her merciful will via Christ's vicars in the church and Order, an obedience culminating in the willingness and readiness to risk martyrdom for the salvation of one's neighbor. Such a form of life, according to one qualified observer,[43] is the most perfect fulfillment of St. Francis' mind for the observance of his Rule today, and provides what Christ wants to sustain and renew his church and the faith of that church under assault, by serving as the focal point for the glorification of his mother the Immaculate and for the promotion of the practice of total consecration to the Immaculate throughout the church.

The point of contact between life in the City of the Immaculate and the Franciscan form of life is to be found in the twelfth chapter of the *Regula Bullata*, where St. Francis states that no one is to be ordered to the mission, i.e., ordered by his superiors to risk martyrdom for the cause of the gospel unless that friar volunteers. This, says St. Maximilian, is not a limit placed on obedience, as it were, a private initiative left to the friars.[44] Rather, it indicates the very apex of the Franciscan way. As the superior can command no one unless a promise of obedience precedes, so the ultimate in heroic obedience within the Order requires a unique promise of obedience

---

observance, but one between observance of the Rule, in particular poverty, in view of the perfect fulfillment of chapter 12 of the Rule concerning the missions, and an observance, equally strict, but which stops short of an obedience for the missions. Perfect observance of chapter 12 of the Rule for St. Maximilian is not simply volunteering for the missions, but allowing oneself to be volunteered by the Immaculate via total consecration. At this point the missionary thrust of Francis' vocation as its final crown coincides with the distinctive purpose of the City of the Immaculate: to be the central instrument at her disposition for promoting her cause as Immaculate. One can be a good Franciscan, even zealous for poverty, without making total consecration or living in a City of the Immaculate (cf. *WK* 314); and one can make total consecration without being a Franciscan or even a religious, and this in a heroic manner (cf. St. Louis de Montfort, *True Devotion*, 86–87). But to be totally consecrated without restriction, and to be actually employed by the Immaculate at the focal point for the promotion of the cause of her Militia coincides with Franciscan life in a City of the Immaculate centered on promotion of the missions. The practical purpose of Franciscan poverty and penance is to conform one to Christ crucified so as to make possible the success of the Militia and of the missions. The successful coordination of these aims rests on the efficacy of total consecration to and obedience of the Immaculate.

43. Fr. Bede M. Hess, Minister General of the Order, 1936–53. His testimony is found in *Beatificationis et Canonizationis*, 532–40.

44. *WK* 398, 399, 402. In addition to *Reg. B.*, 12, cf. *Reg. NB*, 16.

and a particularly intense form of Franciscan life as its immediate basis and preparation. This special promise, his fourth vow, St. Maximilian identifies with total consecration in the third degree.[45] And inasmuch as St. Francis deeply desired this kind of martyrdom in and for the missions as the crown of his calling, and was granted it in his stigmatization, and inasmuch as Francis always asserted the Marian inspiration and guidance of all facets of his vocation, the Kolbean interpretation and application of chapter twelve of the Rule under the aegis of the Immaculate is an insight fully in accord with the mind of his Father Francis.[46]

Within chapter 12 of the *Regula Bullata* St. Francis juxtaposes three aspects of his vocation that have subsequently been recognized on all sides as distinctive of the Franciscan spirit: zeal for the missions, obedience to the pope and exact observance of the gospel, living humbly and in poverty. A part of the genius of St. Maximilian has been to make clear the reason for this linkage: perfect obedience through total consecration to the Immaculate.[47]

For St. Francis, perfect obedience culminates in martyrdom, because one's obedience and the love it proves is only perfect to the extent it coincides with that of the good shepherd and priest on the cross. It is not sufficient merely to admire the sacrifice of the good shepherd; the servant (i.e., obedient religious) must identify with that work in practice for the glory of God and the salvation of souls.[48] This is the goal for which observance of the gospel is the way, viz., a life of humility and complete poverty. Conversely, that observance of the gospel life is only possible under the guidance of the vicar of the guardian and shepherd of our souls, viz., one that infallibly makes known the mind and will of Christ. Thus, obedience is the link connecting the way—poverty—with the goal, love of the crucified. Francis insists that the difference between good and bad, holy and wicked friars is that between living in obedience and outside obedience.[49]

For Francis this obedience is neither mere conformity to the will of another, nor that natural obedience practiced among all men wherein the final reason for obeying is that furnished by the subject obeying; rather it is a total surrender of one's own will including that of intellectual judgment involved in the act of faith to Christ in order that the radical sacrifice begun with the act of faith might be consummated in the penance or atonement of the cross. In this context of perfect conformity to the crucified the intimate

---

45. *WK* 398, 399, 402.

46. *2 Cel.*, 30, 152.

47. *WK* 25.

48. *Adm.*, 6.

49. *Reg. NB*, 5, 13–17; *Reg. B.*, 1, 1.

connection between obedience and poverty is revealed in a characteristic phrase of Francis to describe authentic, gospel poverty: to live *sine proprio*, where "sine proprio" means not only without things, and without the right to possess things, but even without the right to use one's own will and freedom in anything as one pleases, but only as it pleases one's Lord Christ.[50] Thus, to be perfectly obedient is to become like a corpse,[51] as did the Son of God and of Mary in obeying his Father.

How a friar is to accomplish this total surrender is also indicated by St. Francis: in docility, i.e., surrender to the promptings, illuminations and inspirations of the Spirit of Truth.[52] In this the missions of the Son and of the Spirit complement each other. But that same complementarity in the mind and life of Francis can be noted between Christ and the Woman whom Francis addresses in such singular fashion as "Spouse of the Holy Spirit."[53] In practice qualities such as gentle, merciful, sweet, inspirational and intercessory roles are attributed interchangeably to the Spirit and to his Spouse.[54] Once the

---

50. *Reg. NB*, 1, 1; *Reg. B.*, 1, 1; *Adm.*, 11, 4; *Ep. Fid.*, II, 10–15.

51. *2 Cel.*, 152.

52. *Reg. NB.*, 5, 4–8; 5, 14–16; 17, 14–16; *Reg. B.*, 10, 9; *Ep. Fid.*, I, 6; *Ep. Fid.*, II, 48; *Adm.*, 5, 2; 8, 1; *Sal.Virt.*, 14–18; *2 Cel.*, 193.Further reading on the Holy Spirit in the thought and work of St. Francis can be found in these works: Esser, *Temi Spirituali*, 55–57; Schmucki, *Linee Fondamentali*, 183–232, especially 199–216; Van Asseldonk, "De Traditione Vitae Orationis," 55–63; Omaecheverria, "El 'Espiritu.'"

53. Francis, Antiphon, *Off. Pass.*

54. A comparison of the *Salute to the Virgin* and the *Salute to the Virtues* shows that both the Virgin Mother and the Virtues enjoy an identical and unique relation to the Holy Spirit. Our address to them and the action of each in our lives in response to that prayer is inseparably linked with the Holy Spirit. Indeed, what Francis meant by the ideal designated in the virtue can only be grasped by centering the virtue in the person of Mary in whom a certain fullness of grace and virtue is found. In particular the love, mercy, kindness, sweetness traditionally associated with the Spirit are equally associated with the Mother of God. One need only reflect on Francis' devotion to her shrine popularly known as the Portiuncula and on the origin of the indulgence of that name to appreciate the point. And with that observation another parallel important for the Franciscan origins of total consecration is suggested. For Francis St. Mary of the Angels is the "little portion" of his Order (*2 Cel.*, 18). In chapter six of the *Regula Bullata* Lady Poverty is called the "portion of the friars, which leads them into the land of the living." In view of the foregoing the personification of poverty in a manner suggestion the person and role of the mediatrix of all grace is no surprise (cf. also *Ep. Fid. I*; *Leg. maj.*, 8, 5; *2 Cel.*, 83, 85 for other references to Mary's poverty as the focus of Francis' ideal). As soon as it is recalled that in Scripture our portion or inheritance is the Lord (Ps 141:9), and that specifically the Holy Spirit is the warrant or portion already given us to guarantee heaven (Eph 1:13–14), then the significance of calling Mary and Lady Poverty interchangeably the "portion" of the friars which guarantees them heaven is clear. So too why Mary is that in the mind of Francis is also clear: she is Spouse of the Holy Spirit. St. Maximilian simply adds: because she is the Immaculate.

fact of that union is clear, then it also becomes clear how at root St. Francis' ideal of heroic obedience in practice coincides with total consecration to the Immaculate or Spouse of the Spirit are the same. Not only practically, but verbally the coincidence is very close. St. Maximilian speaks of the highest perfection of religious life in the City of the Immaculate in terms of total consecration. St. Francis described the ideal of the Poor Clares as an espousal to the Holy Spirit after the manner of the Virgin who is uniquely, i.e., unlike any other person, Spouse of the Spirit, full of grace.[55]

Rereading the *Admonitions* of St. Francis in view of this equivalence, it is no surprise to discover an exact formulation of St. Maximilian's principles of heroic obedience in a religious community. In the second admonition St. Francis states that the scope of this vow is to counteract the "poison of self-will" that led to the fall of our first parents and to its consequences, continuing wherever it is found to undermine faith and charity. In the third he identifies the most perfect realization of this obedience in executing all the legitimate commands and desires of one's superior as the will of God. And in the sixth he observes that obedience on the part of God's servants, when perfect, culminates in suffering with the good shepherd for the salvation of souls, a suffering and patience whose measure is the perfection of the disciples' humble obedience.

With St. Maximilian it is not difficult to place the Immaculate in this context. For as the first Eve insinuated into the mind of the first Adam the desire to activate the principle of private judgment, viz., the poison of self-will, so the new Eve, the Immaculate, the Woman to crush the head of the liar who rationalized disobedience on principle, inspired perfect obedience in her Son, the new Adam, and in us perfect conformity to him through heroic obedience implied in total consecration to the Immaculate. In the final admonition Francis writes: Blessed the servant who keeps the secrets of the Lord in his heart. These are the exact words St. Luke uses to describe Mary's reflection on the mystery of salvation. Surely, the mystery of her Immaculate Conception, of her love for her Son and his for her is at the center of her reflections, as it should be of ours.[56]

This approach sheds considerable light as well on that special promise of obedience made by Francis to the Lord Pope and found in chapter one of

---

When one is totally consecrated to her as such, she is totally one's portion leading into the land of the living.

55. *Form. Viv.*

56. *Adm.*, 2, 3, 6, 13, 28. The use of the phrase "servants of the Lord" to indicate Franciscan religious in the context of dying as the good Shepherd did, recalls the servants whom Mary instructed at Cana, and the highest command she gives, to give one's life for the salvation of the sheep as her Son did.

the Rule as the succinct identification of that point at which Francis' form of life would sustain the life of the church as established by Christ, particularly when the hierarchical basis of that life of faith began to be attacked violently, systematically and directly by the typical ideologues of Western civilization, viz., the anticlerical puritans of his day.[57] If you love me, said our Lord, keep my commandments. In focusing his obedience and that of his Order on the successor of St. Peter and on the martyrdom of missionary life so as to gain souls for the church and for eternity, Francis merited the title: *vir catholicus et totus apostolicus*. And one may add with St. Maximilian: nowhere is that so fully verified than in total consecration to the Immaculate.

The point of contact and parallel once made clear, then for St. Maximilian as for Francis the complete poverty of common life in the City of the Immaculate as in the home of the Holy Family in Bethlehem and Nazareth—chapter six of the Rule formulates the essentials of this ideal—becomes the connatural context for a life of heroic obedience as the effective love of God and of neighbor, to the extent of giving one's life for the life of one's neighbor, because the Son of Mary first did this for each of us.[58] The act of faith exercised in the practice of this poverty in common is the immediate and indispensable preparation for that exercise of faith demanded in heroic obedience as a response to the love of the Immaculate, and as the greatest work ever asked of anyone by her.

The inspiration and stimulus for this loving faith, as Francis puts it in chapter six of the final rule, is the love of a mother for her child; greater than this should be the spiritual love of a friar for his confrere. In fact, the spiritual love of which St. Francis writes is nowhere so perfect as in that love of the Immaculate for her Son, our brother. Thus, total consecration to the Immaculate on the part of a friar makes common life in poverty the only logical way to live and the only source of perfect joy in this time of struggle, a joy remarkable in the lives of St. Maximilian and his dedicated disciples as it was in the lives of Francis and his.

Further, obedience and poverty become correlative aspects of the faith given at baptism in the promises of Christ and Mary Immaculate, a faith that in conforming to Christ in daily life provides the *"ratio"* of penance: to share in the atoning work of Christ with Mary at the foot of the cross, and under her aegis as indicated by the dying Savior to the beloved disciple: son,

---

57. Esser, "Franziskus von Assisi." This same anti-clericalism pursued in the name of liberation by the heresy of St. Francis' day reappears as the principle of private judgment in the Reformation of the sixteenth century, as the principle of progress in the French and Russian revolutions, and at its most essential is seen to be the heart of the eighteenth-century Enlightenment, the century of freemasonry. Cf. Gay, *Enlightenment*.

58. *WK* 486. For St. Francis cf. *Ep. Fid. I*; *2 Cel.*, 83; *Ult. Vol.*, 6; *Leg. maj.*, 7, 1.

behold your mother, and from that day the disciple took the Immaculate into his home, which is the church. Thus, it is no mystery that both for St. Francis and for Maximilian the mystery of the Eucharist is the practical focus of their daily piety and penance within the home where Mary dwells and is Queen,[59] thus giving distinct form to the Immaculate's command to pray and do penance; that perpetual adoration should be so prominent a feature of Cities of the Immaculate,[60] as visits to and care of churches was so distinctive a feature of Francis' activity; that the inhabitants of these cities, like Francis, should revere and support all priests who live according to the form of the Roman Church, i.e., in union with and in obedience to the pope;[61] and that they should be ready and eager to sally forth to establish other Cities of the Immaculate where the prince of this world least expects them to appear, and that their very success in this should effectively demonstrate the realism of Franciscan poverty and life in common, neither unbearable nor unadaptable without compromise in principle, the efficacious means in any circumstances for attaining the objectives of the Mother of the Church, the Immaculate, and the only way of living evangelical poverty successfully.[62]

Conclusion

Total consecration to the Immaculate and participation in her Militia is the form which cooperation with God's saving grace given at baptism takes as it tends to the highest degree of perfection, particularly revealed in the form of life inspired by the Immaculate in her City, because being the Spouse of the Holy Spirit the Immaculate is the mediatrix of all grace.

If, then, this is the origin, nature and scope of total consecration, why have nineteen centuries of Catholic life and seven of Franciscan passed before an explanation was given of something so essential? In general, it may be said that total consecration was always implicitly present as a principle in the life of the church and of the Order, precisely in the unique intercessory

59. For St. Francis on the Eucharist cf. *Adm.*, 1; *Ep. Ord*; for St. Maximilian cf. *WK* 659, 1145.

60. *WK* 354, 585.

61. *WK* 1038. The importance of his insight into the meaning of national churches and their danger to the faith, and of his identification of the only sufficient corrective for this very alluring temptation is especially apparent in view of the exaggerated emphasis on local churches often encountered since the Second Vatican Council.

62. *WK* 486, 299, 300. The direct linkage of missionary zeal, obedience to the Vicar of Christ, and observance of gospel poverty as these are found in St. Maximilian's ideal for the City of the Immaculate bears a strong resemblance to the manner in which St. Francis juxtaposes them in chapter 12 of the *Reg. B.*

role recognized in Mary for the church and Order, and the consequent dependence on her to cooperate with the grace of God. But like all religious orders and the distinct contribution they make to the clarification of the mystery of grace in the history of the church, the Militia was established through the intercession of the Immaculate at this specific time to meet a specific need of the church now. Hence, anyone who desires a deeper understanding of the Immaculate's plans must make a careful study of the circumstances surrounding the founding of the Militia in 1917, details reflecting a particularly intense confrontation between the Woman clothed with the Sun and the dragon on the scene of history.[63]

It is sufficient here to recall Mary's appearance at Fatima, her promises and requests, prophecies and warnings concerning the triumph of her Son and of his church, the conditions for that triumph, and also the violent tribulations to come until her conditions for salvation and peace are fulfilled, viz., penance and prayer, as a consequence of her enemy's triumph in Russia. How Russia is to be reconquered for Christ through penance and prayer under Mary's leadership, or rather how masses of people are to be so moved as to do what the Immaculate asks so that Russia being freed from totalitarian tyranny might be an agency of evangelization and peace rather than of hellish revolution is very much a matter concerning her Militia and its centers in her Cities.

For the success of Satan's stratagems for his legions in these last times, as in the first days of human history, is only possible to the extent that he can capitalize on the lie that is the principle of private judgment, when it becomes the life of human minds and hearts, what St. Francis calls the poison of self-will. Thus, the threat of violent revolution sparked by Marxist ideology is neither an Eastern nor a root problem, but rather an especially vicious fruit and symptom of that disobedience of all God's laws on principle, justified in the name of personal autonomy, rights, and freedom, but which in fact is the basest slavery to sin, and which to succeed inevitably seeks to destroy that which God has ordained to support his law and sustain its observance, viz., the sacerdotal hierarchy of the church. Once men and women are freed from this slavery and the deception that inclines them to be anti-clerical, the collapse of Satan's power and armies will occur in short order.

Men may be intimidated by arms and wealth; Satan is not. He can turn these to his own advantage, quickly and easily, as the history of the twentieth century demonstrates, if that is all that is opposed to him, particularly when those whom he deals with are infected with the indifferentism symbolized in the ethos of freemasonry and expressed in resentment and opposition to

63. Carroll, 1917.

the Vicar of Christ and successor of St. Peter as the authoritative interpreter of the Lord's mind and directives. But what Satan in no way can deal with is the life and death of those who like St. Maximilian in making total consecration the whole of their lives without any conditions have totally exorcised the vice of private judgment through perfect obedience. This indeed was the final goal of the vocation of St. Francis: to be so conformed to the crucified in penance, poverty and prayer, as to sustain the church and her mission to evangelize all at that point where it was being most violently attacked through the disobedience to Christ's vicars. And so St. Maximilian understood all the spiritual, theological and missionary achievements of the Order in the past as a preparation for the promotion at the right moment of total consecration to the Immaculate and her Militia.

Total consecration to the Immaculate, then, is the distinct Kolbean-Franciscan contribution to an effort, a movement, far greater than the Franciscan Order, a movement inspired, coordinated and led through so many servants and handmaids by the one Woman who is the Seat of Wisdom and Queen of the universe. Her Militia is the providential means by which she will secure a basis for the triumph of her Son's sacred heart, and on that basis all the rest that has been promised us.

2

A Thesis of St. Maximilian Concerning St. Francis and the Immaculate in the Light of Recent Research

IN HIS LETTER TO all the clerics of the Order (1933), St. Maximilian wrote of "The Cause of the Immaculate" as the "golden thread" making of the history of the Order "from its very beginning" a unified, intelligible whole, inspired, protected, and guided by the Immaculate as her instrument for the glorification of her Son.[1] In the view of this cause, according to Fr. Maximilian, the history of the Order can be divided into two parts: the first aimed at making Mary all holy known as the Immaculate and was concluded with the proclamation of the dogma; the second purposes the systematic incorporation of this dogmatic truth into life, both of communities as well as individuals, as the easiest and quickest way to sanctify the greatest number of souls and so to realize the reign of the sacred heart of Jesus.[2] The cause of the Immaculate is her Militia, which, across the centuries, the entire speculative and practical effort of the Order has subserved.

Sources of the Kolbean Thesis

Such a thesis implies not only that the mystery of the Immaculate and her cause in some way function as keys to the spirituality and work of St. Francis and of his Order, but also that St. Francis, not implicitly alone, but also formally and explicitly knew, honored, and served the Immaculate in this context. It is not reasonable to think that the founder of an Order as great as the Seraphic Order, which has as its principal task the cause of the Immaculate as such, should have been ignorant of that mystery, especially a founder

---

1. Kolbe, *WK* 486, 1168. Cf. Fehlner, "Mary in the Franciscan," *CE* 3, chapter 5; McCurry, "Maximilian Kolbe."

2. *WK* 1325.

divinely inspired to know the will of God in this foundation.[3] It is known that St. Francis attributed the clarification of the will of the crucified Savior, and consequently of his vocational grace to the Mother of God, advocate of the Order.[4] And in fact, St. Maximilian believed that St. Francis not only knew and honored the Immaculate as such, but also had consciously and deliberately assigned to his Order as its principal concern her cause. Hence, he could affirm that the Militia and the City of the Immaculate were not incidental accretions to the Order, much less a change in its nature, but organic developments of the very essence of Franciscanism.[5]

It is true that occasionally St. Maximilian cited traditions not accepted by scholars as authentic, to illustrate this thesis, for example, the celebration of the feast of the Immaculate Conception by St. Francis, or its institution in the Order by St. Bonaventure.[6] These assertions, however had been current for centuries and clearly answered a desire on the part of the friars to fill a gap of history: how to explain that the Marian spirituality of the Order, so essentially immaculatist, had its origin in St. Francis. But these citations do not constitute the chief part of Fr. Maximilian's thought. He cites *The Salute to the Virgin* of St. Francis where are found the words "consecravit," "plenitudo gratia" and "omne bonum" which, as we shall see, have been brought into the mystery of the Immaculate Conception by some recent studies.[7] Further, the intimate link which St. Maximilian placed between this mystery and that of the mediatrix of all graces, he also discovered in the life and thought of St. Francis, associating in the mind of the Seraph of Assisi veneration of the Immaculate and her invocation as "Advocata Ordinis," although occasionally he places on the lips of St. Francis words of St. Bernard.[8] Fr. Maximilian

3. Francis, *Test.*, 3.

4. *1 Cel.* 106; *Leg. maj.*, 3,1; 4,5.

5. CK September 4, 1937.

6. WK 1081, 1184. The information concerning the celebration by St. Francis of the feast of the Conception of Mary at Rovigo, with the source for that information included in a footnote by Fr. Maximilian, can be found also in Rossi, *L'Immacolata Concezione*, 16, where Fr. Maximilian probably discovered this. Up to twenty years ago, many scholars held that either at the General Chapter of Pisa (1263) or that of Assisi (1269) St. Bonaventure instituted the feast of the Conception of Mary most-holy in the Franciscan Order. From the liturgical ordinances of these chapters, however, as they appear in the critical edition of van Dijk, *Sources*, vol. 2, 421–32, 441, it transpires that in the General Chapter of 1269 St. Bonaventure only insisted on the Saturday Mass in honor of Mary most-holy. Nothing in these ordinances indicates that such a votive Mass was precisely in honor of the Conception of Mary most-holy, much less the Immaculate Conception, a privilege which St. Bonaventure, like St. Thomas, did not acknowledge. Cf. also Brlek, "Legislatio," especially 8, 25–26.

7. WK 1081.

8. WK 485.

also perceived in the knightly spirit of St. Francis the heart of the Militia of the Immaculate (M.I.): namely, that Franciscans must be vassals of so great a queen and hence fight for her in virtue of the total consecration a vassal always makes to his lord.[9] By way of a biography of St. Francis written by Fr. Honoratus Kozminski, OFMCap., he cited that passage of the *Fioretti* where St. Francis expressed the desire that his followers always be "faithful servants of Mary most-holy," i.e., her vassals.[10]

"It is necessary to pray," he states in a conference of 1933, "and above all to consecrate everything to our Lady. It is necessary often to invoke the all-holy Mother, as St. Francis wished, who knew very well what means would bring one most securely to salvation and sanctity. Hence, he proclaimed, often, the glory of the Immaculate and encouraged his brothers to act accordingly: six centuries before the dogmatic definition of the Immaculate Conception of Mary most-holy."[11]

To the objection that there is no evidence that St. Francis ever used the word "Immaculate," St. Maximilian replied that this is not a question of "Scriptura Sola," but of tradition as well as a source of knowledge:

> From the life of the Order, from its history and activity, we see that our Order excels in the veneration of the all-holy Mother, so that the greatest Marian movement of all time coincides with the Franciscan segment of history, to the extent that the Order's teaching on the Immaculate Conception has come to be called "the Franciscan thesis."
>
> This devotion (to the Immaculate) . . . is a tradition, ancient tradition, rushing back to the roots, to the very first days of the Order. This tradition, moreover, was never sporadic, but constant, throughout every era of its long history.[12]

And to the objection that the M.I. implies an exaggerated veneration of Mary, he replied that not only is it not too much but quite insufficient, and added:

> It is a fact that all the saints, with St. Francis at their head, and all Franciscans are not worthy to fall on their knees and ask Her to allow them to do something for Her. This is no mere hypothesis, but a certainty, because She is the Mother of God, set above all creatures. What an honor to serve so great a Queen![13]

9. CK July 10, 1936.

10. CK July 10, 1936; Kozminski, *Świety Francisiszek Seraficki*, vol., 3, 361.

11. CK August 30, 1933.

12. CK July 23, 1933; WK 1184.

13. CK August 22, 1940.

Although hypotheses other than that of Fr. Maximilian can be formulated as explanations of the immaculatist traditions of the Franciscan Order, it is clear that he held as certain (and not merely as a working hypothesis) that St. Francis knew the Immaculate and had made her Cause that of his Order. For him, it is not sufficient to say that St. Francis had some way anticipated the doctrinal development, because this might also be said of many other saints, and hence would hardly explain why Franciscan Marian spirituality is essentially immaculatist.

Problems of an historical kind, however, remain. For example, not even the term "Immaculate," much less "Immaculate Conception," is found in the writings of St. Francis, nor is there certain evidence he celebrated the feast. And there are those who, while admitting he might have known of the feast, would hardly, as an uneducated man, have been familiar with the niceties of academic discussion of the question. It seems that St. Maximilian was aware of the problems, and wrote Fr. Ephrem Longpré, O.F.M., at Quaracchi, so as to obtain materials for a documented study of his thesis.[14] Had he founded his "Marian Academy" as he had planned, one of its first research projects in history would have been a study of this problem. In a letter of 1933 to Fr. Florian Koziura he wrote: "It is worth the effort to study in depth the relations between our Father St. Francis and our Lady, the Immaculate Conception. This will be our fulcrum."[15]

During St. Maximilian's day, there were few critical studies treating of St. Francis and Mary most-holy. At that time, scholarly monographs in Mariology in the modern sense, had only barely begun to be written. Thus, Fr. Maximilian accurately noted that, notwithstanding all that had been done, everything still remained to be done.[16] The first studies of this kind on

14. WK 564.

15. WK 508, 523. Even if in this review the history of this "golden thread" is not traced after St. Francis, it is interesting to note how, in the view of this clear stand taken by St. Maximilian in regard to St. Francis and the Immaculate, St. Francis becomes the dividing line, although not mentioned by name, in the history of the dogma of the Immaculate Conception prepared in outline form by Fr. Maximilian for his book on the Immaculate. Cf. WK 1313. Before St. Francis, the truth of the Immaculate Conception was believed implicitly; after the work of the Franciscan theologians inspired by the Seraph of Assisi, this truth believed explicitly was called the "Franciscan thesis." For the history of Mary most holy and the Franciscan Order cf. Jean de Dieu, "La Vierge"; Balić, *De Immaculata Conceptione*; Antonelli, *La Madonna nella Spiritualità*.

16. WK 508. In 1923, Felder's *Ideals of St. Francis* was first published in German. (Two years later an English translation appeared.) In this classic of over five hundred pages, only five pages treat of our Lady, and these in a very long chapter on the devotions of St. Francis. Felder was an excellent scholar, and what he says about our Lady is sound. Yet from this one would hardly suspect the Marian dimension to be a major distinctive feature of St. Francis' spirituality, and can easily appreciate how much there

St. Francis and Mary most-holy were published for the seventh centenary of
his birth. Because the thesis of St. Maximilian on the purpose of the Franciscan Order is so relevant, it is worth examining whether and to what extent it
has been documented, or at least shown to be documentable, by the results
of scholarly study of St. Francis and Mary most-holy.

In 1926, for the seventh centenary of the death of St. Francis, Fr. Bede
Kleinschmidt made an excellent study of St. Francis and our Lady in art
history. His perspective cannot but suggest the existence of some link between the Immaculate as such and St. Francis. On the basis of the artistic
tradition, Kleinschmidt claims that of those who venerated Mary in the
depths of their hearts Francis "merits the palm," a judgment repeated in
a number of encyclopedias and dictionaries.[17] He also distinguishes between those who have honored Mary in word, such as theologians and
panegyrists, and those who have venerated her in the depths of their
hearts. Francis he places in the latter category. Interestingly, only when
scholars began to consider Francis' contribution to the veneration of Mary
as a theologian did they begin, as we shall see, to consider his contribution
in both as centering on the mystery of the Immaculate.

In 1927, Fr. Willibrord Lampen published his study on the devotion
of St. Francis to the angels and saints, the greater part of which dealt with
the place of Mary most-holy in the devotional life of St. Francis.[18] From the
results of this study it transpires that, in referring to our Lady almost without
number St. Francis, even using the same title, did not repeat himself once,
a testimony to his literary ability as well as his extraordinary love for the
Mother of God. Lampen assesses the soundness of Francis' piety as follows:
"We can therefore state that the piety of St. Francis for the saints was based on
the doctrine of the church, and in no way disfigured by those exaggerations
not always absent from popular devotions in the Middle Ages."[19]

Shortly after, in a second study, the same scholar, in the course of treating St. Francis as the "cultor Trinitas," as he is described in the *Legenda Major* (3) of St. Bonaventure, briefly mentions Our Lady.[20] But it does not seem
that the author appreciates (as clearly St. Maximilian did) the link between
the devotion of St. Francis to the Blessed Trinity and to the Mother of God.

"was to be done."

17. Kleinschmidt, *Maria und Franziskus*, 13. Cf. Longpré, "Saint François d'Assise,"
coll. 1283–84; Blasucci, "Francesco d'Assisi," 793.

18. Lampen, "De S.P.N. Francisci."

19. Lampen, "De S.P.N. Francisci," 23.

20. Lampen, "S. Franciscus cultor." 452, 454.

Almost twenty years passed before another scholarly study on St. Francis and our Lady was published. During the Marian Year in honor of the first centenary of the proclamation of the dogma of the Immaculate Conception (1954) there appeared the study of Fr. Cajetan Esser on the Marian Piety of St. Francis.[21] In view of its evident scholarship, orderly exposition, and synthetic character, this study soon came to serve as a guide for those which followed. It consists of two parts. The first deals with the theological bases of the Marian piety of St. Francis, namely the relations between Mary and Christ, Mary and the Blessed Trinity, and the role of Mary in the plan of salvation. The second part describes the chief features of the Marian piety of St. Francis in the context of his spirituality and of his work, namely poverty after the example of Mary, poor Lady and Queen, the invocation of Mary, advocate of the Order, and devotional exercises in honor of Mary. In conclusion Fr. Cajetan affirms that the Marian Piety of St. Francis, firmly rooted in the ancient tradition of the church, possesses distinctive features inherited by his Order and which have remained ever present in its history: "Mary, the Mother of Jesus and as such the chosen instrument of the Blessed Trinity for the salvation of men; Mary the poor Lady, and as such advocate of the Order."[22]

Although he does not allude to the question of the Immaculate Conception and St. Francis, and deals only with the practice of addressing Mary all-holy as "Spouse of the Holy Spirit" he does underscore the title "Advocate of the Order" as fundamental to and distinctive of the Marian piety of St. Francis, thus making clear how very Franciscan is St. Maximilian's teaching on the Immaculate, mediatrix of all graces.[23] Fr. Cajetan also remarks on the connection in St. Francis' thought between the title "Spouse of the Holy Spirit" and spiritual maternity: "Because Francis praised the Mother of God as the 'Spouse of the Holy Spirit': by that fact he brought the spiritual maternity of souls and their spousal relation with the Holy Spirit into close relation."[24]

---

21. Esser, "Die Marien Frommigkeit." Before 1954 there were relatively few popular books and articles treating principally of Mary most-holy and St. Francis. Among the books can be listed: Bierbaum, *Franziskus von Assisi*; Benoit, *Le Chevalier*; Christian, *Our Lady*. R. Brown's anthology, *Our Lady and St. Francis*, is very useful. On the eve of the Marian Year of 1954, it was said that all could be said about Mary and St. Francis had already been said; hence, no further study of this point was needed: Brlek, "Legislatio," 3.

22. Esser, "Die Marien Frommigkeit,"190; cf. *WK* 643, 1320.

23. Esser, "Die Marien Frommigkeit,"190; cf. *WK* 1029.

24. Esser, "Die Marien Frommigkeit," 183; cf. *WK* 486.

Esser identifies the divine maternity as the basis of St. Francis' Marian piety: "'He rendered the Mother of God a love beyond words, because she had made our brother the Lord of Majesty' (*Leg. Maj.* 9,3). Thus briefly the biographers set forth the profound basis of the Marian piety of St. Francis."[25]

In treating the themes basic to St. Francis' Mariology more or less the format "New Eve-New Adam" and noting how the thought of St. Francis became typical in orienting the subsequent Franciscan Christology,[26] Fr. Cajetan suggests that such patterns were also normative in the development of Franciscan Marian-immaculatist piety and doctrine, so as to underscore, as St. Maximilian did through this piety and doctrine, the absolute primacy of the Word Incarnate.[27]

Almost simultaneously with the study of Fr. Cajetan Esser was published that of Fr. Octavian Schmucki on the relation of St. Francis with the Blessed Virgin.[28] His observations on the "spiritual maternity" of every holy soul, as taught by St. Francis, are interesting, particularly as they are so similar to the reflections of Fr. Maximilian:

> Hence the faithful soul, through sanctifying grace, a life truly virtuous, and the infused virtues, especially charity, carries Jesus in his heart and in his body in a manner comparable with that in which our Lady carried the Lord in her womb . . . We may conclude that he (Francis) meant this not only in the moral sense . . . but with sufficient clarity also expresses the mystical-ontic aspect, because the basis for this maternity implies a spousal nexus.[29]

Treating for the most part the same themes as Esser, viz., the Marian doctrine, the Marian piety and Marian asceticism of St. Francis, Fr. Octavian also sees in the divine maternity their basis; he adds, however, that there is no evidence to show the Immaculate Conception of Mary had any role in the Marian thought and piety of St. Francis.[30] Finally, in his conclusion he writes: "It is clear, however, to all that his (Francis) Marian piety did not form the center of his spirituality. Further it is evident that St. Clare demonstrated a greater devotion to Mary."[31]

---

25. Esser, "Die Marien Frommigkeit," 176–77; WK 508, 1305.

26. Esser, "Die Marien Frommigkeit," 178.

27. WK 603.

28. Schmucki, "De Seraphici Patris."

29. Schmucki, "De Seraphici Patris," 43–44.

30. Schmucki, "De Seraphici Patris," 18.

31. Schmucki, "De Seraphici Patris," 45.

This perspective clashes somewhat with that of St. Maximilian who became somewhat irked when he realized particular care was being taken always to describe her explicitly "after Christ," as though her position in the spiritual life were no different from that of any other saint.[32] But, as will be seen, more recent studies have tended to show, some explicitly, that Fr. Kolbe correctly understood the mind of St. Francis.

A little before the Second Vatican Council there appeared another interesting study of Fr. Esser on the "ecclesial piety" of St. Francis.[33] And after the Council, in 1976, a parallel study of Fr. Schmucki, "On the Church in St. Francis' experience of Fraternity" appeared.[34] Both authors affirm that the explanation for the notion of "fraternal love" as "maternal" at the center of St. Francis' experience must be sought in his vision of the Mother of Christ as the prototype of the church. Hence the title of Esser's study is very appropriate: "Sancta Mater Ecclesia Romana." Both insist that as the role of the Holy Spirit in Mary is decisive in this vision, so too is it decisive in the church. Both find in each fraternity faithful to the church. Again it is evident how traditionally Franciscan is St. Maximilian's vision of fraternal love in the "City of the Immaculate," as it were rooted in the loving maternal influence of the Immaculate.[35]

Three numbers of *Estudios Franciscanos* for 1961–62 contain a long and very important study of Fr. Felician Rivera on our Lady and St. Francis.[36] In the first part he treats of the doctrinal basis for the place of Mary in the Spirituality of St. Francis. In the second part of the devotional exercises of St. Francis in honor of Mary, and finally, in the third, of Mary as the "Inspiratrix of the Seraphic Ideal." One is rather accustomed to think of Mary having a place in the spirituality of Francis; but the sub-title of this third part suggests as well that Francis with his spiritual work had first of all a place in the Cause of Mary the "Totius bonitatis Mater"—the "Mother of Goodness." This title, says Rivera, is the most significant in interpreting Francis' vision of Mary.[37] Rivera further claims that the *Salute* of Francis to Mary, as to her "in whom was and is fulness of grace and every good" anticipates the classic argument "potuit, decuit, ergo fecit" (he could, it was appropriate, therefore he did it) for the Immaculate Conception: "Scholastic Theology in these three words summarized the complicated arguments of the doctors in favor

---

32. *WK* 603.
33. Esser, "Sancta Mater Ecclesia Romana."
34. Schmucki, "Franziskus von Assisi."
35. *WK* 1284.
36. Rivera de Ventosa, "La devoción a María."
37. Rivera de Ventosa, "La devoción a María," 274.

of the Immaculate Conception. 'Potuit, decuit, ergo fecit.' It seems to us that the affirmation of Francis, that in Mary is found 'the fulness of grace and every good' anticipates this famous recapitulation."[38]

Very similar to St. Francis' style of speaking about the Virgin most-holy is that of our Lady herself at Lourdes, who identified herself thus: "*I am the Immaculate Conception*," a mode of speaking that fascinated St. Maximilian.[39] Rivera, however, does not say St. Francis knew the Immaculate Conception, as Fr. Kolbe says, but only that he prepared the way for the formulation of the dogma.

In the final part of his study Rivera regrets that among students of St. Francis' spirituality few have developed and deepened an understanding of its Marian aspects. Although it would be an error, according to Rivera, to view the Marian aspects of St. Francis' devotion to Mary as the key to his spirituality, nonetheless Mary's place in our return (or conversion) to the Father through the "poor Christ" is essential:

> Devotion to Mary is not the keystone of "Seraphic Spirituality."
> This spirituality formally consists in conversion and in the re-
> turn to the Father who is in heaven . . . no other way is nor can
> be found other than the way that is Christ . . . And in Francis'
> following on the footsteps of Christ . . . There stands the figure
> of Mary as "Inspiratrix," sweetly comforting. The thought of
> Francis evokes the poverty of the Son of God.[40]

As the study of Esser, so this one concludes with the prayer of St. Francis at the Portiuncula to the "Advocate of the Order." The response of this Advocate across the centuries, says Rivera, should be the subject of another study. Such a study, [it] may be noted, had already been planned by St. Maximilian.[41]

The well-known Scotist, Fr. Ephrem Longpré, in the course of a long encyclopedic article[42] writes that in the *Salute* of St. Francis evidence is found that St. Francis knew the Immaculate Conception, and hence had anticipated the scholarship and concepts of his time:

> With St. Francis it is not a question of justification, nor of
> sanctification of Mary, but only of Her Trinitarian "consecra-
> tion" (consecravit), the most perfect possible; and as the saint

---

38. Rivera de Ventosa, "La devoción a María," 267.

39. *WK* 1224, 1319.

40. Rivera de Ventosa, "La devoción a María," 277.

41. Rivera de Ventosa, "La devoción a María," 296; cf. *WK* 1304.

42. Longpré, "Saint François d'Assise."

rightly observes that "in the past as in the present" (fuit et est), there is found in Her the fullness of grace . . . it is no wonder that some illustrious defenders of the Immaculate Conception, such as Wadding, Alva y Astorga, Strozzi and others, cited this text as probative of the Immaculate Conception. Within such a perspective, entirely in relation to the Trinity and Jesus Christ, Francis of Assisi also highly esteemed the predestination of Mary in the Divine plan.[43]

The entire fifth volume of *Quaderni di Spiritualita Francescana* is dedicated to the Marian aspects of Franciscan Spirituality. The essay of Fr. Albert Ghinato[44] recapitulates quite well the "Mariology" of St. Francis. In regard to St. Francis' use of the title "Advocate of the Order" Ghinato suggests that its meaning can be grasped more simply and profoundly by considering it in relation to St. Mary of the Angels. Two citations, one from the *Mirror of Perfection (Speculum Perfectionis)*, the other from *Fioretti (Little Flowers)*, serving as the conclusion of this essay, well describe the veneration, as it were without limits, which St. Francis showed the Mother of God, and which he, called by St. Bonaventure the "Servus Marie," i.e., servant or slave of Mary (*Leg. maj.* 3, 1), desired his sons also to be "faithful servants of Mary." "There (at the Portiuncula) with all your heart, in voices of exultation and faith, confess God the Father and his Son our Lord Jesus Christ, in the unity of the Holy Spirit"; "They must ever honor and magnify in every way and manner possible to them the Blessed Virgin, and hold Her in the highest veneration and devotion. Once again I wish that they ever be her faithful servants."[45]

The study of Fr. Anthony Blasucci in that volume, although not dealing directly with St. Francis, underscores some characteristics of Franciscan Marian piety through the centuries, which have as their source St. Francis and which clearly converge on the thought of St. Maximilian, namely, the knightly and all-embracing aspects of that Marian piety.[46]

The research of Fr. Bernardine Rivellini has identified those elements of St. Francis' Marian devotion which can be discovered in the *Legenda Major* of St. Bonaventure.[47] These elements, effectively an index to the "Mariology" of St. Francis, are: his ineffable love for the Mother of God, because she gave us the Lord of Majesty as our brother; his consideration

43. Longpré, "Saint François d'Assise," coll. 1283–84. Cf. Blasucci, "Francesco d'Assisi," 794.

44. Ghinato, "La Madonna."

45. Ghinato, "La Madonna," 56.

46. Blasucci, "Note caratteristiche."

47. Rivellini, "Elementi."

of Christ as the fruit of purest flesh of Mary; the consideration of Mary as
the font of mercy; the introduction of Saint Francis to the gospel by Mary;
the choice of Mary as "Advocate of the Order"; the continuous meditation
of Francis on the poverty of our Lady. There is no doubt that St. Bonaventure, profound Mariologist that he was, knew how to weave the "Mariology" of St. Francis, as to many other features of the Seraphic Father's life
and work, into the theological and spiritual patrimony of the church. As
regards the Marian heritage of St. Francis Rivellini cites a passage from
an essay of E. Gilson, *La Philosophie Franciscaine*[48]: "Always at the core of
any authentically Franciscan doctrine is hidden the ideal of St. Francis,
the secret principle of the form and life of that doctrine, as the heart is at
the center of the body it animates." Rivellini further comments that in the
picture of the Seraph of Assisi drawn by St. Bonaventure "Mary is linked
inseparably to this ideal, indeed I would say that with Jesus She is the
entire Franciscan ideal." The devotion of the *Angelus Domini*, promoted
in and made universal for the entire Franciscan Order by Bonaventure, is,
concludes Rivellini, the best *Summa* of this Mariology.[49]

Post-Conciliar Studies

In the Capuchin review *Laurentianum* there has appeared between 1969 and
1982 a series of articles, extremely useful both in understanding the Marian
thought and exercises of St. Francis, and in appreciating the Franciscan background of the Mariology and Marian piety of St. Maximilian.

The first of the series, appearing in 1969, is an exhaustive study of Fr.
Hillary Pyfferoen concerning St. Francis and the Portiuncula.[50] The author
affirms that although St. Francis honored Mary at the Portiuncula under
various titles, he did so principally as Queen of the Angels, a title in his
thought strictly linked with the mystery of the Assumption. It is under this
title that Francis experienced and realized the role of Mary, "The Mother
of all Goodness," in the origin and development of his vocation, viz., as the
mediatrix of all grace and "Advocate of the Order."[51]

48. Rivellini, "Elementi," 150.

49. Rivellini, "Elementi," 106, 109. It would be interesting and useful to have a
similar study of Franciscan elements which are present in the Marian sermons of the
Seraphic Doctor. Some of these in the works of Conrad of Saxony have been indicated
in the recent edition of his *Speculum*, 312–13, where reference is made to the antiphon
of the *Office of The Passion* of St. Francis. Cf. Martinez, "El culto a María."

50. Pyfferoen, "S. Maria de Angelis."

51. For the nexus between the mysteries of the Assumption and the Immaculate
Conception in Franciscan Theology in the course of history, cf. Longpré, "L'Assomption."

The next year the same scholar convincingly argued that St. Francis composed at the Portiuncula the vespers antiphon for the *Office of the Passion* (with the title "Spouse of the Holy Spirit" addressed for the first time to the all-holy Virgin Mother) and the *Salute to the Virgin* (with the phrase "Virgin Made Church" and so many other titles, which illustrate the intimate relation between the Virgin and church as palace and tabernacle of God) both directed to the queen and mother, and impregnated by the mystery of the Holy Trinity.[52] Thus the link between the Holy Spirit, Mary most-holy and the church is shown to be characteristic of the thought of St. Francis, and this to have been realized under the influence of his "Advocate" at the Portiuncula.

Finally, in 1971, this same scholar published a commentary on the *Salute to the Virgin*.[53] Given that the primitive reading was not *Virgo Perpetua*, but *Virgo Ecclesia Facta* (for "ever Virgin," the primitive text read "Virgin made Church"),[54] and given that the *Salute* was composed at the Portiuncula, it follows, concludes Fr. Pyfferoen, that the capstone of the Marian thought and piety of St. Francis, namely Mary as the "Mother of all Goodness" and the "Advocate of the Order" is also the key to the "ecclesiology" of St. Francis, and the root of his special loyalty to the church of St. Peter in Rome.

At the International Mariological Congress in Rome, 1975, Fr. Optatus Van Asseldonk, in collaboration with Fr. Pyfferoen, presented a long study on Mary and the Holy Spirit according to St. Francis, published also that same year in *Laurentianum*.[55] Before, and since, others have treated this thesis,[56] but none so extensively and profoundly as these two scholars, who deal not only with this theme in St. Francis, but find the heart of the relation between Mary and the Holy Spirit in the thought of St. Francis to be in the title "Spouse of the Holy Spirit." They expound the history of this title, both before and after St. Francis (this latter only summarily) so as to place in clear relief the originality and influence of St. Francis, particularly in the rapid adoption of the title everywhere Franciscans were found reciting daily that antiphon of the *Office of the Passion*. As these authors note, the better part of that history after St. Francis is still to be written, including, that of this title common with the sons of St. Francis. What they say concerning St. Maximilian is also interesting: "It seems that the person who has best grasped the

---

52. Pyfferoen, "Fuditne S. Franciscus."
53. Pyfferoen, "Ave . . . Dei."
54. Esser, *Die opuscula*.
55. Pyfferoen and Van Asseldonk, "Maria Santissima."
56. Van Asseldonk, "Spirito Santo."

sense of this title 'Spouse of the Holy Spirit' and adapted it to a contemporary
mentality is the martyr Bl. Maximilian Kolbe, O.F.M., Conv. (+1941) . . . In
our opinion, only a charismatic gift of a very high order could have permitted Bl. Maximilian to have discovered among these mysteries of faith the
analogy explained by him in his writings."[57]

Worthy of special note for Kolbean studies is the link perceived by St.
Francis between the chapter of Pentecost, the Holy Spirit as Minister General of the Order and Mary most-holy as the Advocate-Protectress of the
Order: "Here too we find associated the Holy Spirit and Mary, or (according
to the notions of Francis) the Minister General and the Advocate-Protectress of the Order. But in no other thirteenth-century order do we find any
such unity and rather than to attribute it to chance, we prefer to ascribe it to
the attention of the founder, who desired to entrust the government of his
Order to the Spirit Paraclete, and at St. Mary of the Angels. On that Feast
(Pentecost) the sanctuary of Portiuncula is transformed into the Jerusalem
Cenacle where the ministers and custodians gather in prayer as disciples
about Mary, the Spouse of the Holy Spirit."[58]

Although not dealing directly with the mystery of Mary, two studies of
Fr. Dominick Gagnan[59] are quite helpful in understanding the various ramifications of St. Francis' "Mariology." The first article treats of the symbolism of
the woman in the life of St. Francis, and takes as its starting point the parable
of the poor woman in the desert used by St. Francis to explain to Pope Innocent III his plan for a new order. The second examines the personifications
of poverty, as spouse, lady and mother according to the conceptions of St.
Francis. It is not hard to appreciate the importance of this study for deepening
one's sense of Franciscan Marian piety. Fr. Gagnon writes:

> The identification of the spouse (the church, the soul of the just,
> or the saved humanity, cosmic mother) with Mary an aspect of
> what might be called the icon of Jesus, Mary and John. On high:
> Jesus crucified, King of the cosmos, First-Born; at the foot of the
> cross and at each side: Mary, mother of the First-Born, mother
> of salvation, and John become son and heir, prototype just re-
> formed in the likeness of real sonship.[60]

57. Pyfferoen and Van Asseldonk, "Maria Santissima," 438.

58. Pyfferoen and Van Asseldonk, "Maria Santissima," 424–25; cf. Van Asseldonk,
"Spirito Santo," col. 1727.

59. Gagnan, "Le symbole"; "Typologie."

60. Gagnan, "Typologie," 509.

He continues: "The poverty of Christ, loved and changed, and in an altogether unitive way lived in Mary, makes Christ be born in history . . ."[61]

The last article in the *Laurentianum* series is rather a recapitulation, on the part of Fr. Van Asseldonk, of his earlier study, Mary and the Holy Spirit in St. Francis, with a special focus on the title, "Spouse of the Holy Spirit."[62]

Stimulating is the article of this scholar in the *Dizionario Francescano* under the heading *Mother*.[63] Because it is also relevant to the Franciscan background of Kolbean thought, a few selections are included here. "In the first local fraternities, in the hermitages, the Marthas, or superiors, were called 'mothers' and the Mary's, or contemplative friars, 'sons,' with a provision that they would regularly exchange places. Life in the hermitages, fairly similar to that lived by the poor Ladies at St. Damian, was intended to be a model for subsequent local fraternities."

He remarks, further, that the influence of St. Clare in this matter is important: "From the process of canonization it is quite clear that Clare experienced Francis as a 'Mother' . . . For the rest Clare also experienced God and the Holy Spirit 'maternally' . . . and there seems to me to be no doubt about the maternity of Clare towards St. Francis." At the root of this maternal element in the spirituality of St. Francis and St. Clare is the mystery of Mary most-holy: "The deeper sense of the fraternal-maternal vocation must be sought in the mystery of the Mother of Christ, prototype-model of the church." "The virginal, spousal and maternal vocation of the Poor Ladies is a participation in the church of the Maternity of the Mother of Jesus. This mystery of participated motherhood Francis perceived from the very first years of his conversion."

Fr. Van Asseldonk also observes how striking is "the intimate nexus between penance and the Holy Spirit, direct author of the indweller, of Father and Son in us . . ." He notes also, as in his earlier study, that the government of the Order is "maternal," entrusted namely to the Holy Spirit and to the Advocate of the Order, Mary most-holy, who, across the centuries has insisted so much on the necessity of penance.[64]

Also helpful in regard to these aspects of St. Francis' "Marian Spirituality" is the essay of Auspicious Van Corstanje,[65] who explains the "maternity" of St. Francis in its Marian-ecclesial context; so also the study of

61. Gagnan, "Typologie," 510.

62. Van Asseldonk, "Maria Sposa."

63. Van Asseldonk, "Madre."

64. Van Asseldonk, "Madre," coll. 920, 928 note 3, 922–923, 924, 925–926. For the concept of the Immaculate as superior and proprietress of her City according to St. Maximilian, cf. *WK* 314, 319, 436, 1179.

65. van Corstanje, "Dit zeg."

the Poor Clare Sr. Clare Augusta Lainati,[66] who describes the influence of St. Clare on St. Francis.

Recently two studies on the "Mariology" of St. Francis have appeared in *Estudios Marianas*. The first by Fr. Caspar Calvo Moralejo[67] assesses the Marian piety of St. Francis in the light of Pope Paul VI's *Marialis Cultus*. This is an important contribution, not only in view of the themes treated, but also for the perspectives from which the themes are viewed. In the judgment of Fr. Calvo, to align oneself with St. Francis with things Marian is to be fully in accord with the directives of *Marialis Cultus*. Fr. Calvo claims that the title "Mater Ecclesia" given such prominence by Paul VI, recapitulates very well the mind of St. Francis, and he concludes as follows:

> The Cult of the Blessed Virgin has its ultimate justification in the sovereign will of God, beyond all analysis, which being eternal and divine charity, accomplishes all according to a plan of love: "He loves Her and does great things in Her" (Luke 1:44); He loves Her for Herself and loves Her also for us; These words from *Marialis Cultus* can also serve to recapitulate the Marian thought of the Poverello. Mary is the expression of the love of God, Father of Mercy, who has given to us in Her the "Mother of Jesus" and the "Mother of Mercy" . . . For this we are bound to honor Mary as our rightful duty. The cult of our Lady is not understood except in constant relation to the Holy Trinity and to Christ, our Lord. Mary is the "Spouse of the Holy Spirit" who enriches us with her grace. "No other woman on earth has been born similar to you," because you have "all the fullness of grace and every good!"[68]

One can add that this also recapitulates quite well the thought of St. Maximilian.[69] The second study, from the pen of Fr. Peter de Anasagasti[70] expounds the theological principles undergirding the Marian piety of St. Francis. Before doing this, however, the author deals with two preliminary questions, namely whether St. Francis can be considered a theologian, and what importance his Marian piety has in his spirituality. To the first query Anasagasti replies that St. Francis is a theologian, not in the professional style but in the contemplative. Regarding the second query Fr.

---

66. Lainati, "Introduzione."

67. Calvo Moralejo, "La Piedad Mariana."

68. Calvo Moralejo, "La Piedad Mariana," 302.

69. *WK* 508, 1229, 1310, 1318.

70. Anasagasti, "Principios."

Anasagasti writes of St. Francis as an "impassioned lover of Mary"[71] whose Marian piety is essential and central in his spirituality. The "principle of his conversion."[72]

Fr. Anasagasti identifies eight certain principles of St. Francis' Marian piety: Trinitarian Communication, divine maternity, co-redemption, mediation, magisterium, virginity, queenship and dominion. Perhaps Fr. Anasagasti is the only contemporary scholar to treat, in some detail, of Mary as teacher of St. Francis, hence, in some fashion, a source of wisdom, and of the Portiuncula as a school of wisdom directed by Mary.[73] At the end of the study[74] the question of St. Francis and the Immaculate Conception, a mystery already being discussed in the schools at the time of St. Francis, and of the possibility that this is also one of the principles of his "Mariology," is raised. Fr. Anasagasti cites Fr. Longpré as a supporter of the claim. Fr. Anasgasti, however, limits himself to a sympathetic, but conditional affirmation: "If Francis had spoken of the Immaculate (but so far no proof that he did so speak has been adduced), he would have supported the privilege." Fr. Anasagasti concludes thus: "Francis of Assisi was not an academic theologian, but it is very difficult to find any other soul excelling his in understanding the grandeurs of Mary and in the joyful appreciation of her exceptional privileges."[75]

The excellent commentary on St. Francis' *Salute to the Virgin* by Francis di Caccia[76] calls attention, not only to the depth and theological precision of his writings, but also to the marvelous literary production of this "illiterate," particularly evident in this "poetic song," a literary miracle rarely met, as literature to be compared only with the works of Dante.[77] Fr. Calvo observes how Francis linked the incomparable sanctity of Mary with the love of the Mother of God. "If the *Salute* begins with the 'Lady' and ends with 'God,' this is because here—and at this point the poetic inspiration is most creative—is continued the Franciscan faith in the mediatory and in the operational role of Mary."[78]

71. Anasagasti, "Principios," 392.

72. Anasagasti, "Principios," 393.

73. Anasagasti, "Principios," 411–13. Cf. *WK* 1295, 1312. 1313. Anasagasti follows St. Bonaventure. Cf. DiFonzo, *Doctrina S. Bonaventurae*, 123–6 and 139–46, for the texts in question. This idea is also found in Conrad of Saxony, *Speculum*, 189–195.

74. Anasagasti, "Principios," 417; but in the text cited from Longpré the defense is quite brief and does not go much beyond what is found in St. Maximilian, *WK* 1081.

75. Anasagasti, "Principios," 418.

76. Di Caccia, "Il 'Saluto.'"

77. Di Caccia, "Il 'Saluto,'" 59.

78. *WK* 339, 643, 1286, 1310.

Fr. Peter D. Fehlner affirmed in a recent essay on St. Francis and the Immaculate[79] that St. Francis knew the Immaculate and that there are not wanting proofs for this claim. These proofs, some shown from the events of his life, e.g., at the Portiuncula, Greccio, Alverna, and others from his writings, such as the antiphon from the *Office of the Passion* and the *Salute to the Virgin*, converge on that title first addressed to Mary most-holy by St. Francis, namely the Spouse of the Holy Spirit. Once one recognizes the uniqueness or incomparability of Mary most-holy in respect to any other creature (Francis wrote: there is none born among women like you, a Virgin) and her "fulness of grace and all good" which define her and originate from a consecration and special election (namely her absolute predestination) placing her in the midst of the Trinity as the inseparable complement of the Word Incarnate, it follows, that she was such from the first moment of her existence (conception), or she would not be that incomparable woman, full of grace and all good. The reasoning is similar to that which is made of any human being: it was such from the first moment of her conception, or will never be such. In the case of Mary most-holy her nature is her "poverty," namely her "total consecration" to the Trinity, hence totally pure from the first moment of her existence. Francis, then, knew and understood this total consecration of the Spouse of the Holy Spirit, and hence could not but have known the mystery that would afterward come to be known as the Immaculate Conception.

Fr. Fehlner underscores the importance of the relation between the Portiuncula "here Mary most-holy classified the meaning of Francis' vocation to follow Christ crucified and repair his Church, and the mystery of the Assumption of Mary, nothing else but the mystery of the "fullness of grace" in the first moment of Mary's existence in its final development.[80] Whoever like St. Francis had a vision of the Women in heaven and has understood the twelfth chapter of the Apocalypse, understands that the Woman is identical with the Woman of the beginning, and was the possession of God the Creator in the beginning of his ways. This understanding is sapiential and in origin contemplative. Precisely for this reason, writes Fr. Fehlner, Francis was granted a mystical insight through the intercession of the Immaculate, so as to be so great a theologian on this point.[81] Thus is explained how he came to learn what is at the center of his "Mariology" and what is the fountainhead of so many wonderful theological developments.

79. Fehlner, "Saint Francis and Mary Immaculate," *CE* 3, chapter 3.
80. Fehlner, "Saint Francis and Mary Immaculate," *CE* 3, chapter 3.
81. Fehlner, "Saint Francis and Mary Immaculate," *CE* 3, chapter 3.

For the rest the importance of prayer and contemplation for "academic" theology is not without confirmation in the teaching of St. Bonaventure[82] and has been underscored by Hans Urs von Balthasar.[83] With this mystical intuition one can explain the contribution of St. Francis to the development of doctrine, in perfect fidelity to tradition, so characteristic of Francis' Marian piety, and without recourse to a theological "Deus ex Machina."

The position of Fr. Fehlner is confirmed by another study of Fr. di Caccia, but written without knowledge of the study of Fr. Fehlner.[84] Di Caccia writes that:

> It seems proper and useful to focus on the interior aspect of that unique "Woman," whose uniqueness is in particular 'Immaculate,' by approaching Her in childlike simplicity through the limpid teaching of St. Francis of Assisi, whom we consider one of the subtlest, though simple and prudent, theologians the Catholic Church has so far counted among her members . . . St. Francis never used the word Immaculate. Notwithstanding the "lexical lacuna," he taught the basis and nature of the "Immaculate." Francis eludes theological controversy; not out of neglect, but because he lives his Marian belief, if not in the verbalized form of theoretical discussions, nonetheless, in one that falls within limits of this world. As he recognized virginity, in its conceptional purity, as well as in the Word, so too he recognized the Immaculate, even without the semantic presence.[85]

In regard to the question of the Immaculate and St. Francis Fr. di Caccia makes several useful observations on the word "Consecravit" and the parallel which he finds between the all-pure action of Mary in conceiving the Word and the purity which a priest must have in consecrating the Eucharist, and which have parallels in the teaching of St. Maximilian. So too, in regard to the intimate nexus between the Immaculate, poverty and the total offering of one's own will to God in the form of heroic obedience in the thought of St. Francis, because this same nexus is found in the thought of Kolbe.[86] Fr. Di Caccia, however, does not seem to have the importance of the title "Spouse of the Holy Spirit," and its close relation with the uniqueness of the Mother of God.

---

82. *Itin.*, c. 1, n. 7.

83. Balthasar, *First Glance*; Fehlner, Review of *First Glance*.

84. Di Caccia, "Il senso."

85. Di Caccia, "Il senso," 530–531.

86. *WK* 339.

Certainly the most complete treatment of Mary most-holy and St. Francis found in any reference work is that of Fr. Alphonse Pompei in the *Dizionario Francescano*,[87] in which, on the basis of primary sources he recapitulates all the material relative to the Marian thought and piety of St. Francis, thoroughly traditional, yet at the same time a tradition thoroughly impregnated by St. Francis' originality, the synthesis of St. Francis' Mariology formed by Fr. Pompei places the question of the Immaculate and St. Francis in clear relief. Father Pompei writes that:

> The absolute primacy of Jesus Christ in the life of St. Francis, and afterward in his Order, is as it were the natural complement of that very special, and characteristic relation of the Poverello with Mary, embracing a knowledge and love of her crystallized in that title, employed by him for the first time, viz., "Spouse of the Holy Spirit." In other words, in Francis there is missing only the clear formulation which subsequently would be effected with the title "Immaculate Conception of Mary" . . . The strict nexus between the title "Spouse of the Holy Spirit" and the mystery of the Immaculate Conception rests on the fact that with this title Francis, sustained by so many and such wonderful mystical graces obtained for him through the intercession of Mary, seems to have lifted the veil, behind which are hidden the extraordinary relations of Mary with the Divine Persons of the Most Holy Trinity; relations illumined by the incomparable, unique beauty, not only moral, but also of the very countenance and person of the Mother of God and Spouse of the Holy Spirit.

Fr. Pompei concludes:

> In our days the distinctive character of Franciscan Marian piety has been realized in exemplary fashion by St. Maximilian Kolbe. His experience may be described as a "harmonious synthesis of all the various constitutive elements of the Franciscan way and experience across the centuries, and whose point of departure is Francis himself. The perfection of that charity, the central element of Franciscan Spirituality, and whose aim is to die for love of that love of him who did deign to die for love of us, consists in the measure of one's own identification (total consecration) with Mary Immaculate, Spouse of the Holy Spirit, in the history of salvation, the perfect fruit, complement and response to the love of the Father and of the Word Incarnate, as in eternity the

---

87. Pompei, "Maria." Other articles in this Dictionary treating of Mary Most Holy are: "Amore di Dio"; "Dio"; "Gesu Cristo"; "Madre"; "Spirito Santo."

Holy Spirit is the purest fruit, complement and response to the love of the Father and of the Son."[88]

Fr. Pompei insists on the perennial validity of Francis' Mariology: "Certainly he (Francis) articulates and expresses this Marian role in a medieval context; but in his manner of expressing his vision of Mary and his Marian piety are structural features, which can and indeed must form part of any Franciscan Marian spirit in the contemporary world."[89]

Conclusion

Little studied by scholars at the time of St. Maximilian, the subject of Mary most-holy and St. Francis. Since the Marian Year to commemorate the centennial of the dogma of the Immaculate Conception has become the theme of many studies, and notwithstanding the so-called Mariological crisis after the Second Vatican Council, it has been studied more since the council with the return to the sources, and with the critical edition of the writings of St. Francis, done by Fr. Esser.[90]

It remains a fact, however, that "a 'Marian Spirituality' of St. Francis truly worthy of that name has not yet been elaborated."[91] "In recent decades much has been written about the Christocentrism/Theocentrism of the Poverello, yet in the spirituality of the Seraphic Father there is an exceptional place reserved for the Mother of All Good, which in many respects, via the three Orders he founded, is normative for the thirteenth Century."[92]

Nonetheless, the studies reviewed here tend to identify and at least initially describe "the exceptional place" of Mary in the spirituality of the Seraphic Father, his special place in her plans, to study in depth that distinctive element in his Marian piety, the complement of his theocentrism and Christocentrism, namely his love for her who is Spouse of the Holy Spirit, Mother of the Son of God, and chosen daughter handmaid of the most high king and Father. Indeed the recognition of that exceptional place is closely linked to a deeper appreciation of St. Francis as a theologian.

It is not without interest for the thesis of St. Maximilian that some scholars have noted the resemblance between the Marian thought of the

88. Pompei, "Maria," cols. 947–49. The last citation is in part taken from the essay of Fr. Fehlner.

89. Pompei, "Maria," col. 950.

90. Esser, *Die opuscula*. The comments and notes of this edition are very useful for learning and appreciating the thought of St. Francis.

91. Pyfferoen and Van Asseldonk, "Maria Santissima," 413.

92. Pyfferoen and Van Asseldonk, "Maria Santissima," 414.

two saints, a resemblance termed exceptional by one or another of them. Thus, it is only natural to ask if the results of these studies provide a basis for documenting in scholarly fashion Fr. Kolbe's thesis, namely that St. Francis knew the Immaculate Conception as such, and that, under her inspiration, made her cause the purpose of his Order.

It seems to me that the answers should be affirmative, especially when Mary most-holy is contemplated as Spouse of the Holy Spirit and one considers the strict and direct nexus which St. Francis places between Spouse of the Holy Spirit, mother of all goodness and Mother of God, on the one hand, and Advocate of the Order, mediatrix of all graces, inspiratrix and clarifier of his vocation, guide and teacher of the Order; and that the cause of the Immaculate Mother of God is the love of her crucified Son and of the church founded by him, as well as the salvation of souls for whom her Son underwent the death of the cross for the glory of God the Father.

Here are seen the two poles, Christological and pneumatological, from which, according to Fr. Pompei, flow the Marian devotion of St. Francis and via this balanced devotion his ecclesiology.[93] These two poles are the two divine missions of the Word in the incarnation and of the Holy Spirit in the Immaculate, which according to St. Maximilian are at the root of the economy of salvation.[94] In this light one can appreciate the two great privileges of the Order about which Fr. Longpré wrote: "The Seraphic Order, and it alone, has two great privileges in virtue of the merits of St. Francis. The first is to have understood and then defined, better than any other theological school, the central place of Jesus Christ in the work of God, and to have proclaimed, through the pen of Bl. John Duns Scotus, the absolute and universal primacy of the Lord Jesus in the highest form since St. Paul . . . that is the first privilege of the Order, and the second, a consequence and corollary of the first, is to have intuited the Immaculate Conception and to have had that mystery defended after six centuries of discussion."[95]

It remains to be seen, however, how this assessment will be received by scholars and theologians. Some continue to look with great reserve on this title "Spouse of the Holy Spirit," because they think it is dogmatically ambiguous; others are quite oblivious to the part played by St. Francis, both in the formulation and in the spread of this title throughout the Catholic world, as well as in the subsequent theological development. Nonetheless, the stature of St. Francis and Maximilian is such that they cannot be ignored. The structure

93. Pompei, "Maria," col. 950.
94. *WK* 1229.
95. Longpré, "La Sainte Vierge," 552.

of their Marian thought is so similar as to suggest a common source for both and which a few of these scholars think might be the Immaculate herself.[96] In turn, then, another theme to be investigated further is the Marian-Sapiential aspect of St. Francis' spirituality, as an important part of that "golden thread" running throughout Franciscan history.[97]

Mary Immaculate, who is the greatest lover of the Wisdom of the Father, indeed so incomparably so that she is not simply a philosopher, but philosophy itself, our ideal, as St. Maximilian calls her,[98] taught St. Maximilian his wisdom and made him a soul naturally Franciscan (*anima naturaliter Franciscana*). Like his Seraphic Father St. Francis he became a "cultor Trinitatis" (worshiper of the Trinity) because he was so ardent a lover of the Immaculate, a true "Servus Mariae" (slave of Mary).[99] And as to recognize formally-verbally the mystery of the Immaculate theology had need of the contemplative Francis to make, as it were, a translation in human, everyday terms, so to understand and enjoy in daily life the riches and goodness of the mystery dogmatically formulated there was still necessary the help of another servant of Mary, in this case that of St. Maximilian who made possible the "Translation." In this wonderful harmony of mind and heart, so evident in the converging results of so many studies, it is permissible to perceive the hand of the "Advocate of the Order" in response to the prayer of the Seraph of Assisi and of her knight Maximilian.

96. Pyfferoen and Van Asseldonk, "Maria Santissima," 426–27n29; Bengoechea, "Maria, Esposa . . .?" Cf. Dominguez, "La acción común," where one can see how little known yet is the place of Ss. Francis and Maximilian in the history of this title. An excellent theological encyclopedia of Mariology, *Theotokos*, by Fr. O'Carroll, has no entry for St. Francis.

97. The wisdom theme has a prominent place in Franciscan life and theology, as can be seen, for example, in the writings of St. Bonaventure, and also in the ancient liturgical offices of the great Franciscan saints, Clare, Anthony, and Bonaventure.

98. Mary most holy is called our "philosophy" by Odo, Abbot of Bathe Abbey, in a sermon on the Assumption, where is found also the earliest known use of the phrase "Ad Jesum per Mariam" (to Jesus through Mary). This sermon was first published by Leclercq: "Maria Christianorum Philosophia." St. Maximilian often calls the Immaculate his ideal, *WK* 1210, and his model, *WK* 1296; and he finds the basis for this in her predestination, *WK* 1282.

99. *Leg. maj.* 3,3; 3,1.

3

The Immaculate and the Mystery of the Trinity
in the Thought of St. Maximilian Kolbe

THE SUBJECT OF THIS conference is vast, and merits book-length treatment. The conference itself is but a brief summary of St. Maximilian's fundamental positions on this theme. In addition to providing a comprehensive statement of these, its objective is to indicate the manner in which the dictum of St. Bonaventure: *Fides Trinitatis et fundamentum et radix est divini cultus et totius Christianae religionis,*[1] is verified in the Kolbean synthesis of theology, with the mystery of the Immaculate as its hallmark.

Aspects of the theme have been treated by other scholars, but always in the context of other theological questions.[2] This presentation, a digest of a much longer study, begins with the Trinity *ad intra*, the starting point of all theology. Only in view of this mystery can the uniqueness of the Mother of God be properly estimated, despite the fragmentary character of the saint's writings the mystery of the Trinity is expounded by him in relatively complete fashion, and clearly reflects the vision of St. Bonaventure.

A second section deals with the Immaculate. Because of her first privilege she is the Immaculate Conception,[3] as indistant from the three divine persons as all other creatures are distant from the Trinity.[4] Only by considering the mystery of the Trinity first can one appreciate how profoundly orthodox and refreshingly profound are just those features of the Kolbean Mariology to which exception is often taken. A final section is a

---

1. *Myst. Trin.*, q. 1, a. 2.

2. Domanski, "Lourdes"; Ragazzini, *Maria, Vita dell'Anima,* 570–94; Piacentini, *Dottrina Mariologica*; Manteau-Bonamy, *La Doctrine Mariale*; Roschini, *Tuttosanto e la Tuttasanta,* vol. 1, 167–78; Swiecicki, "Prospettive"; Ragazzini, *La Spiritualità Mariana,* 323–63; Philippe, "Il Mistero"; On the importance in general of St. Maximilian's reflection for the study of the mystery of the Trinity cf. the brief but profoundly accurate assessment of Guitton, "Convergenze Mariane."

3. *WK* 1292.

4. *WK* 1286, 1325; CK Feast of the Most Holy Trinity, 1941.

brief presentation of the synthesis of "our theology," as it were the connatural corollary of "philosophizing in the name of the Immaculate."[5]

The Trinity

Theology begins, remarks St. Bonaventure,[6] where philosophy leaves off, with the mystery of the infinite, revealed as the most Blessed Trinity, and continues by constructing from the materials furnished it by philosophy a kind of ladder whose base is on earth and whose summit or apex is in heaven. The mystery of infinity, and the universal exemplarism, cognitive and moral, so basic to the thought of St. Bonaventure and the key to his Christocentrism, pervades that of St. Maximilian as well. The mystery of the Immaculate, as he expounds it, is the elucidation and clarification of that Christocentrism. In this context the importance of the notion of infinity in the thought of St. Maximilian cannot be underestimated.

Mystery, Infinity, Exemplarism

Mystery and infinity go hand in hand. God is a mystery, comprehensible only to the infinite mind, because entitatively infinite.[7] Because the Creator and Exemplar of all is infinite, mystery to a certain degree pervades the whole of the finite order as well,[8] and in a special way the rational creature, whose heart is restless till it rests in the infinite Creator, until it enjoys a blessedness without end.[9] Yet that creature alone is incapable of traversing the infinite distance between infinite and finite, exacerbated by the enormity of sin. And of course no creature can become, and therefore should not aspire to become, entitatively divine, as our first parents were induced to do.[10] But a finite spirit is capable of sharing a mode of life, characteristic of the divine or spiritual *per se*, without limit, i.e., of divinization or spiritualization.[11] If the creature cannot by his own power ascend to the

5. Cf. Leclercq, "Maria Christianorum Philosophia."

6. *Brev.*, p. 1, c. 3; prol. 3.

7. *WK* 1052.

8. *WK* 1305.

9. *WK* 1270, 1295, 1296.

10. *WK* 1086.

11. *WK* 508, 1270, 1296, 1310, 1325, 1331; CK June 23, 1936. In speaking of the Creator St. Maximilian employs almost interchangeably divinity, pure spirit and infinity, contrasting these terms with created, matter (potentiality) and finitude. A created spirit is one capable of being divinized or spiritualized, i.e., of acting in a manner

realm of the divine, or even conceive how this might be done, the Creator can stoop to him.[12]

The secret of the economy of salvation, of how that stooping and subsequent ascent are accomplished, of that final rung in the ladder of creation by which heaven descends to earth, and earth rises to heaven, is the Immaculate, the apex of creation[13] and a "consanguinea" of the Trinity,[14] the bridge across which all roads from and to heaven pass,[15] a ship across infinity,[16] viz., across the infinite distance between the base of the ladder and the Blessed Trinity, between the majesty of God and the guilty sinner.[17]

Though a creature the Mother of God belongs first to the realm of the infinite:[18] she is truly, really, properly the mother of a divine person, and he is truly, properly her Son, and this for eternity.[19] The mystery of the incarnation turns on her "fiat."[20] Thus, she cannot be understood in terms of the finite, for such an understanding would fail to account for her uniqueness. Hence, the revelation of the infinite is also the basis for discovering the answer to the query: who is the Mother of God.[21] That revelation-clarification begins with her appearance on earth as the Immaculate, and is a revelation of the mystery of the Trinity, of the mystery of the perfect love of Father and

---

without limit or end, capable of eternity, of unending progress (cf. *WK* 991 O, 1296). In addition to the qualitative infinity proper to God alone, and the quantitative infinity characteristic of matter and the basis of its finitude, one must in studying the thought of St. Maximilian keep in mind this third type of infinity distinctive of the created person. Just as the created person transcends the material creation in dignity and perfection of being, so the progress of the spiritual creature, radically opening on the eternal, is also radically differentiated from the kind of change and development appropriate to the non-spiritual creature. At the core of that difference is this third type of infinity. That capacity for eternal bliss St. Maximilian centers in the will and in the mystery of love distinctive of the human heart (Cf. *WK* 1295, 1302, 1326). Practically, the problem of how to divinize or spiritualize the created person is resolved through the work of the Holy Spirit-Immaculate Mother of God (cf. *WK* 508). Indeed, the spiritual perfection of the Immaculate Mother of God, incomparably transcending that of any other creature, is the measure of all the diverse grades of perfection or resemblance to the Son of God achieved by the members of Jesus (cf. *WK* 1282).

12. *WK* 1052.
13. *WK* 1325.
14. CK June 23, 1936.
15. CK Feast of the Most Holy Trinity, 1941.
16. *WK* 1291.
17. *WK* 643, 1291.
18. *WK* 605, 1232, 1286, 1320.
19. *WK* 1305.
20. *WK* 1283.
21. *WK* 1224, 1286.

Son.[22] In that mystery of love is discovered the answer to the question who she is who is the Mother of "he who is": she is the Immaculate Conception.[23] She is a part, a complement[24] of the mystery of infinite love, of pure love. Love is not love, if not in some way "without measure"; it is the measureless purity of her love that makes her the Immaculate.[25]

The Essence of God

The infinite essence of the one God when revealed is the revelation of infinite goodness and love. The name of God distinctive of the New Testament according to St. Bonaventure is the Good-*Bonum*;[26] the Trinity, says St. Maximilian, is the mystery of love.[27] The favorite axiom of St. Bonaventure to explain the dual procession of generation and spiration: "Bonum est diffusivum sui,"[28] in the Kolbean synthesis is incorporated within the law of action and reaction, equal and contrary, the *fluxus* and *refluxus* of infinite goodness *ad intra Trinitatis*, and reflected throughout the universe.[29] As an illustration of the Trinity drawn from the physical world, with very obvious links to the Newtonian model of the cosmos,[30] the principle has interesting ramifications, both in respect to contemporary philosophy of science and as a counterweight to currently popular and often abused "psychological" and "sociological" analogies in Trinitarian theology.[31]

But the use which St. Maximilian makes of this "law," as well as the grounds for that use, are in no wise Newtonian. These are thoroughly

22. *WK* 1224, 1286.

23. *WK* 1319. Unlike the divine "Ego sum" the existence of the Immaculate is not her own essence. But in defining her essence as the Immaculate Conception she resembles the divine essence with a perfection superior to that of any other creature (cf. *WK* 1282, 1320) and thus is revelatory of the divine "Ego sum" of her Son and through him of the Father as no other creature can reflect the perfection of God. The metaphysical implications of this Kolbean style of reflection are considerable, particularly for a metaphysics of exemplarism. Cf. Domanski, "Lourdes."

24. *WK* 508, 634, 1318.

25. *WK* 1286, 1318, 1286.

26. *Itin.*, c. 5, 2; c. 6, 1.

27. *WK* 1225, 1310, 1326.

28. *Brev.* p. 1, c. 2; *Itin.* 6; *Myst. Trin.* q.1, a. 2.

29. *WK* 634, 991 O, 1286, 1291, 1310, 1318.

30. Cf. Goretti-Miniati, *Elementi di Fisica*, vol. 1, 230–31. Fr. Goretti-Miniati was St. Maximilian's professor of physics in Rome, and this was the textbook used during the course.

31. Cf. Fernandez, "El Espíritu Santo . . . Boff."

Bonaventurian, resting radically on the complementarity of the dual processions *ad intra*, and reflected objectively in all the works of God *ad extra*, in
particular in the complementarity of the dual missions *ad extra*, by which an
order of salvation and return of creation to the Father is established.[32]

The mystery of the divine essence, of the "I am who am," is the mystery of the undivided Trinity, of the three really distinct divine persons, so
infinitely simple as to be perfectly one, and so perfectly one in essence as
to be really distinct. This mystery of the perfect unity of the three divine
persons is the mystery of love. God is love, says St. Maximilian, the most
Holy Trinity.[33]

The saint goes on to say that the mysterious life of this most pure spirit,
i.e., of the infinitely perfect divine essence, is one of perfect knowledge and
love. God knows and loves himself infinitely, and thus the Father, fontal plenitude of goodness, begets the Son and the Spirit proceeds from the Father and
Son as the nexus or unity of both.[34] In the most Holy Trinity, says St. Maximilian, God is the Father or proceeds from the Father.[35] All proceeds from the
eternal Father and returns to him through the Son and the Holy Spirit.[36] The
Father acts only through the Son and the Holy Spirit.[37]

This double procession he calls the "fluxus" and "refluxus" of infinite
love.[38] The total goodness of the divine essence in the Father is in the Son
by generation; and the total, mutual love of Father and Son for each other,
because the Son is the perfect image of the Father, is in the Holy Spirit by
spiration-conception. Perhaps the difference and relation between the two
processions might be described as an unfolding and enfolding of divine love.
If the terms are not those of St. Maximilian, their sense is surely reflected in
his use of the law of action and reaction, equal and contrary, to point out the
Trinitarian character of the economy of salvation: from the Father through
the Son and the Holy Spirit, and return to the Father through the Holy Spirit
and the Son.[39] Within the Trinity the unfolding of divine love is the generation of the Son; the enfolding is the procession of the Holy Spirit. As the seal
on that mutual, all pure love of Father and Son, the Holy Spirit is God-love,[40]

32. Cf. Fehlner, *Role of Charity*, CE 3, part 3.
33. *WK* 1224.
34. *WK* 1282, 1296.
35. *WK* 1286.
36. *WK* 1284.
37. *WK* 1286.
38. *WK* 1310, 1326.
39. *WK* 634.
40. *WK* 1229.

whose "proprium" is particularly expressive of the nature of love, to complement, to unite in responding or returning to the font of love.

The law of action and reaction enables St. Maximilian to complete and
illustrate the analysis of St. Bonaventure by focusing the mission of the Holy
Spirit in the person of the Immaculate, and to pinpoint the practical character of the mystery of the Trinity in our theology, just where the outer limits
of divine creative love meet an equal and contrary response in the outer limits of created love,[41] namely at the vertex of love which is the Immaculate,[42]
the point at which the return to the Father is begun through the mediation
of the Son of God, conceived in the womb of the Immaculate at her "fiat" by
the power of the Holy Spirit.[43] In the "Trinitas oeconomica" her immaculate
purity is the complement of the Incarnate Word, as the Holy Spirit within
the Trinity is the connatural complement of the love of Father and Son from
all eternity, the sharing of their friendship, the very essence of liberality,
hence the "ratio doni" and of every grace.[44]

Father

St. Maximilian stresses that the Father is the source and end of all,[45] and that
in any discussion of mediation, whether of the Son or of the Holy Spirit, this
absolutely primary starting point and final goal must be kept in mind. Akin
to this is his insistence on the Father as the fontal plenitude of goodness,[46]
a character of the Father dear to St. Bonaventure.[47] In view of this St. Maximilian observes that God the Father alone is properly Father, all others so-
called being but faint echoes of the divine fatherhood, for none of them can
reflect the infinity of fontal goodness in the person whose *proprium* is to be
first or "original," and from eternity to beget a coequal Son.[48] In the Trinity,
he says, God is Father or proceeds from the Father.[49]

---

41. *WK* 1232.

42. *WK* 1318.

43. *WK* 1310. Compare this observation of St. Bonaventure: " . . . ipse Spiritus Sanctus, cum procedat a Filio, per Filium cum aliis (i.e., creaturis) ad Patrem reducitur." *I
Sent.*, d. 31, p. 2, dub. 7.

44. *WK* 634; cf. *I Sent.*, d. 10, a. 1, q. 1; d. 18, a un.

45. *WK* 643, 1291, 1310.

46. *WK* 643, 1224, 1286; *CK* February 15, 1941.

47. *Myst. Trin.*, q. 8 in corp. et ad. 4.

48. *WK* 991 O, 1286.

49. *WK* 1286.

Finally, and perhaps uniquely among theologians, St. Maximilian describes the Father as someone divine in whom there is one person and one nature,[50] a formula that might seem superficially just as applicable to any divine person, and thus useless in distinguishing them, until it is realized that within the framework of the economic Trinity and divine missions the formula is applicable only to the Father, who alone sends and is not sent, and is known to us only through Son and Holy Spirit. For in our theology only in the context of the divine missions can we discern the personal propria of the divine persons *ad intra*.

Son

The second person of the Blessed Trinity is variously named by St. Maximilian as the Begotten, the Son, the Image of the Father, the Word, all names indicating a relation to the Father, called Father precisely because he begets a Son.[51] Each is of considerable importance in the elaboration of his spiritual-apostolic program. One need only recall the importance of the love of truth and desire for wisdom in this program, as the contrary of and remedy for doctrinal indifferentism or pluralism,[52] of the law of imitation as the basic law of spiritualization,[53] and of the fundamental duty of children to obey their parents, both in the natural and supernatural orders,[54] to appreciate the point.

That name of the Son, however, closest to the distinctive features of Kolbean thought, is mediator, to which in the economy of salvation the name Jesus is intimately related. Within the Trinity the Son alone possesses this name Mediator, for he alone because begotten is naturally the middle person and therefore Mediator between Father and Holy Spirit. He is begotten in order to be the Mediator, through whom the Holy Spirit proceeds from the Father. And if he is born again without the Trinity in time, it is also to be the perfect mediator, with a perfect mediation-salvation between the Father and the Immaculate, precisely because she is conceived preserved from all stain of sin, full of the love of Father and Son.[55] This

---

50. *WK* 1286.
51. *WK* 1318.
52. *WK* 1246.
53. *WK* 542, 991 O, 1293, 1295, 1325.
54. *WK* 1232, 1293.
55. *WK* 1310.

Kolbean position is very plainly Bonaventurian in flavor,[56] even if completed by insights of Duns Scotus.

Interestingly, such an analysis indicates that mediation *per se* implies neither separation nor distance (for all three divine persons are simply indistant), but only distinction and order.[57] And where such indistance by grace is verified outside the Trinity, as in the Immaculate, there but one mediator is found, her Son who mediates between her and the Father, and by his merits is preserved Immaculate.

It is only where the factor of infinite distance without the Trinity is verified that the mediation of the Son, absolutely unique without as within the Trinity, because his role is to be between the Father and all others, is complemented by the mediation of the Holy Spirit-Immaculate, whose role is to be between the Son and all others,[58] whose role in Bonaventurian terms is to bring close to the Son by gratifying,[59] in Kolbean terms by purifying,[60] whereas that of the Son is to bring close to the Father by divinizing the one so purified by the Holy Spirit, the Spirit of the Son. That is his nature as "media persona," to be the perfect image of the Father, and hence naturally close to him. Through the Son are reduced or brought close to the Father all others, either by nature—the Holy Spirit, or by grace—the Immaculate and those united to her. In the single work of our sanctification are formally diverse aspects reflecting the complementary actions of Son and Holy Spirit.

A great deal of misunderstanding of St. Maximilian's thought can be avoided simply by clarifying the distinction of persons within the Trinity along the lines of St. Bonaventure. The Holy Spirit is a true mediator without the Trinity, precisely because not one within; but for that same reason his mediation is quite distinct from the unique mediation of the Son. For St. Maximilian the mediatory character of the Son in his divinity, and hence the mediatory work accomplished in his humanity, remain for us impenetrable mysteries, unless complemented by the purificatory-clarifying mission of the Holy Spirit, a mission accomplished not by a second hypostatic

---

56. *Hex.* col. 1, nn. 12–14; *I Sent.*, d. 11, a. un., q. 1; *III Sent.*, d. 10, a. 2, q. 2, in corp. et ad 4.

57. *I Sent.*, d. 10, a. 2, ad 1; *I Sent.* d. 31, p. 2; dub. 7.

58. *WK* 577.

59. *III Sent.*, d. 10, a. 2, q. 2.

60. *WK* 643, 1286, 1310, 1326. St. Bonaventure describes the role of the mediatrix of all graces as one of purifying souls: *Serm. I de Assumpt* (IX, 689b), or the one through whose (pure) hands the body of Christ is offered to the Father or comes to us: *Serm, de SS. Corp. Christi*, 20. Practically, gratification by the Holy Spirit and purification by the Mother of God coincide. The merit of St. Maximilian is to show why in terms of the mystery of the uncreated and created Immaculate Conception.

union, but by a most perfect instrument, the Immaculate, perfectly united to him, ever indistant from him by spousal union.[61] Only through her does the Son come to us (*Incarnatus in ea*),[62] and this not because of any insufficiency on his part, but because of an insufficiency on ours, to be remedied by the action of the Holy Spirit-Immaculate.

As a formula to identify the personal *proprium* of the Son, St. Maximilian employs the dogma of Chalcedon: one person, two natures.[63] That divine person to be begotten in time is that person who is begotten in eternity, thus distinguishing him from the Father who begets. But the formula also distinguishes the Son from the Holy Spirit. Whereas the mission of the Son terminates in the hypostatic assumption of a human nature so as to be his *proprium*, to be his exclusive possession, to be a man who is a divine person, that of the Holy Spirit terminates in a spousal union with a human person, not assumed hypostatically, but so perfectly appropriated as to share the Holy Spirit's name: Immaculate Conception.

Holy Spirit

The naming of the Holy Spirit as the eternal Immaculate Conception[64] deserves to be considered as a major contribution to the progress of theology and an accurate explicitation of one of the pillars of Franciscan theology, the immaculate conception of the Mother of God.

As with the names of the other divine persons, so too this one entails an analogy. Conception among creatures, in particular human, involves two elements: first being the fruit of the mutual love of parents, and second whose mutual love is the beginning of existence of the child conceived. In so far as conception is predicated properly and univocally of created persons, both elements must be present. Angels are not conceived. Neither were Adam and Eve. In his humanity our Lord is conceived as the fruit of the love of the Father and of the Virgin,[65] but is not a conception, because his conception is not the beginning of his origin as a person.[66]

The Holy Spirit, however, in the proper, though analogical sense, is a conception, because the fruit of the mutual love of Father and Son, even if they are not thereby his parents. Secondly, that conception is his origin, even

61. *WK* 634, 1318.
62. CK July 26, 1939.
63. *WK* 1286.
64. *WK* 1318.
65. *WK* 1286, 1296.
66. *WK* 1319.

if being eternal, it is not the beginning of the existence of one who like Father and Son, being divine, has no beginning in existence, but is eternal.[67]

Further, that love of Father and Son being divine, therefore without defect, without any impurity, utterly generous or liberality itself, the conception of the Holy Spirit is immaculate and the person so conceived is the Immaculate Conception. Therein is the peculiar connection with the human person whose beginning of existence is a conception, but whose conception, unlike that of any other creature is immaculate, and she the Immaculate Conception, because in her is the total love of Father and Son that is in the Holy Spirit and makes his purity to be without defect or stain: in her by grace, in him by nature. It is this relation that is the heart of that spousal union so perfect as to give to the Virgin of Virgins, alone among creatures, the name of the Holy Spirit.[68]

Only during the last year of his life, it would seem, did St. Maximilian realize fully why the name of the Mother of God is the Immaculate Conception: because she is the unique Spouse of the Holy Spirit whose name therefore she bears. Earlier he had thought that conception always implied temporal origin, and hence could only be predicated of creatures.[69] There are those who think that this insight was attained only via the influence of infused contemplation.[70]

This analysis of the name Immaculate Conception within the Trinity also serves as a basis for illustrating the nexus, at times implicit, at times explicit, among other notions distinctive of the thought of St. Maximilian and basic to his spiritual-apostolic program with the procession of the Holy Spirit and with each other.

Obedience

In the thought of St. Maximilian obedience, or perfect conformity to the will of God, enjoys a prominent place. The essence of holiness consists in conforming one's will to God's will.[71] Perfect conformity from the first moment of conception, or the formation of a character that could not be more perfect, is the core of the Immaculate Conception.[72] In relating the mystery of the

---

67. *WK* 1318.

68. *WK* 1308.

69. *WK* 1331.

70. Ragazzini, *Maria, Vita dell'Anima*, 573–74; Pyfferoen and Van Asseldonk, "Maria Santissima," 438.

71. *WK* 1232.

72. *WK* 1232.

Immaculate Conception to the procession of the Holy Spirit, St. Maximilian also relates the mystery of obedience thereto.

By obedience, as the saint observes, is not meant servility, or absence of freedom, much less absence of initiative.[73] Where perfect conformity to the will of God is lacking, a creature may indeed experience obedience to God as contrary to freedom and initiative, either because of the imperfection of that conformity or because the creature falsely assumes that conformity (perfect humility) and initiative are contraries.

This conformity to the will of God is not consequent upon, but antecedent to choice and initiative, and is the exact measure of personal perfection and holiness of every created person, occurring as it does at that point where love integrates intellect, being and will.[74] That conformity is the subsisting "velle idem-nolle idem" shaping character and informing every choice. When that conformity is "without restriction" or limit and exists from the first moment of a person's conception without change, as is the case of the Immaculate, "full of grace" and "preserved from any stain of sin," there is a holiness and character which is superlative, that cannot be more perfect, and qualifies her every "fiat" as a choice supremely delighting the divine persons.[75] The capacity of the will for perfect obedience, for spotless conformity to the divine will, is the root of the soul's potential for a blessedness without end, the source of that restless desire of the heart for infinite love, a desire fulfilled without peer in the Immaculate.

If, with St. Bonaventure and St. Maximilian, the procession of the Holy Spirit is considered *active* as the mutual love of Father and Son, and their liberality in spirating is regarded as their agreement or perfect unity of will, then that procession *passive* as their mutual love received in another is their bond of unity, their perfect concord or conformity in loving hypostasized.[76] The consubstantiality of the Son with the Father is just that because he is the perfect image of the Father, being begotten; the consubstantiality of the Holy Spirit with Father and Son is just that because he is their perfect conformity in love, being conceived as the fruit of that love.

73. *WK* 1329, 579.

74. *WK* 1326.

75. *WK* 1282, 1296.

76. *I Sent.* d 10, a. 1–2; d. 11, q. 1–2; *WK* 1229. The nexus or concord of Father and Son of St. Bonaventure is called "God-love" by St. Maximilian, who unites us to Father and Son, as St. Bonaventure says he is the one by whom Father and Son are united (not by whom they are one, i.e., the divine essence). Division or distinction, says St. Maximilian, is for the sake of unification, always creative (cf. *WK* 1318); and St. Bonaventure writes: ratio nexus incipit a distinctione et tendit sive perducit in unitatem. Ultima et completiva ratio est unitas. Cf. *I Sent.* d. 11, a. un., q. 2, ad 2.

Obedience, understood as conformity of will of a person conceived with the divine will, is the essence of love and entails a "perfectio simpliciter simplex," precisely in relation to the position of the Holy Spirit within the order of divine persons. In the Holy Spirit this conformity is majestic in character, for the conformity of will is but the independence and unity of the divine nature. In the created person that conformity is humble and obedient in character, being rooted in the dependence of the creature and proportionate to the perfection of its humility. Where that conformity is perfect by grace, as in the conception of Mary, that person is the Immaculate Conception, because she enjoys as a person a position in relation to the Father and Son parallel to that of the Holy Spirit: the fruit of their mutual love, and in whom their total love reposes, a "part" of the Trinity. That such should be the case outside, as well as within the Trinity, is the heart of spousal union with the Holy Spirit, the focus of his mission in the Immaculate and the basis for the possibility of the Immaculate Conception and for our purification as temples of the Holy Spirit consequently upon her mediation.

As the Holy Spirit within the Trinity, in virtue of his personal *proprium*, may be regarded rightly as the "Giver of gifts" *ad extra*, the "ratio donationis" and whose name, therefore, is also "Donum,"[77] so the Immaculate, in virtue of her unique spousal union with the Holy Spirit, is capable of a "fiat" which is the instrument of that divine donation; and this in a dual manner: as the fecundity of the Holy Spirit in the incarnation and secondly in the spiritual rebirth of Christians or as mediatrix of all graces.[78]

Fecundity

By fecundity of the Holy Spirit St. Maximilian first intends the conception of the Son of God in the womb of the Immaculate.[79] This conception of a pre-existent divine person, not by the seed of man, but by the power of the Holy Spirit, compared to the procession of one divine person from another within the Trinity is the basis for this idea, borrowed by St. Maximilian from St. Louis Grignion de Montfort.[80] Clearly it is only an analogy, for the origin of the person so conceived by the power or fecundity of the Holy Spirit is in eternity, not in time.

What is meant by this comparison can best be appreciated by explaining the infecundity of the Holy Spirit. "Ad intra Trinitatis," this does not mean

77. St. Bonaventure, *I Sent.* d. 18; *WK* 634, 1224.

78. *WK* 1282, 1284.

79. *WK* 1229.

80. *WK* 1229.

that the Holy Spirit is passive or inactive, because receptive of the love of Father and Son, or much less that in acting must supply some insufficiency through the instrumentality of a creature. Rather, this infecundity simply denotes that no other divine person proceeds from the Holy Spirit, because to borrow a patristic term he is the end, the complement, the seal on the infinite perfection of divine goodness.[81] It is just that finality or infecundity that constitutes the line dividing the divine from the created, the difference between the action of divine liberality *ad intra* culminating in the procession of the Holy Spirit and that liberality *ad extra*, or freedom of God in creating, in so far as its term, the contingent cosmos, is outside God.

Because that cosmos does not reveal the divine persons distinctly, that line of demarcation or infecundity of the Holy Spirit functions also as a veil over the entire Godhead, shrouding it in mystery. But because both the creativity of God and the effect of that creativity are associated with the procession of the Holy Spirit via the liberality of love,[82] when the limits of that creativity meet the limits of obedience,[83] there the mystery of love is revealed in the fecundity of the Holy Spirit. The fecundity of the Holy Spirit, then, becomes the removal of the veil over the total love of Father and Son in the Holy Spirit. That unveiling in the world is the Immaculate Conception of Mary culminating in the incarnation, and through the Incarnate Word the revelation of the Father and the entire Trinity. The obedience of the Immaculate, and only of the Immaculate, is the fecundity of the Holy Spirit and the revelation of Father and Son, because her name is also the name of the Holy Spirit.

---

81. Congar, *Je Crois*, 3:200, notes 27–29, lists references to Ss. Athanasius, Basil, Gregory Nazianzenus, Gregory of Nyssa, Cyril of Alexandria, Didymus of Alexandria, John Damascene, Richard of St. Victor, Thomas Aquinas. To these can be added St. Bonaventure, *Hex*. col. 1, n. 12. Only Hesychius of Jerusalem among the Fathers calls Mary the "complement" of the Trinity (PG 93, 1462, in his sermon *De Sancta Maria Deipara*). St. Thomas Aquinas, (*Contra Errores Graecorum*, pars II, 30) states that for this reason, viz., that the Holy Spirit is the complement of the Trinity, the Trinity is likened to a chain, rather than a triangle. And St. Bonaventure, in calling the Holy Spirit the "terminans complementum" of the Father and Son, their bond or nexus, associates with the procession of the Holy Spirit "per viam liberalitatis" the creativity of God *ad extra* and the consummation or perfecting of all these works in their return to the Father through the Son. Here and there the Seraphic Doctor refers to that hypostasized love as immaculate, cf. *I Sent.* d. 10, a. 2, q. 1; *I Sent.* d. 10, a. 2, q. 3. Only St. Maximilian has brought all these strands together in relating the procession of the Holy Spirit to the Immaculate Conception to the creativity of God *ad extra* to the consummation of that creativity in viewing the Immaculate as the complement or part of that chain which is the order of divine persons. Cf. *WK* 643, 1282, 1291, 1318.

82. *I Sent.*, d. 10, a. 1, q. 1.

83. *WK* 1232.

Mediation

The mediation of the Holy Spirit (and of the Immaculate) is not identical with his fecundity in the incarnation, but a corollary or extension thereof.[84] Precisely because no other rational creature, angelic or human, is indistant from the Son, so as to be able to approach him as the one mediator with the Father, so the fecundity of the Holy Spirit is the proximate basis of his mediating between the Son, Redeemer, and those whom he alone redeemed, particularly the human family tainted by original sin. Like the fecundity of the Holy Spirit his mediation is rooted in his name, "Eternal Immaculate Conception," is exercised outside, not within, the Trinity, and when exercised is accomplished through the instrumentality of the Immaculate, and thus is a kind of fecundity, the spiritual maternity of the Mother of God.

Like the fecundity of the Holy Spirit, the mediation of the Holy Spirit is a fact. Whereas in the first case it is the fact whereby the Word comes to us, in the second it is the fact whereby we come to the Word. That mediation, St. Maximilian notes, is designed to deal with two dimensions of our lives separating us from our Savior: the imperfection of our love, exacerbated by sin, and the awesome fear of divine justice offended by our sins. To stimulate a love worthy of the Incarnate Word and to enable us to grasp the depth of the Father's love for us in the passion of his Son is the goal of that mediation.[85] The logic of both facts in the reflection of St. Maximilian rests on the mystery of the Immaculate Conception. Just as within the Trinity the "refluxus" of divine love between Father and Son is the procession of the Holy Spirit, so without the return of creation to the Father through the Son, its refluxus, is initiated by the mission of the Holy Spirit. The predestination of the Virgin Mary to be the Immaculate, i.e., the Spouse of the Holy Spirit, and hence Mother of God and our mother, becomes in such a view the coefficient of an exemplarism, metaphysical and moral, at the heart of the supernatural order. In this the created Immaculate Conception is the most perfect of creatures, the apex of creation, in view of whom every grade of being takes its measure, for whom each was made, and through whom each attains its goal, the love of the heart of God.[86] Placing the mediatrix alongside a mediator no more detracts from the work of the Son, than placing him with a mother by his Father, or the procession of the Holy Spirit implies the insufficiency of that of the Son. Quite the contrary: the cooperation of

84. *WK* 1229.
85. *WK* 1326, 1331.
86. *WK* 1282, 1305, 1295.

the Holy Spirit-Immaculate is the exaltation of the Son, and through the son the glorification of the Father and the entire Blessed Trinity.[87]

Cooperator

With this term St. Maximilian describes the place of the Holy Spirit, and his spouse, in the economy of salvation in relation to that of the one Savior of all.[88] Not only do these roles differ because the two persons are different, but their activities, while inseparable, always occur in a certain order defined by their relation within the Trinity: the Son enjoying a certain precedence, the Holy Spirit or Immaculate Conception a certain "subauctoritas" of the cooperator,[89] whose activities in relation to those of the principal mediator resemble that of a means to an end. This is true not only of the descending mediation by which all good comes to us from the Father, but of the ascending by which our praise and thanks rise to the Father unto his glory. That the return of all to the Father in the economic Trinity entails an inversion in the order of persons, since we must begin through the Immaculate who is closest to us in this order,[90] does not change the relation between the activities of the Holy Spirit and Son.

---

87. WK 577, 605. According to Amato, "Lo Spirito Santo," 94–95, there is currently a strong tendency among Catholic theologians to rephrase the traditional axiom, "ad Jesum per Mariam," as "ad patrem, per Christum in Spiritu Sancto cum et sicut Maria, vel ad Jesum in Spiritu Sancto cum Maria Matre Ecclesiae." The reformation attempts to differentiate between the mission of the Son and that of the Spirit in the economy of salvation, but in so doing by eliminating the "per Spiritum Sanctum," the "per Mariam," leaves the impression that their roles (and by extension the church's role) are merely passive in respect to Christ's, a very traditional Protestant position. The reformulation omits the essential point: the active character of the mediation of the Holy Spirit and of the Mother of God in the economy of salvation. As St. Bonaventure nicely synthesized the matter: the incarnation is the cause of our sanctification, but not the whole cause; our filiation is completed in the mission of the Holy Spirit. III Sent., d. 10, a. 2, q. 2, ad 4. Cf. also De don. Spir., col. 1, 7, where he writes that without the Word inspired into our hearts through the Holy Spirit who is the love of Father and Son and joins us to Father and Son, whatever the Father does in sending his Son to become Incarnate and whatever the Son suffers for us avails us nothing. Once it is clear, as St. Maximilian explains, that the mediatory role of the Holy Spirit coincides with the role of the Mother of God in the "Trinitas oeconomica," because both are the Immaculate Conception, such mediation, far from detracting from that of the Son, enhances and consummates it. The mediation of the church, her necessity for salvation, in relation to that of her head, rests on the truth of the mediation of the Immaculate.

88. WK 1229.

89. I Sent., d. 12, a. un., q. 1; Brev., p. 1, c. 5, n. 5.

90. WK 1284, 1291, 1310, 1331.

Thus, the fecundity of the Holy Spirit is for the sake of the incarnation and Redemption; the mediation of the Holy Spirit is for the sake of our incorporation into Christ as his members. In virtue of the first the created Immaculate Conception is Mother of God and coredemptrix; in virtue of the second Mother of the Church.[91] She becomes each precisely at that moment when the Holy Spirit begins to exercise each role, because she is the Immaculate Conception: at the Annunciation and at the death of her Son.[92] These are the two moments defining the inauguration of the economy of salvation: the advent of the Savior and the initiation of our regeneration. The action of the Savior in both, descending and ascending, unfolding and enfolding the love of God, is contained within that reaction of the Immaculate. This pattern is the hallmark of the Kolbean synthesis. Through her and the Holy Spirit he is born; through her and the Holy Spirit he comes to us and we go to him, and through him to the Father. Hence, we must always seek him in his palace, not without; we pass from her to him, not out of her into him, as though leaving her.[93] She should live in us, as Jesus in her, and the Father in Jesus.[94]

The reason for this order: the Immaculate Conception. Whether one considers the uncreated or created Immaculate Conception, it is the character of that person to receive the total love of Father and Son, to contain the love of each. That is why the Immaculate Conception in the economy of salvation, and only the Immaculate Conception, can be mother of God and our mediatrix, a bridge across the divide between ourselves and the Son. That mediation of the Immaculate by which she purifies our hearts of the multiple imperfections dividing us from the Trinity contains the mediatory action of the Son by which our hearts purified are divinized and rendered acceptable to the Father.[95] The single work of our sanctification embraces a dual moment, ascribed respectively to the Holy Spirit-Immaculate and Word Incarnate in that order.

Formula

In the Immaculate, writes St. Maximilian, there are two persons and two natures.[96] The formula expresses very accurately the difference between the

91. *WK* 1229, 1296.
92. *WK* 1145, 1283, 1296.
93. *WK* 603; CK April 25, 1937.
94. *WK* 556.
95. *WK* 1286, 1310, 1326; cf. *III Sent.*, d. 10, a. 2, q. 2; *De don. Spir.*, col. 1, 7.
96. *WK* 634, 1286, 1310.

mission of the Holy Spirit in the Immaculate and the mission of the Son in the incarnation, between the *proprium* of the Holy Spirit—to be fruit of a conception, and that of the Son, to be begotten, between the image of the Father and the conformity or concord of Father and Son.

The human nature of the Son is assumed hypostatically in the unity of the divine person, thus belonging exclusively to the Son as his *proprium*. In that *proprium* is recognized the one who in his divinity is also begotten. By contrast the Immaculate is not united to the Holy Spirit hypostatically, but in a spousal union so intimate that the obedient humility of the Immaculate reveals the Holy Spirit as the eternal receptacle of the total love of Father and Son. In this union of wills person and nature remain distinct. The Virgin is neither Creator nor Judge as is the Holy Spirit, because he is divine by nature.[97] The mutual possession is in the order of mercy and sanctity, not as something exclusive, but as the basis for the inclusion of others in the kingdom of God. Thus the Immaculate is appropriated by Holy Spirit, for she belongs also to Father and Son. Her appropriation, however, by the Holy Spirit in so perfect a fashion, that she only is the Immaculate Conception among creatures, is the basis and means of our possession by the Spirit of Christ and of our becoming dwelling places of Father and Son.[98] Her love for God is the reason Father, Son and Holy Spirit love us.

The traditional stress in the Franciscan school on the objective character of appropriation, and on appropriation as the only adequate basis for explaining the mission of the Holy Spirit is thrown into relief by this formula of St. Maximilian, and underscores the importance and potential depth of this much-neglected doctrine. Attempts to explain the mission of the Holy Spirit via theories of quasi-propria risk making that mission a mere duplicate or substitute for the mission of the Son; neglect of any reflection at all on the nature of this mission risks leaving that of the Son in a certain relative obscurity. The merit of St. Maximilian rests in showing how the mission of the Holy Spirit, capable of multiple visible forms in contrast to the one visible form of the Son,[99] centers in one person, the Immaculate, and the focus for all the rest; and that mission so centered is best formulated in terms of the doctrine of appropriation.

---

97. *WK* 339.
98. *WK* 1286; *CK* April 9, 1938.
99. *WK* 1229; cf. *I Sent.*, d. 16. a. un., q. 3.

Circumincession

The mystery designated by this term, viz., the real distinction and perfect compenetration of the divine persons in a single communion, is referred to by St. Maximilian as their "simultaneity," and often described by him as a chain, each one of whose links must never be conceived as apart from the others, even if we must think of one after another.[100] Of this chain he says the Immaculate is a part, the complement of the Trinity, because the Immaculate, in conceiving a divine person, became really and properly his mother, forever, and thus entered into "spiritual consanguinity" with the divine persons.[101] With the conception of the Immaculate then, the Trinitarian circle has been widened.

The distinction, however, between Creator and creation is not thereby abolished or confused. For St. Maximilian the creature does not become part of the Trinity in becoming the equal of God, i.e., on the level of God by becoming divine in nature.[102] Thus, in any such "participation" there remains a fundamental distinction between the "Trinitas ad intra" and the economic Trinity, clearly reflected in the formulae for the missions of Son and Holy Spirit.

That distinction, however, between Creator and creature does not preclude special relations on the part of creatures to divine persons, such that the creature, without becoming the equal of a divine person and ceasing to be a creature, nonetheless forms with the divine persons a single communion or order of persons, aptly represented under the metaphor of a single chain. This widening of or participation in the Trinitarian communion is not attained in the creature in virtue of being created (quite the contrary), but in virtue of a creature being the term or receptacle of a divine mission. Only the divine missions, the saint insists, make possible a return of creation to the

---

100. *WK* 603 634, 643.

101. *WK* 1305; CK Feast of the Most Holy Trinity, 1941.

102. *WK* 603, 1086, 1232. The distinction between the "Trinitas in se" and the "Trinitas oeconomica" is fundamental to the thought of St. Maximilian, permeated as it is by a profound sense of the first article of the Creed and of the metaphysical-moral exemplarism resting on that belief, and accompanied by a very clear (and not unexpected) rejection of evolution and evolutionism; cf. *WK* 1186. It is for this reason that the kind of Trinitarian reflection based on "historical consciousness" which views the distinction between the "Trinitas ad intra" and the "Trinitas oeconomica" as of no consequence is profoundly foreign to the saint's thought. The denial of that distinction on evolutionary grounds is effectively a kind of pantheism, tending to formulate the mystery in unitarian or tritheistic terms. For exemplifications cf. Scordato, "Il X Congresso"; Molari, "Riflessioni sul X Congresso."

Father and a fully adequate love of the Trinity by the whole of creation.[103] In the primary sense of the term the *Trinitas oeconomica*, or supernatural order, is constituted by the terms of the two divine missions. Without confusion these terms complement the "Trinitas ad intra," forming a circle from the Father to the Father, attaining that total "immersion" of creation in the love of the Father and the entire Blessed Trinity.[104]

In this restricted sense the two aforementioned formulae indicate two possibilities for describing a creature as "part" of the Trinity. In the first case, that of the hypostatic union, the human nature of the Word is a part or extension of that communion, because in becoming man the Word does not cease to be the Son of the Father.

In the second case, that of the Immaculate, spousally united to the Holy Spirit, a human person is full of the total love of Father and Son, and so stands in a relation to Father and Son paralleling that of the Holy Spirit. Just because she is not the Holy Spirit, and unlike her Son not a divine person, before his conception in time already part of the Trinity, St. Maximilian uses the term "part" (in the sense of partaker of the divine fellowship) of the Trinity only in speaking of the Immaculate. It is the nature of love to unite the lover with the beloved, to make them a part of each other. It is the perfect love of the Immaculate, exclusively for Father, Son and Holy Spirit, that makes her "part" of them,[105] i.e., of their one communion.

But it is just this position of the Immaculate, qua Spouse of the Holy Spirit, that makes the supernatural order or economy of salvation the complement and crown of the natural order and gives us hope of sharing in the divine nature and communion of the divine persons. Through her the Son of God takes flesh; through her the saints are united to him and through him and in him immersed in the Father and the entire Blessed Trinity.[106] For she carries within herself the entire Trinity, so that all which happens in the universe occurs "in the name of the Father, and of the Son, and of the Holy Spirit through the Immaculate."[107] She is emphatically not a fourth person of the Trinity. Rather, as Spouse of the Holy Spirit, the created Immaculate Conception, she is that created person outside the Trinity in whom the purest love of God originating with the Father through the Son begins that perfect return to the Father through the Son. That return once effected, the *Trinitas oeconomica* stands, not simply as another work of God, but as his

103. *WK* 1286, 1326.
104. *WK* 577, 605, 643.
105. *WK* 1296.
106. *WK* 577, 605, 643.
107. *WK* 991 O.

crowning work, a more perfect than which is impossible, because it is an extension of the Trinity, from the Father, through the Son and Holy Spirit, to the Father through the Holy Spirit-Immaculate and Son-Jesus,[108] The point of origin and return, the Father, is the same. That is also why, once effected, the rest of creation whose origin is the Father, can find, through the Immaculate, mediatrix of all graces, and the Word Incarnate, one mediator of the Father and man, a return to the Father.

Summation

While not constituting a finished treatise on the Trinity, St. Maximilian's writings reveal a mind possessing a profound grasp of the mystery as a whole. His fidelity to tradition permits the discovery in this thought of parallels with that of the great saints and doctors of the past, even if these are not cited or known directly by the saint. This is particularly true of the very evident Bonaventurian overtones in the Kolbean synthesis. How these came to be present must be the theme of another study. Here, however, it is only fair to note that the Kolbean is neither a simple repetition of St. Bonaventure (or of any other saint or theologian studied by St. Maximilian), nor an extension of his thought by way of commentary, but a rethinking and perfecting of the Franciscan theological tradition, with its great emphasis on charity, evident at these points distinctive of St. Maximilian.

First, he brings together explicitly the diffusion of good from the Father with the reduction of all to him in a single principle, the law of action and reaction, equal and contrary. In so doing he has provided a fresh perspective on the procession and mission of the Holy Spirit.

Second, in relating the mystery of the Immaculate Conception to the procession of the Holy Spirit he has identified the point of contact between heaven and earth, where the *Trinitas ad intra* and the *Trinitas oeconomica* meet without confusion and the mystery of love, created and uncreated, is consummated. That mystery, in eternity terminated in the procession of the Holy Spirit, in time terminates in the Immaculate Conception, so that the *ratio perfectissimae creationis* becomes the starting point of the recreation or return to the Father through the Son.

Third, in recognizing the mediatory role of the Holy Spirit-Immaculate, both in creation and recreation, as the *ratio donationis ac liberalitatis*, St. Maximilian underscores that in God there are not two, but three persons: and that the Son is only the Mediator "immediate" between Father and us, because the Holy Spirit-Immaculate is mediatrix "immediate" between the

108. *WK* 643.

Son and us. In a word the unity of the work of salvation, and the immediacy of those saved to the Father depends on the complementarity and distinction of the two missions, from the Father—to the Father.

The Immaculate

As in every creature the Trinitarian *appropriata*: power, knowledge and love, are found in the Immaculate, and so noted by St. Maximilian in his earliest writings.[109] They are found in her, however, in the highest degree, as the "omnipotentia supplex," the seat of wisdom, and the one to whom the entire order of mercy has been entrusted by God, precisely because she is the Immaculate, the personification of mercy, hence seat of wisdom and omnipotence at prayer.[110]

To understand how the saint came to realize her uniqueness in this, the Immaculate must be pondered with him, not first in relation to other creatures, as though she were simply one of many, or simply another member of the church,[111] but rather in relation to the divine persons, of whom she is the "consanguinea,"[112] from whom she is ever indistant,[113] and for whom she was exclusively made.[114] Other creatures must be studied in relation to her for whom they were made,[115] so as to understand what it means for God to become man and man to become God through the "fiat" of the Mother of God, the Spouse of the Holy Spirit.

Spouse of the Holy Spirit: The Immaculate Conception

In bringing the dogma of the Immaculate Conception into intimate relation with the procession and mission of the Holy Spirit St. Maximilian has brought to theology considerable depth and freshness. Both the Holy Spirit and the Mother of God can say: I am the Immaculate Conception, because in each is the totality of love of Father and Son, in the first by nature, in the second by grace; hence they are different persons. That is what makes the Holy Spirit divine from all eternity; that is what makes

109. *WK* 41.

110. *WK* 1296, 1331.

111. *WK* 1232, 1320.

112. CK Feast of the Most Holy Trinity, 1941.

113. *WK* 634, 1232; CK July 26, 1939.

114. *WK* 1296.

115. *WK* 1282, 1305.

the Virgin Mary from the first moment of her conception full of grace, the most perfect created person, whose will is never for an instant separated from the divine will by imperfection or sin, and in whom therefore is the total love of creation for God, even if no other creature had been saved.[116] In her the outer limits of Trinitarian love meet the outer limits of created love, at a point called the vertex of love.

This spousal union, called such via an analogy with the love of human spouses, does not mean that the Holy Spirit is either the husband of Mary or Father of her child, inferences contrary to fact (St. Joseph was her husband) and utterly confusing the order of persons and personal identity in the Trinity. The implications of the analogy, intended to underscore the reality and profundity of the relation between the Virgin and the Holy Spirit and always to be interpreted in accord with the certain truths of faith, are these.

1. The core of that union of love is the perfect obedience of the Virgin, i.e., antecedent to any choice, initiative or affection, the perfect conformity or total consecration of her will to the divine will. This is her fulness of grace, so permeating and transforming her entire nature (and not merely its "accidentia"),[117] as to make her as it were the epiphany of grace, a union culminating in the divine maternity.[118]

That transformation does not obliterate in her the distinction between nature and grace. The total love of the Father and Son is in her, not by nature and eternally, as in the Holy Spirit, but by grace, by a creative act of the Trinity so "exhaustive" of the divine omnipotence as to make a creature more beloved of God inconceivable. No created person could be more united or more indefectibly, immediately united in love to God than the Immaculate at and from the first moment of her conception.[119] Whereas all other created persons can be considered both naturally and then supernaturally, because at some time there was in them a real separation as well as formal difference between nature and grace. That is why they are not "full of grace," their natures not being fully permeated by the love of God. The Immaculate can only be viewed supernaturally, for her initial perfection, conformity to the divine will, being full, so permeated her nature as to leave no possible room for such separation, innocent or sinful. Far from being removed from the realm of the human by such a privilege, she becomes thereby the universal norm or model, as well as source for that perfection which, initial in her, is final in others. That is also why she is not, and cannot be, embraced within

116. CK Feast of the Most Holy Trinity, 1941.
117. WK 486.
118. WK 1320.
119. WK 1232, 1319, 1320.

the terms of that law governing our moral inheritance from the first Adam; and not being so affected by that inheritance she can be the instrument of a new beginning, of a better inheritance.

2. That spousal union works such a transformation in the very being of the Virgin Mary, so permeates and shapes her character as to make the Immaculate the personification of the Holy Spirit, as no other creature, rational or irrational, can be the term of the visible mission of the Holy Spirit.[120] Neither dove, nor fire, nor prophet is strictly a personification of the Holy Spirit as his instrument; only the Immaculate who bears his name. That personification is not a confusion of persons or natures. Devotion to the eternal Immaculate Conception for St. Maximilian is always *latria*; to the created Immaculate Conception *hyperdulia*.[121] Rather that personification is the result of a perfect integration of her personality, a superlative formation of character at that point where intellect, being and will are united by love,[122] this from the first moment of her conception so perfectly as to merit the name Immaculate Conception, distinguishing her from every other creature, no matter how holy (whose integration could always be more holy),[123] thus making her entire life and action an epiphany of the eternal Immaculate Conception. Veneration of and devotion to her is veneration and devotion to the Holy Spirit as no other is or can be.[124]

3. In this context the adaptation of certain doctrinal terms, e.g., transubstantiation, quasi-incarnation, originally pertinent to the mission of the Son, to the mission of the Holy Spirit in the Immaculate by St. Maximilian has aroused a certain amount of criticism concerning his theological prudence.[125] The procedure, however, not original with him, is not *per se* illicit, and in his thought is not the basis, but the illustration of an insight, employed analogically, not univocally. Transubstantiation of the Immaculate[126] does not mean that the Virgin on being united to the Holy Spirit represents merely the accidents of human nature pointing to the *proprium* of the Holy Spirit, or that she is an instrument of the Holy Spirit without freedom.[127] Quasi-incarnation[128] of the Holy Spirit in the Immaculate does

120. *WK* 1229.

121. *WK* 1204.

122. *WK* 1326.

123. *WK* 1308, 1320.

124. *WK* 634.

125. Cf. Fernandez, "El Espiritu Santo . . . Algunos Ensayos," 141–43.

126. CK November 26, 1938; *WK* 508.

127. *WK* 1320.

128. *WK* 1286; CK February 5, 1941.

not mean that visible mission is another hypostatic union.[129] Both points the saint denies categorically.

But the phrase "quasi-incarnation" does underscore the uniqueness and visibility of the mission of the Holy Spirit in the Immaculate. "Transubstantiation" of the Immaculate calls our attention to the depth and intensity of the divinization or transformation of her personality at the moment of its formation, as complete and total as that of the substance of bread in the Eucharist, except that in the Immaculate the substance remains human. Both analogies indicate the intimate complementarity of the two missions.[130] That the mission of the Son should have been articulated first in dogmatic formulae is quite logical; the Immaculate calls our attention to him before explaining herself.

4. Finally, that union makes the Immaculate the perfect instrument of the Holy Spirit in the order of salvation and mercy (not judgment).[131] In this order of mercy, in virtue of that spousal union, there is a unity of action between them, such that the action of the Holy Spirit in the economy of salvation is effectively the action of the Virgin, an action in turn most perfectly one of the Holy Spirit.[132] For this reason the mystery of the Immaculate is a key, not only to the unity of the church, but also to the fruitfulness of her sacramental system and missionary effort. Together with the pastoral action of the Redeemer, the purificatory action of the Holy Spirit-Immaculate is basic to ecclesiology and sacramentology. The former action is contained as it were in the latter, or to borrow a phrase of St. Bonaventure: the Word Incarnate is in us as the Word inspired.[133] The sacramental actions of Christ

129. CK February 5, 1941; *WK* 634, 1229.

130. A further confirmation that this term, far from confusing the divine persons and missions, underscores their complementary is found in a passage antedating by several years the first references to "quasi-incarnation," and wherein the Immaculate is described as the personification of the love of Jesus, hence the Mother fashioned to make possible our spiritual childhood. Cf. *WK* 1145. So too the Holy Spirit is the Spirit of Christ, precisely because the "personification" of the love of the Father and of the Son. It is but a small step further to regard the personal relation between the Holy Spirit and the Immaculate as the complement of the mission of the Son in the incarnation and as entailing a spousal union of love so intimate and perfect as to result in the sharing of the same name, Immaculate Conception. Cf. also the very accurate analysis of Philippe, "Il Mistero," 52–55, in particular the differentiation of hypostatic and spousal union, the origin of the second from the first and the complementarity of the spousal union to the hypostatic union. The practical applications (55–59) further clarify this lucid analysis.

131. *WK* 1320.

132. *WK* 634, 1229.

133. *De don. Spir.*, col. 1, 7; the purity and infinity of divine love is particularly associated by St. Bonaventure with the person of the Holy Spirit; cf. *Hex*, II, 12. That

are interiorized by the faithful through the Holy Spirit-Immaculate-Church. That inspiration concretely is a maternal action.

Mother of the Son of God

The Immaculate, the Virgin of Virgins, is Mother of God, of a divine, not a human, person; she is truly, really and properly his mother, who is the Son of God and her Creator, as he is really, truly and properly her Son, and this not for a moment or for a limited period, but forever.[134] Even when physically separated there exists between Mother and Son a very real "indistance." This reciprocity explains their mutual "finality," her purpose in existing as Immaculate is to bear and glorify-clarify him.[135] His reason for becoming incarnate is to honor her, and to enjoy her love (and in saving us to enjoy ours in hers) so achieving the glory of the Father *ad extra*.[136]

St. Maximilian distinguishes three stages in the establishment of the kingdom of God in its fulness, in which Mother and Son are related to each other as New Eve-New Adam: the establishment of the kingdom, or incarnation and redemptive sacrifice of the Son of God, where the Immaculate is cooperator as mother and coredemptrix;[137] incorporation into the kingdom established, where the Immaculate cooperates with the shepherd of souls as the mediatrix of all graces and Mother of the Church;[138] and the consummation of the kingdom wherein the Immaculate is queen as her Son is king, after which consummation the kingdom will be handed over to the Father.[139] In each instance the prior stage is the indispensable preparation and prerequisite

---

association when extended to the created Immaculate Conception explains the universality and necessity of her mediation, cf. *WK* 1321, and by extension the sense of the axiom: Extra Ecclesiam nulla salus. Whoever is saved, is saved through the action of the Immaculate, even if he does not realize this; cf. *WK* 1310.

134. *WK* 1305.
135. *WK* 1229.
136. *WK* 1296.
137. *WK* 1229.
138. *WK* 1296, 1310.

139. *WK* 1331. It is clear that the mystery of the Immaculate effectively excludes from the Kolbean vision of the economy of salvation any taint of Joachimitism or Pentecostalism that would contrast an order of the Spirit with those of Father or Son. There is but one kingdom of God, because God is one. But because he is triune, in the realization of that kingdom and in each of its stages all three persons are involved according to a certain order. That stage in the realization of the kingdom heralding its fulness is initiated with the appearance of the Immaculate, the fulness of grace, whose name becomes more and more evident in the description of that stage as its consummation approaches. Cf. *WK* 644, 1248; *CK* July 3, 1938.

for the subsequent; and in each stage the action of the Incarnate Word is "contained" in that of the Immaculate. He is incarnate in her; he gives eternal life through her and consummates his kingdom through her.

Only-Begotten Daughter of the Father

As with the Son, so too in relation to the Father. St. Maximilian occasionally calls the Immaculate his spouse,[140] but not to indicate that the Father is her husband, much less that the Virgin participates in the generative power of the Father, something he regards as impossible.[141] The metaphor of spouse simply designates the perfection of the Father's love for her and of her love for the Father, the harmony of her "fiat" with that of the Father, an obedient reaction of a creature so perfectly matching the action of love of the divine persons originating with the Father, that its fruit is the incarnation of the Word.[142]

More properly the Immaculate is the "unigenita" and "primogenita" daughter of the Father,[143] beloved for her unique beauty before all other creatures and above all other creatures, precisely because she is absolutely predestined with her Son to be the Immaculate as he is to be the Incarnate, conceived in her womb.[144] This mystery of her predestination to be the exclusive possession of Father, Son and Holy Spirit,[145] in his writings

140. *WK* 1310.

141. *WK* 1291.

142. *WK* 1284; cf. *De don. Spir.*, col. 6, 8.

143. CK Feast of the Most Holy Trinity, 1941.

144. The phrase "absolute predestination" of the Immaculate, like that of "primacy of Christ," does not appear in his writings, but what is commonly understood by those terms is certainly present in his thought. Thus, the Immaculate is created exclusively for the Trinity; her love for the Trinity is the reason for God's loving and saving others (*WK* 1296). She is made for the Trinity, all the rest for her (*WK* 1305). She is the most perfect resemblance among creatures of the perfection and holiness of God (*WK* 1320); all other grades of perfection take their measure from her (*WK* 1282). Even if no other creature were saved, she would have been Immaculate, perfectly saved because preserved from sin (CK, Feast of the Most Holy Trinity, 1941). The trial of the angels was in view of venerating the Immaculate qua most perfect of creatures as their Queen; the seduction of Eve was undertaken by Satan in order to ruin the Immaculate whom he mistakenly confused with the first Eve (*WK* 1293, 1311). The Immaculate alone has the power, because Immaculate, to defeat the wiles of Satan (*WK* 1331). It is a power she has received from the Father through her Son, but it is a power she possesses. In view of that power God could prudently risk creating a world into which sin might enter; under her protection we can reach paradise.

145. *WK* 1296.

hierarchical in the best Bonaventurian sense, excludes any kind of evolutionism, ancient or modern, from his theology.[146]

The Trinitarian formulation of this doctrine, distinctively Kolbean, nicely completes the Christological emphasis characteristic of the scotistic tradition. It is just this Trinitarian formulation that illustrates why in our theology a treatise on the Immaculate is the indispensable introduction to a treatise on the Trinity and on the incarnation, why the "unigenita Filia" of the Father, the source of his Son's humanity, is also the "primogenital" of the Father, exemplar of what it means to be a human person, to love the Son of God perfectly, and through him the Father and the entire Blessed Trinity.[147] She is the "primogenital," exemplar of every follower of her Son, because as the "unigenita" she is the motive of our salvation. No one is reborn in Christ in any other way except by means of the love of God toward the Immaculate and in the Immaculate, that is to say in the same way as the Son of God became her Son because God the Father was so fascinated by her perfect humility.[148] The absolute predestination of the Immaculate *eo ipso* makes her the mediatrix of all graces, because without sharing her fulness no one is incorporated into Christ and accepted by the Father as his child.

Summation

In saving his Mother so perfectly by preserving her from all stain of sin, Jesus widened the circle of the Trinity according to the will of his Father. In making his Mother the Immaculate, full of grace and Spouse of the Holy Spirit, he made her a "consanguinea spiritualis" of the three divine persons, to whom the Father entrusted his Son as to his real Mother, and to whom Father and Son entrusted the entire order of mercy.

That fulness of love in her from God and for God, in a world infected by original sin, appears as preservation from all taint of sin from the first moment of conception, just as the Son of God became incarnate in passible flesh, that jointly they might triumph through the cross over the prince of this world. But even apart from the tragedy of sin that fulness of grace in the Immaculate, the fruit of the love Father and Son, would have set her apart

---

146. *WK* 1027, 1169, 1186, 1276; cf. Swiecicki, "Prospettive," 324, for a very sound evaluation of the abyss between the thought of St. Maximilian and the evolutionary dreams of Teilhard de Chardin.

147. *WK* 577.

148. *WK* 1296; one may also consider in this regard the further implications of the mystery of the Immaculate for ecclesiology, not only the mediation of the church, but for her unity as well. The more we are in the Immaculate, the more we are in each other. *WK* 571; cf. also *WK* 1284, 1326.

from all other creatures, even the holiest, for that union of love would have reached the point where she became Mother of God.

And in being given to us as our mother, as it were, by the last will and testament of her Son when dying on the cross, the fulness of grace won by the perfect Redeemer in a perfect act of redemption is made available to us, and in no other way. Her preservation from sin is the means of our liberation. The sufficiency of Christ's work in her becomes through her efficacious in us. Thus, the mystery of salvation may be articulated with St. Maximilian: in the name of the Father, and of the Son, and of the Holy Spirit, through the Immaculate.

Total consecration is the practical corollary of a Trinitarian view of the economy of salvation. She must instruct us, guide us, transform us every moment, so that we no longer live ourselves, but she lives in us, as Jesus in her and the Father in Jesus.[149]

Summary

In addition to many explanations in his writings,[150] St. Maximilian left several outlines[151] of his vision of the economy of salvation, the "Trinitas oeconomica," all of which verify the dictum of St. Bonaventure that the mystery of the Trinity is the foundation of all Christian faith and piety, both toward God and toward neighbor, culminating in that supreme act of love, viz., of obedience, offered the Father for the salvation of souls by the Son of God on the cross.[152] These outlines, thoroughly and clearly Trinitarian, represent in fact brief syntheses of the whole of Catholic theology, a kind of concentrate, whose richness is made evident to us by pondering that mysterious name: Immaculate Conception.

From a practical point of view, which is the distinctive point of view of our theology (to borrow the phraseology of Scotus), the synthesis in these outlines turns on the person of the Immaculate, the point where heaven touches earth and earth begins to return to heaven, because her holiness is so perfect, because she is the vertex of love, all the love of Father and Son meeting in her all the love of creation. Her character could not be more perfect ever, for from the first moment of her conception the fulness of grace so

149. WK 556.

150. For example, WK 634, 643, 1296, 1310, 1318, 1320, 1326.

151. WK 1283, 1284. These outlines are Bonaventurian in flavor, recalling the *Breviloquium*. By contrast the earlier outline found in WK 1270, with explanations, reflects the *Summa* of St. Thomas.

152. *Myst. Trin.*, q. 1, a. 2, ad 13.

integrates her personality as to make her an example of virtue for all. She is the last rung in the ladder connecting heaven and earth, the bridge between eternity and time, the ship across infinity, the point through which all other roads to and from heaven pass.

In this synthesis all the love of God for creation terminates at the Immaculate in a kind of descending or unfolding movement, a love that could not be more than it is in the Immaculate. That union of love reaches such a point that the Immaculate becomes Mother of God, to whom the Father entrusts his own Son, the Son who descends into her womb, while the Holy Spirit fashions from her body the most sacred body of Jesus.[153] That is why an ascending movement of return, a kind of enfolding of that same love, begins from the same point, indeed reaching the Father through the Incarnate Son, because in its purity it is a reaction equal and contrary to the original love from Father and Son, as in eternity the love of the Holy Spirit, her spouse, matches the love of Father and Son. The Immaculate is the fruit of the mutual love of Father and Son; but it is also true that the incarnation of the Son is the fruit of the love of the Father, and the entire Blessed Trinity, and of the Immaculate.

The heart of this synthesis, then, is a paradox and a fact central to Catholic theology: the "fiat" of the Woman precedes and makes possible the incarnation. The Mother of God is not a merely passive instrument, but an active one. The Son of God is incarnate in her by her consent. It is the mystery of the Immaculate that clarifies this paradox of the unfolding and enfolding of divine love originating with and returning to the Father, passing in both directions through the Son.

The Mother of God is the turning point in this movement that does not return to the Father empty, because she is the created Immaculate Conception, Spouse of the Holy Spirit, outer limits of that love unfolding, and hence enfolding the total love of creation for Son and Father. In her as in his palace we find our Savior, passing not out of her to Him, as we do not pass out of him to the Father, but through each, without leaving each, in the enfolding love of the Immaculate, of Jesus and of his Father.[154]

Because she is the Immaculate, full of grace, of the love of Father and Son, and thus the apex of created love, even if no other creature were sanctified,[155] the practical character of theology begins for us with her maternal action in our regard and our reaction thereto. The power of that action in the capacity of her character (virtue) to attract our hearts from

---

153. *WK* 1320, 1305.

154. *WK* 556, 603, 634; CK April 25, 1937.

155. CK Feast of the Most Holy Trinity, 1941.

within to the love of her Son is shown in the imitation of her Son in loving her and in the implementation of his commands consequent on union
with her will.[156] Thus, the basic law of transformation in the spiritual order
is consecration to the Immaculate.[157] That initial conformation of our will
to hers in virtue of her initiative in our regard in effecting our rebirth
in baptism[158] does not add to the fulness of her love, but is rather our
participation in that fulness, our purification and gratification (liberation
from sin), the indispensable first step in our sharing the life of her Son, the
object of her love, and of ours in union with her.[159]

That verse of the *Canticle of Canticles* (6:9): who is this rising like the
dawn, lovely as the moon, majestic as the sun, may be adapted to illustrate
St. Maximilian's insight in terms of a text traditionally applied to the mystery of the Immaculate Conception. In relation to the Son who saved her,
her loveliness reflects his, as the light of the moon reflects that of the sun.
Her coming, however, heralds his and reveals him, as the dawn the day.
And in relation to us the light which she reflects and the day which she
heralds is the majestic light of the sun, filtered through her to suit our sight.
To identify that person rising like the dawn, lovely as the moon, majestic
as the sun, the Immaculate Conception, as the Spouse of the Holy Spirit,
the uncreated Immaculate Conception, is to give that traditional reading of
the text of the *Canticle* not only a Christological, but Trinitarian context as
well, and so identify the proper and unique place of the Mother of God in
the economy of salvation: between the Word Incarnate, Son of the Father,
mediator-Savior, and the rest of creation.

Much has been written about the dangers of a one-sided Mariology
to the Christocentric character of theology, and of exaggerations in Marian
piety, particularly consequent upon placing a mediatrix alongside the one
Mediator, without whom access to the Mediator, to the love of the crucified
Savior is impossible. The Immaculate Conception of Mary and the doctrine
of her mediation are inseparable; the maximalism of total consecration in the
Kolbean synthesis, it is alleged, tends to sustain such aberrations.

What is not noted sufficiently in all these discussions is the fact that
all Christocentrism is not true Christocentrism,[160] and that a true Christocentrism is one which places Christ between Father and Holy Spirit within

156. *WK* 1295, 1326.

157. *WK* 1285. To be ever more conformed to the will of the Immaculate is our
ideal, our philosophy: *WK* 542, 1210.

158. *WK* 1326.

159. *WK* 1295.

160. Cf. Newman, "Glories of Mary"; *WK* 643.

the Trinity; and without places him between the Father and the Immaculate, and the Immaculate between us and him, for this is exactly how he with the Father wills to come to us by the power of the Holy Spirit, and how he wills to effect our approach to him by the power of the Holy Spirit cleansing us, illumining and perfecting our hearts. The mystery of Mary Mediatrix is the mystery of the Immaculate: not purified, but all pure from conception, being the Immaculate Conception.[161]

If God so wills, that is beyond doubt because it is wisest. The practicality of our theology rests on this mystery, because it is the link completing the Trinitarian character of the economy of salvation and thus constituting the context of true Christocentrism. The incarnation occurs in her, and only in her can the Incarnate Word be found. A theology that or denies the Immaculate and the universality of her mediation entails a false Christocentrism and a false spirituality, leading not to the exaltation of Christ as divine and to the glorification of the Trinity, but to the denial of these mysteries. Who does not belong to the Immaculate, does not belong to her Son, but to the prince of this world. It is the great merit of St. Maximilian, in illustrating theologically the Trinitarian character of the mystery of the Immaculate, also to have shown how and why total consecration to the Immaculate, without restriction, is the only basis for a thoroughly Christocentric spirituality. "Oh, how little known still is the Immaculate! When will it come to pass that the souls of men love the divine heart of Jesus with Hers, and their heavenly Father with the heart of Jesus?"[162]

The depth of St. Maximilian's insights into the mystery of the Trinity naturally opens many other lines of reflection and study, hardly touched upon in this resume of his fundamental teaching. Nor could it be otherwise in dealing with the mystery of the Trinity, for theology is nothing if not about the Trinity. Like all the great treatises on the Trinity his reflection, too, abounds in observations profoundly metaphysical (sometimes erroneously described as a mere exercise in deductive logic). These certainly deserve careful study, particularly because they are not unrelated to the manner in which St. Maximilian draws on the theology of such masters as St. Thomas Aquinas, St. Bonaventure and John Duns Scotus in the formation of his synthesis: from the first the concept of infinity, in particular the infinite distance between God and the sinner; from the second the complementarity of the processions and missions of the Word and of the Holy Spirit, the emanation from and return of all things to the Father, as well as the doctrine of exemplarism,

161. WK 1319
162. WK 1224; cf. WK 647.

cognitive and moral; from the last the Franciscan thesis on the Immaculate and the primacy of her Son, the king of kings.

But the synthesis formed, and the insights into the mystery of love, must also be studied in the context of contemplative prayer. Though a profound theologian St. Maximilian did not lead the life of a professional scholar. The synthesis, moreover, is not explicit in his writings until after 1932, when it appears almost *ex abrupto*, complete except for the crowning element, the relation of the Immaculate Conception to the procession of the Holy Spirit, put in place on the day of his final arrest in a synthesis of thought and life arranged to illumine and be illumined by the mystery of the Immaculate. It is not unreasonable to suggest that St. Maximilian came to grasp this synthesis and how to formulate it on his knees before her who is the Seat of Wisdom, whose spotless clarity of vision is the source of his. The grandeur of his theology begins and ends here: with the incorporation[163] of the mystery of the Immaculate into the life of each believer as it is incorporated into the life of the church by its founder, and with that entry into the paradise of Father, Son and Holy Spirit, the eternal Niepokalanów.

163. *WK* 486.

4

Complementum SS. Trinitatis

THE WRITINGS OF ST. Maximilian, particularly those related to the book projected on the Immaculate, show him to have possessed a facility for the apt phrase, one at once calculated to crystalize a theological reflection and make the mysteries of faith accessible to the believer and to the prospective convert. Undoubtedly this facility contributed not a little to his success as an apologete, and was brought to perfection in him through his total absorption in the cause of the Immaculate. The study of these phrases can contribute to the renewal of theology and of apologetics, an integral aspect of our theology as practical, and ultimately to a deeper appreciation of the relation of theology to the Seat of Wisdom and "Interemptrix omnium haeresum."

Some of these phrases, such as the formulae partly coined and partly adapted by him to give expression to the mystery of the Trinity as it appears in the economy of salvation, viz., in the Father one person and one nature, in the Son one person and two natures, and in the Immaculate two persons and two natures; or to that insight into the mystery of Mary at the heart of his thought, viz., created and uncreated Immaculate Conception, appear to be original with him. Others, for instance the Holy Spirit quasi-incarnate in the Immaculate, or the Immaculate, complement of the Trinity, were already in circulation, the latter for several centuries, but not always with a single meaning. Curiously, his use or adaptation of these two phrases has recently come under criticism, in one case quite violent, almost as though their use by him were the embarrassing innovation of an ill-trained theologian.[1]

More often than not St. Maximilian gives no indication of his sources, because most of the writing for which he had any time: letters, notes, sketches, popular presentations for the non-scholar and for simple folk, did not require this. Indeed, in many instances a scholarly apparatus might have been counterproductive. Nonetheless, he had his sources, and was careful, but not

1. Fernandez, "El Espiritu Santo . . . Algunos Ensayos," 141–43; Hebblethwaithe, "St. Maximilian Kolbe's Doubtful Spirituality."

slavish in their use. Nor is it impossible, by a careful reading of literature mentioned in his writings and study of records of books in his possession or used by him at one time or another,[2] to identify those sources.

But the discovery of those sources hardly constitutes the full explanation of his meaning. He was not a slavish copier of the thoughts of others, nor was he a mere developer of others' insights. Indeed, his use of phrases adapted from other authors appears almost occasional, as that of a tool lying conveniently to hand, when account is taken of the contrast between his insights and those upon whom he depended. The phrase does not so much condition his thought as it itself is conditioned and perfected by his thought. The study of such phrases, however secondary in importance, both in the theological tradition and in his thought, can be very instructive in identifying clearly the original character of his contribution to theology.

This is certainly the case with the title "Complementum SS. Trinitatis" given to the Immaculate as such by St. Maximilian in his writings and conferences. This study comprises four parts: the first an examination of the texts themselves; second the identification of the sources whence he became acquainted with this title; third the broader context of these sources; and fourth a discussion of St. Maximilian's originality vis-à-vis his sources and his contribution to theology.

The Texts

These can be conveniently divided into two groups: those from his writings (*WK*) and those from his conferences (CK) which have the character of "reportationes." The title first appears in 1935, although closely related concepts and phrases appear as early as 1933. Before that time the title does not seem to play any role in his thought, thus indicating that his usage of it is intimately linked to that final period of his life when he was granted such profound insight into the mystery of the Trinity.[3] The title occurs but twice in the writings and thrice in the conferences. And while this does not appear initially to indicate a particularly significant role in his thought, it is important to note that the second appearance in the writings occurs in that final masterpiece dictated the morning of his final arrest; and in the conferences the title appears between 1938 and 1940, when his thoughts were largely occupied with the "material for a book" on the Immaculate.

---

2. Cf. Domanski, "La genesi," 260–61.
3. Fehlner, "Immaculate . . . Trinity," *CE* 6, chapter 3.

The Writings

WK 634: A Letter to Br. Salesius Mikolajczyk[4]

The immediate context in which the title, Complement of the Trinity, appears is a discussion of the study of Mariology: its importance for an understanding of the mystery of the Immaculate, but also a recognition of the limits of such study and the importance of its subordination to "the spirit of prayer and devotion." The point made is exactly that of St. Bonaventure in respect to the study of theology, i.e., of God triune and one.[5] Indeed, St. Maximilian tells us that this is the case because the Immaculate, unlike other creatures, is so close to the three divine persons, that one of the Fathers calls her "complementum SS. Trinitatis."

He goes on to explain that closeness or "complementarity" in relation to the Word who is her Son and to the Father as the key to our closeness to the Word and Father, that is to say her complementarity, is an integral part of the *Trinitas oeconomica*. Quite naturally the question arises: what of the Holy Spirit? Without his presence one can hardly describe the created order of salvation as Trinitarian. The answer, which defines Mary's complementarity, is a recognition that the Immaculate is Spouse of the Holy Spirit in a unique manner, and therefore mediatrix of all grace, something true of no one else. In venerating the Immaculate, we *eo ipso* venerate the Holy Spirit and enter into the dynamism of the order of grace, the sharing in the divine nature of Father, Son and Holy Spirit.

The following observations are particularly worthy of attention. First, it is the closeness of the Immaculate to the Trinity that defines the title "Complement" in the mind of St. Maximilian and serves as a point of departure for other considerations linked to it in his thought. This closeness is utterly unique, setting her apart not only from all other creatures, but even from the rest of those sanctified by Christ's blood. It is not merely that she is close to the Trinity (for in a sense every creature even to exist must in some way be removed from nothing and brought close to God), but that she is uniquely close.[6]

She is uniquely close, because she is Spouse of the Holy Spirit, and only she is such in that unique way. Because she is such, she stands in the same relation to Father and Son in the economic Trinity as the Holy Spirit in eternity. The fulness of their love in the Holy Spirit in eternity is in her in time. She is, as he says elsewhere, an image, the icon, the personification of

---

4. *WK 634.*

5. *Itin.*, prol., 4; *WK* 1306.

6. *WK* 1305.

the Holy Spirit.[7] She is not this because in her alone the Holy Spirit dwells, but because she alone is the Immaculate Conception, through whom the Holy Spirit dwells in all other souls, making of them a single communion in charity.[8] Thus, in this letter he indicates the purpose of that unique closeness, that complementarity, as her spiritual maternity as mediatrix of all graces; elsewhere as her divine maternity.[9] The motive of the Immaculate Conception is the divine maternity; but only in grasping the mystery of the Immaculate Conception can we begin to appreciate the ineffable and "infinite" dignity of the Mother of God.[10]

In other letters from this period where he discusses the "closeness" of the Immaculate to the Trinity, further understanding of the title "complement" in his mind can be gleaned, even if the title itself does not appear. Thus, in WK 508,[11] her closeness to the Trinity is described as being the possession of God (elsewhere the exclusive possession of the three divine persons),[12] such as to make her a "quasi" part of the Trinity. Being not simply handmaid, daughter, thing, property (as we are), but a "part" of the Trinity, she becomes the Mother of God, or as he says elsewhere,[13] so intimately united to the Holy Spirit as to conceive the Son of God and truly be his Mother.

In conceiving and bearing the Son of God, Mary Immaculate enters into spiritual consanguinity with the three divine persons, precisely because with the Father she has the same Son.[14] Him she conceives by the Holy Spirit. Thus her "consanguinity" with the divine persons effectively rests on her relation to the Holy Spirit as his spouse, viz., as the Immaculate. The juncture between the inner and economic Trinity is effected just at this point, the Immaculate Conception, because that spousal union makes her the complement of the Trinity, expanding as it were the family circle.

In WK 603 and 643[15] it is just this analogy that serves as the basis for a profound response to a classic objection to the mediation of Mary, indeed to the exaltation of Mary and to consecration to her, as inimical to the centrality of her Son and as detracting from the sublimity of the Godhead. Rather than

7. Cf. Fehlner, "Immaculate . . . Trinity," CE 6, chapter 3.

8. Fehlner, "Immaculate . . . Trinity," CE 6, chapter 3.

9. WK 1320.

10. WK 1210.

11. WK 508.

12. WK 1296.

13. WK 1320.

14. CK Feast of the Holy Trinity, 1941.

15. WK 603, 643.

imagining each of these persons, he says, as so many objects of devotion on the same plane (which indeed would detract from the divinity were Mary so venerated), they should be represented as links of a single chain, so related one to another as means to a single end: the one God in the Blessed Trinity. Mary is not the equal of a divine person;[16] nonetheless once conceived, she is inseparable from them, for that is why she exists—to be their complement, their exclusive possession, so that access to the inner Trinity is sharing in the economic via consecration to the Immaculate.[17]

In *WK* 643 he further elucidates this observation by insisting that we do not venerate one person after another, but all together; and that "exclusive" consecration to the Immaculate does not exclude, but is also "exclusive" consecration to Jesus, and therefore "exclusive" consecration to the Father, i.e., final immersion in the Father, through the Son, through the Mother, the Immaculate.

Complementarity, then, in the mind of St. Maximilian, is a unique closeness of one created person to the divine persons, based on a spousal union, a union of love, so perfect as to effect an enlargement of the divine circle, without in any way violating the divine transcendence, precisely because it is not by way of addition, but by way of love, not any love, but perfect love, greater than which cannot be conceived.[18] Were Mary not the Immaculate, whose will is so uniquely and completely one with that of her Creator from the first moment of her conception, that love could be greater. Such is the Immaculate Conception, such is the heart of the supernatural order, a sharing in the very nature of God, an insertion into the divine circle through the Immaculate, mediatrix of all graces.

WK 1318[19]

The title "complement of the Blessed Trinity" also appears in that passage of material for a book dictated by the saint the morning of his final arrest in 1941. In this passage the title stands in close relation to that profound insight into the mystery of the Immaculate and the Holy Spirit, viz., of the created and uncreated Immaculate Conception. The Immaculate becomes once and forever the complement of the Trinity at the moment she is inserted into the love of the Trinity, viz., at the moment of her conception, because at that moment she enters an ineffable spousal union with

16. *WK* 1320.
17. *WK* 1168, 1296.
18. *WK* 1232.
19. *WK* 1318.

the Holy Spirit, whose name is Immaculate Conception, and thus she is preserved free of all stain of original sin. She is, therefore, the complement of the Trinity, and although the saint does not note this, it is in fact far the same reason that many fathers of the church call the Holy Spirit the complement of the Trinity.[20]

This union St. Maximilian calls the vertex of love, the point where perfect created love becomes the worthy reaction to the love of the Trinity, where God is adored without compare.[21] The Immaculate as the complement of the Trinity is, then, the vertex of love, the point in creation where the glory rendered the triune God is of a finality and perfection, exactly the counter point of that rendered from eternity within the Trinity by the procession of the Holy Spirit.

The insertion of the Immaculate into the love of the Trinity, making her its complement, consists not in same kind of ontological confusion of created and uncreated natures, something St. Maximilian clearly repudiates, but in the perfect identity of the Immaculate's will with the will of God.[22] It is just this union, expressed in the analogy Spouse of the Holy Spirit, and touching her being and person at its very roots, that is indicated in the auto-definition of the Immaculate: "I am the Immaculate Conception."

The Conferences

Of the three instances where the title occurs in the conferences, the first[23] is found in a relatively long discussion of Mary in relation to the Trinity. The immediate context is the miraculous formation of the humanity of Christ in the womb of the virgin by the Holy Spirit. Her soul is totally divinized. Her relation to the Trinity in the supernatural order is extraordinary, and results from the fact that she is the Mother of God. Pope Pius X calls her the "quasi-complement of the Holy Trinity." He concludes by remarking on the difference between the presence of God by inhabitation in the just and that same inhabitation in the Immaculate. The "quasi" before complement, like the quasi before incarnation, undoubtedly indicates a difference, in this case between the complement of the Trinity *ad intra* and that *ad extra*, i.e., between the Holy Spirit and the Immaculate.

20. Fehlner, "Immaculate . . . Trinity," *CE* 6, chapter 3.
21. *WK* 1318.
22. *WK* 1232, 1320.
23. CK April 9, 1938.

The second is found in another conference of 1938,[24] where he says that her spousal union (inhabitation, divinization) with the Holy Spirit is such that we cannot comprehend it. That union, as it were, "transubstanti-ates" her being, making her one being with him. This relation Pope Pius IX called the "complement of the Trinity." To understand this our intellect is not sufficient, because the Trinity is infinite.

The final instance, in a conference of 1940[25] is very brief. Three phrases form the answer to an initial question: who is the Immaculate? The Mother of God, the "full of grace" and the complement of the Trinity (Pius X).

In each instance the title complement is brought into relation with the person of the Holy Spirit and his action in the Immaculate, above all transforming her in such wise as to be the unique dwelling place of the Trinity. In a word the title identifies the distinctive factor of grace in Mary, meriting for her the name "fulness of grace." The closeness to the Trinity, which in the writings provided a starting point for an analysis of the title is completed in the conferences by the notion of fulness, i.e., so perfect that a more perfect cannot be conceived, hence unique. That fulness is the fulness of the love of Father and Son in her as in the Holy Spirit, because she is the Spouse of the Holy Spirit, the created Immaculate Conception, an insight articulated in the dictation of February 17, 1941.

The Sources

Of the Mariological treatises studied by St. Maximilian three discuss at some length the title complement of the Trinity, and are without doubt his immediate sources for a knowledge of this title. One of these, the textbook of Card. Lépicier, is most probably the source for his vague reference to the Fathers of the church and to Popes Pius IX and Pius X, neither of whom employed the title, but one of whom, Pius IX, is mentioned in connection with its explanation by the Cardinal.[26]

24. CK November 26, 1938.

25. CK September 21, 1949.

26. Lépicier, *Tractatus*, 116–17. The text of Pius IX is taken from the introductory paragraph of *Ineffabilis Deus*.

J. J. A. Nicolas

The first volume of his *Nouvelles Etudes Philosophiques*,[27] treating of the Virgin Mary in the divine plan, contains an entire chapter devoted to the explanation of this title. That plan, set forth in a manner recalling the scotistic tradition re the primary motive of the incarnation and the absolute predestination of the Immaculate with her Son, is first considered in relation to creation and its three ends, and then in relation to the fall of our first parents. In each instance the ministry of Mary is the hinge (in St. Maximilian the "vertex") on which all the rest turns (and thus the key for Nicolas to the understanding of the Christian order from within). On this basis her relations both to God and to the world are outlined, and in both instances those relations are defined in Trinitarian terms. The Virgin Mary is the spouse of the Father, Mother of the Son, and sanctuary of the Holy Spirit, in a word a unique daughter of God. Hence, she is the complement or completion of the divine work ad extra, and thus the complement of the Trinity, not in the sense of adding anything to the fulness of the divine being, an impossibility, but in the sense that that plenitude of God establishes new relations completing and perfecting his manifestation ad extra, and this through Mary. Thus, the Father receives an authority over his Son and is thereby glorified in his humanity as well as in his divinity. Thus, the soul of Mary magnifies both Father and Son. So too, the Holy Spirit who was infecund within the Trinity, through Mary is made fecund and thus is glorified in the salvation of men in the church. "Mary is not only the 'ostensorium Trinitatis' . . . She expands God in his work, glorifies the Trinity in its manifestation" and hence is the complement of the Trinity in realizing the three ends of creation: the glory of the Father, the glory of the Son, and the happiness of man (the glory of the Holy Spirit).

However audacious sounding the title crystalizing this point, viz., complement of the Trinity, it is, Nicolas says, the best word available to describe what it is the Virgin Mary accomplishes by her action, viz., in reaching the frontiers of divinity, and realizing our divinization in humanizing God. *Deus homo factus est . . . ut homo fieret Deus.*[28] In a word her dignity is unique and under God constitutes by herself alone a hierarchy, a grade of being, an order, so uniquely perfect as to transcend the Seraphim as they transcend the Cherubim. The title complement, then, is understood by Nicolas as defining Mary's position as a unique hierarch among creatures,

---

27. Nicolas, *La Vierge Marie*, 347–54. The first edition of this volume was published in 1855. On Nicolas cf. Carreyre, "Nicolas"; Darricau, "Nicolas."

28. Nicolas, *La Vierge Marie*, 343. Cf. *WK* 508, 1232.

the most perfect of creatures, because of her relations to God, triune and one.

A.M. Lépicier, O.S.M.

The second author in this series, although probably the first in whom St. Maximilian encountered the title, is the Servite Cardinal, author of a famous and widely used manual in Mariology, the *Tractatus de Beata Vergine Maria*, first published in 1900, and frequently revised and republished through the first decades of this century.[29] Considerable attention is devoted to the title, complement of the blessed Trinity, in a section of the text dealing with corollaries of the divine maternity, the basis of Mary's relation to God. These corollaries are three: the dignity of the divine maternity *in se*, the duties of Christ to her, and her relations to God. This third point involves a twofold consideration.

First, because she is the Mother of God, she enjoys a certain "affinity" with God: with God the Father, because both the eternal and temporal generation from each respectively bear on the same person, because in each generation the Son is begotten from the substance of the parent, and in each instance is the only Son; to the Son, because she furnished his flesh from her body, because of her familiarity with her Son, her compassion for him, and her present sharing of his glory; to the Holy Spirit, because she received from him her fecundity, shared a common life with him, and a total community of possessions. To summarize all this Lépicier calls (and explains in detail) Mary daughter of the Father, spouse of Christ, sanctuary of the Holy Spirit. While acknowledging Leo XIII's use of Spouse of the Holy Spirit in this context, Lépicier prefers sanctuary citing Terrien[30] who claims the title spouse is found but twice in the entire tradition.

Secondly, Mary is thereby related to the divine persons as their complement, for the same reason that she is daughter, spouse and sanctuary, viz., because she is Mother of God. By her maternity she brings something to the Trinity, not *essentialiter*, but *accidentaliter*, i.e., *ad extra deitatem*, by perfecting the work of creation in relation to each divine person: bringing the Father an authority over the Son otherwise his equal, to the Son his temporal conception, and to the Holy Spirit his fecundity. In this way, he says, citing St. Bernard, glory is given to the Trinity, salvation to man and joy to the angels.

---

29. Lépicier, *Tractatus*, 107–18. The first edition appeared in 1900.
30. Terrien, *La Mère de Dieu*, 202.

Lépicier cites Hesychius of Jerusalem as having first used the title, but in a sense different from a later tradition (that of the French school) which Lépicier himself follows. In a scholion Lépicier cites a number of writers, mainly medieval, in support of his explanation: Ps. Ephrem, John the Geometer, St. Thomas, Peter Martyr. None of these, however, employed the title complement of the Trinity in relation to Mary, and the texts adduced speak not of what she brought to the divine persons, but of her fulness or of her nearness to the Trinity. Finally, he summarizes this entire section with a lengthy passage from Pope Pius IX in the bull *Ineffabilis Deus* where the pope describes how in predestining Mary to be Mother of God he so endowed her with an abundance of graces as to set her far above the Angels, so that preserved from original sin and possessing a fulness of innocence and sanctity she is the most perfect of creatures, more perfect than which none can be conceived and only God can understand. Shortly thereafter in the bull there follows a reference to her relations to each of the divine persons, but none to the title "complement." It is easy to see how in a conference St. Maximilian could have supposed for a moment a text indirectly being used in the conference and supporting the sense of the title also contained mention of it. The reference to Pius X is either a copyist's error or a slip of the tongue. So too, in a letter to Fr. Vivoda (*WK* 508), without any kind of scholarly library at hand, the one Father could become Fathers, particularly as Lépicier cites other pre-reformation authors in support of his exposition, although in fact only one Father used the title and this not in the sense Lépicier gives it. Whether in fact the sense of the title in the thought of St. Maximilian in some ways approaches that of Hesychius will be treated in section IV of this study.

E. Campana

The third major study treating extensively this title, and familiar to St. Maximilian, is that of Lépicier's disciple Campana, in his well-known *Maria nel dogma cattolico*.[31] The work embraces three parts: the mission of Mary, her prerogatives, and her life in the Gospels. The mission of Mary is centered on her maternity, in the context of which a very long exposition of her relations with the three divine persons is found. According to Campana the Trinity was first explicitly revealed in history to Mary precisely so that she might be the Mother of God. And through that maternity she contracted relations with each of the divine persons, setting her apart from and above every other creature.

31. Campana, *Maria nel Dogma Cattolico*, 114–37.

First considered are those relations Campana calls "indirect," viz., that may be subsumed under the title "complement of the Trinity." These consist in what Mary brings to the Trinity, or better what glory the Trinity brings to itself *ad extra* by the work of Mary. Then follow reflections bearing on the direct links between Mary and the divine persons, viz., as "filia unigenita, socia Patris, Mater, Domina et Sponsa Verbi, sacrarium Spiritus Sancti, et proinde Mediatrix omnium gratiarum." His position is in substance that of Lépicier, developed more amply, with several helpful critical observations. In regard to Mary's relation to the Father, Son and Holy Spirit only the title Mother is to be taken in the proper sense designating an exclusive relation to the Son; all other titles, including that of complement, are to be taken as metaphors or analogies, more or less accurate, and as appropriations, i.e., not exclusive to one person. Complement in particular expresses the fulness or perfection of Mary as a work of God, as his instrument. Finally, he includes a brief, but judicious assessment of the historical "status quaestionis": the title "complement" is not as old as some would make it. In effect, the use Hesychius makes of it is not the source of its present usage. None the less there are solid grounds for its current use, despite the fears of abuse by a minority of theologians.

In these three works containing substantive discussions of the title "complement of the Trinity" ascribed to the Blessed Virgin and familiar to St. Maximilian, that title is analyzed in the context of her relations of affinity with each of the divine persons, an affinity according to Nicolas inherent in her absolute predestination to be the immaculate Mother of God, according to the other two authors contracted via her divine maternity. The title itself does not so much describe those relations of Mary to each of the divine persons, as their manifestation via that work (her divine and spiritual maternity) by which she perfects in an absolute manner the work of God *ad extra*, and thus complements the glory of each person *ad extra*.

There is no question but that many of the ideas of these authors are in fact reflected in the thought of St. Maximilian. It is difficult, however, to say to what extent each of them might be or is the major or exclusive source for his information on any one of his ideas. Certainly, the Scotistic tenor of Nicolas' presentation is echoed often in Kolbean thought, especially in the material for a book, perhaps because it provided a very handy statement of that theological current in Mariological form. His information, however, on the title of our Lady, complement of the Trinity, quite obviously is derived from Lépicier. But St. Maximilian does not appear to have been particularly interested in the history of the title, nor is there any indication that he adverted to the discrepancy between the use he actually made of the title, and the interpretation given it by these three Mariologists—and indeed by all Mariologists, pro or con its use since the seventeenth century. The clearest indication of a difference, of usage between St. Maximilian and these modern authors is to be found in St. Maximilian's association of the title with the position of the Immaculate as unique Spouse of the Holy Spirit, a title these Mariologists either do not mention, or only mention in order to discount as lacking deep patristic roots when contrasted with the title, Sacrarium of the Holy Spirit, preferred by each of them as free of possible misinterpretation.

The Title "Complement" in Modern Mariology

Theological discussion of the title "Complement of the Trinity" as addressed to our Lady, has not had a long history. Such discussion first occurred in the seventeenth century, principally in France and in Spain. After the dogmatic definition of the Immaculate Conception in 1854 a renewed interest was taken in the title, first as a result of the success of the work of Nicolas, but later because of the widespread use of the manual of Lépicier.[32] Thereafter, until about the middle of this century a goodly number of prominent Mariologists gave greater or lesser attention to it, either to comment favorably on its use, or to criticize this use as being inopportune.

Almost from the first appearance of the title in the early seventeenth century with Cardinal de Berulle and the French School,[33] and after him J. J. Olier,[34] V. Contenson,[35] Louis Françoise d'Argentan,[36] and in Spain with the Benedictine bishop J. de la Cerda[37] and the Jesuit C. de Vega[38] there has been considerable speculation on the possible antecedents of the title, the possible meanings it might bear to explain its use, and also criticism of its use as an inopportune innovation.[39] It was generally admitted in the seventeenth century that the title had but one verbal antecedent

32. Cf. Wittkemper, "Dreifaltigkeit," coll. 1449–51.

33. St. Maximilian was acquainted with Discourse XI of Berulle's *Grandeurs de Jesus*, reprinted in A. Molien, *Les Grandeurs de Marie*, 114–25, although the word Complement does not appear in the passage reprinted. On the mariology of the French School in relation to the Trinity, cf. Alonso, "Hacia una Mariología Trinitaria."

34. Olier, *Vie interieur*.

35. Contenson, *Theologia Mentis et Cordis*, tomus III, 232–33.

36. d'Argentan, *Conferences theologiques*. The passages treating of the title "Complement" were reprinted by Provin, *Notre-Dame de la Trinité*, 44–52.

37. De la Cerda, *Maria Effigies*, 33–41. On this almost forgotten mariologist who deserves better cf. Alonso, "Hacia una Mariolagia Trinitaria," 238–47.

38. De Vega, *Theologia Mariana*, tomus II, 448–51.

39. Cf. Poiré, *La Triple Couronne*, vol. 1, 146.

(Hesychius), and that with a meaning quite different from the sense given it in the seventeenth century.

Renewed interest in the title during the second half of the nineteenth century was accompanied almost from the start by criticism first expressed by Scheeben,[40] that the use of the title, though licit, is inopportune and in bad theological taste. That criticism was continued in the twentieth century by the Benedictine L. Janssens,[41] the opponent of Lépicier on this point, and was followed in this by J. Müller, the Innsbruck Jesuit,[42] Al. Janssens of the Scheut Fathers,[43] and by the capuchin Jerome of Paris in his study of the Mariology of St. Lawrence of Brindisi.[44] In addition to A. Nicolas, A. Lépicier, and E. Campana, these theologians, all of the first half of the twentieth century, discuss and support the use of the title: F.X. Godts, C.Ss.R., Clovis de Provin, OFMCap., L. Garriguet, J. Bittremieux, G. Alastruey, B.H. Merkelbach, O.P., N. García Garcés, A. Plessis, G. Roschini, O.S.M.[45]

But whether favorable or unfavorable to the title its discussion since the seventeenth century has always occurred in the context of a much broader and older question, viz., that of the relations of the Blessed Virgin to the Blessed Trinity.

A number of authors favorable to the title initiate their analysis by mentioning that the fifth century Hesychius of Jerusalem was the first to use the title complement in conjunction with the Blessed Virgin, but in a sense quite different from that prevalent since the seventeenth century. Indeed, a number of critics have observed there is in Hesychius' use no basis for initiating a discussion of Our Lady's relations to the single divine persons. Whatever the merits of that observation, the principal difference between the only known example of this term in any way applied to Our Lady in antiquity and the relatively modern usage since the seventeenth century was already noted by seventeenth-century writers favorable to modern usage: that it is one thing to *have* the complement of the Trinity, and quite another to *be* the complement of the Trinity. Hesychius uses the term in the first sense; modern authors in the second sense as a personal title.[46]

40. Scheeben, *Mariology*, vol. 1, 181–83.

41. Janssens, *Tractatus*, 487–89.

42. Müller, *De Sanctissima*, 141–42.

43. Janssens, De Heilige, 143–48.

44. Jérome de Paris, *La Doctrine Mariale*, 112–13.

45. Godts, *Marie Complément*; de Provin, "Notre-Dame"; L. Garriguet, *La Vierge Marie*, 60–61; Bittremieux, "Relationes," 18–33; Alastruey, *Tratado*, 110–22 (The original Latin text appeared in 1935); Merkelbach, *Mariologia*, 62; García Garcés, *Titulos y Grandezas*, 62–76; Plessis, *Manuale*, 215ff; Roschini, *Mariologia*, tomus II 173–77.

46. De la Cerda, *Maria Effigies*, 33; De Vega, *Theologia Mariana*, tomus II, 448.

Curiously, with the exception of Bittremieux,[47] neither the defenders nor critics of the title in the nineteenth and twentieth centuries have noted that in the sense of a personal title complement admits of a variety of meanings, many of which had been noted and analyzed at considerable length in the seventeenth century.[48] Bittremieux notes two basic meanings of the title applied to Mary: either she herself is the complement of the divine persons; or the one who brings something to each of the divine persons.[49] It is only in the latter sense that the modern discussion has been conducted, and this in three ways.

a. "Maria causa exstitit cur relationes rationis ad extra divinis personis advenerunt, adeoque cur nomina quibus tales relationes exprimuntur, quaeque non ab aeterno de Deo dicuntur, in tempore de Ipso dici possunt." This is so because she is the Mother of God.

b. "B. Virgo dici potest aliquid SS. Trinitatis contulisse eo quod eius cooperatione divinae Personae novos effectus ad extra produxerunt atque jugiter produceret." This is so because she is mediatrix of grace.

c. "B. Virgo ab extrinseco SS. Trinitati aliquid attulisse potest dici eo quod divinarum Personarum gloriam augmenta verit." This is so because she is the holiest, most perfect of creatures.

These three manners in which the Blessed Virgin adds *ab extra* to the three divine persons correspond exactly to the three grounds identified by Bittremieux constituting her unique relations to the Trinity and thus the basis for her excellence. In virtue of those relations she is either added to the Trinity, or adds to it. After Bittremieux only one theologian appears to have taken note of the distinction in discussing the title, namely Merkelbach, and this in order to clarify the theological use of title. Merkelbach considers the popular use as distinct from the theological to be inopportune, a position somewhat different from that of other defenders of the title from Nicolas to García Garcés, the third edition of whose work appeared in 1959, just before the opening of Vatican II.

No critic of the title has maintained that it has no acceptable meaning per se; rather in every instance the objections have aimed at demonstrating a built-in ambiguity designed to confuse, no matter how much explanation provided, which to be explained must be explained away.[50] These relations

47. Bittremieux, "Relationes," 18–33.

48. De la Cerda, *Maria Effigies*, 33–41; De Vega, *Theologia Mariana*, 448–51.

49. Bittremieux, "Relationes," 19.

50. Bittremieux, "Relationes," 25ff, responds to the major criticisms of the title. The phrase is from J. H. Newman, "Letter to E. B. Pusey," 115, and cited by Aloïs Janssens as

of our Lady to the persons of the Trinity can be expressed better, according to the critics, either without such a title, or with other titles. Perhaps that observation unwittingly calls attention to the reason for the popularity of the title among other Mariologists: it crystalizes a very important theme, viz., the excellence of the Mother of God in her relations to the divine persons, one deeply embedded in the entire tradition of the church. According to Feckes[51] one's interest in the title will to a great extent be determined by the importance one gives to these relations. Ultimately that importance will reflect the place given in theology as a whole to the mystery of the Trinity. Oddly, just at a time when greater place began to be given to that mystery in ecclesiology and in practical theology, discussion both of the title complement of the Trinity, and of the relations of the Blessed Virgin to the Trinity ceased to receive any attention from Mariologists.

Why this should have happened is not entirely clear. No doubt many adventitious factors played their part, and by themselves represent no permanent judgment on the importance of the discussion, or on the ultimate fate of the title. Nonetheless, one cannot entirely suppress the suspicion that even though all the objections have been satisfactorily resolved, there remains a certain aura of defensiveness, or apology for the use of a title that might easily be construed to imply a quantitative addition to the Trinity. And even though that objection is countered by noting that any creature, any created "ens" may be described as a complement of the Trinity,[52] the reply to a certain extent obscures the character of the title as something exclusive to our Lady, as designating in singular fashion her unique relation to the three divine persons. It is the exclusive stress on taking complement to mean "addition" either passively or actively, that is at the heart of the difficulty. So long as that is the focus, so long will the defense remain subtly defensive. But that need not be the case. It is just here that the use St. Maximilian makes of the title indicates another, profounder analysis of the problematic.

The Originality of St. Maximilian

The distinctive use St. Maximilian makes of the title, complement of the Trinity, can be appreciated, first negatively by contrasting his use with that of

applicable to the title "Complement of the Trinity." Many scholars since have included the name of the English Cardinal among those of critics of the title, but in fact Newman never once mentions this title.

51. Feckes, "Die Gottesmutterschaft," 64–67.

52. Bittremieux, "Relationes," 25–26.

his sources, and then positively, by examining the meaning this title in fact assumes in his thought, particularly as it converges on that final elaboration of the answer to the question, who is the Immaculate (*WK* 1318).

Contrasts

1. The title complement in the thought of St. Maximilian is always associated with her unique relation to the Holy Spirit as his spouse, either verbally, or by way of reference to the mystery of inhabitation, in the Immaculate of a perfection not found in any other created person. The authors on whom he drew, or probably drew, for his acquaintance with the title complement did not particularly stress the title Spouse of the Holy Spirit; indeed they tended to discount its use as a potentially dangerous modern innovation (even though employed by Popes Leo XIII and St. Pius X)[53] and insist in this context on the older sacrarium, sanctuarium, templum. "Spouse," on the contrary, is frequently employed by these authors to describe the relations between Mary and God the Father or God the Son, a procedure relatively infrequent in the writings of Saint Maximilian. Authors, such as Terrien, whom St. Maximilian studied carefully, discussed at great length the relations of Mary with the Trinity, but did not mention the title complement, frowned on the use of the title "Spouse" of the Holy Spirit as misleading. Of all those theologians favorable to the title complement, only one, García Garcés with whom Saint Maximilian was unacquainted, also looked favorably on the title "Spouse of the Holy Spirit," and this without regarding the explanation of the title complement as primarily associated with this.[54]

While St. Maximilian fully realized the analogical-metaphorical character of the title Spouse of the Holy Spirit and that it was an appropriatum, predicable also of the other divine persons,[55] nonetheless it indicated something quite unique in the relations of Mary to the Holy Spirit and that something unique is at the core of the title "complement of the Trinity."

2. In none of the instances where St. Maximilian employs the title complement does he mention or imply anything concerning "adding" or "bringing" or "conferring" something on the Trinity or the divine persons singly. Such considerations used almost exclusively by contemporary

---

53. Leo XIII, *Divinum Illud Munus*; Pius X, in an indulgenced prayer to Mary, reparationis causa, in *AAS* 6, 108. Recently Pope John Paul II employed the title, Spouse of the Holy Spirit, for Mary as used in the franciscan tradition: Figlia di Dio Padre, Madre di Dio, e Figlia e Sposa dello Spirito Santo. Cf. *L'Osservatore Romano*, 2 febbraio 1985, 6.

54. García Garcés, *Titulos y Grandezas*, 65–66, 69–70.

55. Fehlner, "Immaculate . . . Trinity," *CE* 6, chapter 3.

theologians to explain the title complement occasionally are found in the writings of Saint Maximilian, but never as explanations for the title complement.[56] One would not be justified in inferring from this that he was therefore opposed to such; merely that when he did use the title complement, it was with other associations.

3. Most of the twentieth-century authors who have discussed the title relate it to a certain closeness of the Blessed Virgin to the Blessed Trinity, unique to her. In this connection a number of texts earlier than the sixteenth century, but not mentioning the title complement, are often adduced in connection with discussions of that title closeness itself, but what Mary brings to the Trinity by being so close in virtue of her divine maternity. This is true even in the case of Bittremieux who notes that the title could designate not only what Mary brings to the Trinity, but that she herself is that "addition."

In St. Maximilian it is the closeness in the first instance that the title complement designates. The Immaculate is as it were a part, within the family of the divine persons, not by nature but by grace, from the first moment of her conception. No other creature can claim such a privilege. That closeness is her first privilege,[57] the basis of her supreme perfection as a creature, the coefficient of her relation to the Holy Spirit; in the explanation of that relation will be found a satisfying interpretation of complement of the Trinity.

The Kolbean Interpretation

The relation between the Blessed Virgin and the Holy Spirit, that union of wills so perfectly and thoroughly transforming her total being, so as to make her the image, the icon, the quasi-incarnation of the Holy Spirit, a union only faintly adumbrated by the analogy of spouse, is ultimately explained by Saint Maximilian in terms of that profound insight into the created and uncreated Immaculate Conception (WK 1318). Mary is the created Immaculate Conception, because in her from the first moment of her conception there was present the total love of Father and Son that from all eternity was present in the Holy Spirit. For this reason his name is Immaculate Conception, and from him she derives her name, because she is the term of his mission *ad extra* as he is of his procession *ad intra*.

1. "Complement" as term: The Blessed Virgin, then, is the complement of the Trinity, not because she adds something or is an addition to the Trinity, as implying a defect therein, but in the same way that the Holy Spirit is the complement —and is called such by the fathers and medieval

56. WK 1229, 1293, 1310.
57. WK 1292.

doctors—as the term of a procession from the Father and the Son, one in whom is their total love, who is therefore the consummation of that love.[58] So also *ad extra* the Immaculate by that fact of being the repository of the total love of Father and Son consummates that love. No more perfect creature is conceivable, and only God could conceive such a creature. Mary, then, is called complement of the Trinity for the same reason that the Holy Spirit is called complement of the Trinity, not because she is a second Holy Spirit, but because, without loss of personal identity, she is perfectly united "in spousal union" to that divine person.

De la Cerda,[59] and after him de Vega,[60] but neither as clearly or amply as St. Maximilian, in their discussion of complement in the context of the revelation of the Trinity, first made explicitly to Mary and through her to us,[61] give as a basis for its use as a Marian title the relation of Mary to the Holy Spirit, who in patristic times and later in the Middle Ages was called complement or term of the Trinity, and whose procession via the will is discussed in relation both to the "creation" of Mary and to her conception of the Son of God.[62] Neither, however, relates this consideration explicitly to the Immaculate Conception, much less call the Holy Spirit the created Immaculate Conception. And although he might have noticed the names of these two Spaniards in a footnote of Nicolas,[63] it is highly unlikely that St. Maximilian had actually read these authors.

2. Complement of the Trinity *ad extra*, however, is not in the thought of St. Maximilian merely restricted to the conception of the Blessed Virgin in the passive sense. Her Immaculate Conception is the first (and dearest) of her privileges, because it is the term of the omnipotent love of God: of no more perfect a creation is his love capable.

58. Cf. Fehlner, "Immaculate . . . Trinity," *CE* 6, chapter 3.

59. De la Cerda, *Maria Effigies*, 37–39; "Spiritus Sanctus complementum Trinitatis, quia complet Trinitatem, quia voluntas ordine originis posterior est cuius optima infinitudo Spiritu Sancto producto cohibetur; nec ultra gradi valet . . . Spiritus Sanctus stagnum superius (est) cum plenitudine gratiae; Maria stagnum inferius per humilitatem . . . Spiritus Sancti super Virgine mansio aeternatur; Imo Circuitio et ambitus, ut tota sub amplexu Spiritus subsideat Maria, et a complemento Trinitatis completa, in ipsius complementi adsurgat attributum"

60. De Vega, *Theologia Mariana*, tomus II, 450.

61. De la Cerda, *Maria Effigies, Academia* I, sectio 1: Publica et solemnis; manifestatio Trinitatis non nisi in Maria auspicatur.

62. De la Cerda, *Maria Effigies, Academia* V: Maria ex amore gignit Filium ei, quem Pater gignit ex cognitione, quae in Deo natura est; et sectio 5 eiusdem Academiae: Prodigium amoris mariani est, non solum velle quod gignit, nec solum gignere velle; sed et gignere, quia velit.

63. Nicolas, *La Vierge Marie*, 347n1.

But that term is also a vertex, a turning point, a counterpoint to the love of Father and Son. The term of the most perfect love of Father and Son ad extra in the Holy Spirit, because total, becomes in the Immaculate the starting point of a reaction, of an act of love on the part of creation equal and contrary to that of the Creator. Thus, the action of the Holy Spirit in his spouse culminates in the conception of the Word Incarnate in the womb of the Blessed Virgin one capable of rendering to the Father all that is or could be desired from creation, concretely in the sacrifice of that Son on the cross for the salvation of mankind.

Contenson[64] in his discussion of complement alludes to this as a reason for calling Mary the complement of the Trinity, but without the explanation provided by St. Maximilian. And in a confused manner the point seems imbedded in the criticisms addressed by Scheeben to the use of this title for Mary by seventeenth-century authors.[65] The term itself, he says, can have an acceptable meaning, but would seem rather inopportune, for in terms of what Mary brings to the Father and Holy Spirit, it is the Son Incarnate who becomes the term or complement of their relations *ad extra*, not Mary herself. Bittremieux[66] in responding to the criticism concedes the point, but insists that Mary in a subordinate way is also the complement of the Trinity, and that because within the Trinity the Son is already related to the other divine persons, the title quite naturally has come to be used only of the Blessed Virgin *de facto*.

By leaving aside the interpretation of complement in the sense of quantitative addition, and taking it first actively as the totality of divine perfection or love, terminating from eternity in the Holy Spirit, and distinguishing between action and reaction, point and counterpoint, we can grasp how *ad extra* the Blessed Virgin is the term of divine love coming forth, whereas in the return, the Word Incarnate, and ultimately through the Word Incarnate the Father, is the term of that love of the Immaculate (and of all united with her). For that love of the Holy Spirit in her leads to nothing less than the conception of the Son of God in her womb, and his rebirth in all of those born again by baptism. In her the Father and the Son love us; in her we love Father and Son, because in us she loves them. And in no other way does this occur for so has God willed.[67] In a word, the Immaculate is the complement of the Trinity, in order to be the Mother

64. Contenson, *Theologia Mentis et Cordis*, 233.

65. Scheeben, *Mariology*, vol. 1, 182–83.

66. Bittremieux, "Relationes," 30–31. In developing a reply to Scheeben's comment, Bittremieux seems to exclude the possibility of Mary being complement of the Trinity qua term of a divine mission.

67. *WK* 1168, 1310, 1326.

of God and mediatrix of all graces. For in her is the totality of divine love of Father and Son in the Holy Spirit, the very "ratio omnium donorum communicandorum, seu ratio donationis."

This interpretation also makes clear what is meant when the Immaculate is described as being introduced into the family circle of the divine persons, or forming with them a single chain: not in the sense of a fourth person added to the three, but in the sense of a complement *ad extra* as the Holy Spirit is *ad intra*, because as Immaculate she is the Spouse of the Holy Spirit. Thus, she reveals the mystery of the Trinity, and in making the Trinity present where she is present makes possible the economy of salvation.[68]

The Immaculate, then, is complement of the Trinity, "non propter additionem, sed propter distinctionem finalem seu terminantem."

3. St. Maximilian refers once to the use made by the Father of the church of this title. No doubt he had in mind the references adduced by Lépicier (and perhaps Campana, Terrien, and Nicolas) to illustrate the background of Mary's relations with the three divine persons, and brought into close relationship to the title complement by Lépicier, Campana and others, a term, however, only employed once before the sixteenth century in connection with our Lady, and then not as a title. In fact, and perhaps unwittingly, the use made of the title by St. Maximilian explains the connection between "having" the complement of the Trinity and "being" the complement of the Trinity, and why Bittremieux's remark that whatever Hesychius of Jerusalem meant by the term his use of it made it available for further development.[69] Because of the indwelling of the Trinity in the soul of Mary, so perfect and thus appropriated to the Holy Spirit in singular fashion,[70] Mary is the complement of the Trinity. Once the singular character of that indwelling in her is realized and seen to consist in the privilege of the Immaculate Conception, as St. Maximilian saw so clearly, and that that privilege is essentially bound up with the title mediatrix of all graces, it is only logical to interpret complement as a title, as well as a term, describing possession by God in the supernatural order, and in the Immaculate the basis of the spiritual and apostolic life for all others possessed by God.

But perhaps more than anyone else, though hitherto unmentioned in this discussion of complement by anyone, Saint Francis of Assisi is the most important antecedent in tradition for this interpretation.[71] For in first addressing Mary most holy as "Spouse of the Holy Spirit" in a thoroughly

68. *WK* 991 O.

69. Bittremieux, "Relationes," 18.

70. *WK* 1286; CK April 9, 1938.

71. Cf. Fehlner, "A Thesis," *CE* 6, chapter 2.

Trinitarian context, in stressing her uniqueness and fulness of grace in a way that can only be understood as indicating the Immaculate Conception, he immerses her in the bosom of the Trinity, in a way that can only be expressed logically as complement of the Trinity. The Antiphon for the Magnificat of the *Office of the Passion* composed by St. Francis, where this usage first occurs, in being recited by the early Franciscans wherever they were, led to its popularization and its widespread adoption outside Franciscan circles. Within the Order this title quickly became and remained, to the days of St. Maximilian, a constant of its Marian doctrine and devotion.[72]

Conclusion

In the hands of a saint a seemingly minor point of theology, considered by some as dated, and even questionable as to its prudence, can be the source of considerable enlightenment in regard to the deepest mysteries of faith. In particular, the discussion of this title helps to illustrate the profound insights into the mystery of salvation and of the Trinity provided by St. Maximilian's teaching on the Immaculate Conception, insights at once speculative and practical. Far from being dated, these are a providential anticipation of reflections which more and more since Vatican II are coming to be a major theme of Mariology, viz., Mary and the Holy Spirit.[73] Little attention has yet been given to the views of St. Maximilian; indeed, it has been suggested that these views have little relevance to the issues raised. The results of this study indicate quite the contrary: in the mystery of the Immaculate will be found not only a sure basis for avoiding errors and exaggerations, but the center of a new synthesis, amply justifying the description of these times since the definition of the Immaculate Conception as a dogma and the two Vatican Councils as the age of Mary, of the church, of the Holy Spirit. Of this age St. Maximilian has been declared the patron.

72. Fehlner, "A Thesis," *CE* 6, chapter 2. Cf. Pyfferoen and Van Asseldonk, "Maria Santissima."

73. Cf. *Maria e lo Spirito.*

5

Niepokalanów in the Counsels of the Immaculate

St. Maximilian once observed that the activities of the Immaculate from the first moment of her existence to the present on behalf of the church and of all members of the human family are little known and that a study of these "acta Immaculatae in universo mundo" would quickly fill a large library.[1] That observation of a half-century ago is still valid, and the need for such study, if anything, even more urgent now. Because the Immaculate is the mediatrix of all graces, her activity is at the very center of history in the age of grace, the final stage in the preparation for the coming and triumph of the Son of God. That observation is pertinent both to the first and second comings of the Savior and to the victory concluding each.

That this activity is not always immediately recognizable as such is perfectly true, and thus the task of discerning and interpreting those acts aright is not always easy. That, however, is not universally so, particularly since the proclamation of the dogma of the Immaculate Conception, a proclamation which in facilitating the recognition of these acts and of the person whose counsels they serve provides grounds for describing the period since 1854 as the age of the Immaculate.[2] And although the entire history of the church may be described as the age of the Immaculate, because the age of grace, there is a certain appropriateness in restricting that appellation to the time when the one whose name is Immaculate Conception, fulness of grace, is not only publicly recognized, but permeates every facet of the life of the church and of her members, thus strengthening her against the attacks of the serpent, making her ready to greet her Savior in glory. And it is in turn the striving after such perfection which in turn justifies the description of this present period as the age of the church.

---

1. *WK* 647.
2. *WK* 664, 1248; CK July 9, 1933.

One of the more significant interventions of the Immaculate in history since 1854, in a particularly significant year, 1917,[3] was to make the inestimable gift of her Militia to the church—and indeed to the entire human family, entrusting this to the care of the Franciscan Order, and consolidating that gift ten years later in the establishment of Niepokalanów, the friary that is her exclusive possession and property. Toward the end of 1927 there arose not far from Warsaw in Poland, through the work of St. Maximilian Kolbe and his confreres, a most unusual Franciscan friary, unusual and different from other friaries, not because in some way "unfranciscan," but because so perfectly Franciscan, as a Minister General of the Friars Minor Conventual, who visited Niepokalanów during St. Maximilian's tenure as Guardian there later testified under oath, that the ideal enshrined in its Rule was perfectly and thoroughly implemented there. Of no other friary could this superior make the same affirmation.[4] And if heroic correctly describes the kind of inner life and apostolic activity to which the Franciscan form of life points, then that word surely describes the tenor of life at Niepokalanów. The heroism of the life led there blossomed in a missionary effort unique in this century. If the size, vitality, rapidity of growth and permanent achievements of this friary, not only in Poland, but throughout the world, in less than fifteen years are any criterion, then Niepokalanów can only be regarded as miraculous in character, and therefore being in fact what St. Maximilian claimed it was, and must remain, the property and work of the Immaculate, a very special mercy for the consolation and salvation of souls in our difficult age.[5] At the heart of Niepokalanów is that love, greater than which none can be conceived, greater than which no one can have for his brother, the love of the Immaculate that was in the heart of St. Maximilian. Thus, it is only natural that the church, and indeed the whole world, should relate the martyrdom of Saint Maximilian to Niepokalanów and that Niepokalanów should have become after the shrine of our Lady of Czestochowa the premier sanctuary of Poland.

The difference which makes Niepokalanów so unusual a community and accounts for its heroic virtue is the observance of the M.I. Statute, more exactly at the level of M.I. 3, not only by each member of the community individually, but by the community as such. Niepokalanów is the M.I. 3 in the form of a Franciscan friary, i.e., where the Statute, as well as the Rule and Constitutions of the Franciscan Order, constitutes an obligatory,

---

3. Cf. Carroll, *1917*.

4. Hess, *Beatificationis et Canonizationis*, 533.

5. Domanski, "Niepokalanów." This is an important source for appreciating life at Niepokalanów as lived under St. Maximilian.

public norm, regulating the life of the community and of each of its members.[6] That Statute places this friary and each of its members totally and exclusively at the service of the Immaculate and of her cause, the conversion and sanctification of souls through the incorporation of the mystery of the Immaculate into their lives and the fabric of society, so much so that that friary exists solely for that purpose, and would cease to be Niepokalanów, did it not exist in that way, for that end.

That service can only be total, and therefore adequate, if it is the service of total consecration, whereby the consecrated becomes the "res et proprietas" of the Immaculate (whence the name Niepokalanów in Polish— property of the Immaculate). That consecration can only be totally effective where it is unlimited and unconditional apostolically as well spiritually. In terms of the inner life, in terms of a common form of life, in terms of missionary effort, this can only mean heroism. The heroic character thus imparted to Franciscan life, communal as well as personal, by the daily living of the Rule in the spirit of the M.I., is exactly what is necessary in the counsels of the Immaculate for securing her cause, the incorporation of her mystery into the life of the church. And it is also what secures the sanctity and vitality of the Franciscan Order, enabling its members to strive as well as aspire to be the greatest possible saints.

Almost from its beginning Niepokalanów met with opposition. That is hardly surprising. History is but the story of the conflict between the Woman and the serpent, and that the evident acts of the Immaculate in the world should attract the attention of the prince of this world and provoke his wrath is only to be expected. The absence of such attention would render them suspect. Moreover, those attacks, however inconvenient and painful to the servants of the Immaculate, cannot destroy either her or her work, indeed serve rather to promote it.[7] Nothing is so evident than this in the publicity and favor won for the cause of the Immaculate by the martyrdom of Saint Maximilian on the eve of the Assumption in the darkest of circumstances.

But there was another form of opposition, encountered almost from the beginning, far more dangerous than the attacks mounted from without by masons, Nazis and communists, because this opposition came from within the Order, and if once successful in attaining its objectives, would spell the end of Niepokalanów and constitute a mighty blow to the cause of the Immaculate in the world. That danger was the proposal to level the differences

6. *WK* 333, 336, 475.

7. Cf. Domanski, "Niepokalanów," 393ff. Neither Nazi nor Communist tyranny has been able to destroy Niepokalanów.

between Niepokalanów and the other friaries of the Order, that is to say by eliminating those features which made Niepokalanów the sole property of the Immaculate, to be used solely in her cause.

Such proposals were not always motivated by the same concerns. Some thought Niepokalanów too demanding and strict and that the daily sacrifice demanded by a heroic lifestyle should be a matter of personal option, rather than obligation, and hence sought to liken Niepokalanów to other friaries in the manner of observing the Rule.[8] Others, however, proceeded in an opposite direction: because of its exemplary character and productivity Niepokalanów should be available to reinforce common life and apostolic work elsewhere in its province, for example by educating in its seminaries the future friars of the province, by providing key personnel and resources in the promotion of other works of the Order.[9] Those so thinking sought to liken the discipline of other friaries to that of Niepokalanów.

But in both instances of leveling the essential feature of Niepokalanów would be eliminated: the observance of the M.I. Statute as a basis of community life, not as a Rule other than that of St. Francis, but as that whereby this friary is constituted in its totality the exclusive property of the Immaculate, to be used by her for her cause. The first tendency negates the Statute by placing personal limits on the degree of sacrifice total consecration may demand; the second does the same by restricting in practice the availability of the community for the work of the Immaculate. Whatever the pragmatic considerations rendering such proposals attractive and plausible, their theoretical justification rested on a major premise touching the need and importance of unity in any society. There cannot be a single Order, unless there is a single law observed by all members wherever they may be. The observance of the M.I. Statute in those friaries known as Niepokalanów introduces differences into the manner of leading Franciscan life and must either tend to the formation of a different kind of community, or introduce into the single community a divisive, sectarian spirit, in which one group might well consider itself holier than another.

For St. Maximilian the success of any proposal to "level" would be the equivalent of a tragic disaster, the implementation of a colossal error, with incalculable harm for the cause of the Immaculate, for the good of the church, the salvation of souls and the authentic tradition of St. Francis and of his Order. Thus, not only is the use of every licit means and available energy in defense of the true character of Niepokalanów permissible,

8. WK 325, 348.
9. WK 325, 449.

it is necessary.[10] That defense, as conducted by St. Maximilian himself, includes a sound apologetic, not directed polemically at the motives of his critics, nor organized about a superficial rebuttal based on pragmatic considerations, but grounded on a deep appreciation of the Immaculate as Mistress of history, the queen of heaven and earth, and of the place of Niepokalanów in her counsels.

The saint's defense is not, then, a criticism of the intentions of those who proposed to level the differences between Niepokalanów and the practice of Franciscan life elsewhere. Rather that defense is an explanation of a point those proposals failed to comprehend. In such proposals total consecration is to the Rule and Constitutions, what a private revelation or private devotion is to the teaching of the church, a matter of private faith rather than public law, binding on all. St. Maximilian, on the contrary, shows that total consecration can have a public place in the life of the Order, and indeed does occupy such a place in any Niepokalanów by definition. It can do so, without in any way changing or adding to the Rule, because the Immaculate as such is a public figure in the Order, its advocate and patroness. Qua Immaculate, she is the mediatrix of all graces and therefore mistress of history. The Order and her cause, as well as a principal instrument of that cause, the M.I., are not identical, but in her counsels they are nicely coordinated so that the distinctions do not divide, but rather perfect each other in that community known as Niepokalanów, in the words of St. Maximilian, the M.I. not attached to a friary, but in the form of a friary.[11] For that reason the friars and the Order can follow no better counsel than that of the Mother of good counsel in fostering M.I. 3 communities within and without the Order.

The Mistress of History

"Beatam me dicent omnes generationes." For St. Maximilian all history is but the fulfillment of this prophecy of the *Magnificat*. No interpretation of history is correct unless it takes into account the place which God has given to his mother in the plan of creation and of salvation. All generations viz., all history, must praise and glorify her "because he who is mighty has done great things for me," viz., given her a preeminent place above and before all other creatures.[12] She is preeminently a public figure, and hence her actions enjoy a special, key significance in the unfolding of history. Her "fiat" and her

10. *WK* 485.

11. *WK* 1380.

12. *WK* 1210, 1232, 1305.

actions in the entire world stemming from each of these, precisely because they are the actions of this person, the Immaculate, the mediatrix of grace, the mistress of history, constitute not only for individuals, but for communities, nations and the entire human family the coordinates for the interpretation of history. All this is but a logical and practical corollary of her position as mediatrix of all graces, a position she holds because she is the Immaculate Conception. Three considerations illumine this public role of the Immaculate as mediatrix of all graces and queen of heaven and earth.

All the actions of the Immaculate in history from the first moment of her existence center on two "fiats" of her will, that at the annunciation, on which the incarnation is conditioned, and that at the crucifixion, wherewith she accepted us as her children, and on which our salvation is conditioned.[13] In both instances the perfection and efficacy of that "fiat" is directly proportionate to the perfection of her will, i.e., to its sanctity or degree of conformity to the divine will. That conformity could not be more perfect in each specific choice, because it was so perfect in the first moment of her conception.[14] The sanctity of the first "fiat" made her the Mother of God and completed her consecration to the Son of God. No one could ever love him more perfectly. The sanctity of the second "fiat" made her Mother of the Church, and the term of our consecration, whereby we are able to love Jesus with the same purity of heart. Preserved free of all stain of original sin, she is at once the goal of the incarnation, and also an agent thereof. The perfect fruit of the perfect redemption, she is not only the fulness of grace, as no other saint, but for that very reason a source of grace for all saints.

Her unique relation to the Lord of history as its mistress rests secondly on the mystery of her name, Immaculate Conception, a mystery consisting in her espousals with the Holy Spirit, the Spirit of the Father and of the Son, the fruit of their mutual love in eternity, the eternal Immaculate Conception. She is, as it were, the personification of that Spirit, his visible instrument in pouring forth charity in our hearts.[15] It is that love that motivated creation and salvation. It is that love that is their goal. And hence, with the Incarnate Son, the Holy Spirit, the Paraclete-Advocate, acting through his spouse, the Immaculate, guides the course of history to the Son, and through the Son to the Father, viz., to the final consummation of the kingdom. That guidance is not a substitute for that of the head and Savior of the church, but

13. *WK* 1296. Cf. Fehlner, "Immaculate . . . Trinity," *CE* 6, chapter 3.

14. *WK* 643, 1232, 1331. Cf. Fehlner, "Immaculate . . . Trinity," *CE* 6, chapter 3.

15. *WK* 1326. Cf. Fehlner, "Immaculate . . . Trinity," *CE* 6, chapter 3.

the complement, as the procession and mission of the Holy Spirit is not the alternative to, but complement of that of the Son.[16]

Finally, the proximate goal of history is the glorification of the Immaculate: in Kolbean terms not only her recognition for the person whom she is, i.e., the recognition of her name, but the incorporation of that name into life, viz., our sharing in that perfect redemption through her and in her. The goal of history is the Immaculate, under the direction of the Immaculate. In this way the God who made us without us, does not justify us without our cooperation. Without the Immaculate such cooperation is beyond the reach of sinners. Through her merciful activity, essentially purificatory, we are capable of cooperating with our Savior in preparing for that final triumph, at once the glory of God and the everlasting bliss of the saints, the second coming of Jesus, just as the preparation which preceded his first coming passed through the Immaculate Virgin to reach its final term.[17]

Does such a view substitute a Mistress of history for the Lord of history, alone the Christ? Only, St. Maximilian would reply, if the will of the Immaculate is conceived as actually or potentially separate from God's will, i.e., in sin, however minimal for however brief a time. Just because She is the Immaculate, that is exactly what is never so, not because she is not a creature, *ex nihilo*, but because by grace she is so perfect a creature in her humility in her identification with the divine will, none more perfect being conceivable. That degree of perfection in her is a matter of the spiritual order. The possibility and the fact of such a degree of perfection in a creature is an aspect of the mystery of charity, where the perfect love of the triune God meets in the perfect love of a created person a response "equal and contrary."[18]

The Immaculate, precisely because the Immaculate, is not a supplement, but the complement of the Trinity. Inseparable from the three divine persons in the economy of salvation, and thus unlike any other created person, angelic or human, she shares their position as a unique figure in that economy and therefore in history.[19] Indeed her appearance in the world at her conception marks the line dividing the two great periods of history; the old dispensation and the new, or age of grace. Within that new age of grace, whether it be his first or his second coming the Savior comes to us through her and we go to him through her. That is what is meant

16. Fehlner, "Immaculate . . . Trinity," *CE* 6, chapter 3.

17. *WK* 508, 1310, 1326.

18. *WK* 634, 991 O, 1286, 1291, 1310, 1318. Cf. Fehlner, "Immaculate . . . Trinity," *CE* 6, chapter 3.

19. *WK* 603, 643.

when our salvation is said to be conditioned by her "fiat." In that "fiat" is the realization of divine mercy "in facto esse," the perfect fruit of a perfect redemption, of the mutual love of Father and Word Incarnate, viz., the Immaculate Conception. That mystery in the church is the radical basis for her mediatory character and fruitful work, why the holier and more fruitful the church becomes, adorned as a bride ready to meet her spouse, the more evident the mystery of the Immaculate in the life of the church. To the extent that our wills are one in the church with that of the Immaculate, we also share in that mystery of divine mercy and of the triumph of the Father's love for us in the victory of his Son.

In that consists the realization of the primacy of Christ, of the kingdom of the Sacred Heart, of Christ's mercy and love: not simply in his divinity, nor simply in the fact of the incarnation or of his exaltation alone in him, but in the Immaculate as the perfect fruit of a perfect redemption, and in all those united to her, i.e., who are her possession and property, as she is Christ's and Christ is God's.[20] That primacy of Christ's love in the Immaculate St. Maximilian, with so many great saints and doctors, contrasts with his primacy of judgment, a primacy verified precisely in those who are not one with the Immaculate.[21] This is the Father's will that we believe his Son and observe his commandments. This is accomplished through and in the Immaculate, through and in the church, which is the Immaculate's home and of which she is the mother. Salvation, not judgment, is the object of the Son's mission, or in Kolbean terms, the incorporation of the mystery of the Immaculate into the church. Judgment occurs only because a person refuses to believe and to do Christ's will, viz., refuses his mercy by refusing to have God's mother as his own.

The Immaculate, then, is a public figure in history together with her Son, because the consummation of Christ's kingdom is effected in the fruit of his work, the reign of the Immaculate Heart of Mary. This is the will of God, because she is the Spouse of the Holy Spirit, the eternal Immaculate Conception, in eternity the bond of love between Father and Son, and in history through the Immaculate the bond of love between the Father and the Word Incarnate, and all who are brothers and sisters of Jesus, guaranteeing them eternal life. The kingdom of mercy is wholly entrusted to her[22] because she is the Immaculate, not because Christ does not exercise mercy, or worse is not merciful, but because he is merciful and exercises mercy through her, the wisest and finest manner of exercising mercy in our midst.

20. *WK* 556, 643. Cf. 1 Cor 3: 22–23.

21. *WK* 339, 643, 1331.

22. *WK* 1331.

The mystery of the Immaculate occupies a central place in the true history (and philosophy of history) of the entire human family. Her "I am the Immaculate Conception" and her "fiat" are the counterpoint of the "I am who am" and the "fiat" of the Creator, a reaction of love perfectly balancing the action of divine love in creation.[23] The closer the world comes to its final goal, the more imperative becomes the need of "incorporating" that mystery of the Immaculate into every dimension of life, that the beauty of the communion of saints might be pleasing to the divine groom and the joy of the saints. In view of this the opposition met in this work of incorporation appears as a part of the final effort of the malignant one, begun at the beginning of history, to triumph over the Creator and Redeemer by ruining the fruit of his work, indeed by depriving him of its fruit. That the devil, the prince of this world, cannot do, precisely because the Immaculate is the fruit of that work. Her place in history as Queen is God's warranty, the sign placed in heaven and on earth, of victory over the dragon, namely that the primacy of the Word Incarnate can and will be realized in those who are one with the Woman, rather than with the prince of this world. Her power in history as mediatrix is but the exercise of her Son's, the implementation of Christ's love capable not only of converting those currently deceived by Satan, but of keeping them safe from his wiles and preparing them for the final coming of her Son. For against the Immaculate even the subtlest stratagems of the deceiver are powerless.[24] In the light of the mystery of the Immaculate, and of the opposition between her and the serpent from history's beginning to end, foretold in Genesis 3:15, the course of human events attains a singular clarity.

The theology here expounded is not merely theoretical; it serves as an eminently practical basis for contributing to the final triumph of the Savior, both by individuals and by communities. The key to such responsible cooperation is to be found in the will of the Immaculate, always one with that of her Son, and in conforming oneself in all things to her desires by allowing her to act in oneself, in Kolbean terms by making oneself the instrument of the Immaculate via total consecration.

The will of the Immaculate in history is neither in opposition to nor a substitute for the hierarchy of the church. Rather, as the visible representative of Christ in the church that hierarchy confirms for us the will of Christ in the Immaculate. Conversely, the Immaculate, as Spouse of the Holy Spirit, in extending the love and mercy of Christ to all souls, sees to it that her wishes receive the approval of Christ's vicars, particularly the successors of

---

23. *WK* 1283, 1284, 1318.

24. *WK* 1210, 1331.

St. Peter. Many examples might be adduced to illustrate how the work of the mediatrix of all graces in the economy of salvation is discerned and verified in an objective manner by means of the hierarchical structure of the church. Two works, however, without any doubt the fruit of her intervention in history, are particularly pertinent to an understanding of the historical role of Niepokalanów: the foundation and history of the Franciscan Order; and the recent establishment of the Militia of the Immaculate (M. I.), entrusted to the care of that same Order.[25] The link between these two works of the Immaculate came to be consolidated in those friaries known as "Niepokalanów," viz., the property of the Immaculate, her portion or "Portiuncula" wherein every person, resource, thought and action characteristically Franciscan is at the disposal of the Immaculate and employed by her exclusively for her cause. Why there should be a certain affinity between what St. Maximilian called the M.I. 3 and a Franciscan friary will illumine the place of Niepokalanów in the counsels of the Immaculate; in turn the understanding of Niepokalanów's place therein will reveal more clearly the ultimate purpose of all her activity in history: the reign of the sacred heart.[26]

The Franciscan Order in the Counsels of the Immaculate

Although only a sketch of the briefest kind, St. Maximilian has left a very profound outline of the history of the Order seen from the perspective of the Immaculate.[27] So viewed that history embraces two great periods, the first extending from the founding of the Order in 1209 to 1854, the year of the dogmatic definition of the Immaculate Conception; and the second extending from that year until the coming of Christ in glory. In the view of St. Maximilian the general purpose of the Order is the promotion of the primacy of Christ, a purpose, however, to be achieved in two stages: in the first by securing the public acknowledgment on the part of the church of the mystery of the Immaculate Conception as a truth of salvation; and in the second the incorporation of that mystery into every phase of life. By "acknowledgment" St. Maximilian understands not only intellectual, but affective acknowledgment as well in the form of devotion guided by sound doctrine. By "incorporation" he means a progressively deeper realization and implementation on a habitual basis of the practical import of this saving truth, both in the lives of individuals and in that of the entire church, an implementation by definition calculated to perfect the sanctity of believers and of the believing

25. *WK* 486.
26. *WK* 486, 1224.
27. *WK* 21, 486.

community and so to ready it for the coming of Christ, in the process depriving Satan of his power to manipulate, and hence providing the conditions
for an era of peace and justice and for the resurgence of a Christian culture.[28]
That purpose constitutes for St. Maximilian the ideal of the Order. The more
effectively it motivates the thoughts and desires and activities of the friars, the
more they will grow without limit in holiness and in the love of St. Francis,
and the more the Order itself, instead of growing weaker in the spirit as its
history advances, will be strengthened therein.

The justification of this vision of Franciscan history ultimately rests
on the intimate nexus between the mystery of the Immaculate and the primacy of Christ, between the activity of the mediatrix of all grace throughout
the world and the realization of the reign of the sacred heart, culminating
in his triumphant return in glory. On that basis the two coordinates of the
Franciscan vocation, viz., conformity to Christ crucified—the contemplative
coordinate, and repair of the church—the apostolic coordinate,[29] appear in
a marvelous harmony whose focal point is indeed the mystery of the Immaculate, and toward which all the characteristic features and activities of the
Order gravitate so as to form a very distinctive way of life.

St. Francis is known as the Seraphic Saint, because in him love for the
heart of the Savior reached such heights as to be described by Christ in a conversation with St. Margaret Mary Alacoque as the saint closest to his heart, a
point long meditated by St. Maximilian and one significantly bearing on the
foundation of the M.I. in 1917.[30] The degree of sanctity granted St. Francis
has a purpose and was not granted, so as to make other saints appear less
holy or less Christocentric,[31] but in order to make clear that the repair of
the church is to be understood not so much as the correction of abuses and
defects, a necessary task, but next to impossible of accomplishment when
undertaken directly as an end in itself, as the attainment of that same holiness in the Catholic community and in each of her members. That holiness is
none other than the mystery of the Immaculate, under whose guidance and
inspiration the task of repairing the church will be accomplished.[32]

The fact of the influence of the mediatrix of all graces at the center of the
Order's history justifies the division of that history into two great periods, not
in view of secular events, or even religious events and persons, but specifically
in view of the Immaculate and of her triumphs, and in terms of this those

---

28. Cf. Domanski, "Niepokalanów," 391–3.

29. Cf. Poulenc, "Conformità"; Szabo, "Chiesa."

30. Cf. Domanski, "La genesi," 248; Pius XI, *Rite Expiatis*, April 3, 1926, Introduction.

31. Pius XI, *Rite Expiatis*, April 3, 1926, Introduction.

32. Cf. Vatican II, *Lumen Gentium*, c. VIII, nn. 55, 56, 62, 65.

other events are interpreted. Thus, the survival and resurrection of the small-
est and humanly speaking weakest of the Franciscan families after the French
Revolution and secularizations of the nineteenth century is interpreted by St.
Maximilian as being effected by the Immaculate for a very definite objective.
That that family should have been chosen and so honored is a mystery of her
love, the motive and goal of that history.[33]

The object of her love in guiding the history of the Franciscan Order
is the triumph of her Son, viz., his primacy, and the repair of the church.
To make the mystery of that love of the Immaculate qua Immaculate for
these two objectives known and revered publicly and explicitly in and by
the church secures the proximate basis for attaining what is the ultimate
aim of the Order founded by St. Francis, the incorporation of the mystery
of the Immaculate into the life of the church. That goal, in the mind of
St. Maximilian, embraces two distinct aspects: the conversion of non-
believers and sinners to the church; and the sanctification of all members
of the church. It is an aim extending far beyond the confines of the Franciscan Order, but it is also an aim whose attainment cannot but affect the
character and degree of sanctity within the Order. If the miracle of the
stigmatization of St. Francis reveals the depth of his love for the Crucified
and the degree of conformity of his heart to that of Jesus, then the miracle
of the martyrdom of St. Maximilian reveals the way to the attainment of
that ultimate objective for which St. Francis was inspired to found his Order, viz., total consecration to the Immaculate.

Thus, the goal of the Franciscan Order is not one that is self-contained,
as though the "incorporation" of the mystery of the Immaculate into the
life of the church would make church and Order identical. Nor is it one that
can be accomplished without the help of the mediatrix of all graces. On the
contrary, the Order, in such a view of history, belongs to Christ and to the
Immaculate as their instrument, to be employed in one way by them before
1854 to obtain the dogmatic definition of the Immaculate Conception, and
in another way after 1854 to attain the incorporation of that mystery into
the life of the church. There is, then, an antecedent probability that the
Order will work in conjunction with other instruments of the Immaculate
for this end, and this in a way transcending the wisdom of this world. In
fact, the special, foreordained instrument for this is the M.I. The nexus
between the M.I. and the Franciscan Order rests on the role and activity of
the Immaculate in the economy of salvation, more proximately on the public recognition of that role, and of its certification in particular instances
by the church, rather than on the merely private faith and inspiration of

33. WK 485.

individuals. It is just that certification that has been given to the Franciscan Order and its Rule (whose interpretation is reserved to the pope), to the Militia of the Immaculate and to the fusion of the two in the approval of the M.I. 3 in the form of a Franciscan friary, wherever a Niepokalanów has been authorized to exist and in fact exists.

The Militia of the Immaculate

Founded in 1917 in Rome by St. Maximilian Kolbe, the M.I. enjoyed a spectacular growth during the lifetime of the saint, though in his estimation next to nothing in comparison with what it had still to accomplish in winning all souls, living or to live, for the Immaculate.[34] The heroic death and subsequent canonization of the founder without doubt is intended in the counsels of the Immaculate to call attention to and function as a sign of heavenly approval for the M.I. There still remains a considerable work to be done, however, in making clear the deepest significance of St. Maximilian's witness. Often enough the M.I. is thought by many to be but another in a long line of pious associations or sodalities, an extension of a traditional Franciscan spirituality in the circumstances of the early twentieth century, as belonging to that dimension of religious life commonly described as devotional, important but always to be adjusted and adapted to the context in which it is practiced. Others, perhaps linking the M.I. to the personal charism and mission of the founder, see it as primarily a coefficient of that charism, dated therefore by his times and the specific needs that charism met then, in want therefore of renewal and adaptation.

St. Maximilian would be the first to note that such considerations, however superficially plausible, rest on a serious misapprehension of fact. The M.I. is not his, nor is it the property of the Franciscan Order, to use and modify as it pleases. The M.I. belongs exclusively, totally, to the Immaculate, who is its principal foundress, the one who gave it and who defined its character to meet a specific need of the church in a period far from ending before Vatican II, indeed a need more urgent since.[35] Hence, it is not in the power of the Franciscan Order to whom it has been entrusted, as it was not in the power of the saint inspired to organize and launch it, to tamper with its essential character, but only to accept it and then nourish that gift of the Immaculate. The M.I. is not the coefficient of the Kolbean charism; rather that charism is a coefficient of the M.I., for which he was chosen by the Immaculate and favored with such great graces. His death as well as his

34. *WK* 1222, 1225, 1328.
35. *WK* 943.

life witnesses to the M.I. and as a sign of salvation can only be understood in relation to the M.I., to the kind of sacrificial love for souls, for all souls the Immaculate inspires and teaches.

The essential character of the M.I. distinguishing it from other Marian associations and movements can only be understood correctly in terms of its place in the counsels of her to whom it belongs. It is intended by her as an instrument whereby all souls will be conquered for her, viz., converted and sanctified, and the power of Satan rendered utterly useless.[36] That instrument does indeed take the form of an association, whose essence is constituted by "total consecration." Both essence and scope are expressed by the wearing of the miraculous medal, symbol of the power of the Immaculate to convert even the most indifferent and hostile of souls and to break the hold of Satan over them. In a word, the ideal of the M.I. is the Immaculate, ever closer union with the Immaculate, ever greater love and honor for the Immaculate, not simply by reinforcing the devotion of the faithful to the Immaculate, but by incorporating that mystery into life, in such wise as to make the mystery the cornerstone of Catholic spirituality, the practical basis for the sanctification of oneself and of others, and the cornerstone of an apostolate aimed at the conversion of non-believers, particularly those most ill-disposed to the church, such as masons and communists.[37] To conquer the whole world for the Immaculate is to make it her possession, to consecrate it totally to her in fact as well as in theory, so that in belonging as closely to her as she does to Christ, that world might be entirely His, to be returned by him to his Father.

Although the M.I. is a pious association for the laity, it is not simply another lay organization supplementing others with different ends. Much less is it the Marian dimension of the Third Order Secular of St. Francis, to be administered and/or guided by an officer of the First Order.[38] Even if statistically the M.I. is primarily a lay movement, because lay persons are most numerous in the church, in virtue of its form, total consecration, it embraces clergy and religious, individuals and communities, and hence is not simply a lay organization to be related to the Order as any such organization might be related in view of its canonical structure or assigned goals. The M.I. indeed employs every licit means of reaching its goal, but none of the activities it sponsors constitute its essence. It is indeed related to the Franciscan Order, but in a relationship *sui generis*, crystalized in what has come to be known

---

36. *WK* 1326, 1330.

37. *WK* 1329, 1330. Cf. *WK* 1168, 1210, 1220.

38. St. Maximilian clearly distinguished the Militia and the Third Order. The first is neither an adjunct of the second, nor a substitute for it. Cf. *WK* 136.

as Niepokalanów. On the one hand the M.I. is by no means an exclusively or primarily Franciscan association; it is intended to penetrate all sectors of society; lay, religious and clerical.[39] On the other hand no effective direction and promotion of the M.I. as defined by the Immaculate has ever occurred apart from that centered in a Niepokalanów. Niepokalanów, then, assumes a role of central importance, both for the distinctive features of the M.I. as a truly Catholic movement and for the central purposes of the Franciscan Order at the present time.

The circumstances and context of the founding of the M.I. provide clues as to the nature of that affinity between the M.I. and the Franciscan Order intended by the Immaculate. Of all those circumstances bearing on the formation of the M.I. ideal in the mind of St. Maximilian and leading to the establishment of the M.I. in an "upper room" of the International College of the Order in Rome, surely the Franciscan exerted a considerable influence.[40] For the M.I. was founded by a Franciscan in a Franciscan context and entrusted to the Franciscan Order by the Immaculate, not because the M.I. is only or primarily for Franciscans, for it is intended for everyone; but among other reasons to make possible the comprehension of its nature and purpose.

At the heart of the M.I. ideal, firstly, is the mystery of perfect love; of God and of neighbor, so wonderfully disclosed in Sts. Francis and Maximilian. Such love is not perfect except in the degree it entails conformity with the Crucified, i.e., sacrifice for the same motives and for the same objectives as Jesus died.[41] Such conformity is only perfect when in fact it has the purity of the love which is in the heart of the Immaculate for Christ, a purity only attainable under her influence as mediatrix of all graces.[42] The love of St. Maximilian was so perfect in death, not simply because he gave his life for another, but because he gave his life as Christ gave his. That he could do at the end of his life, because during his life he had become so perfectly the possession of the Immaculate, and so perfectly reflected that sacrificial love in even the minutest circumstances of a common life defined by heroic observance of poverty. Saint Maximilian loved Jesus with the heart of the Immaculate; or better she loved Jesus with

39. *WK* 991 Q.

40. Cf. Domanski, "La genesi," 248–51, 259–63.

41. *WK* 643, 1190, 1303, 1326. St. Maximilian repeatedly calls attention to the original penitential character of the Franciscan Order and its connection with the pardon of sins and mercy of God, and the appeal of the Immaculate at Lourdes for penance. Cf. *WK* 486, 1297.

42. *WK* 1310, 1326.

his heart purified.[43] To aspire to be the greatest saint possible, as did St. Maximilian,[44] implies no invidious "holier than thou" comparisons, but an ever more intimate union with the Immaculate, the greatest of saints in loving Jesus and therefore the humblest.[45] It is that union that explains how St. Francis attained such conformity with Christ as to typify this for the entire church. It is in the promotion of such love universally that the repair of the church requested of Francis by the crucified is achieved. Thus, the repair of the church in the final sense effectively postulates the "incorporation" of the mystery of the Immaculate into life, i.e., the progressive conquest of the world for her by subtracting souls from the influence and power of the prince of this world, and this under the immediate direction of the Immaculate, always efficacious when deployed. This is just what the M.I. via total consecration is intended to accomplish.

For St. Maximilian the coordination of the M.I. and the Franciscan Order as regards their common objectives is rooted in the counsels of the Immaculate. The work of the Order as an instrument of the Immaculate in promoting the primacy of Christ, beginning with St. Francis, initiated a Marian movement in the church distinctive both for its character and for its impact. That movement, nourished at each of its critical junctures by the Order, culminated in the triumph of 1854. And that work, begun at St. Mary of the Angels, where St. Francis came to understand Christ's call under the guidance of her whom he named the Advocate of his Order, has rightly come to be symbolized by the Portiuncula indulgence, the sign of that super abundance of divine mercy and pardon for all in the most trying of circumstances, arranged by the mother of mercy.[46] It is in view of that mercy that St. Maximilian explains the intimate, perfect unity of will of the Immaculate qua Immaculate with the divine will.[47] One might say the dogma explains the meaning and purpose of what the famous indulgence symbolizes.

The ultimate purpose of that indulgence, however, is not attained with the proclamation, but only with what St. Maximilian calls the full "incorporation" of the dogma into life. In this the Order, in the plans of the Immaculate, will have a special role, one central to all its other responsibilities, and that role is the support and promotion of her Militia. Like the famous Indulgence, the Militia St. Maximilian saw as the special

43. *WK* 508, 647, 1310.

44. *WK* 647.

45. *WK* 1232.

46. CK July 23, 1933. Cf. Fehlner, "Mary in the Franciscan," *CE* 3, chapter 5; "Saint Francis and Mary," *CE* 3, chapter 3. On the Portiuncula and its link with the M.I. cf. *WK* 1099.

47. *WK* 339.

instrument entrusted to the Order for the salvation of souls and the good of the church, as well as the prosperity of the Order itself. For without the M.I. the Order would be hard put to maintain its spirit, much less to realize in any proper manner the "repair of the church" in the triumph of the cross. Compared to the M.I. the famous Indulgence is but a foreshadowing of the mercy to be granted in days to come.

The affinity of the M.I. and the Franciscan Order is also evident in the choice of times for the accomplishment of her aims by the Immaculate, particularly with respect to the repair of the church. Thus, the proclamation of the dogma occurred not before, but after the French Revolution, when the "secularization" symbolized by the ethos of freemasonry was in full swing and when the typical reaction of the "liberated" adult to the proclamation of the dogma of the Immaculate Conception was one of disbelief that anyone could possibly imagine such events to be anything but empty gestures of a dying piety. The world was growing cold, yet after the proclamation the flame of that love for the Savior and his teaching grew bright so quickly that even the enemies of the church could no longer ignore her in cold indifference. Indeed, as a further illustration of the power of the Immaculate, St. Maximilian indicates her choice of the smallest and the then weakest, humanly speaking, of the Franciscan families to be the guardian of her cause and of its subsequent progress, and suggests that the Immaculate intended thereby a striking example of her power at the service of her love for the entire Order and the church.[48]

As the Order of St. Francis may be regarded as an antidote to the vice of self-will, particularly as that takes the form of a choice of the goods of this world in place of those of the life to come, so the M.I. was entrusted to that Order at the very moment when the fruits of that self-will, assiduously cultivated by the prince of this world, were beginning to manifest themselves with satanic violence against the church and against all those faithful to the teaching of the Savior. The year 1917 chosen by the Immaculate to found her Militia was the fourth centenary of Luther's revolt against the authority of the church, the second centenary of freemasonry, and the year of the October revolution in Russia where a "militia" of another kind established itself in control of a Christian people and proceeded to abuse that people as a base of operations for conquering the world for another master.

However unconnected these events might superficially seem, one religious, one secular, one totalitarian, they are in St. Maximilian's vision linked by a single, common error, insinuated by a single source, the father of lies: truth in matters of religion and the morality based on it are radically a matter

48. WK 485.

of personal faith and private judgment or choice alone, a matter solely of the interior order, in no way shaped or regulated by any authority or law outside the experience of the human individual or community, an error first passing under the guise of piety, then of pleasure, and finally of tyranny, in each stage ever more determined and violent in its efforts to destroy the church of Christ, and to overturn the rock upon which Christ erected that church during its time of pilgrimage.[49] Thus St. Maximilian realized the particular significance of the anti-clerical demonstrations with satanic overtones, sponsored by the freemasons in Rome during 1917.

That error, correctly described by John Henry Newman as "liberalism in religion," the view that one religion is as good as another, because no religion is true, all being matters of private taste,[50] initially was introduced under the allure of "private inspiration and judgment" in the interpretation of sacred Scripture, in the name of church reform. Subsequently, to remedy the problems of sectarian division in religious matters, it developed into a system of tolerance, and pleasure, without the constraints of any authority. Any religion might be practiced, so long as it made no claim to teach dogmatically the truth that is one only. And then, when the abuse of unrestrained freedom in intellectual, cultural, economic and political affairs had sufficiently matured, that error showed its true face in the form of a tyrannical social system which can only be described as the enslavement of the human family. The refusal of obedience to God who is the truth and one only, and to his church, which is one only and proclaims the truth authoritatively, is not freedom as it is made to seem at first, but license and then slavery.

Contemplating this error, the poison of self-will, variously appearing as naturalism, modernism, secularism, St. Maximilian sought a means to make the truth, viz., of obedience to God and to his Son known and accepted most of all by those most deeply caught in this snare. Good strategist that he was, he realized that if the "troops" could be detached from the "general," the latter would be powerless to promote and enforce his errors. The prince of this world would be rendered powerless. Under the inspiration of the mediatrix of all graces, the leader of God's hosts, he came to understand, while meditating on the miraculous conversion of the Jew Alphonse Ratisbonne, the means and methods to be deployed in this battle with the ancient liar.[51]

The principal instruments of the devil for the promotion and enforcement of his power are twofold, and apparently contrary to one another: independence of church authority, particularly that of St. Peter, promoted

49. *WK* 1328, 704 note 1.
50. Newman, *Addresses*, 64–69.
51. Cf. Domanski, "La genesi," 251–54.

in every sector of human endeavor, within every stratum of society, even within the church via the corruption of morals; and totalitarianism. The first is made alluring by an offer of pleasure to follow on the acquisition of autonomy from authority in principle; the second is made to seem attractive in the name of idealism and the need for justice. The first in fact appeals to greed, the second to envy. The means of freeing souls from the tyranny of this error are spiritual, not in any vague sense, but in a definite form provided by the invincible Woman of Genesis, viz., the M.I. If the serpent insinuates, as he has from the formation of the first man and woman, the superior pleasure of a pseudo-freedom from divine law, viz., disobedience on principle, culminating in religious indifferentism as the only basis of a mature existence, with intellectual and moral relativism as its corollary, the Immaculate proceeds in contrary fashion inculcating and demanding unconditional service to the truth who is her Son, via total consecration to herself and the practice of penance. It is an approach that to the materialist, like that of David to Goliath, will always seem ridiculous, but in fact always works, because it is the appeal of true love to sacrifice. For if the appeal to self-indulgence is, as it were, the "come-on" to adopt a radically indifferent (and unnatural) stance in religion, it is one which because of its falsehood can only end in social tyranny.[52] Whereas the appeal to sacrifice via consecration to the Immaculate can not only stop, but can also reverse the process in minds and hearts, when that true love is contemplated visibly in the form of a true paradise on earth—Niepokalanów, the garden of the Immaculate, and where the real connection between sacrifice and joy, disobedience and tyranny, can be perceived.[53] For true love in its highest form is capable of moving sinners as well as saints. Such a love, when it is perfect, as it is in our Savior, is truly irresistible, except by a Satan or one totally in his power. Short of that it will always elicit a response in love and a desire for conversion. It is our Lord's will that such love should be encountered in his Mother, and in all those purified by her to be his brothers and channels of that grace.[54] Hence the urgency of the church's mission and the need for saints to undertake it. Such saints will be available, if they are formed by the Immaculate. That Christ should have so ordained is eminently wise, and that wisdom is nowhere so evident than in the humility of obedience, first shown in faith, exercised via the teaching of his vicars, and consummated in charity, done to him in the neediest of his brethren, not only by sharing, but by taking their place in suffering, not so that they might live a while longer on earth, but so

52. WK 1328.
53. WK 184, 1222.
54. WK 1326.

that they might share the hope and promise of life everlasting and have the courage to observe faithfully the commandments of God.

It is that reversal through the unmasking of false love by sacrifice which spells the ruin of Satan's stratagems for subverting the primacy of Christ in the hearts of men and impeding the repair of the church in preparation for the final coming of her head in glory. If the form of consideration based on a comparison of objectives illustrated an affinity between the M.I. and the Franciscan Order in view of a perfect conformity to Christ, this second consideration illustrates an affinity in relation to the repair of the church. That sacrificial love which poverty in common is designed to foster for Christ and for his brethren the M.I. focuses on the mystery of the Immaculate and her merciful plans for the conversion and sanctification of all, and the cultivation in all of a spirit rooted in and reflecting the love of her own heart for Jesus.

Finally, the affinity between the M.I. and the Franciscan Order is particularly evident in the manner of implementing the M.I. in the third degree. Total consecration, the essential condition for participation in the M.I., is by definition unconditional. But in so far as that consecration is translated into practice of an apostolic kind directed toward the conquest of the world as an instrument of the Immaculate, St. Maximilian distinguished three degrees of zeal.[55] In each of them the consecration is unlimited, but in fact for various reasons there remain objective limits in the first two degrees beyond which the individual or group in question is not available for service to the cause of the Immaculate as such, viz., for activity in promotion of the specific objectives of her Militia.

The first degree, M.I. 1, is that in which the knight exercises his own discretion, according to the dictates of prudence and conscience, in choosing and implementing work or projects to be done for the cause of the Immaculate. But neither the choice itself, nor that which might be chosen, entail any obligatory character. Lack of any such definite obligation to translate the consecration into specific works, performed singly or in cooperation with others constitutes a limit on the effectiveness of the M.I. as an instrument for the conquest of the world for the Immaculate. Whatever its reason, such a limit does not diminish the value and importance of total consecration for the spiritual life of the knights; it does, however, point to other dimensions or degrees of the M.I. without which the movement as a whole will remain incomplete and relatively unproductive.

---

55. WK 402, 1272, 1330. Cf. Domanski, "Lo Spirito"; Domanski, "Milizia dell'Immacolata."

A second degree, the M.I. 2, attends to the social dimensions of the M.I., not because the M.I. 1 involves no elements of association, but precisely in order to give the social form of the M.I. a more definite and stable character in view of specific tasks to be undertaken by the members in concert. The organization and scope of such groups is to be well defined in specific statutes and by-laws, according to which the activities of the members are to be directed and carried out, and according to which each is obliged, but beyond which there exists no further obligation. The limit in no wise diminishes the value of the total consecration, but the organization of the group does not in fact remove every limitation on the availability of the group to the Immaculate as an instrument of her cause. It is the unlimited availability of the M.I. to the Immaculate to use solely at her discretion, without conditions placed antecedently by others, however legitimate, for her cause that is at the heart of the effectiveness of the M.I. at every apostolic level.

Thus St. Maximilian distinguishes a third degree, the M.I. 3, in which the knight makes himself available for unlimited service of the Immaculate, not at his discretion, but at that of the Immaculate, and not within the limits dictated by human prudence, or obligations deriving from other states of life, or limits dictated by statutes or risk of life. In a word, M.I. 3 is essentially characterized by the willingness and constant effort to practice heroic virtue habitually in the cause of the Immaculate, to never lose an opportunity to use any licit means on behalf of that cause.

The exercise of such zeal is undoubtedly capable of many forms, not excluding participation in an M.I. 2 group. But such a presence in an M.I. 2 group does not thereby change the essentially limited character of that group as an instrument of the Immaculate. Nor does the willingness to be available to the Immaculate at her sole discretion always resolve by itself in every instance the problem of discerning what in fact is her will. Thus, the implementation of M.I. 3 potential, so central to the actualization of the M.I. as the effective instrument for incorporating the mystery of the Immaculate into life at every level quite logically points to a social unit wherein not simply the individual members, but the community as such is totally, without restriction, at the disposal of the Immaculate for her cause. This points quite naturally to a religious community wherein a form of life shaped by heroic sacrifice and governed by principles of supernatural obedience at once maximizes the fruitfulness of each member in the hands of the Immaculate and serves to channel her will effectively and objectively so as to bear directly on the work of the community and of its members. The essential point cannot be stressed too often: the fruitfulness of the work of the M.I. depends not primarily on the work itself, no matter what the talents of the workers, or on the quality of the organization, but rather on the degree in which both factors are available to the Immaculate, in such wise that she works through and with them. Where that availability is unconditional, and the Immaculate in fact employs such an instrument, the results will be stupendous, as in fact occurred in the Niepokalanów under the direction of St. Maximilian. This is but a practical corollary of the mystery of the Immaculate as mediatrix of all graces. If our wills, individual and collective, are as one with hers as hers is with the divine will, then our work and our cooperation, with the Immaculate and with each other, will no longer be merely natural, but the instrument of divine omnipotence at the service of divine mercy in pursuit of souls.

It is this aspect of cooperation with the mediatrix of grace that Niepokalanów in fact supplied, and thereby became the natural center of the movement and the archetype of total consecration, a kind of vision of paradise and the joy of the communion of saints. It is not to be inferred from this that only members of Niepokalanów can be M.I. 3, or that only Franciscan communities can be cities of the Immaculate. Nonetheless, the choice of a Franciscan community by the Immaculate to be the archetype of the movement is not without instruction for understanding both the M.I. and Franciscanism.

Niepokalanów

Niepokalanów arose in 1927 to meet an immediate need of the M.I.: adequate quarters for a publishing house, one of the principal means of providing unity and direction among the members of the fast growing Militia of the Immaculate.[56] Under the terms of its erection that friary was to serve exclusively the needs of the Militia, that is to say to be as its name implies the exclusive possession of the Immaculate, in which for this reason she might function as proprietress and her eucharistic Son be "citizen no. 1."[57] In so founding Niepokalanów, however, the event of its foundation becomes not simply another in the history of the M.I., but obtains a special place as that whereby in fact the M.I. was so consolidated as to achieve the results intended by the Immaculate. Wherever other communities of this kind have been established and conducted in the same manner, similar marvelous results are not slow in appearing.

It is important to underscore the purpose for which Niepokalanów was established: the service of the Immaculate, not the reform of the Order. In fact, however, the renewal of Franciscan life in the perfect observance of

56. *WK* 1222.
57. *WK* 313, 314, 1239.

the Rule and Constitutions naturally followed upon this, because without a heroic observance of the Rule, Niepokalanów would not be itself the possession of the Immaculate, completely at her disposition, and its members would not be living fully their total consecration. The form of that heroic observance is but the result of fusing the dedication of an M.I. 3 spirit with the Rule and Constitutions as the basis of community life, as the obligatory norm of life at Niepokalanów. Without that obligatory character the total consecration can hardly be described as unlimited in every respect; without the statute of the M.I. 3 the community can hardly be described as totally at the service of the Immaculate.

The nature of the Franciscan friary is not changed thereby. Nothing divisive or sectarian is introduced into the Order, although the dedication of the inhabitants of Niepokalanów, like anyone genuinely practicing virtue, do become an example of goodness for others. That example, however, has nothing of the sanctimonious about it, for the discipline observed is not an end in itself, but to an end, in this case ever closer union with and ever more zealous service of her who is the zenith of humility and simplicity, the Immaculate. That this discipline in theory should include those visible or external elements traditionally associated with the Franciscan Order and with heroic observance of the Rule of St. Francis should not suggest hypotheses about "externalism" and "rigid uniformity," because no religious tradition is purely interior; wherever it appears, its unity will quite naturally include a typical uniformity in discipline as its form of expression. That uniformity at Niepokalanów is but the conjunction of total dedication or consecration of self to the Immaculate with Franciscan poverty, the outer form of this inner heroism.[58]

The objective of that heroism is the cause of the Immaculate, anywhere in the world, in any circumstances, even the worst humanly speaking, including those entailing an immediate risk of life. In a word that heroism is missionary in nature and thrust, nor could it be otherwise and still be described as total service in the cause of the Immaculate.[59] Hence, the primary difference between Niepokalanów and other friaries, as St. Maximilian repeatedly stressed, rests in the removal of that restriction chapter 12 of the definitive *Rule* of St. Francis places on the power of the superior to assign a friar to a mission in the strict sense without the friar's prior agreement. Such a restriction does not exist at Niepokalanów.[60] In effect a friar

---

58. WK 299, 348. When that occurs, the various Franciscan families will rediscover their unity and no longer argue over poverty, but practice it perfectly. Cf. WK 991 R.

59. WK 475, 512, 603.

60. WK 300, 398, 399.

at Niepokalanów is asked to live a form of life, adapt his lifestyle, even in minor particulars to the requirements of a missionary assignment for which he must be habitually prepared. That is why St. Maximilian required a special training, in special seminaries, for anyone desirous of joining Niepokalanów.[61] This is also why those unwilling or unable to sustain this form of life were asked to go elsewhere. The heroic by definition transcends the natural capacities and tendencies of human nature, and without the specific graces of the M.I. and a willing acceptance of the mode of life these imply, life at Niepokalanów as it should be is not possible.

This difference between Niepokalanów and the other communities of the religious order to which it belongs is not a difference of ends or of nature, but of the degree of perfection by which that community is intent upon one particular end that is central. It is the contention of St. Maximilian that the goal of Niepokalanów is indeed the central aim of the Franciscan Order, and that the position of the Immaculate in the economy of salvation not only justifies such intensity, viz., total consecration in her cause to such a degree that diversion of any resources to other ends, however good, by the superiors is an act of injustice, but that the degree of perfection in the observance of the *Rule* will be of the purest kind, because of the mystery of the Immaculate.[62]

That difference in degree of perfection or intensity in the pursuit of a central goal of Franciscanism manifests itself in three features of the Franciscan way of life, and this in a manner eminently practical for maximizing the human contribution to the cause of the Immaculate.

First, poverty.[63] The practice of poverty at Niepokalanów entails the reduction of all personal needs to the bare minimum and the elimination of any mere convenience of a personal kind, together with the observance of perfect common life. So practiced it is the means of attaining in fact that spirit of sacrifice typical of a love "usque ad victimam" and which conforms one so intimately to the crucified. Apostolically, it is the means by which great and stupendous projects are undertaken, "capitalized" and administered, with the most sophisticated of equipment in the cause of the Immaculate without in any way compromising the exactitude wherewith poverty is observed personally and in common. Paradoxically, that exactitude in the practice of poverty is the "capital"[64] of the Immaculate by which great projects, such as the complex publishing houses and

61. WK 475.
62. WK 314, 439, 991 R.
63. WK 300, 339, 486.
64. WK 299.

communications media, as well as missions, are supported and become financially viable. Poverty functions as a sacramental symbol, a visible sign of a unique presence in that community, worthy of respect. It is that presence of the Immaculate and of her Son, however vaguely grasped by others without, that serves as a beacon guiding their generosity toward Niepokalanów for the sake of the Immaculate. Poverty conceived as an aspect of unconditional dedication to the Immaculate becomes in fact the effective sign of the one who is the "Omnipotentia supplex" and the means by which she works the miracle of Niepokalanów. A miracle, of course, is a work of grace, something not to be taken for granted, and something for which to be deeply grateful and appreciative.

Second, obedience.[65] The heroic character of life at Niepokalanów is also evident in the practice of obedience, one placing no limit on the scope of legitimate commands of the superiors, or in the perfection, exactitude, generosity and imagination to be engaged by the subject in executing the tasks assigned. There is no doubt that the obedience demanded is that of a soldier, but one who is a knight, whose love for his commander knows no limits, nor suffers any doubts, because his commander enjoys a wisdom and a power fully justifying such confidence. The personal views and interests of the subject are never to be so presented as in any way to influence the decisions of the superiors representing the supreme commander of Niepokalanów, not in the name of blind obedience qua blind, but in view of not allowing personal bias of any kind to limit the wishes of the Immaculate. Obedience at Niepokalanów, then, is not so conceived as to exclude responsibility, intelligence and initiative, but to place all this wholly at the direction of the Immaculate rather than of self. This is only possible because the will of the Immaculate is one with that of God, and because she occupies a unique place in the economy of salvation as mediatrix of all graces. As poverty is not an exercise in misery at Niepokalanów, but plays a very crucial role in a very sensible plan for the repair of the church, so obedience is not an exercise in slavery, but a very intelligent exercise of responsibility in the love of God and of neighbor, responsibility to the Immaculate. Both poverty and obedience are as reasonable as the faith exercised in their practice, a faith whose object is the credibility of God's word, of the Immaculate's word to care for those consecrated to her and to use the decisions of the superiors as a channel for making God's will known in the service of her cause. For Niepokalanów to work it is enough for subjects and superiors to be faithful in the performance of their duty.

65. *WK* 339, 486, 487.

Third, the spirit. Permeating all these elements of Franciscan life fully at the service of the Immaculate is a distinctive spirit, one of perfect charity for God and for neighbor, of profound joy in adoring through and with the Immaculate the Son of God and her Son, citizen number one of Niepokalanów, the prisoner of love ever present in the sacrament of the altar.[66] Neither poverty nor obedience nor discipline (the fusion of the first two) are ends in themselves, but means of attaining the spirit of sacrificial love "usque ad victimam." Niepokalanów, then, is not only the effective instrument of the Immaculate in directing and promoting her cause throughout the world, the natural center and headquarters of that missionary movement,[67] but is archetypical as well of the paradise to come, a kind of foretaste of the divine family life, a more than effective countermagnet to the false allurements of "liberalism in religion" and the deceptive idealism of the secular "paradise of the working classes."[68] At Niepokalanów both aspects of total consecration: the interior of union with the Immaculate, and the exterior of work for her, both without limits, are harmoniously integrated, not simply in theory, but in practice. And that practice is also the integration of the contemplative and apostolic dimensions of the Franciscan calling: conformity with the Crucified in the service of the church. Niepokalanów is an exemplification of the Militia of the Immaculate as "a global vision of Catholic life under a new form, consisting in its link with the Immaculate, our universal mediatrix with Jesus."[69]

It is this spirit that makes Nepokalanów so totally the Immaculate's and thus totally Christ's, and thus totally the Father's in the manner they desire.[70] That spirit is the spirit of sacrificial charity, which is distinctive of the holy family at Nazareth as it is distinctive of the paradise to come. That distinctiveness makes that family not less human, but more so, not merely in an idealistic fashion, but in fact. So too, when this spirit appears in any Franciscan community, it will have just those distinctive disciplinary features touching the practice of poverty and obedience found in Niepokalanów under the guidance of St. Maximilian. Nor is there any valid reason to think any other Niepokalanów could do ought but follow that tradition and still remain a Niepokalanów, except nominalistically. To do otherwise is to repudiate an inheritance whose source is the Immaculate, not simply another friar.

66. *WK* 1239. Cf. the many texts in Domanski, *Per la Vita.*
67. *WK* 1376.
68. *WK* 1222.
69. *WK* 1220.
70. *WK* 508, 1284.

Nor is there any reason to fear that such differences will divide the Order, any more than the asceticism of any missionary is objectively a cause of division for those not sharing his form of life. Quite the contrary, differences stemming from a more heroic observance of the Rule tend to unite the friars of the Order at a deeper level, provided these differences are the coefficient of a deeper charity and profound humility. For charity, the more perfect it is, comes more promptly to exercise itself humbly and sacrificially, and because it is by nature unitive,[71] tends in that form to attract and unite more. Why this should be so at Niepokalanów, how St. Maximilian came to live and die for a love and with a love greater than which none can have, find their explanation in the mystery of the Immaculate. Ask her for that explanation, he would tell us.[72] Each of the distinctive disciplinary features of Niepokalanów, far from being an exercise in zealotry, is an index of true love and fidelity. It is love in this form that eventually will lead to the full "marianization" of the *Constitutions* and not only to a deeper unity of charity among the friars of one Franciscan family, but of all Franciscan families.[73]

St. Maximilian was very insistent on the priority of the interior life.[74] It is often wondered how he could reasonably aspire to unite with an intense practice of contemplation, an equally demanding involvement in the work of the apostolate and in the direction of the worldwide M.I., the first requiring great stability, the second just as great adaptability. The secret, again, is the Immaculate. And what is true of the original Niepokalanów, will be true of any community that implements in its life the M.I. 3 statute. The level of perfection in that community will attain marvelous heights as to make it abundantly fruitful, according to its particular character, in serving the cause of the Immaculate. The mixed character of Franciscan life, simultaneously contemplative and active, makes it, once fused with the M.I.3 statute in the service of the Immaculate, an apt instrument in the direction and promotion of the M.I.

Whatever the service to the cause of the Immaculate, the opportunity to render this service is not something the Immaculate owes us, but something we owe her out of charity and gratitude. For in the view of St. Maximilian even the greatest saints were unworthy of themselves to render even a small service of love to the Mother of God.[75] How great must be her love for us to request our cooperation with her in the M.I. It is only

71. *WK* 1229.
72. *WK* 1168.
73. *WK* 485, 991 R.
74. *WK* 878, 991 Q, 1210, 1306.
75. CK August 22, 1940.

in this perspective that St. Maximilian's firm and unyielding opposition to "leveling" must be seen. It is one thing for the Immaculate to bring Niepokalanów to an end; it is quite another for the friars to do this by radically redefining it on their own initiative.

Leveling

At Niepokalanów the friars must not aim merely at being as holy as St. Francis, or as St. Maximilian, but at a love of God without limit—as in fact the Immaculate loves her Son.[76] Such a way of life requires an adequate preparation, a distinctive form, and a competent direction, i.e., a distinctive system of formation, a heroic observance of poverty and perfect common life, and a system of supernatural obedience, one in which the motive of obedience is the authority of God alone, and the commands are given solely in view of the cause of the Immaculate. The first is for the sake of the second, and the second for the sake of implementing the will of the Immaculate in the service of her cause. Because of their interconnection, "leveling" applied to any one of these points is bound to affect the others.

First, as regards the system of formation St. Maximilian considered necessary to the survival and growth of Niepokalanów and to the foundation of other Niepokalanów throughout the world.[77] That training must be distinct because it is geared to meet the needs of Niepokalanów as the "res et proprietas" of the Immaculate. To refuse to Niepokalanów the right to provide such preparation is equivalent to a denial that the distinctive features of Niepokalanów have any place within a Franciscan context, i.e., is tantamount to "leveling the differences." So too, to make the educational system of Niepokalanów operate according to standards perhaps adequate for the observance of the Rule elsewhere, but clearly insufficient as a preparation for a heroic missionary life in the service of the Immaculate, is the equivalent of "leveling."

In the final analysis St. Maximilian's defense of a system of formation appropriate to the needs of Niepokalanów stands or falls on the validity of his defense of Niepokalanów as a distinct, but not divisive manner of observing the Rule of Saint Francis. Such a form of life, as a coefficient of a love for the Immaculate and for her Son, far from dividing will unite; and far from making the graduates of its program of formation less loyal and fraternal, will make them more so.

76. WK 647.
77. WK 475.

Second, as regards differences of discipline, St. Maximilian did not insist on certain disciplinary practices as ends in themselves, nor did he fail to recognize the need to adapt externals to meet changed circumstances affecting more effective methods and organization of work or the health of the sick friars. What he did not admit as grounds for such adaptations were considerations reducible to the convenience of the friars, nor did he admit as licit changes in discipline affecting the priority of the interior life, or those practices invariably associated with the observance of the Rule and maintenance of the common good.[78]

No one could seriously regard differences in disciplines resulting from licit adaptation of externals for sound spiritual and/or apostolic motives as a source of division within an Order. If it should be the occasion of disunity, that is because other factors are undoubtedly operative. But neither are differences of the second type, resulting not from adaptation so much as from insistence on that uniformity which a heroic style of life demands a cause of divisiveness where that discipline is but the natural expression of heroic demands made in the observance of the Rule out of love for the Immaculate and her cause.

A process of leveling in the program of formation and in the disciplinary norms observed at Niepokalanów, if implemented, could only point toward an eventual diversion of the energies and resources of Niepokalanów to other goals and to other ways of life with no immediate bearing on the cause of the Immaculate. It is that diversion which St. Maximilian opposed with all his might, at every stage of its development, as incompatible with the nature of Niepokalanów as the property and possession of the Immaculate and with the donation which so established it. It matters very little whether such leveling is for a good or evil end. It is in itself simply an abuse, amounting to nothing more or less than betrayal.[79]

Once established authoritatively, the existence of Niepokalanów imposes a condition on the activities and commands of the superiors of the Order in its regard, analogous to their obligation to command always in accord with conscience (i.e., the truth of the gospel) and the Franciscan Rule. That condition is this: to command always in accord with the nature and purpose of that total and unconditional donation of a friary to the Immaculate for the service of her cause for which reason the friary is known as Niepokalanów. As in the case of the Rule, when the superiors fulfill the two conditions laid down by Saint Francis, what they command is indeed the will of Christ and when rightly fulfilled by the subject truly serves Christ's

78. *WK* 337, 339, 366.
79. *WK* 300, 325. Cf. Domanski, "Niepokalanów," 387.

goals and the friar's salvation, not because the superiors are perfect, but because in those circumstances Christ, true to his promises uses the superiors as his instrument in making his will known, so too when the superiors fulfill that condition governing their guidance of Niepokalanów, the Immaculate makes her will, one with Christ's, known there in the same way. Even the best of human counsel cannot compare with those of the Immaculate in guiding us to do what is most pleasing to her Son. The history of Niepokalanów and Mugenzai no Sono under St. Maximilian provides striking illustrations of the validity of this faith in the merit of supernatural obedience. The accomplishments of these Niepokalanów represent a practice confirming theory and amply justifying the permission and support given St. Maximilian by his major superiors in establishing the M.I. and Niepokalanów on the solid foundation of authentic obedience.[80]

Such an establishment does place a condition or limit on the exercise of authority, just as total consecration in its own way places a limit on the personal discretion of the person making that consecration. Such a condition, to be respected by the superior once a Niepokalanów exists, differs "toto coelo" from the kind of condition laid down by an applicant to the Order who aspires to join, but only if a career is guaranteed him, or a certain kind of work, or a certain place or type of residence, etc. These are private conditions incompatible with any kind of true religious life; the condition in question here is one inherent in the nature of religious life, and specifically, the nature of a Franciscan community totally in the service of the Immaculate. If the consecration of that community in that manner is valid, so is the condition, for the second is but the formal effect of the first.

Wherever men gather, religious not excluded, grounds for criticism can be found. But what has not been proven by anyone is that the ideal of Niepokalanów, when seriously implemented, is the source of problems, the origin of divisiveness, or inappropriate to the times. Indeed, experience, where the Kolbean tradition has been implemented authentically, without specious interpretation and adaptation, argues quite the contrary, that it is a source of great blessing in this difficult age. To pursue a policy designed to alter essentially its nature and necessary conditions of existence and growth would represent a disaster of tragic proportions for the M.I., the good of the church and the salvation of souls, and above all for an Order ungrateful for the love and honor shown it by the Immaculate, and unfaithful to a promise made and gift given. In the face of such a contingency, St.

80. WK 487.

Maximilian believed, he, and with him every Niepokalanów, had the right and duty to use every licit means of defense.[81]

The grounds for this position are to be found in his belief in the Immaculate as mediatrix of all graces, and therefore Mistress of history. All generations are to call her blessed; and indeed her Son points the way to the fulfillment of this prophecy in consecrating-donating the entire church and every soul for whom he died, to his Mother when about to consummate the work for which he was conceived of the Holy Spirit and born of the Virgin Mary, and give his life, and all he won by that death, i.e., the Immaculate and those united to her, to the Father. The implementation of that donation, the making of the entire world and each soul in it wholly the Immaculate's (totus tuus) governed, St. Maximilian believed, the history of the church during her time of pilgrimage. So too, the implementation of that donation ever more fully he understood to be the purpose of the dogmatic proclamation of the Immaculate Conception in 1854: to authoritatively recognize her by name whose possession of the church and of every soul to be saved must become ever more perfect in preparation for the coming of Christ and the consummation of his kingdom. Once the Immaculate is acknowledged publicly by name, the M.I., her foreordained instrument for the final incorporation of this mystery into life and the means of a spiritual-cultural second spring, might be publicly launched. In this movement the total consecration of an entire Franciscan friary, viz., its total segregation from other uses so as to be exclusively at the disposal of the Immaculate, has a privileged place, not only possible, but actual, because in fact the donation has already been made by the Order. Rescinding that donation is unthinkable, said St. Maximilian.[82] Rather the aim of the Order, as of every Niepokalanów, should be the multiplication of such friaries throughout the world, so that the blessings the Immaculate would bestow in the spiritual and temporal orders might be realized as soon as possible. In that perspective his desire to see the M.I. statute eventually a part of the *Constitutions* of the Order and the entire Order an instrument of the Immaculate, a Niepokalanów, can be understood.[83]

81. *WK* 485.
82. *WK* 485.
83. *WK* 485.

Conclusion

Niepokalanów exists to realize the scope of the M.I.,[84] viz., the plan of the Immaculate to hasten the triumph of her Son, just when it appears to many that he cannot triumph at all in saving in fact a race of sinners, that it is useless to belong to the church or to observe her commands and counsels, that spiritual renewal is a mirage masking psychological or social impoverishment and injustice. Niepokalanów exists, however, not only to give the lie to such despair, but to reveal the vision governing the counsels of the Immaculate. Who wishes to understand and apprehend concretely rather than theoretically what a paradise the Son of God and Son of Mary has prepared for those who love him, need only visit the sanctuary that is every Niepokalanów, where he will begin to experience a foretaste of heaven, of the beauty of the truth which is one and the charity that sustains the believer in the truth, and where one will come to understand, if never fully in this life, at least sufficiently, to be able to admire the mercy of God in the acts of the Immaculate, nowhere so evident than in her Niepokalanów, and thirst even more for the living waters springing from the heart of the Savior.

To the questions and doubts raised concerning Niepokalanów almost from its beginning St. Maximilian saw three possible solutions: either the entire Province and Order would be totally consecrated to the Immaculate as Niepokalanów; or Niepokalanów would be suppressed either directly or by a process of leveling; or Niepokalanów in virtue of its status as the possession of the Immaculate would be allowed to continue in this distinctive mode of life.[85]

The first would have been for him the ideal solution. The second would represent a tragic disaster, to prevent which all licit means of defense could and should be employed. The third solution, the one actually followed, is a viable one, precisely because the entire concept of total consecration, not only of an individual, but of an entire community to the Immaculate is a valid one. That a particular friary should be exclusively reserved to a special cause of the Immaculate is no more strange than that one should be reserved to a particular project of our Lord, for their wills are one and their proprietorship of the Order absolute. Nor should differences of lifestyle arising from the degree of perfection and intensity of the observance of the *Rule* pose a problem of unity, any more than the existence in the church of different states of perfection pose a problem for the unity of the church. St. Francis in the twelfth chapter of the *Rule* would

84. *WK* 337.
85. *WK* 485.

seem to have anticipated in some way the very mode of life realized at Niepokalanów, once the limit on the superior's authority to assign to the missionary life without prior consent of the subject is removed. St. Maximilian would simply add that such a possibility is only realizable under the guidance and direction of the Immaculate.

That Niepokalanów, then, should merit a defense by its knights on earth, and in heaven, should surprise no one, a defense hinging on the position in history and in eternity of the Woman who has crushed the head of the serpent and has overcome every heresy in the whole world. That defense, far from being the polemics of fanatical zealotry, is instructive and inspiring: instructive, because the response of St. Maximilian to radical proposals aiming at the leveling of differences between Niepokalanów and other friaries however strict, but not exclusively in the service of the Immaculate's cause, illumines the true nature of the struggle governing the history of the world from its beginning to end, the battle between the Woman and the serpent, which as the Seer, St. John, so well saw, must and will conclude with the final incorporation of the mystery of the Woman into the life of the church in virtue of her total victory over sin and Satan from the first moment of her conception; inspiring, because in pondering that defense our hearts are stimulated by a profound sense of gratitude to the Immaculate for the gift of the M.I. with Niepokalanów at its center as a sign and vision of victory and of the glory of the saints, and moved to labor zealously for that cause of the Immaculate by consecrating ourselves ever more perfectly as the property and possession of the Immaculate.

6

Vertex Creationis: St. Maximilian and Evolution

MANY PERSONS ACQUAINTED WITH St. Maximilian during his lifetime testified to his native intellectual ability and to the depth of insight characteristic of his thought.[1] After winning doctorates in philosophy and theology, however, he did not pursue an academic career. Nonetheless, his mind continued active, and what his contemporaries noted during his lifetime can be observed by us in his writings. This is particularly the case with the many short apologetic essays, for the most part contributed to "The Knight of the Immaculate." These certainly indicate on his part a very sound grasp of the place of the intellect in the work of conversion and sanctification, and of the need to integrate the intellectual activity of every person, however simple and unsophisticated, into the "rationale obsequium," the heart of the life of faith. During his lifetime, and since, his Marian devotion and work have been criticized as exaggerated and pietistic. Even a superficial acquaintance with his thought would show how unfounded is such a view in fact. Rather it is just that profound love of the Immaculate that is at the root of his mental clarity.

Sound apologetics, particularly in a pastoral and missionary context, is a delicate operation. If the apologete does not possess the requisite grasp of philosophy, but even more important a profound sense of the analogy of faith and of the connection of mysteries, even the best mastery of technique will not serve to communicate effectively reasons for the hope that is within us (1 Pet 3:15), and draw others to embrace that faith which is the substance of things to be hoped for. Nurtured by her who is the Seat of Wisdom St. Maximilian conjoined competence in theology and philosophy with a delicate charity for others and appreciation of their point of view, enabling him to enter easily into conversation and draw them toward the Truth. It is only natural, then, to find embedded in such apologetics the contours of a rich and illuminating thought.

---

1. Cf. Domanski, "La genesi," 263–65.

One of the perennial problems of modern apologetics is the question of evolution.[2] Since it was first explicitly formulated in the eighteenth century, the basic issues have not changed, if the details of argumentation have varied from generation to generation. Not only are the basic issues the same, but the relative positions possible in respect to these, and the argumentation to be employed on behalf of each likewise so. This assessment of St. Maximilian of half a century ago[3] is still valid. And despite the many periodic announcements that evolution is now a proven fact and the controversy may be regarded as closed, speculatively speaking, it continues as vigorously as ever. Surprisingly, however, within the last quarter century, more theologians have been found defending evolution than attacking it (in contrast with the earlier period), whereas an increasing number of scientists, some non-Christian, have been among skeptics calling into question the "fact" of evolution, even the possibility of demonstrating evolution scientifically.[4]

Perhaps St. Maximilian would not have been so surprised. Science, for him, did not naturally tend to discover facts inimical to Catholic belief and tradition.[5] Quite the contrary. But when science appeared to "discover" such facts, such discoveries are rather to be regarded as the projection of a false philosophy and intellectual pride, rather than the interpretation of the real itself.[6] For St. Maximilian evolution is not a true fact, but in the first instance part of a religious-philosophical creed contrary to that of the church. What he might have found strange is the decided proclivity of many Catholic theologians to insist on a reinterpretation of Scripture and tradition on the basis of what at best can never be more than a mere hypothesis, when excellent scientific considerations demonstrate the plausibility of creationism to be as much or more, scientifically speaking, than evolutionism.

The purpose of this review of St. Maximilian's remarks on evolution, however, is not to assess what might have been his position in the current phase of the controversy. The objective is rather to call attention to another aspect of the discussion, often overlooked, but clearly present in the thought patterns of St. Maximilian, and which is critical to any fair estimate of the issue.

Evolution as a theory of origins is twofold. It may serve as an explanation of the origin of the world, or as an explanation of the origin of the

2. Cf. Bethell, "Agnostic Evolutionists," 61.

3. *WK* 1186.

4. Cf. for example, O'Connell, *Science of Today*; Lammerts, *Why not Creation*; O'Connell, *Original Sin*; Morris, *Scientific Creationism*; Johnson, *Crumbling Theory of Evolution*; Bethell, "Agnostic Evolutionists."

5. *WK* 607.

6. *WK* 1180.

species, i.e., of the differentiation among living beings to be found within
the world. The first quite obviously assumes the truth of the second, and
in fact constitutes a vision of reality directly opposed to that affirmed in
the first article of the Creed, viz., that the world began because created by
an omnipotent God out of nothing in the beginning of time, not in order
to gain something he did not have or to develop, but in order to share his
love and goodness.

The second, however, at least not in all its versions, does not rest on
the truth of the first. One may, for instance, argue to the existence of God
the Creator, prescinding entirely from the question of how the differences
among creatures came about. The plausibility of what is called theistic evolution is linked to this distinction. So long as the question is simply that
of origins, the repudiation of evolution in the first sense need not entail
repudiation in the second. Indeed, the theistic evolutionist often maintains
belief in creation constitutes a kind of antecedent probability for evolution
in the second sense.

St. Maximilian appreciated the distinction, and as will be seen, made
use of it in setting forth his arguments against evolution in the first sense.
But as we shall also see, St. Maximilian is not a theistic evolutionist. He
is adamantly opposed to evolution as an explanation of the differentiated
structure of the world of living beings, as he is opposed to evolution as an
explanation for the origin of the world. The reasons he gives for making not
merely evolution in the first, but also in the second sense the object of an
absolute "non credo," merit examination, because they underscore a crucial
aspect of the discussion: the theory of evolution is not simply a theory of
origins; it is also a theory of ends, and of how to reach those ends. Only when
it is examined with respect to both can its true character and concrete veri-
similitude be assessed. The value St. Maximilian's brief remarks on evolution
is to be found in just this analysis, one intimately linked to wider dimensions
of his thought and work, especially that of mediation.

The Texts

There are four texts in which St. Maximilian mentions or deals directly with
the theme of evolution.[7] These may be arranged in two groups, the first treating of evolutionism as an explanation for the origin of the world opposed
to that of creation *ex nihilo*; the second treating of evolutionism as a theory
explaining the origin and differentiation of the species and of the rank of perfection among them. This second version of evolution is not directly opposed

7. *WK* 1124, 1169, 1186, 1276.

to the fact of creation *ex nihilo* as it is to a special intervention (creative or miraculous) of the Creator as principal cause in effecting the differentiation of the species and their ranking by levels of perfection.

1. Only one text, a 1926 article in *Rycerz Niepokalanej* in the form of an apologetical dialogue, a genre in which St. Maximilian excelled, deals with evolutionism in the first sense.[8] The reference to evolution occurs in the context of remarks bearing on the teleological argument for God's existence. Toward the end of his reflections on intelligence and design found throughout the universe and illustrated particularly in the biological science, he says: "Were we to amuse ourselves in adopting the evolutionistic position and were to assume that all this (the mysteries of biology) had developed from a certain primitive matter, the same question would remain to be answered: who gave existence to this matter? And who with such wisdom had endowed it with such power, that after the passage of so many years, across so many transformations, as to be able to attain the set goal?"

The theme of the article is not the truth or falsity of the "fact" of evolution as an explanation for the origin of the species and in a broader sense as a paradigm for understanding the world, but the existence of God and the validity of the arguments thereof, pro and con. Evolution of the species figures in the dialogue only in view of the use to which the atheist puts it, viz., to disprove the existence of God, the Creator. Thus, the position of the atheist might be recapitulated as follows: if the species could have evolved from non-living matter, then that matter could have begun to exist by evolution as well. Hence, the existence of God cannot be proved from a consideration of the world as an effect.

For the sake of argument St. Maximilian assumes the truth of evolution in the second sense. The phrase he employs, "Were we to amuse ourselves in adopting . . ." clearly indicates this to be but a logical device to illustrate the utter lack of support for atheism in the argument adduced. It implies nothing as to his personal view of evolution of the species, whether in fact such occurred in the past, or even could occur. "Amuse" points rather to a negative stand on both counts, one quite explicit where the saint deals directly with the evolution of the species.

In retorting the argument St. Maximilian argues as follows. Evolution is a natural process, i.e., whose subject is a non-intelligent, free, or personal agent. To reason otherwise is to ascribe design to chance, intelligence to non-intelligence. The evolution of the species is a process terminating not in random activity, but in design, in a living organism, whose major feature is design, organization for an end. Evolution, then, is

---

8. *WK* 1124.

not self-explanatory, but presupposes the existence of an intelligent agent outside the process of evolution itself, capable and willing to initiate the process not by a natural, but by a creative act.

This is a position commonly known as "theistic evolution," admitting the evolution of the species, but far from denying God's existence serves to prove that point. Whether or not such a view correctly expounds or adequately expounds the notion of creation is open to question. St. Maximilian, however, is not concerned with that issue in his "contrary to fact" argument, but with the illustration of a distinction crucial to his thought, viz., the difference between the natural and the voluntary (intelligent) action, the physical and spiritual orders and the essential difference in their modes of action and transformation.[9] It is this irreducible difference, factually true, which renders the evolution of the species in the eyes of St. Maximilian, not a "fact" of science, but an article of an unreasonable "credo."

In three texts St. Maximilian deals directly with evolution of the species, not as a basis for explaining the existence of the world independently of a Creator, but of explaining the differentiation and ranking of orders of being, of the essences of created being, viz., of species according to their proper perfections, without a special intervention of an intelligent, all powerful agent, viz., the Creator, to effect that differentiation.

The first text, entitled "Non Credo," is a *Rycerz* article of 1933, apologetic in character.[10] Rather than a dialogue, this is a simple, but forceful and thoughtful affirmation of Catholic truth via a direct challenge of its contrary as false. Six points are made, the third of which deals directly with the question of evolution of the species. The first two points treat of the creation of the world by God alone and of the impossibility of explaining it by chance alone, i.e., as the result of the interaction of blind powers; the fourth affirms the immortality of the soul, the fifth the impossibility of total, perfect atheism, and the sixth the universal, human desire for a happiness that is infinite.

The third "non credo" reads as follows: "I do not believe that chimpanzees or other children of Darwin (the apes) will compete with us in building airplanes or other inventions, because no progress is noted in them. After so many centuries they are not even capable of writing the modest history of simian progress."

Despite its brevity this passage expresses the fundamental argument of St. Maximilian against the theory of evolution as an explanation of the origin of man, in his body as well as in his soul. Progress and change are

9. *WK* 991 O, 1285.
10. *WK* 1169.

not the same. Progress implies action in view of a higher level of perfection. Change that is not progress may entail variation, but it is a variation (or development) that does not alter the level of perfection of the subject acting, and thus is radically monotonous. All natural development or evolution is of this kind, limited within the bounds describing its original perfection. The ape at the end of its development has not progressed, i.e., the level of final perfection is no greater than that of its original.

Progress on the other hand, its accomplishment and its recognition, is of a different character from evolution. It is the characteristic fruit of activity by an agent that is spiritual rather than natural, capable of transcending the limits of nature in a manner that is potentially infinite. If progress is noted in the world, first in the grades or levels of being, and second in the modes of acting characteristic of intelligent creatures within the world, capable of a perfection or happiness touching on the infinite, then this is a sign that progression in the world as a whole is not a matter of uniform, natural processes, that the explanation for the origin of such differences in levels of perfection in being and in acting is not a theory of evolution, but in the final analysis the special intervention of an intelligent agent who mediates that progression, at each higher level with or without the cooperation in some way of less perfect agents.

The analysis rests on the radical discontinuity between the material and the spiritual, the natural action and the voluntary, and the inherent superiority of the latter over the former. Man, both in body as well as in soul, is inherently superior to the beast, in the same way as the spiritual (or personal) is inherently superior to the material or physical world, and man's origin or appearance cannot be accounted for naturally, i.e., by evolutionary processes.

In such a perspective the world cannot be viewed as a single, uniform whole, of which each being found therein is a part in the same manner, as though the world might be conceived as a single, complex organism. Rather, it is organized "hierarchically," by grades of being, each higher grade being in the world, but not of it in the same manner as the lower grades. This is particularly the case with that spiritual being called man, in the world, but also transcending the rest of the visible creation: in the world in virtue of his body, but transcending it in virtue of his soul. That is nowhere so evident as in the fact that man is capable of progress, not only of adapting the material world to his ends, and thus perfecting in a certain sense beings less perfect, but of advancing in perfection himself, toward a happiness that is infinite, without ceasing to be human. Hence, St. Maximilian distinguishes two laws of transformation, one proper to the material world, and one proper to the spiritual.[11] Paradoxically, natural change or transformation in the material order is rooted in the instability of matter and is monotonous in character, i.e., incapable of progress, a kind of defective immutability. Spiritual change or transformation is rooted not in the mutability of the agent, but in the relative simplicity and stability of the intellect and will, and opens on the infinite rather than the finite. Only when intellect is infected by skepticism and will by sin and cynicism does change, instead of being progress, become regression or decadence.[12] That spiritual transformation, however, which is truly progress, while always the fruit of a "voluntarium," remains ever dependent on the power of the Creator, and where in fact it does progress to the infinite itself, to the point of divinization,[13] dependent on that power in a special way, viz., on grace. The problem of spiritualization in the sense of divinization, is to discover the special mediation which makes this possible.[14]

The second and third texts in this group date from 1934. The second is entitled "I cannot believe" and was published in *Mugenzai no Seibo no Kishi*.[15] The third, entitled "I do not believe" and never published represents the original version of the second.[16] The points treated are substantially the same, but not without certain differences in the manner and order of presentation.

Both texts begin with a reference to the saint's days as a student of philosophy in Rome,[17] followed by a discussion of truth, the love of which makes one a philosopher. Truth is one only, objective and immutable. These are its characteristics and only in the context of such a mode of thought can one understand, as he says in the published version, the sense of the universe. Hence, the theory of evolution, like all the positions rejected in this "non credo," is very much linked to basic issues of truth, and not merely to the working hypotheses of scholars.

Both texts, the published text at somewhat greater length, conclude with a discussion of truth and charity, viz., the recognition of the duty of observing God's commandments. The intellect naturally tends to recognize the Truth. God being the truth itself, atheism is not natural to the intellect. Its strength is directly proportionate in practice to the desire to be free of God's commandments. This is why a counter-strength or special courage is necessary in order

11. *WK* 1285.

12. *WK* 1086.

13. *WK* 1270, 1296.

14. *WK* 1295.

15. *WK* 1186.

16. *WK* 1276.

17. *WK* 1186, 1276.

to affirm that "natural" credo of the human intellect, to resist the stratagems of the serpent and prince of this world.

Only the mediatrix of all graces can obtain that requisite courage for us. Thus, the pursuit of truth and the attainment of happiness, true progress, revolve about the place of the Immaculate in creation. Her work makes possible our progress by securing our solidification in grace, the harmonization of activities with the will of God, and thereby crowns as it were, is the vertex of love[18] in that system of mediation exercised by the human family and by angels, in the world as a whole, and in a special way within the church, as it verges on the infinite, reached in the Incarnate Word, through the "fiat" of the Immaculate.

Both texts, in contradistinction to that of the first of the group, mention the existence of the soul. But in the third text evolution is treated after the existence of the soul and before the question of its immortality is broached. In the second, or published text, evolution is treated after the immortality of the soul and after pointing out that physical-chemical forces, as such, though found within and without living organisms, cannot explain the origin of life, in particular the life of the human body, any more than they can explain the origin of matter.

On the matter of evolution the texts do not duplicate, but complement each other. In the original, unpublished text, Saint Maximilian comments as follows to explain his reasons for not "believing" evolution.

Were evolution a fact, it would be possible to duplicate the process and make the ape human. So far no one has observed such a duplication, or duplicated the evolutionary process at any level of being, let alone the human, nor is there the slightest indication such might be accomplished in the future. In so far as evolution and the evolutionary thought it is alleged to justify are matters of present rather than past reality they are not only lacking in demonstration, but appear to be indemonstrable. What happened in the past to bring about the differentiation of the species, in particular the human, is not primarily a matter of scientific observation and analysis, but of witness and faith: the traditional faith of the church, or the new faith of the evolutionists. The contention of St. Maximilian is simply that the traditional Catholic faith in a direct divine formation of Adam and Eve, is a reasonable faith, because the testimony of God is always reasonable; and that the faith of the evolutionists is quite unreasonable, because the real world is not evolutionary.

The sub-human, for instance the ape, to take the beast alleged to be most similar to the human, is incapable of writing the history of his modest

18. *WK* 1310, 1318.

progress. Hence, there must be a fundamental difference, or discontinuity, between man and the rest of the visible world, which no amount of natural activity can bridge, however exceptional. That difference is the soul, a difference reflected in the body informed by it, and which therefore cannot be classified simply as another composite of physical-chemical forces.

In the published version the saint makes the following points in support of his belief that man did not evolve from a lower species of animal life.

First, 120 years of scholarly analysis and debate over evolution, far from clarifying our knowledge of human origins (and of what man is) has only served to muddy the waters, this despite the innate tendency of science and technology to progress.

Further, the theory of evolution is not supported by the results of experimental science, itself in continual progress.[19]

What was initially only proposed as a hypothesis by Darwin, has been elevated by world-famous scholars to the level of fact, on no other grounds but that of an alleged "possibility." *A posse ad esse non valet illatio.*[20]

It is increasingly more urgent, he concludes, to stress and illustrate the basic, or essential diversity between man and ape (and the rest of creation) than similarities. Only man is made in the image and likeness of God in the proper sense. The failure to stress this point is what permits so arbitrary a theory as evolution to gain credibility. And it is the failure to think in terms of that difference that leads to confusion over the sense of the universe and of the destiny of man, to be achieved via the "mediation" of the Immaculate, who among all the levels of perfection in the universe holds the highest, because of all created persons most perfectly the image and likeness of God.[21]

Grades of being exist, then, precisely in order to permit the exercise of that mediation without which the world as a whole would not progress toward that fulfillment willed for it by its Creator. The presence of the highest grade of being indicates that such a fulfillment is to be the highest, as in fact it is in the incarnation. Progress does not effect, but presupposes the differentiated grades of being. The less perfect can never be the principal

19. This is recognized by a great many scientists today, even if they personally believe evolution. Cf. Bethell, "Agnostic Evolutionists," passim.

20. The evolutionary hypothesis is peculiar as a scientific hypothesis dealing with a non-observable phenomenon of the past, incapable of repetition and direct verification by scientific means. The transition from possibility to fact can only be on the basis of authority, a matter of faith rather than science, or on the basis of reconstructions (fossil evidence, geological time periods) which presuppose the truth of what the they propose to demonstrate, an evolutionary frame of reference. The argument is circular, and hence inconclusive. Cf. Klotz, "Philosophy of Science."

21. *WK* 1232, 1282.

cause of the more perfect. This is why an evolutionary mode of conceiving the world and its development and one based on a hierarchical system of graduated mediation at whose vertex is the Mother of God, the Immaculate, mediatrix of all graces, are naturally incompatible.

Commentary

Evolution as it is proposed in modern times purports to be a scientific theory explaining the origin of presently existing species of living beings, of their variety and relative perfection in terms of self-contained natural processes. Its supporters claim that it is at once a demonstration and a reflection of a coherent vision of the world. Its critics have always maintained that there is a *petitio principii* involved in these claims: that the theory of evolution in science is employed to justify an evolutionary vision of the world; in turn without such a vision the theory is lacking in any kind of apodictic proof, that evolution in fact is not, nor ever was, a scientific question, but one of apologetics. At the heart of the argument is not a question of scientific fact versus an obscurantist faith, but two competing faiths, both of which cannot be true simultaneously.

This is the position of St. Maximilian as well. Evolution is not primarily a question of scientific research, but the object of a "credo." Evolution is part of a complexus of views forming a philosophy of life, the exact antithesis of that taught by Christ the Savior. It is, therefore, preeminently a question of apologetics, a defense of the reasons for the hope that is within us. And in this case the defense offered by St. Maximilian is not simply a presentation of the evidence for the reasonableness of the Christian credo and of its contents, but a challenge to its adversaries to provide convincing reasons to the contrary.

His contention is that there are none, that the atheistic "credo" being arbitrary and capricious, is worthy of a "non credo," that its inspiration is a desire to be free of God's law, and that the most effective manner of rationalizing so arbitrary a human choice is to prove the "non-existence" of God. "Evolution" is perhaps the most popular of contemporary intellectual props for modern infidelity.

That is perfectly clear in respect to evolution construed as an alternative to the dogma of creation. But the theistic evolutionist would contest the validity of that position in regard to evolution as a possible explanation for the origin of the species. He might even consider St. Maximilian inconsistent, in so far as in his first text on evolution he seems to have admitted the hypothetical possibility of such as not incompatible with God. Indeed, teleological analysis might strike some as being substantially the position of a theistic evolutionist. Why, then, did St. Maximilian make the theory of evolution of the species the object of so forceful a "non credo"? The answer is: precisely because of teleological analysis.

There are many arguments employed to demonstrate the implausibility of evolution.[22] That St. Maximilian should have chosen to develop just that point seemingly pointing to the contrary can perhaps be accounted for by three considerations. His practical bent would naturally incline him to favor the argument from design. As a good apologete he would be inclined to turn the strongest argument of his opponent to his own view. Finally, the argument from design against evolution illustrates a pattern of thought congenial to one who conceives the return of creation to God as a series of progressive stages crossed not by evolution, but by mediation.

The use of this argument depends on a recognition that the problem of evolution is not simply a question of origins, but also of ends, not simply how the world came to be, but why it came to be and how it will reach that end. The remote origin of the world is a creative act of God in the strict sense, not an evolutionary process.

The world, however, did not simply come forth from the hand of God; it was made to return to God. In Kolbean terms the creative action of God is designed to find a reaction in the creature.[23] Except in the most perfect of creatures, that reaction is never "equal and contrary," i.e., could always be more perfect. It is a reaction always contained within the limits of creaturely powers, limits not determined by the creature, but principally by the Creator, and only within the power of the Creator to modify. A more perfect return to God, a greater immediacy and intimacy with the Creator, with Father, Son and Holy Spirit, is only possible to the degree that higher grades of perfection are introduced into the world. That is a work of the Creator, mediating rather than making. The differentiated structure of the world, the varied strata of perfection, though not necessarily the fruit of a creative act in the strict sense, are not the term of a natural evolutionary process. Each step in the process is a further special grace. Each higher grade of perfection in respect to subsequent interventions of the Mediator is a potential instrument, whose activities are a kind of cooperation with the divine mediation, and in respect to lower grades of being exercise in their regard a secondary, but true mediation, each according to its proper nature.

In such a scheme the most perfect creature, the one in whom the reaction to divine love in creating is equal and contrary, is the one in whom

22. Cf. e.g., Lammerts, *Why not Creation*, for summary presentations.
23. *WK* 1291, 1318, 1326.

the mediatory grace of the Savior is fullest, the one who is the "perfect fruit of a perfect redemption," the Immaculate, preserved free of all stain of sin, Spouse of the Holy Spirit, Mother of God, first-born daughter of the Father, perfect cooperator with the Redeemer, mediatrix of all graces and perfect instrument of the Holy Spirit in the sanctification of sinners. The perfection of her love, viz., of her "reaction" is evident in the fruit of her womb, the Word Incarnate, the humanization of God, the divinization of man.[24] And in such a scheme the progressive purification effected by the Immaculate as mediatrix of all graces in all those who have become her "property" is but the complement of that "divinization" or "infinitization" effected by the Savior in recapitulating all things and offering them to his Father.[25] That action on her part is not the result of our progress at any level, but its premise. That is why the mystery of the Immaculate as mediatrix of all graces precludes an evolutionary explanation of the origin of the species, of the grades of perfection in the world. Such a theory is radically Pelagian in its tendency to deny the need of grace, viz., the need of mediation in approaching God as our last end.

In a Kolbean perspective, then, theistic evolution fails to take account of the order of grace, because though recognizing the origin of the world in a creative act of God, it fails to note the term of that act is not, without further intervention of God as mediator, capable of a reaction equal and contrary to that of the divine action, or of autonomously advancing in perfection so as to be capable of such.

In St. Maximilian's view there is, even prescinding from the mysteries of grace, a clear confirmation of this scheme of things in the book of nature, the irreducible difference between the human and non-human, between natural evolution and progress, between two laws of transformation, one of the material or physical order, the other of the spiritual, and in the mediatory role exercised by the more perfect order of beings in respect to the less perfect. That fact excludes evolution as a plausible explanation for the origin of the species, for the differentiated structure of the world. But it does more than that; it acts as a foreshadowing of that even more perfect mediation to be exercised by the Incarnate Word, with the cooperation of his Mother and all those one with her, in bringing to pass the final triumph of God's kingdom.

This vision of creation can aptly be described as hierarchical, one entailing the recognition not only of the difference (and inequality) between Creator and creature, but of the relative difference (and inequality) between

24. *WK* 508, 1318.
25. *WK* 1310.

creatures in perfection. Further, that vision includes a recognition that the source of that difference in perfection is an act of the Creator, the premise of progress, not its fruit; and that the purpose of that differentiation is precisely to make possible a higher and higher level of progress, or return to him from whom all creation originally came.

That such a return should be by "steps" rests on the fact that such a return is a passage from the less perfect to the more perfect. Each grade of being represents a step, whose limits are passed, not by natural evolution, but by an ever more special act of divine love, a grace, terminating at an ever more perfect kind of being. That love, at heart a mediation between the less perfect and the more perfect, finds in the "reaction" of the creature a cooperation, to the extent that such a "reaction" is informed by obedience. In relation to its own immediate finality that creature in reacting is the principal cause of its action. In relation to the higher purposes of God, that agent is a potential instrument, whose potential is realized to the extent its obedience is perfect in responding to an ever-special love on the part of the Creator. Finally in respect to less perfect agents, that cooperation itself is mediatory, for the lower creation is fulfilled not in becoming the higher, but in serving the higher in attaining its perfection.

The most important difference in the natural order is that between natural and voluntary agents. The obedience of the natural agent can never be more than an imperfect obedience in contrast with that of a creature endowed with free will. That difference matches the difference between the general love of the Creator for his work, and that special love which he has for the human family, for the creature made in his image and likeness.

The recognition of the difference in the "natural" or created order between a merely natural agent and the intellectual or voluntary agent, viz., the agent capable of contributing with his Creator not only to his development, but also to his progress or advance in perfection toward an infinite goal, toward an eternity,[26] also entails a recognition that this higher level of perfection is unattainable apart from the possibility of a still more particular love or grace on the part of the Creator, to which corresponds on the part of the rational creature not a change of essence, but a degree of "spiritualization" or "divinization"[27] whose measure is the distance between limited and unlimited conformity or obedience to the divine will. From revelation it is known that this grace of mediation par excellence is realized in the incarnation and redemption, and the correspondence with this grace is fully, without limit, achieved in the Immaculate Conception.

26. *WK* 1296.

27. *WK* 1295. Cf. Fehlner, "Immaculate . . . Trinity," *CE* 6, chapter 3.

The recognition of this difference between natural and voluntary, mere development and true progress in view of the supernatural order of salvation, also leads to the recognition of another difference, that between a merely natural limitation, defect or privation (physical evil) and disobedience (moral evil). The limitation of the voluntary agent in the natural order, includes a potential for sin, for disrupting the whole of creation as the natural agent cannot. Such a disruption, in fact tragically verified in the fall of Adam and Eve and the transmission of original sin to their descendants, breaks as it were the order by which the whole of creation might contribute to the final glory of the Creator, because it renders, at least from the mere standpoint of reason, cooperation in the work of mediation impossible. Either the mediation, so the argument runs, by which we are saved is exclusively the work of the Savior-God, or such mediation is unnecessary, an affront to human dignity. Both positions have been and still are adopted by many who do not understand the axiom of St. Augustine, that the God who created us without us does not justify us without us. Neither incarnation nor redemption occurs without the cooperation of a creature, viz., the Mother of God and mediatrix of all graces. In the context of such thought patterns there is evident the mystery and genius of the Immaculate Conception: the Spouse of the Holy Spirit, the fruit of the mutual love of Father and Son in the economy of salvation as the Holy Spirit is the fruit of that love in eternity, the personification of their mercy and love for a race of sinners, the perfect fruit therefore of a perfect redemption because preserved from sin so as to be Mother of God and mediatrix of all grace, the vertex of creation's love for its Creator, a reaction equal and contrary to the love of the triune God, whose perfection as such is evident above all in her love for sinners and in the power of her prayer and obedience to work the conversion even of the worst of these provided he is capable and willing to respond to this Mother's love, something every person short of a sin against the Holy Spirit, i.e., a deliberate and final repudiation of such love of the Immaculate, is capable of doing.[28]

In such a vision the doctrine of Mary's absolute predestination with Christ, and of her cooperation with him as mediatrix in the work of redemption from beginning to end, is inextricably linked to the mystery of the Immaculate Conception, her preservation from all stain of original sin. This is the not unexpected pivot, on which turns the final progress of creation toward its end. For a sound vision of the world is "mediatory," not "evolutionary."[29]

28. For the sources of these various phrases in the Kolbean corpus cf. Fehlner, "Immaculate . . . Trinity," *CE* 6, chapter 3.

29. How unsound the evolutionary vision is evidenced in one of its current postulates, viz., polygenism, adjudged by the Magisterium of the church to be incompatible

Though not the saint of modernism,[30] Maximilian is a very modern saint, alive at once to the best efforts of science and of theology, because alive to the one person who is queen of heaven and earth.

Conclusion

Behind the arguments over origins, of the world, but especially of the species, is an issue of anthropology, of how the only creature in the visible world capable of progress, viz., of perfecting the nature with which the Creator endowed him, will perfect that nature in fact and reach the end for which he was placed in this world: eternity. One approach, which serves as the basis for the evolutionary credo (and not merely hypothetical speculation), holds that man's power to change and be changed by his own initiative is radically unlimited, and seeks to rationalize this by appealing to the unlimited change in nature and in the order of ideas. With respect to the human will and human science, neither things nor concepts enjoy any immutability or "fixity." The other affirms indeed that the human heart opens on the infinite, but denies that the intellectual and affective powers of the soul are capable of reaching that infinite autonomously, without mediation.

That denial is based on the difference between the voluntary and the natural, and on the radical dependence of the natural on the voluntary, viz., on love, not only for existence, but also for the perfection of its existence. The limits within which any creature acts are set not by the creature, but by its maker, by a will. Only the same will can intervene to modify these limits, i.e., the order of nature. The distinction between the natural and the miraculous,

---

with the historical facts of Revelation touching original sin, its origin and inheritance by descent from Adam and Eve. In order to avoid an overt denial of the Immaculate Conception in subscribing to polygenism, attempts have been made in recent years to redefine the dogma of the Immaculate Conception without reference to original sin as traditionally understood in the teaching of the church. Lately it has been suggested (Cf. for example Pancheri, "Nuances et Problèmes"; "Cristocentrismo"), that St. Maximilian's thought can be construed as providing implicit support for such a position, even though verbally he continues to employ the received phraseology to explain the Immaculate Conception. But it is just the anti-evolutionary character of his thought which shows its implicit direction to be quite the contrary. Far from being an embarrassment to him the historical data of Revelation concerning original sin fit well in a mediatory vision of a creation disrupted by original sin, where the Immaculate mediatrix at its vertex, preserved from every stain of original sin, is not simply a model of grace and mercy in a created person, but one whose personal, human actions bespeak the beauty of love and obedience toward the Redeemer, through whose merciful love for the conversion of all sinners the cooperation of mankind, and through man the rest of the cosmos, with the Savior is assured and articulated.

30. WK 13, 968.

and ultimately the supernatural, rests on this point. Human science and technology, however great, are incapable of transgressing those limits.[31] But the potential for development and integration to which they point, and sometimes aspire illicitly, is already realized in the person of the Immaculate, full of grace. Her perfect love, a reaction equal and contrary to the love of the Creator and Redeemer, not only the fruit of the love of Father and Son, but the totality of love from creation for the Creator possible in any created order, is not the fruit, but the premise, measure and stimulus of any other development within creation, in particular spiritual progress. This vision of the mediatrix and queen of the world, in correcting the radical misconception represented by the evolutionary vision, puts that which makes that vision attractive viz., progress, in its proper context.[32]

Two objections to the Catholic theology of cooperation with the Creator implied in the mediatory vision of the world and of its development, in particular with the Savior as that is fulfilled in extraordinary fashion by the Immaculate, are often heard. One commonly stems from those protestant circles which, while often rejecting all theories of evolution, also insist in such wise on the uniqueness of Christ's mediation as to exclude the possibility of any cooperation with him on the part of creatures in the work of salvation. Theirs is a failure to note that the rejection of evolution as an explanation for the origin of the species indicates the natural basis, a quasi-anticipation of that cooperation with the Redeemer in the economy of salvation, which far from detracting from his uniqueness is its connatural complement and glory.

The other proceeds from exactly the opposite stance, one inclined to give full credence to theories of evolution, because these seem to sustain the proper autonomy of the world. In doing so they effectively erase the distinction between nature and grace, and render incomprehensible the character and possibility of a principle of action from without the subject acting, not within his power, such as is grace, the fruit of a special act of love of the Creator and Savior, not of evolutionary development. Here again the insights of St. Maximilian are helpful in showing such a view of the "autonomy" of the world is not evidently reasonable. Quite the contrary the world does not possess a simple, uniform immanent structure, but within it are found a variety of beings differing greatly in specific or essential perfection. One of these, man, from the beginning of history, has exercised just that kind of "mediatory" role in developing (sometimes for the worse) the less perfect creatures entrusted to his care.

31. *WK* 1080.

32. Cf. Swiecicki, "Prospettive," 323–25.

St. Maximilian's final comments[33] on evolution concerned truth and charity: each point of the false credo, as each point of the true faith, ultimately involves issues of truth and of charity. There is a choice to be made by the believer of a standard of truth which is the eternal Word through whom all things were made, who is the exemplar and end of all, or to repudiate that standard. The false credo is just that repudiation. So too there is a choice to be made by the believer of true charity which consists in doing the will of God rather than one's own, or to repudiate that charity, i.e., to love oneself, even if it is necessary to hate God. The false credo is just that repudiation, indeed it is the rationalization of a choice to disobey God so as to be as free as God, a choice which cannot be other than arbitrary in fact. It is the choice of that false freedom originally offered to Eve by the serpent. The right choice and the right faith is that of the Immaculate, the new Eve. To accept her as mediatrix, to be totally consecrated to her, is to find the grace to unmask the deception and deceiver and the courage to serve God with a love "usque ad victimam," rather than offend him. That love does not evolve, it is a gift mediated. The difference between the physical and the spiritual, the natural and the voluntary, of which true love is the finest form, the mediatory role which that difference implies in the "reaction" of creation to the love of the Creator, and the consequent anti-evolutionary stand of St. Maximilian are but logical complements to his profound appreciation of the mystery of the Immaculate, and how the cooperation of the universe with the Savior in the work of salvation unto the praise of the glory of his grace, nowhere more so than in her who is full of grace, is to be orchestrated through her and in her who is full of grace, who is his palace.[34] May all generations call her blessed!

33. *WK* 1186, 1246, 1276.
34. *SalBMV*, 4; *WK* 603.

———— 7 ————

Hereditas Kolbiana: Novus Impetus Influxus Mariae Immaculatae in Ordinis Spiritualitate

The Impact of the Kolbean Heritage in Relaunching the Influence of Mary Immaculate in the Spirituality of the Order

THE TITLE OF THIS conference, a statement of its central theme, is in fact an answer to a question, the solution for a problem. To speak of "relaunching," however generically, assumes something that ought to be flying is not; i.e., something desirable or necessary in our spirituality is missing or not functioning properly—in this case the Marian dimension. To say that the Kolbean heritage could or should have some impact on resolving such a problem is also to raise a question: why such a "relaunching" is desirable or necessary, and why the Kolbean heritage should provide the solution. Before we can state precisely what that impact is or should be, or what this chapter might do concretely to facilitate that impact, a certain number of preliminaries must be examined: what is the nature of the problem to be resolved; what the Kolbean is; and why it is the resolution of the problem. Thus, the conference has three sections: the first dealing with the nature of the problem, the second with the bearing of the Kolbean heritage on its resolution, and finally a series of practical considerations bearing on what must be done if the "relaunching" is to be realized.

The Nature of the Problem

The figure of speech chosen by the organizers of this chapter to formulate the theme of this conference, whatever its literary merit, is appropriate to the space age and does call our attention to one of the unchanging, eternal truths, ever valid whatever the culture, not subject to adaptation: heaven is our true home, not earth. We must seek first the kingdom of heaven and its justice; and to do this we must find the wings of angels and fly. If a spirituality does not contribute to this goal, whatever else it might accomplish, it is a failure.

No spirituality will accomplish this wherein the influence of the Mother of God is absent, or, worse, in which that influence is neglected or deliberately rejected. This is a key theme of St. Maximilian: Mary Mediatrix of all graces. There is no access to Christ and therefore to the Father, except through Mary. But it is not simply a key theme of St. Maximilian; it is one of the church in the first instance. It is useless to argue, as some do, that because all the details of this mystery are not clear to us, therefore the fact is not clear either, or that God might have devised a plan of salvation without a divine maternity. In fact the only salvation available to us had its beginning with the "fiat" of the Virgin to become the Mother of God, a "fiat" which in constituting her in fact Mother of God not for an instant but forever, constitutes her in fact as the mediatrix of all graces. Through her he comes to us: through her we find our Savior. Once inaugurated, the mystery of our salvation involves both the Savior and his Mother. It is one thing not to realize this; it is quite another to repudiate this fact, to imagine one can approach Jesus alone. Such presumptuous pride, and the despair of ever seeing God, so often its fruit, are but a denial of the reality of sin, original and personal, in life, a reality best appreciated in the light of the Immaculate Conception. Thus, it should also be perfectly clear that in practice a spirituality consciously giving greater place to the Immaculate, the mediatrix of all graces, is an *a priori* one calculated to procure greater fruit in respect to the kingdom of God and his justice (to which all the other things will be added).

To speak of the integral place, indeed necessary place of Mary in any Catholic spirituality, is not simply to speak of her as a mystery to be contemplated, although surely this is a necessary preliminary to any living of the spiritual life. Who does not believe and contemplate that mystery will never really live an authentic spiritual life. But beyond that contemplation there is a need to recognize her as a person, a subject who acts, who intervenes in interceding, just because she stands in so unique a relation to her Son and Savior, and ours. On her love and intercession-intervention we depend. Prayer to the Virgin without cessation, a life of prayer with the Virgin, is an indispensable prerequisite for launching, and relaunching, any spirituality, individually and in common, and for reinvigorating the apostolate of which it is the soul. Typically Kolbean, this is also thoroughly Catholic.

But in a special way this is particularly pertinent to Franciscan spirituality, because the basis for the Virgin Mary's position as mediatrix of all graces is her privilege of the Immaculate Conception. The Immaculate

Conception historically and spiritually is the "Franciscan thesis." Why was Mary preserved from all stain of original sin; what is the point of preservative redemption as contrasted with liberative? The response: to be the Mother of God and mediatrix of all graces. How can a mere creature be Mother of God, coredemptrix and mediatrix? By being preserved from all stain of original sin. She was so saved as to be able to cooperate actively in the entire work of redemption. Of her alone can this be said. But because it can be said of her, it can also be said of the redemption that it could not be more perfect, that the love of Father and Son for the human family could not be greater than it is in the Immaculate. In her and through her we find the ultimate expression and realization of the love of God and mercy of God for us. Franciscan spirituality is built around and progresses via a clearer and clearer recognition of the mystery of the Immaculate Conception and its implications in practice for the interior life and for the apostolate. The mystery of the Immaculate conception is central to the Franciscan charism. That is why the influence of the mediatrix of all graces is particularly crucial to the vitality of that spirituality and to the realization of its full potential. Thus, the "relaunching" of her influence in the spirituality of the Order, both at the level of the individual member and at that of corporate institutions of the community, is key to the revitalization of Franciscan spirituality as such and the source of renewed energy in undertaking the missionary apostolate of the Order. And just because the ideal in loving Christ crucified is the love of the Immaculate for him, the measure of that revitalization cannot simply be the level of achievement of times past, but an ever more perfect "incorporation" of that mystery into the lives of the friars and of the community as such. This was the point grasped so clearly by St. Maximilian. His heritage provides the means, appropriate to the Order in this period of its history in view of its role in the church, for realizing that potential. Total consecration to the Immaculate so as to form a part of her Militia, to be with others her instrument unconditionally at her disposition for the conversion and sanctification of all souls, living and to live, is just that method, a gift of the Immaculate herself. When implemented, not only personally but at the level of community, the result may be described in a single word: the property and possession of the Immaculate, the M.I. in the form of a friary. In such wise the M.I. is not simply the instrument of conversion and sanctification, but the type, the effective symbol of the paradise which is the goal to which the Immaculate would guide all.

The Appropriateness of the Solution

What it means to be the possession and property of the Immaculate, why
one word "Niepokalanów" describes exactly what a Franciscan community
ought to be if it is striving for a sanctity that is heroic, of the kind exemplified in the life and death of St. Maximilian, can only be appreciated as the
key to the relaunching of the influence of Mary Immaculate in the spirituality of the Order by viewing it in terms of the relation of the Immaculate to
St. Francis and to the Order which he founded.

St. Francis

The love and attachment of St. Francis to the Mother of God was not simply
remarkable, it was so exceptional according to St. Bonaventure and Celano
as to be beyond description. According to some modern scholars it must
be regarded as unique among the saints for its intensity and extent. But
it is not merely the testimony of his contemporaries and first biographers
to acquaint us with so mysterious an experience as this one of St. Francis;
his writings, e.g., the Magnificat Antiphon of the *Office of the Passion*, the
Salute to the Virgin, and its companion piece, the *Salute to the Virtues*, the
Letter addressed to the whole Order with its magnificent comment on the
Virgin Mary, purity and the Eucharist, the *Last Will for St. Clare*: all these
are eloquent witnesses. So, too, the most important events and places of his
life are all intimately associated with the mystery of Mary: the Portiuncula
where he discovered the sense of his calling by Christ crucified to repair
the church, to embrace the leper, where he made the Queen of the Angels
advocate of his Order, her whom he called Spouse of the Holy Spirit, the
Minister General of the Order, the place for which inspired by the Spouse
of the Holy Spirit he sought and obtained from the pope that special indulgence and largesse of mercy, and near which he himself died; Greccio where
he celebrated the joy and poverty of the Mother of God; and Alvernia where
he came to share her compassion in loving the incarnate, crucified Son of
God and Son of Mary, so intimately as to be conformed in his own flesh to
that of the crucified Savior—all this for the conversion of sinners and the
repair of the church. No greater love could anyone have for his brother than
Francis in fact had for them in loving his God and Savior in obedience and
poverty. In him that love is the manifestation of divine mercy for sinners.
No wonder the Portiuncula indulgence has come to symbolize the characteristic Franciscan devotion to the Mother of God.

However ineffable that devotion of St. Francis to the Mother of God, it is neither vague nor indeterminate, as though any kind of generic Marian devotion might well define it. Quite the contrary; it is her love as Spouse of the Holy Spirit for Christ; it is her love as the uniquely consecrated Daughter of the most high king to be the mother of his Son. This espousal, this consecration defines and measures the vocation of Francis and of his followers who in embracing the gospel life become spouses of the Holy Spirit, capable of giving birth to Christ in the souls of sinners and non-believers, because capable of compassion with the Savior. The secret of this love is that of the perfect fruit of the perfect redemption. The mystery of the Immaculate Conception, as the unique sanctity (consecration) of the Virgin Mary recognized by Francis would come to be known, is that of the incomparable Woman in whom is all good, whose love for God is so untainted by sin, original or actual, as to be greater than which none can be conceived in a mere creature and only God can understand; to be so great as to offer not only her life, but that of her Son, the heart of her heart, for the salvation of sinners, for the conversion and sanctification of the rest of his brethren. Spouse of the Holy Spirit, Advocate of Sinners, Francis addressed her: Immaculate Conception and mediatrix of all graces epitomize the distinctive Franciscan experience of charity, for God and for neighbor. Why poverty, why obedience? To be pure, i.e., to love as the Immaculate loves the crucified, so as to be able to love one's brethren as Christ loved them in loving and saving her so perfectly, preserving her from all stain of original sin. The perfection of the Immaculate's love, like that of God's, is seen in her capacity to stoop to sinners, to love them and to effect their conversion, their spiritual rebirth and resurrection. That love of the Immaculate is the clue to the intimate association of the contemplative and apostolic in the Franciscan form of life: a form of prayer and devotion centered on the crucified so as to labor for the repair of the church, to prepare it for the final coming of the groom. Thus the Franciscan form of life is perfectly integrated in its two poles, the contemplative and apostolic, because it is a reflection of Mary's love qua Immaculate for the crucified. The heart of Franciscan spirituality and missionary zeal is the mystery of the Immaculate Conception. In a word, Franciscan spirituality and with it Franciscan activity, is immaculatist, or it is nothing but an exercise in mystification and sentimentality.

The Order

St. Francis' vocation was not only one to personal sanctity of the highest order, viz., to be the saint closest to the heart of the Savior, but to found an

Order, a community whose form of life in common would illustrate, by partial anticipation, the joy of heaven, of living in the company of the three divine persons, together with the Mother of God, the Immaculate, the one creature never outside that paradise. That community established by St. Francis is at once to illustrate within the church what kind of love is that which the most perfectly redeemed has for the most perfect Redeemer, and to serve as the instrument for incorporating that love into the very life of the church and of believers. Chapter 6 of the *Regula Bullata* gives profound expression to this ideal of paradise, wherein as St. Bonaventure and St. Maximilian tell us, God is our Father, Mary our Mother and Christ our Brother. If a Mother so loves her child according to the flesh, how much more our brothers according to the Spirit with the love the Immaculate of God has for us.

It is not difficult to document the essentially Marian character of the Franciscan Order and of the charity at its core from its first beginnings at Rivo Torto and the Portiuncula, and which gives to the Franciscan movement of penance and repentance, prayer and devotion its typical flavor, so well summarized in chapter six of the definitive *Rule*. It is enough to recall such devotions as the Angelus, the Portiuncula Indulgence, the Franciscan Crown, the commentaries on the Angelic Salutation (Conrad of Saxony, *Speculum B. V. Mariae*), the Marian sermons of St. Bonaventure, especially his exposition of Mary's participation in the mystery of the cross, her Assumption and her position as mediatrix of all graces, James of Milan in his *Stimulus Amoris*, the *Stabat Mater* of Jacopone da Todi, the Marian preaching of St. Bernardine of Siena, the propagation of the title Spouse of the Holy Spirit through the widespread use of the *Office of the Passion* composed by St. Francis, the stimulation of interest in the figure of Mary at the foot of the cross, devotion to the crib of Bethlehem and to the divine maternity, promotion of the feast of the Visitation, so intimately associated with the title "mediatrix," and commentaries on the Magnificat (e.g. Cornelius Musso, Eleutherius Albergoni) with particular stress on the humility and poverty of the Virgin as her outstanding virtue most pleasing to God and the reason for his having done great things for her, the interpretation of passages of the Canticle of Canticles in an immaculatist key (*Tota pulchra es—et macula non est in te*), even with a complete exposition of this song celebrating the love of Christ and his spouse verse by verse in terms of the Immaculate Conception (St. Francis Anthony Fasani: *Mariale* I), and the theological and devotional elaboration of the mystery of the Immaculate Conception, associated above all with the name of the Subtle

Doctor-Marian Doctor, John Duns Scotus,[1] and culminating in the solemn dogmatic definition of 1854 by Pope Pius IX.

It is this last which has come to be known as the Franciscan thesis, not simply in Mariology, but in theology, the feature of Franciscan thought and devotion most distinctive of the Order's ethos, an insight fully reflecting St. Francis' manner of loving the crucified and those for whom he gave his life: that is as the perfect fruit of a perfect redemption loves the Savior. At the core of Franciscan spirituality, viz., Franciscan charity, is the mystery of the Immaculate. The genius of St. Maximilian was to see and state clearly that the cause of the Immaculate, of the one who is not simply immaculate, but the Immaculate Conception, of the one creature not merely as full of grace as she can be, but who could not be made to be greater as a receptacle of grace, is the ideal of the Franciscan Order: to be an example of what that mystery means in practice, viz., Paradise opened to us, and to be the instrument of the Immaculate, the mediatrix of all grace and advocate of the Order, in restoring the church and preparing it for the triumph of the sacred heart.

The first stage in that history, according to St. Maximilian, is orientated toward the dogmatic definition of the Immaculate conception. It is an orientation primarily the choice of the Order's advocate rather than of the Order, but whose implementation by the Order is its principal glory and privilege. About this all else comprising the life and work and history of the Order gravitates. And without this all else, in particular Franciscan thought and devotion, would cease to be more than private opinion and personal taste. The definition of the Immaculate Conception, however, is not the glorification of one private taste in piety rather than another. The work of the Order is rather that of an instrument designed and selected for something far greater than the Order itself: the mystery of the Immaculate Conception and the realization of her cause in the church, whose first step is the explicit and solemn confession of this mystery by the church. This step once taken leads not only to a deepening of the thought and devotion preceding it, as signaled at Lourdes by the "I am the Immaculate Conception" and the request for penance, but to a further, final goal: the incorporation of the mystery into life.

This incorporation, like the preparatory elaboration of the doctrine, is a work greater than the Order, and like the doctrine has a characteristic form, viz., the Militia of the Immaculate based on total consecration to the Immaculate, with the Miraculous Medal the sacramental of its goal, a form

---

1. Hopkins, *Duns Scotus's Oxford*: "Of reality the rarest veined unraveller; a not Rivalled insight, be rival Italy or Greece; Who fired France for Mary without spot."

authoritatively defining and expressing the incorporation of the mystery of the Immaculate into life, the formation of a global vision of Catholic life under a new form, consisting in its link with the Immaculate, our universal mediatrix with Jesus. This is the second stage of Order history focused on the work of realizing that incorporation of the dogma of the Immaculate Conception into life and every dimension of life and mission of the church, to conquer every soul for the Immaculate, and through this to achieve the maximum love and glory of Christ in the church. All else in the life of the Order today gravitates for better or worse about this incorporation.

According to St. Maximilian, then, the central goal of the Order, toward which everything in it is orientated and toward whose achievement it must constantly move, the reason for its institution, as the continuation and exemplification of the vocation of Francis to repair the church, is to be found in the mystery of the Immaculate, i.e., in the mystery of the perfect love of the Redeemer by those for whom he gave his life. The achievement of the goal constitutes the repair, restoration and perfecting of the church for the final glorification of Christ's heart and of his love for the Father and for his brethren. The first stage in the history of the Order is but the condition for the second, as it were the preparation of the plans according to which the house will be built.

It is perfectly true that the Order has contributed to goals other than the cause of the Immaculate, for the simple reason that there is no necessary contradiction between these and the cause of the Immaculate. Indeed, until the first stage of the history was concluded in the solemn definition of the dogma, total consecration to the Immaculate in corporate form was not fully possible. Naturally it is possible to theorize about a central goal of the Order other than that of the cause of the Immaculate, for the simple reason that the Order is not necessary to the plans of the Immaculate and is not compelled to agree to these plans. Whether one can argue that the acceptance of these plans by the Order is not necessary for the Order to be genuinely and fully Franciscan, or whether failure to support these plans with anything less than full cooperation could be anything but tragic for the Order in every way, is quite another matter. In fact, speculation about other possible central goals for the Order is mere speculation. For the fact of the matter is simply this: in the entire span of time stretching between the founding of the Order and its near demise at the time of the French Revolution and subsequent secularizations, the central, outstanding contribution of the Order to the life of the church was the dogma of the Immaculate Conception. There were indeed other contributions, none, however, to equal this in importance and solemnity for the church itself. What the dogma articulates was true, a part of revelation, before Franciscan thought and devotion came to be. But the truth did not come to be expressed with the clarity presupposed for a dog-matic definition, except via the instrumentality of that theology and devo-tion. Apart from the dogma, that theology and devotion lose their vitality and raison d'être.

That being so, the proclamation of the dogma not only points to, but de-mands the second step (as dogma naturally guides praxis): incorporation into life, particularly where that dogma is the mystery of the person who identifies herself as the Immaculate Conception. The existence of the Order can indeed be construed apart from the mystery of the Immaculate; but it is no more likely to come alive in fact than the theology and devotion of the Order can flower apart from the mystery of the Immaculate. And what dogma is to the theology and devotion of the Order, in its own way the M.I. is to the life, spirituality and mission apostolate of the Order. For the M.I. is nothing more than the form that spirituality takes when the mystery of the Immaculate is incorporated into life. And Niepokalanów is nothing more or less than the M.I. when it is incorporated into the spirituality of the community as such, not an apostolate aside a friary, but in the form of a friary.

Of course, the M.I. is far broader than the Order, just as the dogma extends far beyond Franciscan thought and devotion. Nonetheless the Order in each case is the chosen instrument of the Immaculate for attaining and for illustrating each. Why should this be so? Because the Order of penance and poverty, of unconditional obedience, is uniquely disposed, where that *Rule* is lived heroically, to promote the cause of her whose love is so deeply entwined with the suffering of her Son and the purposes of the suffering of that Son, the Word Incarnate: the conversion and salvation of sinners.

What St. Maximilian calls "incorporation" is but the construction of a way of life and apostolate with the Immaculate as the person at its origin, its center and end, in a word, as all-encompassing as an atmosphere, in such wise that the Immaculate in fact possesses each individual friar and each com-munity totally consecrated to her to use unconditionally as she best knows how for the conversion of all and for the triumph of the sacred heart. The M.I., a gift of the Immaculate, was given to achieve just that kind of spiritual-apostolic life, one in which the Immaculate would love Jesus and sinners with our hearts, and we would love Jesus with hers. Such a love would lead us to offer our lives for our neighbor and his eternal life, as Jesus gave his life for us. Such love on our part is but the fruit of a mystery, that of the Immaculate Conception, the loveliest of God's works and the ideal of the Order. *Tota pul-chra es, Maria, et macula originalis non est in te.*

Niepokalanów: Practical Implementation
of the Kolbean Heritage

The Kolbean heritage is a gift of the Immaculate to the Order, in the same way as the vocation of Francis was a gift of Christ at the intercession of the Immaculate, Advocate of the Order. It is Kolbean precisely because given to us through St. Maximilian, because lived so perfectly by him so as to exemplify its implications on the practical level. Saints are given us to be imitated, not merely venerated. Imitation of him is asked of us precisely because correspondence with the wishes of the Immaculate, mediatrix of all graces, completes and fulfills the Franciscan spiritual tradition. Indeed, that gift, the M.I., stimulates the growth and perfection of that tradition; that growth and perfection serves as an instrument of the Immaculate to sustain the M.I. In this sense the Kolbean heritage may be regarded as a natural outgrowth of the Franciscan tradition. One word describes it in its entirety: Niepokalanów, total consecration on our part to the Immaculate, without limits or conditions; total possession of us by her as her property, to use as she sees fit for the consummation of the kingdom of the sacred heart and for rescuing all souls from the influence of the prince of this world. Niepokalanów is no mere theoretical insight into Mariology; it is above all a dynamic, living spirituality resting on the acceptance and incorporation of the truth of the Immaculate's mediation into every dimension of our lives.

To many, Niepokalanów suggests a specific place in Poland, or perhaps as well the activities entailed in operating a large publishing venture which among other things made that particular place so famous. But if all those activities initiated by St. Maximilian in his lifetime are to be duly appreciated and understood in proper perspective, then we must, as he always insisted, define Niepokalanów primarily from a spiritual point of view. Rather than a place or an activity, Niepokalanów is first of all a way of life, a way of living Franciscan life, a way of observing the Franciscan rule, precisely incorporating the mystery of the Immaculate as consciously, deliberately and fully as possible into that way of life. In so proceeding we do not retreat from the practical to the theoretical, from the concrete and specific to the vague, general and indeterminate. Niepokalanów so defined is a very thoroughgoing practical norm and functional formula of Franciscan life: it is the Kolbean charism imitable and imitated in Franciscan life, as Pope John Paul II says it must be for all.

As a practical norm Niepokalanów focuses our attention, our thoughts, our desires, our actions on that mystery of faith, which, as we have seen briefly, is the central, distinctive feature of Franciscan spirituality at its core, viz., the Immaculate Conception. Of course, if one does not see this point, chooses to neglect it, or worse, deny it, then of course the Kolbean heritage will not have much meaning for him as a major contribution to Franciscan spirituality and spiritual living. But is such neglect or denial justifiable? Quite the contrary. Hence we have been given the gift of the Kolbean heritage, the M.I., and ultimately the M.I. in the form of a friary, viz., Niepokalanów, to bring us back to our true origins. By implementing that heritage, we will indeed come to understand the core of our vocation better. The starting point of that implementation is an acceptance of the truth that the Immaculate should possess us and our community totally, in fact and practice as well as in theory. Niepokalanów as a practical norm means total consecration, total possession.

As a functional formula Niepokalanów is a form of life, specifically the M.I. in the form of a friary. A Franciscan spirituality accounting only for the personal, interior dimension or apostolic, exterior dimension of the friar's life is incomplete. The element of fraternity, of what is best described as the "vita perfecte communis" is indispensable both as the instrument and major support at once of the interior and apostolic dimensions of that life, and as the concrete exemplification of what Franciscan charity is when realized: an anticipation of paradise, of the communion of saints. Chapter six of our Rule cannot be underestimated as one of the finest summations of the Franciscan form of life in practice, and it is just this kind of paradise St. Maximilian understood any Niepokalanów should be to deserve the name, and which any friary could be provided it truly became the exclusive possession and property of the Immaculate. That formula, "res et proprietas Immaculatae," is neither vague and indeterminate, nor subject to interminable change, revision and unpredictable applications, such as deprive any religious community of the last shreds of credibility. The specifics of that formula are the elements whose presence or absence will determine, whatever the circumstances or cultures, whether or not we as a community as well as individuals, are acting as true heirs of Francis and Maximilian.

1. The priority of the interior life of contemplation. Citizen number one of Niepokalanów is the Son of Mary. To take the Immaculate as our ideal is first of all to strive to be as uninterruptedly absorbed in her Son as she is, and concretely by centering that attention on his real presence in our midst. The desire to remain before the blessed sacrament with the Immaculate in adoration, reparation, petition and contemplation is crucial to Niepokalanów. Other duties required by obedience may determine the relative amount of time available for this; but that no time should be available, or that the desire to be present before the blessed sacrament whenever possible is not the operative desire of all persons in that community

whatever they might be doing surely indicates a failure to implement the Kolbean heritage.

2. A sacrificial life postulates an objective form or rule of life, observed as the ascetical basis for the devotion at its center. No spirituality has ever succeeded without disciplinary uniformity. The love of Christ crucified made possible by the vow of celibacy within the context of the Franciscan form of life has as its ascetical basis poverty and obedience. This is their fundamental reason within this form of life: to promote the love of Christ and of the church for which he gave his life, and effectively counteract the influence of the serpent under the efficacious direction of her who has destroyed all heresy in the whole world by destroying its root: inordinate self-love.

But the discipline so constituted in the faithful implementation of the vows of poverty and obedience is not without its functional value on a practical, day-to-day basis. Poverty has as its objective the use of only what is strictly necessary for the community and its members, so that whatever else may accrue to it can be devoted exclusively to the cause of the Immaculate. It is, in the view of St. Maximilian, the means employed by the Immaculate to further her projects throughout the world, for effectively extending the mercy of God even to the most abandoned of sinners. And while there is a certain amount of relativity in assessing the material or corporal needs of each community and friar in mathematical terms (e.g., the sick friar objectively has needs the healthy friar does not), there is certainly nothing relative about assessing what is not necessary, i.e., what is simply a personal convenience and in no way pertains to the efficient operation of an apostolate. The careful distinction of the material goods pertaining to the life of the friars and those to the work of the apostolate, in such wise that the latter never formed an excuse for "broadening" the personal needs of the friars, and the zeal to always restrict personal need to the minimum required by objective standards, together with a cheerful willingness to leave the provision of such minimal needs to divine providence, the care of the Immaculate, work and begging rather than "investments," "insurance" or fixed revenues, at once constituted the secret of the admirable observance of poverty at Niepokalanów under St. Maximilian and the source of so much dynamic energy in and support for the apostolic and missionary projects of that community. And if the luxuries forbidden at Niepokalanów by St. Maximilian, often regarded—then and now—as prohibitions tending to "rigidity," e.g., liquor, tobacco, outside entertainment, dress other than habit, work clothes or clerical garb, the modern version of the peculium, P.M. (Pocket Money), etc., are regarded in this light, none of these "negations" will seem particularly unreasonable, or repressive. What they seem to the worldly and/or imprudent is quite another matter. But the perceptions of such do not constitute appropriate norms for assessing what should or should not be the standard of the discipline of objective perfect common life.

If poverty is the "capital of Niepokalanów," whereby it is sustained materially by the Immaculate, obedience constitutes the method by which it is governed by her. By obedience is meant supernatural obedience, where the motive for prompt, cheerful execution of legitimate commands is simply that they are the will of God. It is not a system in which suggestions are excluded, where initiative and responsibility are suppressed, but in which these are exercised as perfectly as possible in view of what is known to be the will of the Immaculate rather than one's own pleasure; rather where one's own desires are conformed as exactly as possible to the clearly objective indications of the will of the Immaculate. Nor is obedience of this kind merely an exercise for the subject; it is also the obligation of the superior, to command only what he knows with certainty to be the will of the Immaculate, i.e., to issue legitimate commands that serve her interests. While he may not know her will perfectly, he certainly must not act contrary to what is her will, or make use of his position for personal advantage. When he so acts, the Immaculate will guarantee that what in fact is commanded does in fact secure her ends. So, too, those, for example teachers, theologians, academics, who enjoy, if not the authority to command, at least analogous positions of influence, ought not to use such positions merely to promote personal opinion as a basis for conduct, or worse to undermine confidence in the patronage of the Mother of God. Their influence should be placed at the service of the truth under the direction of her who understands so well the truth who is her Son.

No matter how unpalatable to the worldly mind, there is no question, if we judge by the experience of Niepokalanów under St. Maximilian, that such a system works, when the conditions for its functioning are fulfilled, viz., a humility on the part of all objectively based on the truth as that is known in the Catholic Church, and works with considerably less friction, artificiality and tension than more worldly-wise approaches to community management and administration do.

3. As the motive of such discipline is the love of the Immaculate for her Son, shared by the members of a Niepokalanów, so its goal is nothing more or less than the promotion for the Immaculate of her mission to conquer for her the entire world and every soul. So oriented, the heroic observance of poverty and obedience become as well a living testimony to the message preached, the power and drive giving effect to the missionary effort of the community. And just because Franciscan life is missionary by nature, that life lived heroically entails the waiver of the condition placed by chapter 12 of the Regula Bullata on the authority of the superior to

assign a friar to a mission without his prior consent. Who joins a Niepokalanów has by the fact of its total consecration to the cause of the Immaculate already embraced a permanent missionary status with the attendant
risk of total sacrifice of life in that cause. In such a status such a condition,
as St. Maximilian more than once observed, makes no sense. How could
a general (and he regarded the Immaculate as the supreme Condottiera of
the Niepokalanów) of an army fight a battle (and the battle in this case is
that of the Woman with the serpent), if the soldiers can place conditions on
the circumstances in which they will fight? Likewise, the missionary objective of Niepokalanów, so universal in scope, implies the need to expand
and multiply throughout the world. To deny such a community (or groups
or communities organized as a province within the Order) the right to
seek out recruits, and to make new foundations is to consign this idea to
stagnation and ultimately death within the Order.

4. Just because it is a heroic, missionary form of life, those preparing
to enter upon it require a special preparation and formation, including
the intellectual and theological dimensions. And just because Niepokalanów is not simply an apostolate, but a way of life, a spirituality, this is a
formation which in its essentials can only be imparted within the City of
the Immaculate itself. As with the former three points, so, too, failure to
account for this element in the definition of Niepokalanów as a functional
formula will effectively impede the successful continuation of the Kolbean
heritage within the Order.

Two objections are often heard to the Kolbean heritage so defined
in functional terms: it is divisive and it is fossilizing. As regards the first I
would with St. Maximilian simply deny the charge. So long as every friary
of the Order does not in fact accept the Militia statute, viz., to live the Rule
as perfectly as possible for the exclusive purposes of the Immaculate, then
of course the style of life at a genuine Niepokalanów will be distinctive. But
a distinctive style demanded by the exigencies of a special cause is not divisive, if that cause is proper to the Order, especially if that cause is central
to the Order, as I have tried to indicate here, no more so than the sacrifices
Franciscan missionaries make in their form of life is divisive of the Order.
We should carefully consider if at times our way of understanding provincial
divisions in the Order does not lead to a far worse provincialism. Nor does
a specialized preparation in a Niepokalanów constitute any more of a threat
to the unity of the Order than the present system of formation systems for
each national or geographic unit in the Order. Two distinct questions must
be considered: whether all friaries should become Niepokalanów; and in the
event that response is presently negative, whether the Order can afford to
be without any Niepokalanów, and afford not to promote their expansion

throughout the world. A negative answer to this second would constitute a repudiation of the genuine Kolbean tradition, surely a grievous step foreboding a gloomy future for our Franciscan community.

As regards the question of fossilization: the foregoing view of Niepokalanów and the Kolbean tradition hardly precludes legitimate adaptation, where there are objective grounds for this and where we have the authority and responsibility to make prudent changes. But such authority and such adaptations are not unlimited, nor do they, when they occur, occur other than within well-defined limits, in particular when the M.I. takes the form of a friary.

The character of those limits, as here sketched, is objective, i.e., transcending the variable circumstances subject to change and adaptation, and reflects the nature of the M.I., not within our power to change, but only to accept as the gift of the Advocate/Immaculate of the Order and faithfully nurture, or reject. To pretend that we can modify the essence of such a gift by way of adaptations or "restructurings" as some would say, so as to bring it up-to-date and make it more acceptable to a contemporary mentality is not a position capable of defense. Should the Order choose not to accept the M.I. as given by the Immaculate through St. Maximilian, then the only honest course of action is that of repudiation, because the essential elements not subject to change by us, viz., total consecration as the possession and property of the Immaculate, to be used by her as she sees fit in her battle with the ancient serpent to win all souls for her Son, an ideal and goal well symbolized by the miraculous medal, are judged, for whatever reasons, to be irrelevant and inappropriate to the Order and to the times.

But that is a judgment whose correctness and justice have not only not been demonstrated; it is one contradicted by many evidences of the appropriateness of the M.I. as given: for the Order, for the church, for the times. To take up such a position in support of the prudence and foresight of the Immaculate, clearly a rejection of the philosophic evolutionism, epistemological relativism and legal positivism necessary to rationalize adaptation without limit, does not preclude legitimate and appropriate adaptation; indeed, it provides the only secure basis on which to identify those elements subject to change and to make those adjustments, particularly in the organization of work and in the daily guidance of a multitude of persons and groups, each with their unique character, history and experience, required in fact for the successful realization of the M.I. goals.

Before proceeding to questions of adaptation or "restructuring," an understanding and acceptance of those principles of the M.I. ideal not subject to change must be acquired, lest decisions taken in the name of adaptation, of practical "common sense," in fact modify the M.I. beyond recognition in its essentials, particularly as it comes to be incorporated in the Order as a Niepokalanów. The above four points constitute a set of limits within which responsible authority within the Order—and this General Chapter is one of those authorities—must act. So acting such authority will indeed contribute to the preservation and development of the Kolbean heritage, in a manner faithful to Catholic tradition and orthodox theology (as St. Maximilian ardently wished in underscoring so often the immutable character of truth) and equally zealous for the realization of the greatest sanctity conceivable, viz., one taking the holiness of the Immaculate as its norm. Precisely because Niepokalanów is the practical heart of the Kolbean ideal translated into a daily form of life, it is on this reality that chapter discussions must center. To the extent that Niepokalanów is successfully promoted in accord with its authentic character as set forth by St. Maximilian under the inspiration of the Immaculate, to that extent will the mystery of the Immaculate be incorporated into the life of the Order. So also that effort successfully pursued will enable the Order to do effectively what the Immaculate asks of it: the dynamic guidance of the M.I. under her direction. If the Order so acts, St. Maximilian foretold unheard of blessings and prosperity, not excluding the ultimate reunion of all friars, to be granted by the Immaculate and her divine Son.

Points for Discussion

1. The mystery of the Immaculate Conception and the distinctive features of the Franciscan way: life, spirituality, thought.

2. The mystery of the Immaculate Conception, and the distinctive, essential features of the M.I.: total consecration, unconditional obedience under the direction of the Immaculate, generous engagement in the battle between the Woman and the serpent for the minds and hearts of men and in the work of preparing the church for the final triumph of the Sacred Heart.

3. Niepokalanów, the M.I. in the form of a friary, i.e., the incorporation of the mystery of the Immaculate into the life of a Franciscan community qua talis; the constituent elements of a Niepokalanów where the Rule is observed exclusively to promote the cause of the Immaculate. Niepokalanów: The Kolbean charism as imitable and imitated in the Order.

8

The Immaculate and the Extraordinary Synod 1985

A SUPERFICIAL READING OF the acts of the recent extraordinary Synod of Bishops in Rome might lead one to conclude that questions of Mariology and of Marian devotion did not figure prominently in the discussions and decisions of the Synod. Such an impression is just that because superficial. An attentive meditation on the mystery of the church in the light of the Cross and Resurrection of our Savior, the very center of those discussions and the key to a genuine understanding of the teaching of Vatican II and of the renewal that teaching is to guide and of how it differs from a merely mediocre adjustment to the fashions of the day, reveals how intimately present the Immaculate was in the deliberations and Acts of the Synod. That presence without doubt was a response to the prayer of the Holy Father at the opening of the Synod: "Mary most holy, Mother of God and Mother of the Church, help today the bishops, as once you helped the Apostles in the Cenacle, and intercede for all Christians that freed from divisions they might achieve unity; relieved from suffering and oppression they might live in peace; assembled in the bond of love of the Trinity they might display to the entire world the church, the body of Christ and living temple of the Spirit, to the praise and glory of Father, Son and Holy Spirit. Amen."

That prayer to the mediatrix of all grace followed immediately on a plea to our Lord Jesus Christ to send "His Spirit, the Spirit of love and truth, upon the bishops so that they might accept what the Spirit is saying today to the churches, allowing themselves to be guided by the whole truth, that through their ministry the faithful, purified and sustained in their assent to the Gospel of salvation, might become a living sacrifice to the Father."

The link between this plea for the sending of the Spirit of truth and love and the prayer to Mary most holy is the point of departure for that profound commentary on the significance of the Synod offered by the Holy Father himself at its conclusion last December 8, the feast of the Immaculate Conception: "The Holy Spirit will come upon you and the power of the Most High will overshadow you" (Luke 1:35) (Introduction to the Homily). That Spirit of truth and love is uniquely present in Mary all holy, the Immaculate, and does nothing in this final age of salvation history, the age of the church, except through Mary all holy, Mother of God, through whom the Savior comes to us, comes to the cross. Further, what he the Savior has done for us, what he has made it possible for us to become, is what is contemplated in the mystery of the Immaculate: the mystery of the beginning, the beginning of a better world, the world of God (The Angelus, December 8, 1985). That is why "the church looks to Mary, the Mother of God, as her prototype," no more so than under her title of Immaculate, who is all fair, in whose beauty the church comes to understand her own (Address to Mary, Piazza di Spagna, December 8, 1985). For this reason the pope, with the bishops, desired on the feast of the Immaculate Conception "to entrust this time in the life and mission of the church to the Mother of the Church, to her who is uniquely present to the mystery of the church, because uniquely present to the mystery of Christ" (Address, December 7, 1985). "This is the truth given expression in the final chapter of the Conciliar Constitution *Lumen Gentium*." It is the key to the mystery of the church, a truth the Holy Father desired to underscore at the conclusion of a Synod dedicated to the understanding, appreciation and implementation of the Second Vatican Council: "because the Synod closed on the feast of the immaculate Conception and because in so doing the work of the Synod would find its crown" (Homily, December 8, 1985).

No more than a brief summary of that homily deserving far more extensive comment is possible here. The descent of the Holy Spirit on Mary Immaculate, began the Holy Father, is the model and figure of the church, born on the day of Pentecost, born in human history through the descent of the Holy Spirit on the apostles assembled about Mary, and this in order to strengthen them in view of their weaknesses and of the contradictions to come upon them for the sake of the gospel message: the truth of Christ crucified and risen. The solemnity of the Immaculate Conception turns our minds to reflect on the beginning of the history of creation and of salvation: indeed to go behind this beginning to the eternal thought of God. For the greeting of the Angel Gabriel: "Hail, full of grace," deals with the singular election of the Virgin Mary to be holy and Immaculate in Christ, before the creation of the world, to be immaculate in the first moment of her conception, to be in the mystery of the incarnation mother of divine grace.

The liturgy of the Immaculate Conception guides us to the very heart of this mystery, appropriately called the mystery of the beginning, announced on the first pages of Genesis. In the context of this beginning is described the sin of Adam and in this context is also found the foretelling of a Redeemer. The Immaculate Conception is thus depicted via a contrast with original sin, and signifies freedom from the effects of the disobedience of Adam, a freedom achieved through the obedience of the second Adam, Christ. In consideration of the price of that redemption the spiritual death of sin in no wise touches the mother of the Redeemer. That privilege, however, does not remove her from the economy of salvation; rather her presence is thereby engaged at the very center of the spiritual struggle with the prince of darkness, in a perpetual enmity with the enemy of the human family which will bring her to participate at the foot of the cross in the culminating moment of that enmity when Christ achieves a definitive victory over Satan and the Immaculate crushes the serpent's head. According to the Holy Father Vatican II teaches that through her suffering Mary, the Immaculate, cooperates in a manner unique to her in the work of the Savior, and for this reason the Mother of God is intimately united to the church as its figure. The church is mysterious, because Virgin and Mother; it is Virgin and mother to the extent it is linked to the mystery of Mary Immaculate. The Immaculate Conception is the prism through which the church grasps the mystery of grace: of union with God, of communion with the three divine persons, without which that created communion which is the church would not and could not be.

It is through this prism as well that the church comes to grasp the nature of her mission for men in the contemporary world, not only created and conserved in existence by the power of God, but also under the slavery of sin, from which it can be and is liberated by the power of the cross. The preservation of Mary from original sin, her fulness of grace, is the figure and means of our liberation from sin. It is only in being the sacrament of unity with God (*Lumen Gentium*) that the church can minister effectively in the contemporary world (*Gaudium et Spes*). And in seeking to enter more fully into the mystery of the cross, the church, and every believer in the church, seeks to make her own the response of the Immaculate to the divine election and call: "Behold the handmaid of the Lord," because the church looks to the Immaculate as her prototype in the Holy Spirit.

The church so acts because she desires to be at the end of the second millennium the same church born of the Holy Spirit when the apostles in the Cenacle were united in prayer about Mary, the Immaculate, from the very beginning at the center of the apostolic community. The church so acts, because at this time she desires to be the church in the contemporary world, but can only be so to the extent she is, in Christ, the sacrament of union with God for all mankind. So concluded the homily.

Who is in any way familiar with the thought and action of St. Maximilian Kolbe will not fail to note how the saint's insight into the mystery of the created Immaculate Conception, Mary, the Spouse of the Holy Spirit, the uncreated Immaculate Conception, into her role qua Immaculate as Coredemptrix, the unique associate of the Savior under the cross, the mediatrix of all graces, the beginning not only of a better world, but of that created paradise where God is Father, Mary our Mother and Christ our Brother, of that created communion with the uncreated communion of Father, Son and Holy Spirit which could not be better (where sin abounded, grace has superabounded: Vespers Meditation, St. Mary Major, December 8, 1985), is the basis of a spiritual-apostolic program for incorporating the mystery of the Immaculate Conception into the life of the church and of every human being, viz., the M.I., providentially prepared for just this moment when the mystery of the church and her relation to the cross and resurrection of Christ are supremely important. Who lives the mystery of the Immaculate Conception will discover the Mother of the Church, and thus the paradise of her Son, our Savior, and of his Father who so loved us as to send his only-begotten Son into this world to give his life in expiation for our sins. May our love for him and his Father be always that of the Immaculate, so that we too might love our neighbor as the Savior does, as that herald of the great king, St. Francis, that Knight of the Immaculate, St. Maximilian, have illustrated in their lives.

9

Mother of the Redeemer and *Redemptoris Mater*

I. ON MARCH 25 of this year the Holy Father published the Marian encyclical announced earlier (January 1, 1987) in conjunction with the first news of a Marian year in preparation for the second millennium of the birth of our Savior. The feast of the Annunciation was chosen for this event because the encyclical in essence is a meditation on that mystery of salvation communicated first to the humble Virgin of Nazareth during her memorable conversation with the Angel Gabriel on that occasion. The inauguration of the work of salvation in the mystery of the incarnation was dependent then, as it continues to be ever since, on the "yes" of the Virgin, a "yes" with which history entered upon the "fullness of time." That "yes" at the moment of the annunciation was a conscious, deliberate act of faith, a confession of the triune God and of the Incarnate Son of God and Savior, the most perfect act of faith ever made, the finest flower of the "fulness of grace," of the Immaculate Conception, an act of faith consummated in the compassionate love of the Mother of God at the foot of the cross. Our understanding of, and more importantly, our participation in that mystery of salvation is directly proportionate to the degree our faith coincides with the faith of Mary and is nourished by her fulness of grace. At the very core of the church's life of faith and of that of each of her members is an orientation indispensable to every other aspect of that life: the contemplation of the Savior and of his work of salvation through the eyes of his Mother, an orientation mirroring a fact of salvation history: her appearance always precedes his and heralds his quick advent on our horizons.

That contemplation, however, has another side. The church contemplates Mary through the eyes of Jesus. For the church is the body of Christ and the Mother of God is her Mother. Only in him can we understand and love her, the most perfect fruit of a most perfect redemption, and thus understanding her mystery at the heart of the church come to appreciate and esteem what Christ has made the church in saving her and giving her over to the care of his Mother. Thus, the love and veneration shown by the church to the Mother of God seeks ever more to be that shown her always by the Savior, because such veneration is the secret of the church's vitality as mother and virgin, sustained by the never-ceasing maternal mediation of the Theotokos.

This reciprocal contemplation of the unending union of Jesus and Mary at once enables the church, and her members, indeed all who are called to be members of the church and share the life of faith, to deepen their understanding of the patrimony of truths they believe and extend in their own lives the range of that "obedience of faith," so perfect in the life of Mary, from Nazareth to Ain Karim, in the Temple, at Cana, on Calvary, in the Cenacle. In this the all-holy Virgin is the model, guide and support of the people of God throughout its history, no more so than in its more diffi-cult and significant moments. During the church's time of pilgrimage Mary is the effective, never-failing sign of hope founded on faith, the evidence of things unseen, the "stella maris," the divine guarantee seen by the Seer of Patmos in the very Tabernacle of God, that the church born on Pentecost will reach the glory of the assumption.

As the Holy Father remarked in his discourse at the General Audi-ence of March 25, 1987, the encyclical so meditated is a re-proposal of the teaching of Vatican II on the mystery of Mary in Christ and in the church, and under certain aspects a deepening of the conciliar teaching in chapter 8 of *Lumen Gentium*. The study of the mystery of Mary in Christ and in the church reveals the grandeur and perfection of the salvation wrought by the Son of Mary on the cross and of the glory one day also to be that of the church formed from his side on the cross.

The encyclical, however, has a very particular, concrete goal: to en-courage, to stimulate, to illumine, to deepen in the church in view of the bimillennium of the birth of her head that Marian spirituality and corela-tive devotion appropriate to the body of Christ, a spirituality and devotion rooted in the very origins of the church, witnessed by every generation of believers, and at the core of that spiritual discipline to which the Council exhorts us. That spirituality and devotion is, in the words of St. Louis Gri-gnion de Montfort cited by the Holy Father in the encyclical, but our con-secration to Christ offered through the hands of Mary. It is this spirituality which the Marian year is intended to cultivate, a spirituality so appropriate and necessary, because the life of the church between Pentecost and her Assumption in glory at the coming of Christ on the last day is first of all and above all a life of faith whose coefficient is obedience to the word of God. In this the Virgin Mary anticipates and precedes the church. For she is indissolubly and actively linked to the salvation wrought by Christ in its

every moment, first in effecting the work of salvation and in the formation of the church, then in caring for the growth of the church and of her
members in the life of faith.

II. The life of faith characterizing the church's time of pilgrimage enjoys
a vitality whose measure is the perfection of that obedience—practical love—
motivating it. From this perspective the obedience of faith is the central
theme of the encyclical. That obedience is a very special and crucial instance
in the sanctification of the human person, viz., in conforming the human will
to that of the Creator-Savior. Faith as an assent of the intellect, viz., dogmatic
faith, the act motivated by that obedience, is both a manifestation of and a
guide to that unconditional love of the truth which is God. A manifestation,
for in subordinating personal judgment (the root of personal liberty) unconditionally to the judgment of God, the assent of the intellect to the truth for
its own sake could not be purer or more perfect; a guide, for in its purity such
understanding cannot deceive or disappoint.

The choice entailed by the obedience of faith marks the difference
between humility and pride of mind and intellect, between Catholic belief
and private judgment, the spirit of faith and that of heresy, in a word between salvation and damnation at the point where one or the other first appears in the soul. That difference is the one between acceptance and refusal
of the grace of salvation wrought by Christ Jesus. Thus, the obedience of
faith is the initial response to the prior salvific love of God, to our election
in Christ Jesus before the constitution of the world to be holy and immaculate in his sight, to our predestination to be adopted sons of God, to the
praise of the glory of his grace wherewith he has graced us (Eph 1:1–14).
That grace, the basis of our cooperation in the work of salvation and sharing in the victory of our Savior, the Son of God incarnate, over the prince
of this world, over sin and death, is a participation in the divine nature, in
the fellowship, of the divine persons (2 Pet 1:4).

The faith of our Lady is a privileged instance within this context of
divine election. Before all others she was an object of divine love, greater
than which none is conceivable. For she was chosen to be the Mother of the
God who saves, so that when the fulness of time came God would send his
only-begotten Son to be born of the Woman, to be born under the law, that
he might redeem those under the law, that they might receive the adoption of
sons, and with the Spirit of his Son cry out, Abba Father (cf. Gal 4:4–6). That
election of the Woman in Christ Jesus from all eternity is in time the mystery
of her Immaculate Conception, of that fulness of grace wherewith she could
not have been graced more unto the praise of the glory of his grace, i.e., of the
Son whom she would conceive by the Holy Spirit and bear. She received fully
of his fulness of grace (John 1:16), and in addressing her as "Full of grace" the

Angel Gabriel revealed and synthesized the height and the depth, the length and breadth of that unique love for her of him who sent his only Son to be born of the Woman, to be a propitiation for our sins.

In linking these texts the Holy Father shows how the exemption of Our Lady from original sin in her Immaculate Conception is the basis of a life of faith, of obedience, of humility on which the mystery of the incarnation and of our redemption depends, and which therefore is the divinely willed means of our life of faith. The life of faith of Mary most holy issues in the conception and birth of the Son of God as man, but is consummated at the foot of the cross in the compassion of the Immaculate for her Son. It is this faith that first merits for her the title "Blessed": from her Son (Luke 11:28) and from all generations (Luke 1:45, 48). It is this faith, which anticipates, precedes and makes possible the faith of the church. That faith defining the history of her interior life is the pattern for the church's history, for the history of every soul, and so affects the whole of history. It is this faith of a mother which accompanies and is an active part of every mystery of the Savior's life, from his conception at Nazareth to his death on Calvary outside the holy city, when he entrusted-consecrated his church and her members to the care of his Mother, the moment when the beloved disciple received the Mother of God among his most treasured possessions (cf. John 19:26–7). The grace of the Immaculate Conception by which as it were Mary is a contemplative from conception, wrapped up in the life of the divine persons, is also the grace by which is fulfilled the promise-prophecy of Genesis 3:15. As the Immaculate, whose will is perfectly conformed to that of her Son's, perfectly one with the divine will, the Virgin Mary becomes the "interpreter" of her Son's will to us.

As the perfect fruit of a perfect redemption, then, the Virgin Mary is the type and exemplar of the church. Her faith is the model of that of the church, the basis of the church's own virginal maternity. But Mary is more than a model of the church; she is also Mother of the Church. Her faith exerts a causal influence on the faith of the church and of each of her members, at the formation of the church on Calvary and at the birth of the church at Pentecost. That she should be found in the midst of the Apostles and disciples at Pentecost (Acts 1:14) is the consequence of our Lord's own final will and testament on dying (John 19:26–7). The church herself recognizes this maternal mediation not as a substitute for the authoritative teaching and work of the apostles and their successors, but as its premise. Mary is the memory of the church and by making Mary's faith her own, the church remains faithful to her head and Savior. That is the reason for the veneration of the images or icons of Mary in the church, for frequent chanting of her Magnificat, the hymn of faith and praise for the

Savior, for the frequenting of sanctuaries of our Lady, milestones as it were on the road of faith, the geography matching its history. It is that faith that must animate the church's appeal to all men to repent and believe and be baptized as disciples of the Savior and children of his Mother. It is the faith of Mary and the love for Mary which will unite all who believe in Jesus in the one sheepfold founded and organized by him.

The maternal mediation of the Immaculate is not a mediation other than Christ's but a unique cooperation with his, one which makes ours possible. Her preservation from sin in the Immaculate Conception makes possible our liberation from sin in fact, that we might be holy and immaculate in God's sight. As the final crown of that Immaculate Conception the Virgin's Assumption bodily in glory must be meditated as the logical premise for the continuance of that maternal mediation on our behalf until the church too reach that glory which already is her mother's. It is a mediation carried out not apart from her Son, but always with him: at his conception and birth, in the visitation of Elizabeth and John, in the Temple, at Cana inaugurating the public ministry, at the foot of the cross and now in heaven. It is preeminently a work of intercession, unique of its kind, universal in extent, and continued effectively in the mediation of the church. Just because it is an extension of that active mediation of the victorious Woman (cf. Rev 12) the church herself is assured of and can assure her members of a certain victory over the dragon, over sin and death. In a word the church is an anchor of hope because the Virgin Mary, the great sign in heaven, the "stella maris" (star of the sea), is in her midst, because the church is the house of Mary, because the knowledge and love of Mary gives us a saving knowledge and love of God.

III. Even a summary study of this encyclical will not fail to disclose striking affinities with key elements of Franciscan-Kolbean spirituality. To be consecrated to Jesus through the hands of Mary: what is this but to be perfectly plunged into the mystery of salvation, to be perfectly conformed to Christ crucified through the intercession of the Spouse of the Holy Spirit and as far as possible in a degree directly proportionate to the degree of one's consecration to the Immaculate, or better incorporation of the mystery of the Immaculate into one's life? In making the Immaculate Conception, the fulness of grace in the Virgin the key to our appreciation and participation in the work of the redemption the Holy Father in effect has drawn out the implications of the celebrated argument of Scotus for the truth of that mystery: God the Father willed a perfect Redeemer and perfect redemption, more perfect that which none can be conceived. That redemption is the Immaculate, preserved so holy so as to be Mother of the God-Redeemer and Mother of the Church. That point once grasped, then it is not difficult to begin to appreciate why that absolutely singular Woman, addressed by St. Francis as elect daughter of the Father, Mother of his Son and Spouse of the Holy Spirit should also be greeted by him in his "Salute to the Virgin" as the "Virgin made Church," and why that Virgin so intimately bound up with the mystery of salvation at the Annunciation and at the cross should also be intimately involved in the mystery of the Eucharist in the church, as both St. Francis and the encyclical insist.

The maternal mediation of Mary in the Church, the ultimate practical implication of her Immaculate Conception, of her perfect love for her Son and his Father's will, a mediation so stressed by the pope in the third part of the encyclical, St. Francis regarded as the key to every conversion to the faith, a mediation whose extension is to be found in the church and in the missionary zeal of her members. To seek to make converts and to live for their sanctification is to "beget" Christ in one's neighbor. Is not this the essence of "repairing" the church? And how else can such repair be effected, except by a life of faith, of prayer, of penance? Thus it is no surprise that the Franciscan thesis: the maternal mediation of the Immaculate based on her unique election in Christ to be his Mother and her unique participation in the work of redemption because preserved free of the stain of original sin should find such clear confirmation in the first and second parts of the encyclical where the predestination of the Virgin as the Immaculate in Christ and her place in the church are treated.

What that means today, when fully implemented in the circumstances of the time in view of preparing the church for the third millennium, can be seen via the life and death and glorification of St. Maximilian Kolbe whose Militia of the Immaculate was inspired and founded so as to realize more effectively the maternal mediation of the Immaculate by incorporating that mystery into the life, of the church and of every soul. The essential condition for realizing that goal, the conversion and sanctification of every soul now living or to live or in purgatory, is the practice of the radical consecration of oneself to the Immaculate as her property and instrument. The radical consecration of Mary to Christ is the Immaculate Conception.

Our consecration to the Immaculate by Christ: of the church at the crucifixion and of each of her members at baptism, made ever more explicit and full during their life, is the progressively more perfect realization of our consecration to Christ. The triumph of Christ's love, the love of the heart of God, is the incorporation of the Immaculate into life, for to live that mystery is to live the mystery of salvation in Christ and in the church. By the will of the Father and of the Son that life is the fruit of a maternal mediation of the very one preserved immaculate, and whose preservation as the Immaculate is the very root of the possibility of such mediation, whose consummation is the complete conformity of our wills to that of the Immaculate as hers is to Christ's and thus the "interpreter" of his will to us.

This spirituality is at heart contemplative. The language of the encyclical and that of St. Maximilian nearly coincide: to know and to love Jesus with the mind and heart of Mary Immaculate; to know and to love Mary with the mind and heart of Jesus. Or to go one step further with St. Maximilian: to let Jesus and Mary know and love each other with our minds and hearts. The secret of sanctity is perfect, unconditional obedience, or conformity of our wills to that of the Immaculate as hers is one with the divine will, in a word the obedience of faith whose consummation, a dark night in this life, is the sharing of the cross of the Savior, and in the life to come paradise. It is Mary Immaculate whose faith did not waver even in the slightest during that darkest of dark nights on Calvary, as the Holy Father notes; and it is the witness of that triumphant faith in the midst of the Apostles and disciples at Pentecost which is the instrument of the Spirit of truth in sustaining all who believe in Christ. And in that triumph of the love of the Sacred Heart over hatred and lies, so marvelously prefigured in the Niepokalanów of St. Maximilian and confirmed in the miracle of his martyrdom is the person of the Immaculate, from whom that saint learned how to love as Christ loved with a priestly love of God and of neighbor.

And in relating the Immaculate Conception to the maternal mediation of Mary consummated in the mystery of the death and resurrection of Jesus the Holy Father shows exactly how and at what point contemplation and action, love of God and love of neighbor—as the Son of God and of Mary loves—are integrated as they were so perfectly in the lives of Sts. Francis of Assisi and Maximilian. Total consecration to the Immaculate qua Immaculate cannot but have an apostolic side, one involving even the most cloistered of contemplatives in that struggle between the Woman and her seed on the one hand with the prince of this world and his seed on the other. Our consecration to Jesus through the hands of Mary Immaculate cannot but be in the form of a militia. And without the support of the Immaculate-Mediatrix (cf. the words of the Marian antiphon cited at the end of the encyclical: *succurre cadenti, surgere qui curat populo, Alma Redemptoris Mater*) as St. Maximilian saw so well, no apostolate, no mission will bear fruit, and the course of history will not be changed from death to eternal life.

Every knight of the Immaculate, every Franciscan on pondering this encyclical will be deeply grateful to the Holy Father for this profound and moving document, the fitting *complement* of his three great encyclicals dealing with the divine persons of the Blessed Trinity: *Dives in misericordia*, *Redemptor hominis*, and *Dominum et vivificantem*, a document about her whom the "patron of our difficult age" so often called the "complementum Ss. Trinitatis" (Complement of the Blessed Trinity in the economy of salvation).

— 10 —

A Proposal

THIS PAST YEAR THE announcement and inauguration of the Marian Year, respectively on the solemnity of the Mother of God and the feast of Pentecost, together with the stupendous encyclical *Redemptoris Mater* written to introduce and explain that event, overshadows all the other events of the "Marian world" even such as the International Mariological and Marian Congresses at Kevelaer (September 11–20, 1987). For this reason, the Marian Year reveals more than any other what is at the heart of that history and geography of faith: the maternal mediation of the Immaculate. Practically the fact of such mediation at the very center of the church explains why, as the Holy Father stressed in his address, December 22, 1987, to the Cardinals and other members of the Roman Curia, the Marian profile of the church takes precedence over every other, including the Petrine and apostolic, and is at once the point of departure and arrival for every activity and service in the church. In a word all activity of believers must be Marian and marianizing, for the same reason their lives cannot be Christian, viz., consecrated to Christ, if their spirituality is not Marian, viz., vivified through the hands of Mary. All this is an elucidation of "total consecration," or if one wishes the motto of the Holy Father: "Totus tuus."

Such total consecration, the core of that spirituality appropriate to the entire Church as she prepares to celebrate the second millennium of the birth of her Savior and head and awaits his second coming in glory, is also the foundation of a pastoral-missionary program, at once cultic and cultural in its ultimate ramifications. In his discourse to a group of Polish Bishops, December 17, 1987, the Holy Father discussed the significance of the act of consecration at Jasna Gora, the bearing of "Marian slavery," the "slavery of love" on the problems of our difficult times and explained how paradoxically this slavery of love only possible through the mediation of the Mother of the Church is the indispensable condition for genuine freedom and everlasting happiness. In the course of this talk the Holy Father named the two masters of the spirituality and doctrine of Marian slavery in and for our times: St. Louis Grignion de Montfort and St. Maximilian Kolbe.

It is from this perspective that the history and geography of the human family should be viewed, if understanding of the true nature and course of our world is desired. And it is on this basis that the fruits of the redemptive work of the Savior will be shared: via the Marianization of every aspect of life, ordained by the Savior himself when dying as the key channel of grace. In the above-cited address to the Roman Curia the Holy Father discusses several events of the year, the Synod on the laity, the many beatifications and canonizations, the visit of the Patriarch of Constantinople to Rome, December 3–7, 1987, noting how the Marian dimension of each, even if not immediately evident, is the root and goal of each and the key to its correct evaluation. He also notes a forthcoming event, the publication of an encyclical on the social doctrine of the church to commemorate the twentieth anniversary of *Populorum Progressio*. This encyclical will be entrusted to the Mother of the Church, for the same reason that every activity and service must be rooted in and aimed at the marianization of life, particularly when there is a question of the orientation of culture and public life to the person and family.

In all of this St. Maximilian with the Militia of the Immaculate, as then Card. Wojtyla noted in his press conference of October 14, 1971, anticipated the teaching of Vatican II. St. Maximilian always insisted on the doctrine of our Lady's mediation as the practical basis for the spirituality and apostolate of the M.I., a basis given concrete form in the total, unconditional consecration of each member to the Immaculate as her possession and property.

In illustrating the maternal mediation of the Mother of God in Christ as the centerpiece of post-conciliar Mariology the Holy Father has effectively corrected the gross error of those who in recent years have downplayed that doctrine to the point of suggesting it be quietly dropped in the interests of ecumenism.

In vindicating devotion and services to the Mother of God qua mediatrix he has shown such a life of prayer to be the most effective and rapid means of attaining the goals of a genuine ecumenism. And in the process he has also vindicated the continued relevance of the original ideals and activities of the M.I. Perhaps it is more than coincidence that the bicentennial of the death of St. Alphonsus Liguori occurs this year. He is the author of *The Glories of Mary*, one of the most widely diffused books ever written, and one which contributed so much to the solidification of the "sensus fidelium" about the doctrine of Mary's mediation at a period when it was coming under increasing attack from "theologians" within the household of the faith.

Because the doctrine of our Lady's mediation is so crucial both to the church and to the M.I., the majority of articles published in this issue of *Miles Immaculatae* deal in one way or another with this doctrine, almost always with frequent reference to the recent encyclical *Redemptoris Mater*. In subsequent issues it is planned to treat other dimensions of the "Marian world" from the perspective of this mystery.

Though the efforts in recent years to promote the cause of St. Louis Grignion de Montfort as a Doctor of the Church came as a surprise to many, the reasonableness of such efforts and the favor they reputedly enjoy with the Holy Father become quite clear in the light of the centrality to be given to the mediation of the Immaculate Virgin and the spirituality which in the church and the life of every believer is the direct counterpart of that mediation. Who is rightly called the master of such spirituality is indeed a "doctor" of the truth that saves, of the science of the saints. St. Maximilian M. Kolbe is also justly regarded as a master of this spirituality. Would it not also be appropriate to consider him as a candidate to be proclaimed one day Doctor of the Church? And would not the proclamation of these two masters of the Marian spirituality appropriate to the church in our times constitute another step toward the much hoped-for solemn definition of the mediation of the Mother of God?

Such a definition, like that of the Immaculate Conception and Assumption, would do great honor to the Savior who entrusted his Church and beloved disciples to his mother and bring great blessings on the church and all mankind.

11

Marian Geography of Faith

The Kolbean Perspective

1. MORE THAN ONE commentary on the encyclical *Redemptoris Mater* has remarked the fresh perspectives, originality, depth and breadth of the Marian themes expounded therein. Those characteristics are evidently the fruit, not of doctrinal innovation, but of a meditative, protracted contemplation of exactly the kind the encyclical (n. 26) affirms has always been practiced by the church in perfecting its faith: contemplating Jesus through the mind and heart of Mary, and contemplating Mary through the mind and heart of Jesus. Some, therefore, refer to this encyclical as a spiritual rather than theological document. Without in any way denigrating the value of what St. Bonaventure (*Itin.* 1, 7) calls intellectual theology, one may with the Seraphic Doctor regard this kind of spiritual contemplation of the truths of faith a mode of theologizing more truly theological than that which is characteristic of the classroom or lecture hall. While it is surely necessary that the conduct of prayer be guided by the truths of faith, it is also a fact that those truths are never so fully and profoundly grasped as when the activity called "theologizing" is thoroughly imbued with the spirit of prayer and devotion, is carried out, i.e., in a contemplative rather than academic mode. Thus, it is preferable not to contrast spiritual and theological documents in this instance, but to ascribe an even greater theological value to this encyclical, precisely because it is so spiritual, because it has expounded the symbol of faith in the spirit of prayer and devotion.

It is this mode of exposition by the highest authority in the church that brings to our attention so many dimensions the mystery of Mary hitherto rarely or never the subject of more academic discussions, which enables us to see not only the whole of "Mariology" in better and broader perspective, but the whole of theology as well. For to the extent any theology of men is genuinely such, it is a Marianized theology, one realized in and through the

Mother of God. What the Holy Father calls the Marian history and geography of faith are instances of such perspectives set in relief.

2. The historical dimensions of faith and of theology have been subjected to study and analysis for centuries, particularly in modern times. And in modern times historical studies of the faith: of its origin and development have often enough been used to undermine the faith, its certainty and immutability, and the authority of the divinely appointed organs in the church entrusted with its "confirmation" and "preservation."

This has been possible, not because historical study is by nature inclined toward the denial of the objective, of the factual, and even more the factual which is miraculous and supernatural, but because such studies have been pursued in a metaphysical and spiritual vacuum. In underscoring that the faith of the church is above all a Marian faith, the faith of Mary and the faith for which Mary is the primary witness: at the annunciation and at Pentecost, the Holy Father has introduced into this discussion a necessary and radical corrective of the imbalance so often found in it. For it is the person of the Mother of God who stands at the point where dogma, metaphysics and history meet. Nothing can be more historical, factual and objective at the same time as a human conception; it is the start of every history. And no event of history can be more metaphysical and potentially supernatural. For the history which begins there, the fact and event which occurs, is the first moment of existence of a person made in the image and likeness of God, enjoying a dignity and potential for sanctity, setting him apart from the rest of creation, showing that conception to be not the simple term of an evolutionary process in nature, but a unique event effected by a unique activity called procreation, of which a woman is the "mediatrix." Whoever has a firm grasp on the dignity and importance of a mother in the scheme of the universe and a respect for the dignity of every person, such because his existence is begun by and at conception, will not misuse historical study or be deceived by abuses of it. For he will be already disposed to recognize the eminently historical character of the miraculous events surrounding the incarnation of the Son of God, the central mystery of our faith, the very basis of our redemption and salvation. The Virgin Mother is the "mediatrix" par excellence of all history and of every history, because she conceived not a human person, but a divine. In her personal identity as Virgin Mother and in the faith in the message of the Angel whereby she undertook the responsibilities of mother of the divine Redeemer she is the ultimate sign guaranteeing the faith of the church and of each believer in the person and work of her Son: this man is the Son of God who after dying for our sins on the third day rose for our justification.

Contrariwise, those who denigrate the dignity of the Virgin, and attack in the name of "liberation" the very foundations of motherhood and of human existence, who deny the teaching of *Humanae Vitae* particularly in regard to the intrinsic evil of contraception, are already disposed to deny the historicity of the Gospel and the truth of the incarnation. In the final analysis the reason for the denigration of the one and denial of the other is the same: a love, a preference for self-will rather than the will of God. At this point we clearly glimpse the supreme importance of being drawn to invoke the Mother of God, so that we might indeed desire and be able to accomplish what we are taught by the Savior to ask incessantly in prayer: Thy will be done on earth as it is in heaven.

3. Unlike the history of faith its geographical aspects have almost in inverse proportion been neglected by students of theology in modern times. Pilgrimages, sanctuaries in particular, have either been relegated to the ash heap of a discredited tradition, or assigned as a theme of applied theology dealing with the piety of unscholarly. With his felicitous phrase "Marian geography of faith" and even more his implementation of its meaning on his every journey throughout the world the Holy Father has effectively restored to its proper place in theology the geographical dimensions of the faith. This is not a minor point. For just as archeological studies tend to bring to the historical research on the scriptures a healthy sense of the objective, so the practice of Marian devotion at those places where in fact her maternal presence is exercised and felt in a special way complements and reinforces the perception of the objective and supernatural character of those events constituting the mysteries of salvation: in the lives of Jesus and Mary, and in the life of the church and her members, a life eminently sacramental. In a word the Marian geography of faith where it impinges in fact on the lives of believers effectively fills that metaphysical and spiritual vacuum so inimical to sound historical perception of the supernatural and miraculous, above all the incarnation.

What is true of the church is also true of religious orders, and is certainly true of the Franciscan Order. One need only recall the role of the Portiuncula in the life of St. Francis and the role that saint expected it to play in the history of his community as model friary to appreciate the point. As Mary's "little portion" in Assisi was her favorite spot in relation to St. Francis, so every friary was to be her "little portion," her possession to be used and guided by her in the service of her Son for the good of his church. There exists, then, a Marian-Franciscan geography of faith shaping and guiding the patterns governing the successful implantation and growth of the Order of Lesser Brothers throughout the world in every age. In our times Niepokalanów is an obvious example of that geography, an example whose stress is exactly that of St. Francis. The presence and influence of the Immaculate at Niepokalanów is not in the first instance by way of some relic of her life there preserved, or by way of some miracle or miracles worked there by her, or because there she has appeared. Rather it is to be found in the mode of observance of the Franciscan form of life there as an exemplification of the spirituality of total consecration: heroic poverty and obedience so as to be totally at her disposition for the conversion and sanctification of all, to be an effective continuation of her primary witness to the identity of her Son and to the truth of the reasons for our hope in the Resurrection. That this is the meaning of Niepokalanów is made perfectly clear in the miraculous witness whereby the Founder of Niepokalanów ended his life in Auschwitz in a priestly act of sacrifice to save the life of another, above all the eternal life, by restoring his faith and hope in God.

4. Hitherto, little scholarly attention has been given to this Marian geography of faith in the life and work of the Founder of the M.I. This issue of *Miles Immaculatae* offers two studies dealing with aspects of that Marian geography of faith in a Kolbean context.

If it is true that a sincere believer cannot remain unaffected in certain places sanctified by the special presence of our Lady, a knowledge of those places, an understanding of the peculiar features defining the Marian presence and influence there is especially valuable for assessing the formation, particularly interior, of a Marian saint like Maximilian Kolbe who came under the Immaculate's influence at one or another of these shrines. In the article treating the "Haghiosoritissa" Fr. Luigi Meloni presents the first of a series of essays on the Roman icons of the Mother of God St. Maximilian surely knew and venerated during his frequent visits to the ancient churches of Rome during his student days there. Those who ponder these icons with the guidance of Fr. Meloni will gain a more exact appreciation of subtle, but real influences of the Virgin in the life of this great saint.

A second article, "The Other Page," investigates a long-forgotten volume familiar, however, to St. Maximilian, undoubtedly a work suggesting to the saint important elements later incorporated by him into a "philosophy" of Franciscan history, one structuring that history in radically Marian terms, on the premise that the ultimate reason for the existence of the Franciscan form of life and of the Franciscan Order is to be found in the interests of the Immaculate. This article, in addition to underscoring the refined sense of history in the thought of the saint, and clarifying a number of details forming the background of his analysis, reveals how in the thought and writings of that saint there is also to be found a "Marian geography," of no small help in appreciating the historical significance of the miracle that is Niepokalanów, indeed of the special presence of the Immaculate to be encountered in any Franciscan friary truly organized on the model initiated by St. Maximilian in 1927 at Niepokalanów.

In 1971 the then Cardinal Wojtyla observed in a press conference that this humble son of St. Francis anticipated prophetically the Marian thought of Vatican II, especially the eighth chapter of "Lumen Gentium." To share this saint's sense of the Marian history and geography of faith surely is no small aid to the discovery of the way of salvation and to walking in that way by consecrating oneself totally to her who was conceived without stain of original sin and who conceived without loss of her virginity the Son of God, indeed who was thereby united even more fully to her Savior in his consecration consummated on the cross.

12

Marian Slavery

Slavery of Love

I. It is by no means original to observe that we live in a post-Christian era, that the distinctive feature of "modernity" (at some time every era was "modern") is the secularization of life, in particular of human culture.

What does this mean in terms of the salvation of souls, the one thing necessary, the supreme law of life (*suprema lex—salus animarum*)? And how does this effect the proclamation of the straight and narrow way of the cross leading to salvation? In former times and in other places that proclamation may have fallen on uncomprehending ears. Such a fact defined the initial problem to be resolved: the relief of ignorance, a not insuperable problem, for ignorance is naturally relievable by the effective exposition of the truth. Right reason (*recta ratio*) in the form of a missionary apologetic accounting for the hope that is in us (1 Pet 3:15) was and remains an appropriate remedy for that malady.

Today the initial reception of the gospel and its practical side, the moral and social teaching of the church, in the increasingly secularized cultures of the modern world is not one of mere incomprehension, but of inhospitality, of incredulous resentment.

The connatural tendency of the human mind and heart, the reason the soul may be described as "naturaliter christiana," to respond positively to the truth of the gospel of salvation, the only fully adequate philosophy of life leading to blessedness under the influence of the light of faith, is blocked by commitments embedded in a secularized culture subscribed to in ever-increasing numbers, even by persons calling themselves Christian and Catholic (clergy and religious not excluded). Those unspoken commitments represent a mindset, a sensibility, an interior matrix, potent even if rarely recognized as such, in terms of which proposals utterly incompatible with the eternal welfare of souls and calculated to lead to hellfire, are judged *a priori* acceptable in conscience and far preferable to the traditional Catholic norms. Contraception, abortion, infanticide, divorce, marital infidelity and premarital sex, sodomy, and euthanasia, *inter alia*, not only are considered permissible for the "sincere," the well-intentioned (who do no physical violence and harm to others), but as "rights" whose denial is thought a coefficient of the tyrannical and cruel. And in the name of such liberty, or better license, social-political ideologies are espoused and violently promoted, ideologies in diametric opposition to the dignity of the person, the welfare of the family and the very existence of the church of Christ. The inhuman and depersonalizing character of such propos-als is so obscured in and by that culture to those living it that even the spontaneous warnings of a human nature abused are denied, even when they cannot be suppressed, The deliberate attempt to stifle those groanings intended by the Creator to protect man and to stimulate a desire for salva-tion cannot but entail as well the systematic resentment and elimination of any presence of a form of life contradicting the essential direction and shape of that culture, such as is Catholic life.

Disobedience and its rationalization, rather than any insuperable problem in knowing the existence of God and the advent of the Savior, is the radical source of atheism and of its militancy.

How does so perverse an attitude come to be accepted by so many? What makes so unnatural a mentality seem so more plausible and attractive than the truth?

No doubt many factors have been operative, but among the more prominent is a purely subjective (and false) concept of freedom, one iden-tifying blessedness with unrestricted permissiveness and unhappiness with obligation, restraint or restriction of any kind on the part of another person. For large numbers personal autonomy has replaced obedience as the key to blessedness and the context of freedom. It matters not what I love, so long as whatever I love coincides with my pleasure and I do no harm (physical) to others. My will, rather than the divine will, has become the final criterion of right and wrong; right is in that context whatever I like and wrong whatever I dislike, viz., subjection to another. Freedom no longer is most of all the love of God "usque ad contemptum sui," but love of self "usque ad contemptum Dei," practically in the repudiation of the moral law as the supreme inconvenience and restraint on one's self-glorification as divine. Happiness and salvation be-come identical with present pleasure; misery with present suffering (physical evil). All signs and reminders of sin, such as guilt, such as the proclamation of the Gospel and of the moral law, which render evident the falsity of such equations, must be violently, if necessary, removed.

The plausibility and attractiveness of this inhuman vision rests, as in the case of the first human temptation in the garden of Eden, on the success with which the lie embedded in an equivocation can be disguised and as it were sold: if you only repudiate the law of God on principle you will be truly free and god-like yourself, Since the fall of our first parents, the cumulative consequences of that fall have not always left the task an easy one. For the very suffering endured as a punishment tends to reinforce the desire for a true redeemer, the one promised by the Creator. And where that redemption is given expression even at the level of civilization the light of faith easily unmasks even for the greater number of sinners the radical flaw in the arguments of those who would deny the reality of sin and the certainty of a final accounting before the judge of the living and of the dead. It is rather the conjunction of two things in modern times that accounts for such plausibility: the hubris of the human heart and the illusion that human science and technology can remedy the unfortunate consequences of disobedience. Concupiscence no longer need be feared, nor its indulgence felt as sinful and shameful. Hedonism as a philosophy of life can be vindicated.

II. Clearly there is a gap between the mentality of those who subscribe to the traditional norms of right reason illumined by faith, and those who have opted for a secularized culture, whose guiding norm is the autonomy of the human conscience in the name of freedom and whose goal the pleasures of this life. In so materialistic a vision that tradition of Catholic life can only be conceived as "against all reason." Can anything be done to bridge the gap separating those blinded by such a vision from the truth? Is it practically possible to hope for the conversion of the contemporary world? Some have despaired of this and been converted to the world. Others, despairing of altering or reversing the progressive secularization of a once Christian civilization, have decided to modify (via evolution) the character of the gospel message, so rendering it palatable to the secular mind.

Neither of these courses has been followed by the Holy Father. In a discourse to a group of Polish Bishops making their "ad limina" visit last December he reiterated in particularly incisive language the basis of his approach to this problem of contemporary evangelization, thus illustrating a very important dimension of the Marian Year and the encyclical published to guide our observance of it. In this discourse (December 17, 1987) the Holy Father proposes the Marian slavery of total consecration, the "slavery of love" in its highest form as the key to a missionary-pastoral program of "fighting for the right use of freedom."

The objective of this struggle is not solely dialogue with the individual and his conversion, but the creation of an entirely new cultural sensibility in the face of which even our de-Christianized contemporaries will find their hostility evaporating and their hearts and minds once more disposed to listen to the truth of the gospel. That slavery of love has its

Christological and cultic side: Marian slavery is the profoundest participation in the paschal mystery possible. But just because it is so thorough an introduction to the mystery of Christ, it has a profoundly authentic anthropological side as well. It is the foundation of true freedom: in the family and in society (including the economic), because where it is accepted and lived consistently it inevitably sets human freedom in its only valid context, that of the truth of salvation. And in living the humility and the obedience of Mary Immaculate the great lie—you will be like gods if only you repudiate obedience on principle—is unmasked for what it is, powerless in the face of the love of Christ crucified.

Why this Marian dimension of our interior lives and of the life of the church should be so fundamental to the evangelization of the nations and to our salvation was explained at great length in a discourse of the Holy Father to the Cardinals and other members of the Roman Curia on December 22, 1987. In a very true sense, the Marian character of the church precedes every other, even the apostolic and Petrine. Every missionary effort, every pastoral service, beginning with that of the pope and the Roman Curia, must keep this in mind. For Christ has willed his Church to be consecrated to him and to be for him the instrument of the salvation of all by entrusting it to his Immaculate Mother, by commanding the beloved disciple to take that Mother unto himself. For the same reason he preserved her Immaculate to be his Mother, so she was preserved Immaculate to be Mother of the Church, the heart of a fruitful, efficacious, maternal influence and advocate in the work of salvation, of snatching souls from the domination of the Father of lies and transferring them into the kingdom of light. Missionary, pastoral apostolic work of any kind will be that much more effective to the degree it is marianized, i.e., rooted in and directed to that total consecration or Marian slavery, a slavery of love capable of overpowering that slavery of sin so carefully disguised in the secularized culture as a "divinization of man," capable of such a victory, because an extension of the mystery of the Immaculate into the church and thereby into time, of the Woman conceived without sin, never deceived or overpowered by the lie. One such person is enough to make the dominion of Satan collapse.

Herein is the practical fulfillment of the protoevangelium, the original promise of salvation made to our first parents after their fall (and ours). In the light of this we can understand better the furious contemporary attacks on the dignity of the maternal vocation, of the virginal Mother in particular, the importance of the naturally mediatory role a mother always plays—for better or worse, of the intimate association of purity of heart and mind, an association only to be maintained perseveringly through the mediation of the Mother who is immaculate. That is why paradoxical as it sounds genuine freedom, spiritual and cultural, is only possible on condition of this slavery of love effected by total consecration to the Immaculate. Only the humble love of a will united with the divine will, as is that of the Immaculate and of those her property and possession, is capable of undoing the effects of that self-will, of that self-love "usque ad contemptum Dei eiusque imaginem" (to the point of despising God and one's neighbor made in his image).

III. In his discourse to the Polish Bishops cited above the Holy Father refers to St. Louis Grignion de Montfort and "our own St. Maximilian Kolbe" as the two great masters of this spirituality in our time. In a special way the saint whom the Holy Father has declared to be the special patron of our troubled times illustrates in his life and above all in his death the power of this Marian slavery of love to overcome the cruel deceit of a secularized culture and reverse what appears to so many to be a hopeless situation, correcting both the presumption and the despair inherent in it: presumption that one can in virtue of human expertise flout divine justice with impunity; despair that with the help of God's grace and mercy the slavery of sin cannot be broken and the direction of a secularizing culture be reversed. St. Maximilian gave his life for another not as a humanitarian but as a priest in order to bring the hope of eternal life to many, first of all to the other nine who were to die by starvation and expected to do so cursing God. In fact, they did so blessing him, like the good thief, because like the good thief they had come to know through the Knight of the Immaculate the priestly love of the sacred heart and so found themselves in paradise.

If we would understand what the Immaculate has in mind in giving that slavery of love the form of her Militia and what great things the almighty will work in us thereby, we need only contemplate the martyrdom, the ultimate testimony of faith, of its founder to realize that that martyrdom is the sign of hope appropriate to our troubled times, to a culture and way of life founded on the premise that salvation is a threat to human liberty, a premise in fact coinciding with that of despair. The premise is not an inevitable necessity of nature as it comes of age, but the fruit of a choice. The testimony of St. Maximilian is that with the help of the Mother of God even the isolated, persecuted individual can choose the contrary and save his soul; and if enough persons do this, culture and the social-political-economic order can be purified and once again humanized. The "struggle for the right use of freedom" will be victorious.

In his classic biography of St. Thomas Aquinas, G. K. Chesterton wrote:

> The saint is a medicine because he is an antidote. Indeed, that is why the saint is often a martyr; he is mistaken for a poison because he is an antidote. He will generally be found restoring

the world to sanity by exaggerating whatever the world neglects, which is by no means always the same element in every age. Yet each generation seeks its saint by instinct; and he is not what the people want, but rather what the people need . . . Therefore, it is the paradox of history that each generation is converted by the saint who contradicts it most . . . So, as the nineteenth century clutched at the Franciscan romance, precisely because it had neglected romance, so the twentieth century is already clutching at the Thomist rational theology because it has neglected reason. In a world that was too stolid, Christianity returned in the form of a vagabond; in a world that has grown a great deal too wild, Christianity has returned in the form of a teacher of logic . . . In the first case, they dimly perceived the fact that it was after a long fast that St. Francis sang the Song of the Sun and the praise of the fruitful earth. In the second case, they already dimly perceived that, even if they only want to understand Einstein, it is necessary first to understand the use of understanding . . . Thus, in our time the two great saints (Francis and Thomas) have appealed to two generations, an age of romantics and an age of skeptics; yet in their own age they were doing the same work; a work that has changed the world.[1]

We may add: when that world of skeptics turned to despair, then the Mother of holy hope gave it the gift of the saint of the two crowns, the patron of our troubled time. His life and death are the sign of hope adapted for our age, because they indicate that antidote the age needs, total consecration to the Immaculate in her Militia. That is the medicine, often mistaken for psychological poison, which taken will successfully alter that horrendous choice embedded in a secularized culture. In order not to despair of man it is first necessary to hope in God: through the Mother of God. This our contemporaries have already dimly perceived in the figure of the martyr St. Maximilian. Undoubtedly, the Savior had in mind this "ultimate weapon" of the Prince of this world, a secularizing culture, when he entrusted-consecrated his church and his beloved disciples to his Mother and enjoined on them the obligation of taking her "unto their own" (John 19:25–27). God our Savior has placed our salvation in the hands of a Woman, the "Alma Redemptoris Mater."

Hail, our hope!

---

1. Chesterton, *St. Thomas Aquinas*, 22–24.

13

The Other Page

AMONG THE MANY INTRIGUING insights scattered throughout the literary heritage of St. Maximilian that explains in terms of his theory of the "two pages," the nature, purpose and history of the Franciscan Order, a theory taking as its major premise the role of the cause of the Immaculate as the "golden thread," the foundation, the raison d'être of the inner logic and unity of that history. That theory is a part of a larger view of the Order and its founder St. Francis of Assisi in relation to the mediatrix of all graces, the Immaculate. In that perspective the essence of St. Francis' spirituality is Marian, indeed immaculatist, and the existence of the Order is an immediate fruit of an intervention of the mediatrix of all graces, whom St. Francis quite logically named "Advocate of his Order" because "Spouse of the Holy Spirit," on behalf of the church, or more precisely, in view of the repair of the church.[1]

In such terms the theology-philosophy underlying the history of the Order is fundamentally Marian, more specifically in function of the privilege of our Lady's Immaculate Conception and her "Cause" resting on "total consecration" to the Virgin qua Immaculate. Every division and organization of that history must be worked out about the mystery of the Immaculate, and only secondarily and subordinately in relation to other dimensions of the life of the Order. Consistent as always in his thought St. Maximilian more than once[2] expressly refers to the Marian character of Franciscan history, to the radically Marian finality of that Order. The best known of these references is found in his Letter to the Clerics of the Order of Friars Minor Conventual (*WK* 486). Though relatively brief it is rightly admired for its forceful and convincing interpretation of the core of Franciscan spirituality, both historically and theologically, in terms of the Immaculate. The basic division of Franciscan history there presented is twofold, the two parts

---

1. Cf. Fehlner, "Mary in the Franciscan," *CE* 3, chapter 5; "Saint Francis and Mary" *CE* 3, chapter 3; "A Thesis," *CE* 6, chapter 2.

2. *WK* 21, 485, 486, 991 R, 1081, 1313.

respectively the two "pages" of that history. The first page deals with that history from the founding of the Order in 1209 until the proclamation of the Immaculate Conception as a dogma of the church by Pope Pius IX in 1854. The second page continues that history after the great event of 1854 and deals with the incorporation of that mystery into life, a goal for which the Militia of the Immaculate is a key instrument. The first goal, achieved in 1854, is the condition for the achievement of the second, currently in process; thus, the first page of the Order's history is a kind of indispensable preliminary for the understanding of the second.

It is perfectly obvious that the theories espoused and expounded by St. Maximilian are not set forth in terms of merely pragmatic grounds for a "praxis," viz., of the Immaculate the central concern of the Order and of each of its members, in particular the most recently professed engaged in the study of the sacred sciences in view of ordination to the holy priesthood. The adoption of such a "praxis" cannot but entail its "institutionalization" at the very center of the Order's life in the form of a "Niepokalanów," the model friary of the second page of Order history, as the Portiuncula was in the former period, that is to say the friary organized about the person of the Immaculate, under the direction of the Immaculate and for the cause of the Immaculate, exemplifying how the Rule or form of life of the Friars Minor is to be observed in the highest degree. Hence, the emphasis of St. Maximilian on a singular intensity in the formation, in the practice of poverty and obedience on unconditional availability for missionary assignment required of members of a friary where total consecration to the Immaculate and to her Cause on the part of both friary as well as friars regulates every aspect of life and work there. At least by implication the Marian interpretation of the history of the Order is complemented by a Marian interpretation of its geography centered on a particular place where the presence of the Order's Advocate, the Immaculate, is particularly evident and from which radiates her influence for the sake of the entire church and all souls.

Naturally the views of St. Maximilian have not been lacking sharp criticism both in his day and since. Many of these criticisms are of a directly practical character, e.g., the institutional changes that his suggestions imply are divisive of the Order, introduce a radically new and different orientation into the life and work of the Order via total consecration, an orientation not intrinsic to the Rule or vows professed by Franciscans. But like the theory criticized these criticisms also have a theoretical base: the Franciscan Order is not an essentially Marian Order, much less immaculatist, in its spirituality and apostolate. The Marian dimension, though present from the beginning, is one among many facets not the central one. Which view is supported by the factual, objective evidence bearing on the

relation between Franciscanism and the Immaculate, above all in the life of
St. Francis? The matter has been examined elsewhere.[3] It is enough to note
that the facts favor St. Maximilian, not his critics.

There is a second, theoretical criticism of St. Maximilian's proposals,
viz., there exist no concrete antecedents for reconstructing the tradition of
the Order as he does, for positing a "two-page history," of which the first
narrates in essence the preparation for the launching of the Militia of the
Immaculate and for the total consecration of the Order to that cause. The
first page did not exist until St. Maximilian wrote it, not as an objective reconstruction of historical events, but in view of an apologetic for a practical
proposal. In a word it is an arbitrary reconstruction.

Do the facts bear out the critics, in particular the fact that hitherto no
one had ever thought of making the "Franciscan thesis" about the Immaculate Conception the basis for understanding the total history of the Order?
Without a continuous, historical link between St. Francis, seen as one of
the greatest of Marian saints, and St. Maximilian as founder of the Militia,
the Cause of the Immaculate, it is difficult to meet fully the objection that
the spirituality and apostolate of total consecration to the Immaculate does
not enter intrinsically into the very warp and woof of Franciscanism. Some
of the sympathizers[4] with the Kolbean ideal, in order to get around the
objection, have made use of rather dubious theories of evolution to justify
the concept of the two pages and their logical nexus. Aside from the weak-
ness of that approach in principle it also has an unfortunate side-effect in
contributing to a tendency to relax the original austerity of Niepokalanów
and loosen its exclusive dedication to the Cause of the Immaculate as St.
Maximilian understood and promoted it.

Another approach is a study of Order history so as to determine
whether or not such a reading is possible apart from any consideration
of the second page in the Kolbean sense. That this is possible will become
immediately evident if some precedent for the first page, particularly one
known and used by St. Maximilian, can be indicated, a kind of testimonial
that not only could the history of the Order be understood in a primarily
Marian key, but in fact it was quite naturally illustrated in that manner by
competent scholars, long before the Militia of the Immaculate had been
conceived and launched by St. Maximilian in 1917. In other words, before
St. Maximilian "wrote" the first page as a prelude to the second, he had
already read that page elsewhere, explained in such detail from a Marian perspective that one may justly say it was the first page that initially

3. Fehlner, "A Thesis," *CE* 3, chapter 2.
4. Cf. Pancheri, "S. Massimiliano Kolbe"; "L'eredita Kolbeana."

suggested to him the second, not the second to originate a Marian-immaculatist reading of the first as the justification for making the Cause of the Immaculate the central concern of the Franciscan Order.

The precedent in question exists in the work of Fr. Filippo Rossi, O.F.M. Conv., *L'Immacolata Concezione di Maria ed i Francescani Minori Conventuali dal 1210 al 1854*,[5] a work that enjoyed wide circulation in its day and was still well-known when St. Maximilian was a student in Rome, and is today completely forgotten, tragically, for according to a scholar, expert in things Marian and Franciscan,[6] it merits remembrance. More important is the fact that St. Maximilian was acquainted with this study, indeed quoted from it verbatim on occasion,[7] and pondered its contents at length. Reading again this study of Fr. Rossi we will become aware of the contents of that "first page" of Franciscan history, the detail the saint had before him, but did not include in his brief summary, detail indicating the objective grounds suggesting how the "golden thread" of the Cause of the Immaculate does indeed bind the whole of the Order's life from within, not from without. Further, that reading of a prior exposition of the first page of Franciscan history will help appreciate how the Marian geography of that Order, apparently implicit in the saint's writings, in fact was explicit in his mind.

P. Filippo Rossi, "Sacerdote Umbro"

Relatively little is known of the life and personality of this Umbrian friar. At the time he wrote the work under consideration he was Secretary General of the Order, thereafter Assistant General. Six works, at least, from his pen are known. They show him to have had better than average mastery of theology and history, a person endowed with considerable spiritual insight, capable of a pleasing literary style. Nonetheless, despite his relative prominence in the Order little more than a century ago and his literary activity he managed to practice "intellectual humility" to such a degree—always signing his work "sacerdote umbro"—that according to Fr. Sparacio,[8] even after considerable research it cannot be determined when and where he was born, who were his parents, when he was professed in the Order, when

5. Rossi, *L'Immacolata Concezione*. As the author confesses in his foreword to the reader the composition of this volume was only completed on the last day of December, 1854. It seems hardly likely that it was also actually printed that year.

6. DiFonzo, *La formazione romana*, 109.

7. *WK* 1081, in particular the curious note 2, identical with that found in Rossi, *L'Immacolata Concezione*, 16.

8. Sparacio, *Frammenti Bibliografici*, 164–65.

ordained a priest. Only three dates in his life can be determined exactly: that of his doctorate in theology (June 15, 1836), that of his term in the General Curia of the Order (1851–1857) and that of his death in Rome (January 26, 1872). Fr. Sparacio speculates that he may have been born c. 1812. Questions, however, touching his biography or his other works do not directly concern this study, as they had no direct bearing on St. Maximilian and the formation of his vision of the Order, and of its geography. Undoubtedly Fr. Rossi had his sources, indeed in a certain sense "precedents" or inspirations for the synthesis of Franciscan history and geography he sets forth so coherently and in such detail. The idea had been in the "Franciscan air" for quite some time, as the recently "discovered" writings of St. Francis Anthony Fasani clearly indicate.[9] What primarily concerns this study is the synthesis itself, set forth by a friar well-trained in the schools of the Order before the centuries-old tradition these represented was definitively interrupted by the last suppressions of the nineteenth century in Rome, 1873, a friar capable of expounding his views with a certain enthusiastic calm, but never as an instance of that itch for "revolutionary innovation" so common in his time and to which he was adamantly opposed.

The Friars Minor Conventual and the
Immaculate Conception: 1210–1854

This modest work, as its author himself describes it, written in the space of one month, December 1854 (but no doubt meditated over a much longer time previously), was intended to serve as a souvenir of the most memorable year and month in the history of the Order, celebrated in splendid fashion throughout December, 1854, at the Basilica of the Twelve Apostles, Rome, since the days of Cardinal Bessarion and Fr. Francesco della Rovere, later Pope Sixtus IV, center of devotion to the Immaculate in the Eternal City.

In addition to a three-page dedication to the Minister General, an introductory note to the reader and a number of appendices containing discourses and poetry recited during these celebrations, a partial chronicle of the celebrations and a rhythmic hymn of Pope Clement XIV in honor of the Immaculate (modeled on the Lauda Sion of St. Thomas Aquinas) the work principally consists of five chapters and a series of concluding reflections. The purpose of these chapters is to show why, historically speaking, this year, 1854, and this month of December are to be put on a par, as the title of the

---

9. St. Francis Anthony Fasani, *Mariale*; *Le 7 Novene Mariane*; Fehlner, "St. Francis Anthony Fasani," *CE* 3, chapter 8; DiFonzo, *L'immagine di S. Francesco*. Cf. also the review of this last work in *Miles Immaculatae* 23 (1987) 505–6.

book indicates, with that of the founding of the Order in 1210 (Fr. Rossi claimed 1210 rather than 1209 as the foundation date of the Order, as have some scholars since); why this event, the dogmatic definition of the Immaculate Conception is the true glory, the real triumph of the humble Poverello, St. Francis, and of all his sons; why such an event should have been celebrated in Rome in the Basilica of the Twelve Apostles; in a word why Assisi should be linked so profoundly with Rome and St. Peter because of the Immaculate, why the glory of St. Francis is so great in the church because it is realized in the exaltation of the Immaculate Conception.

The thesis of this "Umbrian priest," basis for a response to such queries arising from the realization of the place of the Immaculate Conception in the economy of salvation which presented with clear evidence the importance of a dogmatic proclamation for the life and worship of the church,[10] may be summarized as follows: the service rendered Our Lady qua Immaculate by St. Francis is his greatest claim to glory. Indeed, his Order was founded principally to continue and complete that service distinctive of St. Francis' devotion to the Mother of God, a service Fr. Rossi considers consummated in the dogmatic definition of 1854, a stupendous act of worship rendered the Father through Christ. So formulated the thesis also clarifies the grounds on which rests the essentially Marian character of Franciscan spirituality, in St. Francis and in his Order in its two main features: conformity to Christ and repair of the church. Conformity to the crucified is achieved via this service to the Immaculate, for she is the perfect fruit of a perfect redemption by a perfect Redeemer; and in reflecting that mystery the Franciscan form of life effectively promotes the repair of the church as desired by the crucified in calling Francis to this way of life. Not only the founding of the Order in 1210, but even more the stigmatization of the Poverello in 1224 which Fr. Rossi with St. Bonaventure regards as the divine seal of approval on the sanctity of St. Francis and the Rule of the Order (1223), an infallible guide to an exceptionally exalted degree of holiness, find their complement in the great event of 1854.

What makes the thesis so stated particularly attractive is not merely its undoubted consistency at a conceptual level, but its exposition and verification in terms of two conditions essential to the existence of any community: its history and geography and the coordination between these two. It is in relation to this service to the Immaculate that events and personalities and places significant for that history and geography can be identified and their significance explained, or in Kolbean terms that the golden thread of Franciscan history can be found and traced. Once we are sure of the first and last

10. For example, Alimonda, *Il dogma dell'Immacolata*.

event of that history, we are in a position to identify the intermediate links. The dates 1210 and 1854, according to Fr. Rossi are mutually illuminating the key to a recognition of its subdivisions and patterns. Their discernment cannot not suggest the probable directions that history should take as well as an evaluation of the heart of the unity of the Franciscan Order.

It is this same service that constitutes the focus of the Order's geography: the interaction of its many and various friaries and the shifts in its geographic poles over the centuries in relation to Assisi not by happenstance, but then also to Paris-Rome, in Fr. Rossi's perspective. Even more than the temporal factor the question of the unifying principle of the Order stands under this logic: it is the presence of the Immaculate mediatrix of all graces in the founding and unfolding of the life and work of the Franciscan Order. That unfolding in turn is the expression (or lack thereof) of the spirituality and devotion appropriate to a community and religious professing the Rule of St. Francis. Because one word says all that is realized therein: Immaculate, that unfolding is a triumph of holiness "greater than which none is conceivable."[11]

Franciscan History and the Immaculate

Although very brief, the first chapter of this study dealing with the history of the mystery of the all-holiness of Mary in the church prior to St. Francis shows how Franciscan history and geography are part of a larger context, that furnished by the church. Franciscan service to and promotion of the Immaculate Conception are, therefore, to be situated and explained in relation to that larger context, or in the words of the Crucified in S. Damiano to St. Francis, in his command to repair the church, its consummation in holiness. Fr. Rossi's exposition in this chapter is open to criticism on many details. But his general vision is correct; subsequent research on the early history of the Immaculate Conception (before the time of St. Francis) only tends to confirm the principal point made by Fr. Rossi: this mystery stands at the very center of the plan of salvation and the life of the church. The elucidation of the unique sanctity of the Virgin Mary, doctrinally and devotionally, is something that began in the church at Pentecost. St. Francis invented neither doctrine nor feast; but the spirituality that was his special

---

11. Cf. Pius IX in the Bull *Ineffabilis Deus*, paragraph 1. In this sense the Immaculate is St. Maximilian's ideal of sanctity (cf. *WK* 1210) as he believed she was St. Francis' as well. Hence, without any trace of envy he could seek to honor the Immaculate with a holiness greater than that of the greatest saints, and strive to encourage others to exceed his own. Cf. *WK* 1305.

charism and the distinctive character of that spirituality can only be grasped when it is first seen as an instrument for the final effective elucidation of that unique sanctity of the Mother of God in the church: doctrinally via the dogmatic definition, devotionally via her cult under that title. The dogmatic definition, though, certainly prepared by the liturgical celebrations of Mary, is in the ultimate analysis the condition and means of a definitive incorporation of the mystery into the life of the church. With the background for the appearance of the Franciscan phenomenon in the church at a certain place and time clearly identified, the second, third and fourth chapters proceed to deal respectively with the three fundamental subdivisions of that great period of Franciscan history later to be called by St. Maximilian the "first page" of the Order's history. Each of these periods is introduced by a person and an event whose activity in each instance is the controlling influence shaping the direction of that period toward the next proximate goal in the plan of divine providence for the glorification of the Virgin Mary and the salvation of souls and serving as the key point of reference for interpreting and organizing all other events and activities of the Order in that period. Evidently, in the case of St. Francis the influence exerted extends not only to the first sub-period, but to the entire history.

For St. Francis' influence, source of the entire subsequent development of the story, may be described as the spirituality of the Immaculate Conception, one whose rapid propagation throughout the Christian world during and shortly after the death of the Seraphic Patriarch would realize the indispensable conditions not only for the universal adoption of the feast of the Conception of the Virgin, but also for a correct and more express theological elaboration of that mystery (and its implications for Christian thought and culture as well as Christian conduct), in effect the preparation (given the nature of the principal intellectual objection to both the feast and the doctrinal profession of the mystery celebrated in it) necessary for dogmatic as well as theological recognition of the truth of this mystery of faith, always believed. Thus, the work of St. Francis, above all as the embodiment of the "spirit of prayer and devotion," whose exemplar is Mary Immaculate, was the stimulus of a Marian piety singular both in its intensity and extent.

From the point of view adopted by Fr. Rossi that spirituality of St. Francis is the antecedent rendering possible the work accomplished by John Duns Scotus, the defense of the Immaculate Conception in the very center of medieval intellectual life at Paris (chapter three), a work culminating at Rome in that of Fr. Francesco della Rovere, disciple of Scotus in theology and metaphysics, St. Francis' successor as Minister General of the Franciscan Order. When he became Pope as Sixtus IV, he inserted the feast of the Conception of Mary into the universal calendar of the church and forbade the description of the "Franciscan thesis" as heretical, in effect giving that "thesis" its first express doctrinal recognition by the ecclesiastical magisterium, a recognition which would effectively guide the actions of the Council of Trent and subsequent Pontiffs whenever they made further decisions concerning the profession of this belief and the devotion concomitant with it. The evident conclusion of this story is the dogmatic definition of 1854, a final, solemn recognition of this mystery, an act of worship of him who preserved his Mother free of original sin for the sake of a most perfect redemption and an act of thanks by the church for so great a gift, an act therefore far transcending a merely academic exercise, a victory not of a party but of the Woman, who, as Fr. Rossi notes more than once, made use of the efforts of humble disciples of the Poverello in order to secure the greatest blessings and mercy for all souls.

With the hindsight subsequent research permits, it is not difficult to note errors and defects in the exposition, particularly chapter two. There is a misreading of the *Salute to the Virgin* (*conservavit* for the correct *consecravit*, a mistake not repeated by St. Maximilian in *WK* 1080, where his source is this work of Fr. Rossi), the use of a rather questionable story of St. Francis' visit to Rovigo and his building of an altar there in honor of the Conception of Mary, his lack of any reference to the title "Spouse of the Holy Spirit," his crediting of St. Bonaventure and other theologians of the Order during the thirteenth century as supporters of the Immaculate Conception, when in fact they opposed it as an erroneous theological opinion. Nonetheless, that same research on the whole supports the basic insights of Fr. Rossi. Even if there is no documentation for St. Francis' use of the term Immaculate Conception or his celebration of the feast there is evidence more than sufficient to justify the affirmation that his spirituality is at root informed and permeated by the mystery so designated doctrinally and theologically and that even where some major Franciscan theologians opposed the thesis of the Immaculate Conception (often faulty explanations rather than the mystery itself), their work in fact prepared the way for the contribution of John Duns Scotus.[12]

But even if under the pressure of composing an essay in the span of 30 days filled with celebrations of every kind the author may have succumbed to the temptation of supporting his thesis regarding St. Francis with a number of proofs less than apodictic, his exposition is not without value today. Its correct estimate of and stress on the role of Our Lady in the life and work

12. Cf. Fehlner, "Mary in the Franciscan," *CE* 3, chapter 5; "Saint Francis and Mary," *CE* 3, chapter 3; "A Thesis," *CE* 6, chapter 2.

of St. Francis at the Portiuncola and his desire to die there, on the intimate link between the role of the Virgin in Francis' life, his perfect conformity to the crucified and the stigmatization, a miracle at once explaining and giving divine approval both to the Founder of the Order of Friars Minor and to the Rule of life which he gave to his fraternity, and finally on the Marian significance of the place of his final burial on what was once a hill known as the hill of hell and after his burial there called the hill of paradise. For Fr. Rossi the glorification of the humble Francis in the magnificent Basilica in Assisi is the fruit of a unique intervention of the Immaculate, mediatrix of all graces and advocate of Francis' Order, a revelation of how one passes from the slavery of sin and power of hell to the freedom and joy of paradise. Such factual considerations, more than the presence or absence of the title Immaculate Conception in the surviving documentation, provide solid, objective grounds for linking St. Francis and the Immaculate Conception directly. Ultimately these help us to perceive the correctness of the traditional interpretation of the Salute to the Virgin, as well as the *Antiphon to the Office of the Passion* in an immaculatist sense.[13]

Geography of Franciscan Faith

So viewed the Assisi of St. Francis is a Marian city, nowhere more so than at the Portiuncula where the Poverello came to understand his vocation and where the Mother of Mercy helped him to conceive and beget the spirit of gospel truth.[14] The desire, indeed command of Francis that the friary at the Portiuncula about the Queen of the Angels be a model of regular observance[15] reinforces this insight. But it is equally a Marian city in virtue of the glory of the Poverello celebrated about his tomb, a glory that is a triumph of the Mother of Mercy.

But what the Franciscan Order is at its center, it is also intended to be at its furthest extremities: Marian, for the sake of the Immaculate Conception. That Order is not merely contemplative: but apostolic because essentially missionary in purpose. Its mission, in the light of this geography, is primarily the service of the Immaculate and the promotion of the glory of the Mother of God under that title. As "conformity with the crucified" and "service of the Immaculate" are practically convertible, so the mission of preaching penance, of virtue and vice, punishment and glory to all

13. Cf. Fehlner, "Mary in the Franciscan," *CE* 3, chapter 5; "Saint Francis and Mary," *CE* 3, chapter 3; "A Thesis," *CE* 6, chapter 2.

14. *Leg. maj.* 3, 1.

15. 2 *Cel.* 18.

mankind, above all sinners and non-believers, is practically convertible with the promotion of that service of the Immaculate.

The missionary expansion of the Order was not haphazard. Quite the contrary the "terminus a quo," Assisi, of all that effort tended always to find a complementary "terminus ad quem" for each of the three historic periods Fr. Rossi identifies in the history of the Order from its founding to its greatest triumph in 1854. Paris was the *terminus* of the first period with the successful work of John Duns Scotus in defense of the Immaculate Conception in the capital of the theological and intellectual world of medieval Christendom. From that center, during the one hundred and seventy years of the second period that missionary effort had its greatest triumph in the conquest of the Catholic theological world for the Immaculate Conception, an effort terminating in Rome, with the accession of a disciple of Duns Scotus and successor of St. Francis to the chair of Peter, an event initiating in Fr. Rossi's vision the third and final period of the Order's history and the beginning of official recognition of the mystery of the Immaculate Conception on the part of the Magisterium, a process to be concluded by the solemn dogmatic definition of 1854.

A bare half-century before that triumph of St. Francis and his Order in 1854, an event Fr. Rossi considered the omega matching the alpha of 1210, that Order, like so many others nearly disappeared in the cataclysms of the French Revolution and secularizations in its wake. The renewal of the Order, its restoration to a future even greater than its past, was heralded by two events, both Marian. The first was the rediscovery of the body of St. Francis in Assisi, the original Marian center of the Order. The other was the apparition of Our Lady, the Immaculate, mediatrix of all graces, to St. Catherine Laboure in Paris and the revelation of the design of the miraculous medal, the "sacramental" of that mediation, particularly in the spiritual order, and the almost immediate increase of conversions to the faith among the now secularized and atheist intellectuals of the academic and social world, still centered in Paris. For Fr. Rossi these events in those places constitute a "recapitulation" of the entire history of the Order on the eve of its greatest triumph, the immediate stimulus for the preparations preceding the solemn definition of 1854. That recapitulation signaled in particular the final goal of Franciscan missionary effort: the repair and renewal of the church, the conversion and sanctification of all souls, the triumph of the church over her enemies, especially the masonic-revolutionary forces unleashed by the French revolution, and the re-Christianization of culture.

It is with this in mind that Fr. Rossi in his fifth chapter explains why the solemn celebrations in Rome in thanksgiving for the dogma took place at the Conventual Franciscan Basilica of Santi Apostoli. Here since the days of Fr.

Francesco della Rovere and Cardinal Bessarion devotion to the Immaculate in Rome had been centered and promoted.[16] Here symbolically is where the ancient eastern traditions concerning the sanctity of the Mother of God from the first moment of her existence again met and fused with the western forms of the same devotion, forms whose initial source was in the east. Thus, the first Roman acknowledgment of this mystery as an article of faith by Pope Sixtus IV in a true sense is the confirmation of a single tradition of the whole Church. Here, too, for centuries the study of theology and metaphysics in the tradition of St. Bonaventure and John Duns Scotus was systematically combined with the study of the Immaculate Conception and a solemn, public devotion to our Lady under that title. During his student days in Rome St. Maximilian also participated in those activities.

St. Maximilian and the Thesis of Fr. Filippo Rossi

Is this the end of the story? Is there nothing else to be done but act as curators of the mementoes of past glory, repeating the accomplishments of the great friars of the past, but not building further on the foundation they laid? In view of the foregoing summary of Fr. Rossi's synthesis of Franciscan history and geography it is not too difficult to appreciate how a negative reply would suggest itself to the Founder of the Militia of the Immaculate, that a second page of Franciscan history was being currently written under the direction of the Immaculate, for which the first page serves as introduction. What St. Maximilian meant in describing the apostolic-missionary efforts of the Order during that first page of history as radically orientated toward the dogmatic definition of the Immaculate Conception, the prelude to the even greater work of incorporating that mystery into life, also entrusted by the Immaculate to the Order, and in what way he made use of, but also corrected and enlarged the insights of Fr. Rossi, can best be appreciated by examining the five texts where the saint clearly makes explicit use of Fr. Rossi's work (though never citing him).

The first occurs in a letter of 1918 to his brother, Fr. Alphonse Kolbe (*WK* 21). There he mentions that "our Order" has had the great good fortune to be under the special protection of the Immaculate qua talis, this from the time of St. Francis and St. Bonaventure who made devotion to the Immaculate the characteristic feature of the Order. Duns Scotus and the Franciscan school after him defended the privilege theologically until the goal of that devotion and defense was reached, the solemn dogmatic definition of 1854. This characteristic piety and thought in respect to the Immaculate represents

16. Cf. Mazzucco, "Note."

the "golden thread" of the Order, and perhaps the concrete beginning of the renewal of our corrupt society. With the exception of the metaphor "golden thread" (evidently a Kolbean phrase nicely synthesizing the insight) the reflection expressed here is that of Fr. Rossi.

The second instance (in chronological order) is found in *WK* 1081, an article originally published in the *Kalendarz Rycerza Niepokalanej* in 1925 (and reprinted in *Rycerz Niepokalanej* in 1932). It is an article that locates briefly, but clearly the significance of the work of Duns Scotus and his followers on behalf of the Immaculate Conception and its dogmatic definition in the broader context of St. Francis' devotion to Mary Immaculate and the purpose of his Order, the conversion and salvation of souls, and that also of the Militia of the Immaculate founded by St. Maximilian. The historical information used in this article and its organization about three key figures and periods in the history of the Order in relation to the Immaculate Conception depend in every detail on Fr. Rossi. The three major figures (and periods) in St. Maximilian's presentation of the facts are St. Francis, John Duns Scotus and Pope Sixtus IV. The facts of this history presented by St. Maximilian are an accurate summary of the materials contained in the book of Fr. Rossi, particularly evident in the remarks concerning St. Francis and St. Bonaventure (citing the Salute to the Virgin, the discussion of St. Francis' visit to Rovigo with Rossi's reference in a footnote, St. Bonaventure's institution of the feast of the Conception within the Order). The article is obviously not a work of original research or a critical evaluation of earlier research here summarized. It is rather a popularization of ideas the saint considered sound. It is also an indication in the saint of an interest in and appreciation of the historical aspects of the cause of the Immaculate. From the content of a subsequent letter to Fr. Ephrem Longpré and from proposals for an Academy of the Immaculate it is clear he was quite conscious of the considerable research yet to be undertaken for a more adequate verification of basic historical truths bearing on the mystery of the Immaculate and her intervention in the life of the church and Order.[17]

The third case is that of the Letter to the Clerics of the Order (*WK* 486). Here we find again a brief summary of the thesis of Fr. Rossi, practically a paraphrase of the title of his book so as to make clear the direct and immediate relation between the founding of the Order and the dogmatic definition of 1854, two dates perfectly complementary. But there are also found here a number of original elements, not changing, but significantly nuancing the thesis of Fr. Rossi so as to provide logical interpretation of the subsequent history of the Order. In addition to the metaphor "golden thread" already

17. *WK* 564, 647.

used by St. Maximilian fifteen years earlier to synthesize the thesis of Fr. Rossi, a new metaphor occurs for the first time in this letter of February 28, 1933, viz., that of the second or other page of Franciscan history of which the first page (that effectively narrated in Fr. Rossi's book) is the prelude and introduction. That second page now in course is, however, no mere extension or repetition of the first page. While it builds on the definitive triumph of St. Francis and his Order in the dogmatic definition of the Immaculate Conception, it does so by recapitulating that history in view of an even greater triumph of the Immaculate which St. Maximilian calls the "incorporation" of the mystery of the Immaculate into the life of the church and of all souls. That recapitulation is bound up with the founding of the Militia in 1917. The more fully each friar, each friary, indeed the whole Order becomes the exclusive property of the Immaculate for the sake of this "incorporation," her Cause, which for St. Maximilian is the Militia of the Immaculate, the greater will be the realization of the ultimate purpose of the original foundation of the Order in 1209, indeed we may say of the sanctity originally envisioned as the final goal of the vocation of St. Francis to be perfectly conformed to the Crucified for the sake of the repair of the church. In the mind of St. Maximilian, the still greater accomplishments of the Order to be achieved in the sanctification of its members and through its apostolate are linked to this gift of the Militia entrusted to the Order, just as the original founding of the Order and its subsequent preservation from extinction on many occasions were linked to the special love of the Immaculate for St. Francis. The correspondence of the Order with this love by placing itself totally at the service of her cause and doing nothing to harm it are the conditions for the realization of these still greater accomplishments.[18]

The triumph of 1854, the dogmatic definition, is not the end of the story begun in 1209, but only the end of the introduction to that story. The public recognition of the mystery of the Immaculate Conception by the church is not the final triumph of the Immaculate, but the foundation for that final triumph, the incorporation of that mystery into the life of the church, naught else in fact but the final realization of the kingdom of the sacred heart of Jesus. The ideas governing the nexus between Franciscanism and Mary Immaculate outlined in the Letter to the Clerics (*WK* 486) serve as the doctrinal stimulus for the observance of the Rule of St. Francis by an ever more profound Marianization of that observance, a Marianization to be effected via the M.I.

Their manner of presentation also suggests certain parallels, left implicit by St. Maximilian, but nonetheless sufficiently evident. The year 1209

18. *WK* 485.

has a counterpart in the year 1917, that of the founding of the M.I; 1854 will find its counterpart when Christ finally comes to consummate his kingdom. St. Maximilian does not mention 1224, the stigmatization which Fr. Rossi underscores as a divine seal on the work of St. Francis. The parallel in the life of St. Maximilian is his martyrdom on August 14, 1941, vigil of the Assumption of our Lady, a divine seal at once guaranteeing and "explaining" both his life and death in the service of the cause of the Immaculate.

In the last of a series of meditations made two months later during a return to Europe by sea (*WK* 991 R) St. Maximilian briefly refers to the first and second pages of Franciscan history. Both this and the preceding meditation (*WK* 991 Q) reveal how deeply convinced was St. Maximilian of the essential link between St. Francis, Franciscan religious life and the mystery of the Immaculate, in the second great period of the Order's history, more precisely with Niepokalanów as the ideal or model friary, the Portiuncola of this period. At the heart of Niepokalanów is the fact and spirituality of total consecration to the Immaculate. The reality of Niepokalanów rests on the initiative of the Immaculate, an initiative, however, whose origin is to be found in the charism of St. Francis.[19]

A fifth and final appearance of Fr. Rossi in the writings of St. Maximilian occurs in *WK* 1313, part of the material for a book-length study on the Immaculate Conception. The piece in question deals with the role of the Immaculate as mediatrix across the centuries. Among the interventions of our Lady considered by St. Maximilian as more important are those touching the events leading to the definition of the Immaculate Conception as a dogma. The outline followed is that of Fr. Rossi, calculated to illustrate the contribution of the friars of St. Francis to what has come to be called the "Franciscan thesis."

In the final paragraph St. Maximilian mentions the extraordinary interventions of the Immaculate, immediately preceding and following the definition: the revelation of the miraculous medal, the miraculous conversion of the Jew Alphonse Ratisbonne and the apparitions at Lourdes. Fr. Rossi also mentions these extraordinary interventions of the Immaculate preceding the definition, as it were providing a final stimulus and guide toward that definition and indicating its purpose, a presentation suggesting a certain parallel with the extraordinary role of the Immaculate in the life of St. Francis centered on the Portiuncula as the shrine particularly dear to her ("her special portion," as it is the friars') and implying another page of Franciscan history still to be opened. It is not inconceivable that the idea

19. Cf. Fehlner, "Mary in the Franciscan," *CE* 3, chapter 5; "Saint Francis and Mary," *CE* 3, chapter 3; "A Thesis," *CE* 6, chapter 2.

of a "second page" was in part insinuated in the mind of St. Maximilian by the study of this work of Fr. Rossi. At the least, however, our awareness of the significance Fr. Rossi assigns the manifestation of the miraculous medal (and the many subsequent conversions to be ascribed to its wearing) in relation to the rediscovery of the body of St. Francis in 1818, viz., to the Franciscan charism, will make clear the Franciscan-Marian role of Rue du Bac, Paris, S. Andrea delle Fratte, Rome (place of conversion of Ratisbonne) and Lourdes in the mind of St. Maximilian.

Attentive reading of these five writings of St. Maximilian in relation to the book of Fr. Rossi clearly reveals the extent to which the Founder of the M.I. had absorbed the ideas of the "Umbrian priest" and the manner in which he utilized these in elaborating a coherent theology of Franciscan history as primarily a history of the interventions of the Immaculate in behalf of the kingdom of her Son, that is to say, in favor of the "repair or the church." Was he also influenced by Fr. Rossi's Marian geography? More exactly did he think of Niepokalanów as a "Portiuncula" occupying in the second page of Franciscan history a role comparable to Paris in the first?

Since the saint never once expressly mentions Fr. Rossi in his writings,[20] it is difficult to construct an apodictic argument in favor of an affirmative answer. Given his attention to detail, his clear and logical mind, and his deep reflection on the contents of Fr. Rossi's study, it is difficult to imagine how he could not have been aware of certain parallels with his own work suggested by the insights of Fr. Rossi.

The Militia was founded in Rome, in a friary and school of the Conventual Franciscans the lineal descendant of the Sistine College at Santi Apostoli where for so many centuries the study of the mystery of the Immaculate and its defense was carried out in close conjunction with devotion to the Immaculate at its Roman center, a devotion in which popes regularly participated and whose beginnings there enjoyed significant links with the traditions of the Catholic Orient. St. Maximilian not only knew of this; he also lived this tradition while in Rome.[21]

Further, there appear indications[22] that St. Maximilian was aware the renewal of the Order, foreshadowed in the rediscovery of the body of St. Francis in 1818 and the manifestation of the miraculous medal in 1830, according to Fr. Rossi, would be consummated in Rome, where according to Fr. Rossi the triumph of St. Francis in 1854 had occurred. Rome, then, is

20. Cf. DiFonzo, *La formazione romana*, 109; Kolbe, *WK* 1081, in particular, again, the curious note 2, identical with that found in Rossi, *L'Immacolata Concezione*, 16.

21. DiFonzo, *L'immagine di S. Francesco*.

22. Cf. Domanski, "La genesi," 250–51, 270n47.

the geographic point where the two pages of the history of the Franciscan Order are joined.

Whatever the merits of these particular considerations, together they tend to focus attention on the analogical roles played by Paris and Niepokalanów respectively in the first and second pages of Franciscan history. What the great friary of Paris (where the work of sanctifying the intellect in the spirit of prayer and devotion was so successfully accomplished, especially during the thirteenth century) symbolized and effected for the Order (Assisi) and the church (Rome) during the first period of the Order's history, Niepokalanów, the friary totally consecrated to the cause of the Immaculate (or "the M.I. in the form of a friary"), symbolizes and accomplishes during the second period of that history.

And as Paris represents during the first period the typical form the ideal Franciscan fraternity (Portiuncula) takes in the course of achieving the immediate goal of the fraternity during that period (the dogmatic definition of the mystery of the Immaculate Conception), so during the second period Niepokalanów represents the typical form that ideal fraternity takes in view of the definitive goal of the Order (the incorporation of the dogma of the Immaculate Conception into life). Just as those precise goals are not alternatives, but stages in the achievement of the overall purpose of the Franciscan charism, viz., "repair of the church" and "perfect conformity to the Crucified," so the typical forms of Franciscan community life in each period are not contraries, but rather complementary one to another, the first, minus its imperfections, being recapitulated in the second. Both the renewal of the Order and its contribution to the life of the church in this second period (for which the first is but the preparation) will come about in direct proportion to the progressive Marianization of the Order, i.e., its consecration to the cause of the Immaculate, its acceptance of Niepokalanów as the type of its life and work.

Because the specific goal of the Order during this second period of its existence, viz., the incorporation of the mystery of the Immaculate into life, occurs at a time of maximum tension between the Immaculate and the Serpent, between the claims of true spirituality articulated about total consecration to Christ via the hands of the Immaculate and the pretensions of pseudo-spiritualities dispensing with this consecration, the typical Franciscan friary of this period, Niepokalanów, is "the M.I. in the form of a friary."

Nor are these the only possible points of contact between Fr. Rossi and St. Maximilian. Both insist on the fundamental unity of the Order among its various families and branches as resting on their common devotion to the Immaculate and service of her cause and whose defense and exaltation none have ever betrayed and all have shared. Thus, not the dates signaling the divisions within the Order, e.g., 1517, but the Marian dates have primary significance for the period divisions of Franciscan history in the thesis of Fr. Rossi. On this assumption one can readily comprehend why St. Maximilian insists that the renewal of the Order (above all the Conventual family) in respect to poverty, for the sake of which the divisions originally occurred, would be achieved fully precisely in the degree the unity of the Order about the standard of the Immaculate is perfected.[23]

Fr. Rossi envisions the Marian devotion of the Dominicans and their promotion of the Rosary, indeed even their historical role as "critics" of the initial formulations of the "Franciscan thesis," not as competitive, but as complementary to the role of the Friars Minor. So too, St. Maximilian saw the M.I. not as another Marian movement in substitution of or in competition with other similar groups in the church, but as complementary of them, precisely because the M.I. is uniquely centered on the mystery of the Immaculate Conception.[24]

Finally, both Fr. Rossi and St. Maximilian insist on the gratitude, love and service all Franciscans should have toward the Immaculate, for in the final analysis her love for St. Francis and each of his disciples is the proximate basis for all that the Order is or ever will be.[25]

Whether all of these points of contact between the ideas of Fr. Rossi and those of St. Maximilian also indicate an influence of the first upon the second is not entirely certain in the light of the present evidence. The coincidence of thought, given the initial premises of the "Franciscan thesis" in historical and geographical terms as Fr. Rossi formulated it (whose acceptance by St. Maximilian is in part due to the influence of Fr. Rossi's book), might well be in respect to single points the fruit of a logical meditation on that thesis sustained by unique graces of a saint, granted him during contemplation of the Immaculate so as to grasp the theological and historical grounds of that mystery and expound these clearly and convincingly.[26]

23. Cf. *WK* 343, 485.

24. Cf. *WK* 662.

25. Cf. *WK* 485, 663.

26. Cf. Joseph de Sainte Marie, *La Vierge du Mont-Carmel*, for a similar approach to the interpretation of Carmelite history within the church and the economy of salvation. According to this learned Carmelite Our Lady first makes her presence felt in the church via prayer in the context of a humble, simple life. Only thereafter do the theologians and historians come to understand the particular dimension of the mystery of salvation which the intervention of the mediatrix of all grace makes clear initially. Both the contemplation and intellectual activity are ultimately oriented toward advancing the church to her final goal (cf. 15.). One may usefully compare this observation with the general approach outlined by St. Maximilian for the study of the mystery of the Immaculate, *WK* 1306.

Conclusion

From the foregoing it is clear St. Maximilian was thoroughly acquainted with the "Umbrian Priest's" vision of the Immaculate Conception and the Order of Friars Minor Conventual. In the synthesis of Fr. Filippo Rossi he undoubtedly found an initial point of departure and stimulus for the eventual refinement of his own history of the Order and of its geography, the complement of a theology and metaphysics, culture and science primarily at the service of the Immaculate, the Seat of Wisdom. Unlike Fr. Rossi he did not ever write a systematic exposition of his views; rather they are to be found scattered throughout a mass of occasional pieces, fragments as it were to be collected and set in proper relation one to another. Acquaintance with his initial source of inspiration and knowledge of the history and geography of the "Franciscan thesis" is a precious help not only in identifying the fragments and seeing their relation one to another in the mind of St. Maximilian, but of appreciating what else he might have had in mind when utilizing these himself, or making practical applications based on that intuition of Franciscanism as Marian at root, a gift of the Immaculate, "Mother of mercy," and for the sake of her Immaculate Conception. The greatest glory of the Order, as the greatest triumph of St. Francis, is its service to the Immaculate. That service is at once key to perfect conformity to the Crucified, perfect sharing of his consecration in the passion and to the "repair" of the church. The more perfect that service, that consecration, the greater the sanctity, the more fruitful the apostolate, the more effective the victory over the enemies of the church and the salvation of souls. Practically, that service, that triumph is accomplished in two steps: (1) dogmatic, cultic recognition of the mystery of the Immaculate Conception by the church; (2) formation of the Militia of the Immaculate for the incorporation of the mystery of the Immaculate into the life of the church, its history, geography and culture. The first step, the record of its accomplishment and final consummation, was sketched by Fr. Rossi. St. Maximilian in pointing to the second step and the factors involved in its accomplishment, has also deepened the vision of Fr. Rossi and set in relief its fundamental and enduring value. In meditating on that vision, in the knowledge and love and service of the Immaculate, the Franciscan Order and its members will find an inexhaustible font of spiritual strength, the indispensable support for any genuine renewal, and an authentic criterion of missionary vision and zeal. That criterion is the cause of the Immaculate. The Franciscan Order did not first come into existence and only subsequently become involved with that cause; that cause is the primary reason for its existence, the justification of the Franciscan form of life. To understand the Marian character of the Franciscan Order, it is not enough to ask how the Virgin fits into that community's life and work; it is necessary to ask how that form of life fits into the plans of the Immaculate, why service of the Immaculate is the Order's greatest honor. On those terms it is the miracle of Niepokalanów which clarifies in theory and practice the meaning of Assisi.

14

The Immaculate Conception

Outer Limits of Love

IN AN ARTICLE ENTITLED "The Will of God and the Will of the Immaculate,"[1] originally contributed to the *Informator Rycerstwa Niepokalanej* for September 1938, St. Maximilian attributes to St. Bonaventure the *Speculum Beatae Mariae Virginis* of Fr. Conrad of Saxony, more exactly according to recent scholarship[2] Konrad Holtnicker of Braunschweig (Brunswick). In a footnote the editors of St. Maximilian's writings correct the error, observing that for many centuries the work had been considered the Seraphic Doctor's. They give no explanation of how St. Maximilian came to make such a mistake some thirty-four years after the publication of the first critical edition of the *Speculum* at Quaracchi in 1904.[3] That edition prepared by Fr. Lorenz Schmitz, O.F.M., leaves no doubt at all about the authorship of Brother Conrad or about the late fifteenth-century origin of the attribution to St. Bonaventure. One might surmise that the Founder of Niepokalanów might have used an older edition prior to the great critical edition of St. Bonaventure a century ago at Quaracchi, or one of the many nineteenth-century translations (French: 1854; German: 1865; Italian: 1877) all of which ascribed the work to St. Bonaventure. This, however, is unlikely, as none of these editions ever appears in any list of books used by St. Maximilian,[4] who for the rest admired scholarship, particularly in the fields of the sacred sciences and natural science, and was generally familiar with the work of the Fathers of Quaracchi in the field of Franciscan studies.[5]

---

1. Kolbe, *WK* 1232.

2. Cf. Conrad of Saxony, *Speculum*, 11–24.

3. Conrad of Saxony, *Speculum Beatae Mariae* (1904). This is the second volume of the "Bibliotheca Francescana Acetica Medii Aevi."

4. Cf. Domanski, "La genesi," 259–62.

5. Cf. *WK* 564 and 992 D, viz., his letters to Fr. Ephrem Longpré, OFM at Quaracchi.

There is another peculiarity about this text of the *Speculum* in *WK* 1232 not noted by the editors of St. Maximilian. Though appearing in the article of this saint as a direct quotation, it is in fact a paraphrase of Conrad's text, adapted to illustrate the mystery of the Immaculate Conception rather than the divine maternity which is its subject in the original of Conrad.[6] The original Latin text in both critical editions[7] reads as follows:

> Maiorem mundum posset facere Deus, maius caelum posset facere Deus, maiorem matrem quam matrem Dei non posset facere Deus.

It is clear from the context that Conrad intends the divine maternity as absolutely the greatest work of God in any possible world for one who is merely a creature.

The text in St. Maximilian appears in this form:

> Dio —come afferma san Bonaventura—può creare un mondo più grande e più perfetto, ma non può elevare nessuna creatura ad una dignità piu elevata di quella a cui ha elevato Maria.

For St Maximilian in this article the exalted dignity of the Virgin involves the divine maternity, but the stress in the article in precisely on the sanctity of Mary qua Immaculate as the basis of that dignity, the reason why in any possible creation other than the actual one her dignity could not be greater. As we shall see, St. Maximilian, knowingly or unknowingly, in his use of Conrad has in fact recaptured the sense of this citation in Conrad's probable source, St. Anselm,[8] where the accent is not on the divine maternity so much as the sanctity of the Mother, "greater than which in a creature none is conceivable." This text appears quoted by St. Bonaventure in his first sermon for the feast of the Purification of Our Lady in this form:

> Decebat, ut illius hominis conceptio fieret de Matre purissima ea puritate, qua maior sub Deo nequit intelligi.

Whether St. Maximilian was familiar with the text as used by the Seraphic Doctor is difficult to ascertain.[9] Once, however, St. Maximilian's source

---

6. Conrad, in fact, held that Mary was freed from original sin after conception, being sanctified in the womb like Jeremiah and John the Baptist. Cf. *Speculum*, 165, 330, 374.

7. In the 1904 edition, 135; in the 1975 edition, 317. In this section Conrad drew especially on Ss. Anselm and Bernard.

8. *De Conceptu Virginis*, c. 18.

9. Cf. Domanski, "La genesi," 260. St. Maximilian possessed a copy of the study of DiFonzo, *Doctrina S. Bonaventurae*, but it is not clear to what extent he familiarized

is identified, it will be easier to grasp how he came to recapitulate the line of reflection followed by St. Bonaventure in exalting the dignity of the Mother of God, a line of thought that ultimately culminates in the formulation of the great thesis of Franciscan theology, the Immaculate Conception, and how his recapitulation advances the understanding of that thesis.

I. After his student days in Rome, St. Maximilian never had at his disposition library resources adequate for the kind of scholarly research he desired to undertake or that should be undertaken to honor the Immaculate and advance her cause.[10] Often in citing representatives of the church's tradition, or in dealing with historical questions he relied on anthologies and secondary sources which he believed to be and were generally accepted as reliable.[11]

A number of studies he considered valuable for the study of Mariology he listed in a letter of September 25, 1940, to fra. Alexander Zuchowski, then a student of theology in Krakow.[12] Among the works listed is that of Emilio Campana, *Maria nel dogma cattolico*. Canon Campana was a very well-known and influential Mariologist in his day. Among other features his volumes provided extensive quotations from the Fathers and ecclesiastical writers of the past dealing with the mysteries of Mary.

In a review of this same scholar's *Maria nel culto cattolico*[13] Fr. Amadeus Teetaert a Zedelgem, O.F.M.Cap., remarks that Campana is perhaps the only serious twentieth-century Mariologist still to ascribe the *Speculum* of Conrad and the *Stimulus Amoris* of James of Milan to St. Bonaventure.[14] The same attribution of the *Speculum* to St. Bonaventure is also made in the volume, *Maria nel dogma cattolico*, "già communemente ritenuto di S. Bonaventura,"[15] and later on,[16] without qualification.[17] And in the same work the following citation from the *Speculum*, in Latin and Italian, is found:

> Esse mater Dei est gratia maxima purae creaturae conferibilis. Ipsa est qua majorem facere Deus non potest. Majorem mundum posset facere Deus; majus coelum; majorem matrem, quam

---

himself with the numerous citations in this work from the sermons of the Seraphic Doctor.

10. Cf. *WK* 508, 647.

11. Cf. Fehlner, "Other Page," *CE* 6, chapter 13.

12. *WK* 906.

13. Campana, *Maria nel culto cattolico*; Teetaert a Zedelgem, Review.

14. Cf. vol. 1, 317, 557; vol. 2, 176.

15. Campana, *Maria nel culto cattolico*, 76.

16. Campana, *Maria nel culto cattolico*, 225.

17. DiFonzo, *Doctrina S. Bonaventurae*, 348n225.

Matrem Dei non posset facere. Essere madre di Dio e tale grazia, che Dio non può farne un'altra più grande. Egli potrebbe fare un mando ed un cielo più grande; fare una madre più grande della Madre di Dio, e anche per lui una cosa impossibile.[18]

The source of this quotation is given as book X of the *Speculum*, but no edition is indicated. Evidently the citation does not correspond with either critical edition of this work.[19]

That this very citation adapted by St. Maximilian in an important reflection on the grandeur of the Immaculate should appear in a work he esteemed expressly ascribed to St. Bonaventure, master of the Franciscan school of theology, lends great probability to the hypothesis that this study of Campana was the saint's immediate source for the quote in *WK* 1232. This is further confirmed by the context in which Campana cites the *Speculum*. That context is an extended discussion of the excellence of the divine maternity, a subject recurring in various writings of St. Maximilian from this period,[20] particularly in relation to the question of the study and knowledge of the Mother of God. In at least one of these, *WK* 1210, a passage of St. Thomas on the infinite dignity of the divine maternity cited by Campana just before that from the *Speculum* seems to be reflected.

But that discussion in Campana is intimately bound up with a study of the sanctity of Mary, one whose transcendent excellence in relation to the rest of the entire creation (actual or possible) is rooted in the Immaculate Conception, a point recognized in the bull of definition of the dogma by Pius IX in 1854. It is not too difficult to see how this presentation by Campana of a series of texts to illustrate related ideas might be reworked in the retentive and reflective mind of St. Maximilian to explain the mystery of the Immaculate Conception. The infinity associated with the divine maternity, so overwhelming to the powers of reason unaided by the light of faith represents in fact (in Kolbean terms) "the outer limits of God and creation"[21]: the greatest dignity the creative power of God can bestow on a creature, the ultimate limit of divine love in regard to any creature, and conversely the ultimate limit of the love of creation for the Creator, in a word the vertex

18. Campana, *Maria nel culto cattolico*, 76.

19. Until Campana's source is identified it remains difficult to correlate the first two sentences of his citation with anything in the critical edition.

20. Cf. Kolbe, *WK* 1210, 1305, 1318.

21. *WK* 1232.

of love.[22] That outer limit is the mystery of the Immaculate herself, whose name coincides with that of the Holy Spirit.[23]

Naturally, there is a certain value in identifying St. Maximilian's sources for the materials forming the material upon which he reflected. Often enough these sources are not easy to identify, but when they are they often enable us to reconstruct many of the points comprising the contents of his conscious thought, but not expressly reflected in his writing. But it is equally obvious once these sources have been read that the saint never merely transcribed what others had written, or simply restated their views. This is the case with the citation probably taken from the *Speculum* of Conrad via the study of Campana. Maximilian goes far beyond his source in his use of this citation. This perhaps is the greater value stemming from an identification of these sources. The "originality" of the saint becomes more evident.

How is it, then, that St. Maximilian did not advert to the mistake in attribution? One explanation might be that he had never heard of the critical edition of the *Speculum*, and thus uncritically accepted the attribution of Campana. A more likely explanation might be this. Not being occupied regularly over the years in questions of textual criticism, and probably recalling from memory a passage read in Campana rather than copying directly from the volume in question, a passage interesting primarily for its content rather than author the saint might easily have forgotten at the moment of composition the common view of scholarship in 1938 concerning the authorship of the *Speculum*, as he indeed seems to have overlooked even Campana's qualification: "già communemente ritenuto."[24]

II. Even a superficial reading of those passages of St. Maximilian's writings where thoughts encountered by him in the works of others are reflected is sufficient to demonstrate that he neither simply repeated nor commented on these. Rather he habitually recast and deepened them by associating them with or incorporating them into a line of thought his own. In these instances, it is not what he was reading which suggested the line of thought; rather the line of thought he was pursuing—under the influence of the Immaculate[25]—enabled him to perceive an aspect of the truth about Our Lady suggested by the content of his teaching. One example of

22. *WK* 1318.

23. *WK* 1318.

24. If the saint saw the correction of Campana by Fr. DiFonzo, that most probably occurred after the composition and publication of the article where he cites the *Speculum*.

25. This St. Bonaventure calls the "contemplative mode of theologizing." Cf. *Itin.*, c. 1,7: theologia symbolica, propria et mystica.

his method is to be found in the use he made of a study of Fr. Filippo Rossi.[26] Another is that of the material found in Campana's *Maria nel dogma Cattolica*[27] in *WK* 1210, 1232, and 1318. In none of these cases do we find a direct citation, even when so indicated as in *WK* 1232, but a paraphrase more of less based on the contents of Campana's study. Indeed, in *WK* 1318 there may not be so much a conscious recall of the book of Campana, as a use of materials already transmuted into his own thought so completely that their source would not be suspected unless their affinity with earlier uses traceable to that source had been verified.

In the article "Our Ideal"[28] first published in *Maly Dziennik*, June 24, 1936, the day after St. Maximilian's definitive return from Japan, and then reprinted in *Rycerz Niepokalanej*, August 1936, is to be found a particularly important definition of the M.I. ideal of holiness: the Immaculate herself, and why that ideal so crucial to the church and to every believer, actual or potential, is so difficult, even after years of asceticism, to comprehend and therefore pursue. All the privileges of the Virgin Mary, first of all her Immaculate Conception, he writes, have been granted her in view of the divine maternity, and of her spiritual maternity in our regard. While we can grasp the essential note of motherhood, our intellects, unaided by the grace of faith implored on one's knees in humble prayer, cannot grasp what "Mother of God" might mean, because the notion of God entails that of infinity. This is why the vocation of the Mother of God, and the sanctity appropriate to it, that of the Immaculate Conception, "our ideal," viz., the measure of the holiness to which we aspire, is so difficult to grasp, even for a good person.

Here is the text of St. Maximilian:

> Noi conosciamo bene il significato del termine "madre," ma la nozione di "Dio" contiene in essa stessa l'infinito, mentre la nostra intelligenza è limitata e non sara mai in grado, quindi, di comprendere appieno il concetto di "Madre di Dio."

If we set this text alongside that of Campana, citing a well-known passage of St. Thomas,[29] the source of this notion of associating infinity with a mere creature becomes apparent.

> Maria ex hoc quod est mater Dei, habet quamdam dignitatem infinitam ex bono infinito quod est Deus, et ex hac parte non potest aliquid fieri melius; sicut non potest aliquid esse melius

---

26. Cf. Fehlner, "Other Page," *CE* 6, chapter 13.
27. Campana, *Maria nel culto cattolico*, 75–76.
28. *WK* 1210.
29. Thomas Aquinas, *ST*, I, q. 25, a. 4.

> Deo. Maria per ciò che è madre di Dio ha una dignità pressochè infinita per i suoi rapporti con Dio bene infinito; e sotto questo riguardo non è possibile niente di meglio; come non è possibile trovare cosa alcuna che sia migliore di Dio stesso.

The remark of St. Thomas originally occurs in a discussion of the outer limits of divine omnipotence, beyond which the Creator cannot improve on his handiwork in any possible order. These the Angelic Doctor says are three: the incarnation, the divine maternity of Mary, and the fruition of God in the beatific vision by the saints. To each in a certain relative sense can be applied the term "infinite," not as the divine being is infinite, but in comparison to other works of God "ad extra," all of which admits the possibility of further perfecting.

It is possible St. Maximilian might have developed his thoughts in *WK* 1210 directly from the text of St. Thomas, or from Lépicier's manual of Mariology with which he was familiar.[30] His description of the outer limit of God[31] directly reflects the context of St. Thomas' original thought. But St. Maximilian's use of this idea in *WK* 1232 juxtaposes with the outer limit of divine power (action) the outer limit of creaturely response (reaction) to the creative initiative of God. The Immaculate is the "outer limit between God and creation." Two powers of loving and doing meet and fuse here in the Immaculate. And in Campana, 75, just preceding the citation from St. Thomas is one from Cajetan:

> Ad fines divinitatis propria operatione attigit, dum Deum concepit, peperit, genuit et lacte proprio pavit. Toccò le regioni della divinità e divenne affine con Dio quando lo concepì, lo generò e lo nutrì della propria sostanza.

Thus, it is also likely that his reading of Campana suggested a line of thought encountered in the articles under study here, a supposition confirmed when one recalls his use merely two years later of the text of the *Speculum* (attributed there to St. Bonaventure as in Campana) to illustrate the "infinite" character of the unique sanctity of the Immaculate. Thus, a discussion by St. Thomas of the omnipotence of God, employed by Campana to underscore the excellence of the divine maternity, is recast by St. Maximilian to illustrate the unique sanctity of the Immaculate as such. In fact that recasting gives us a glimpse of certain aspects of the depth of his theological insight.

---

30. Lépicier, *Tractatus.*
31. *WK* 1232.

To appreciate this it is necessary to examine briefly why and how he came to recast these texts in an *analogous*, but wider context touching the practical order: the incorporation of the mystery of the Immaculate into life. It is the "infinity" associated with our Lady which is the source of the difficulties many encounter in regard to the prerequisite understanding of this ideal. In *WK* 1210 the saint briefly refers to the resolution of these difficulties: recourse to prayer and contemplation as the appropriate context of study. It is a theme to which he returned at greater length in April 1938, in *Rycerz Niepokalanej*[32] and again in the "Material for a Book" in 1940.[33] How exactly these difficulties, even for reasonably devout persons, in making the M.I. ideal their own can be resolved in the practical order St. Maximilian explains in *WK* 1232, the article where he cites the passage from Conrad of Saxony's *Speculum*.

There he intends to treat of the identity or union of wills between God and the Immaculate. Precisely in virtue of the Immaculate Conception that union is so perfect that none more perfect is possible or conceivable between God and a creature. Her "infinity" consists not in the fact she ceases to be a creature, "infinitely inferior," as the saint writes, to God, but in her unique sanctity as Mother of God, viz., in the fact she is the Immaculate. She is the utmost possibility of divine creativity, the "outer limit between God and creation," and "the faithful image of divine perfection, of divine holiness." Hence to do her will is to do God's will, and he remarks the Son of God himself did the Father's will in doing his Mother's, in entrusting himself to her as her possession for our salvation, a salvation wrought by obedience unto death on the cross.

So too the measure of our perfection, our holiness depends on the union of our wills with God's will. Nowhere is this greater than when our wills are identical with that of the Immaculate, when we are her "possession and property," when in fact we live continuously total, unconditional consecration to her. Such a degree of holiness on our part increases (rather than decreases) the glory of God, and in that veneration we recognize the omnipotence (and infinity) of God who has given existence to a creature so sublime and perfect as to represent the outer limit of divine creativity and goodness. In admiring so beautiful a work of holiness we admire and begin to grasp the genius of the maker. And with that living of the ideal in prayer we begin to grasp its nature.

---

32. *WK* 1228, 1305.

33. Kolbe, *WK* 1306, entitled "How to Study," a reflection very similar to thoughts of St. Bonaventure in the prologue of the *Itinerarium Mentis in Deum*, n. 4.

Here we see how two complementary ideas, one from St. Thomas the other from Cajetan: the outer limits of divine creativity (action) and the outer limits of created response (reaction) meet in the Immaculate and terminate in the incarnation. That meeting in the Virgin is the mystery of the Immaculate Conception, the foundation of the very possibility of Marian mediation, viz., cooperation in the work of salvation centered on the incarnation, first on the part of the Virgin, and then on the part of all others who unite their wills with hers via "total consecration."

In what that meeting might consist we are given a fleeting, but ecstatic glimpse in *WK* 1318, entitled "The Immaculate Conception," dictated the morning of the saint's final arrest by the Gestapo and regarded by many scholars as the fruit primarily of contemplation rather than academic study.[34] This reflection of the meaning of the name Our Lady gave herself at Lourdes: I am the Immaculate Conception, is indeed a profound insight into that mystery, not hitherto granted in the history of theology, and one destined eventually to have a far-reaching influence on the thought and conduct of Christians, so intimately bound up is it with the mystery of the Holy Spirit within the Trinity and within the economy of salvation.

In no way does this reflection, intended by the saint as a chapter in the book he was preparing on the Immaculate and her Militia, directly depend on the materials found in the volume of Campana. The only link is an indirect one: the "outer limits of divine creativity" of *WK* 1232 appear reinterpreted here as the vertex of love, the point where all the love of the Blessed Trinity, that is of Father and Son, converging in the procession of the Holy Spirit, and all the love of creation, that is in a creature whose will is most perfectly united with the divine as Spouse of the Holy Spirit, as the "Full of grace," meet and are so united as to conceive and give birth to the Son of God in the flesh. It is this vertex of love which in humble prayer and total consecration to the Virgin we begin to grasp in her name: Immaculate Conception. It is also the name of the Holy Spirit. Once we begin to grasp the relation between conception, person and holiness, ultimately consummated in the paschal mystery, then we are in a position to begin to appreciate the ideal of the M.I. and why our paradise can only begin when that ideal is incorporated into every aspect of life.

In summary St. Maximilian has borrowed reflections on the "infinity" of the Mother of God, originally set forth in contexts dealing with the omnipotence of God or the excellence of the divine maternity, to illustrate the grandeur of the Immaculate. So proceeding, he has not betrayed the sense of these ideas in their original context. Rather his recasting in terms of

---

34. Pyfferoen and Van Asseldonk, "Maria Santissima," 438.

profound insights into the mystery of the Immaculate Conception enables us to see more clearly not only the excellence of the divine maternity, but the coordination between those three works of God St. Thomas claims enjoy an absolute perfection among all the actual and possible works of God. For the Immaculate being the "vertex amoris" through which the divine and created pass is by that fact the "Mediatress" of heaven and earth. Her only reason for existence is to be in fact the Mother of God. That is why she is so perfect. Her perfection enables us to appreciate both the greatness of our Savior and of his love for us, as well as the unsurpassed excellence of the salvation which he has won for us, the preservation of the Mother from sin being the means of our liberation and its immediate goal. To the extent our lives, our wills more precisely, are focused exclusively on that mystery, to that extent do we share the glory of God. That consecration of our wills in this fashion is the core of humility, fully achieved in the consecration of the Virgin, or her Immaculate Conception.

III. From the foregoing it is evident St. Maximilian throughout a lifetime of reflection on the mystery of the Immaculate and of following Christ crucified as a disciple of St. Francis of Assisi pursued a line of thought not contrary to, but certainly not identical with any of the contemporary writers from whom he often drew for the contents of that reflection.

But neither is that line of thought a purely original creation of his. It is rather a continuation of a line of thought at the heart of the "Franciscan thesis" in theology: the Immaculate Conception and the absolute primacy of Christ, a line of thought intimately associated with the Cause of the Immaculate, in our time taking the form of the M.I, but initially entrusted by the Immaculate to St. Francis and his Order according to St. Maximilian.[35] His ability to perceive the key elements of conversion and sanctification. of prayer and mission, not only theologically, but within the Franciscan tradition considered historically, and advance these significantly both in a theoretical and practical way is illustrated by his use of a text he mistakenly attributed to St. Bonaventure, but which in using advances one of the characteristic features of Franciscan and Bonaventurian thought: progress in sanctity for the Christian depends of the mystery of the divine maternity; promotion of such progress (work of conversion and sanctification of souls) is an extension of the maternal mediation of the Virgin consummated at the foot of the cross in her compassion, that is a giving birth to Christ in the minds and hearts of those who are baptized.[36]

35. Cf. Fehlner, "A Thesis," *CE* 6, chapter 2.

36. Cf. Bonaventure, *Sermo I in Purificatione; De don. Spir.*, col. 6, especially nn. 15–21.

In its original context, a commentary on the Angelic Salutation (whether St. Maximilian ever read this commentary is not known), the citation from the *Speculum* of Br. Conrad of Saxony stands in close relation to two features of Franciscan theology distinctive of that thought not only in the history of the Order, but in the life of St. Francis as well. The well-known antiphon composed by St. Francis for use in his *Office of the Passion*, in which the Virgin Mary is addressed as firstborn daughter of the Father, Mother of his Son and Spouse of the Holy Spirit, is the immediate basis for reflections on the "Dominus tecum" where the remark about the impossibility of making a mother better than the Mother of God in any possibly better world or heaven. The transcendent dignity of the Virgin qua Mother is evidently based on her sanctity, viz., the uniqueness of her relation to the Blessed Trinity. No one else among women, according to St. Francis in this antiphon is comparable to Mary in holiness. Hence in his *Salute to the Virgin*, a kind of commentary on the Angelic Salutation in certain respects, he addresses her as full of grace, in whom is all good, i.e., God. Between the divine maternity (and with it the spiritual maternity) of Mary and her unique sanctity there is an intimate nexus in the mind of Francis, a nexus reflected in the meditations of Br. Conrad, first on the fullness of grace in Mary, and then on the divine maternity, a fullness of grace to be appropriated to the Holy Spirit under the title of Spouse. We may summarize thus: the sanctity of the Virgin is the source of our sanctity, precisely because she has become Mother of God. That sanctity, called by St. Francis her consecration by the Father with the Son and Holy Spirit, is the *ne plus ultra* of God's creative love, taken to its final limit in the paschal mystery, a limit suggested by the Office for which the famed antiphon just cited was composed. In Franciscan spirituality and thought the Virgin Mary, whom St. Francis calls the "Virgin made Church," at once is the most beautiful fruit of the most perfect work of God, the Redemption, and the instrument of that same redemption wrought by the Incarnate Son. This is why the "Franciscan thesis" qua Christocentric has been given a Marian coefficient, the Immaculate Conception. She is the Advocate of St. Francis and his Order, the key to that distinctive prayer and missionary work associated with the Franciscans across the centuries.

Even if neither Conrad of Saxony nor St. Bonaventure arrived at an express confession of the Immaculate Conception in theological terms, indeed plainly denied it in such terms, nonetheless, the inner logic of their thought prepared the way for Duns Scotus in linking a maximum love of God for creation in the incarnation with the sanctity of the Mother of God and her maternal mediation.[37] Here is found the reason for the appropri-

---

37. Cf. Fehlner, "Mary in the Franciscan," *CE* 3, chapter 5; "Saint Francis and Mary,"

ateness of a holiness in the Virgin Mother transcending that of the rest of creation, such as to constitute her an "order" or "hierarchy" apart.[38] The maximal degree of perfection in any created being is found in the perfection of the will in the love of God precisely because there, as the Seraphic Doctor notes,[39] we are dealing not merely with an image of God, but the similitude, not with an analogy or proportion admitting always of more or less, but of an identity or union in a single perfection: charity. It is this union of wills that is at the heart of the supernatural order of grace a union of wills based on a love of the divine goodness (for St. Francis the "summum bonum, omne bonum"), a love "appretiative summus."

All that remained to be done was to point out how in fact the maximum union of wills in charity could be achieved and in what that consisted concretely, so as to identify the "infinite" in created excellence, the utmost limit of divine love and creativity in respect to his creatures in a human order infected by original sin. The objections to the Immaculate Conception of Mary were resolved by Duns Scotus in showing that the preservation of our Lady from all stain of original sin from the very first moment of her conception was neither an obstacle to her descent from Adam nor a detraction from the universality of her Son's redemptive work, because her preservation from original sin was the perfect fruit of a perfect redemption, the utter limit of divine mercy for all those whom his Son would free from sin.

Rightly, then, does the Angel of the Lord, Gabriel, address her reverently as "Full of grace," a title feared by that other brilliant spirit who refused her honor from the beginning, who because of her could not frustrate the incarnation nor the redemption.

Theologically the reflections of St. Maximilian recapitulate the key elements involved in this history and take the synthesis one step further in showing that the positive complement to the definition of the Immaculate Conception as "preservation from the stain of original sin" is "Spouse of the Holy Spirit," both of whom share the same name: Immaculate Conception, because the Holy Spirit in eternity and the Immaculate in time are the fruit of the mutual love of Father and Son, and because the fruit of that love of Father and Incarnate Son in time in the Virgin who virginally becomes by the power of the Holy Spirit his Mother.

We need only add that that speculative advance is ultimately for the sake of loving God as the Son of God loved his Father, and as he loved his Mother, so as to give his life for his brethren; indeed, this was achieved by a

---

CE 3, chapter 3.

38. St. Bonaventure, *II Sent.*, d. 9, a. 7.

39. St. Bonaventure, *II Sent.*, d. 16, a. 2, q. 3. Cf. Rezette, "Similitudo."

saint in just such a context where he had consecrated his life to his Mother and would give that life for the salvation of his brothers, thus illustrating in deed as in word the nature of the greatest love: of God for man and man for God. When understood, such love has the name Immaculate Conception, created and uncreated.

15

Mulieres Dignitatem

THE APOSTOLIC LETTER TREATING the dignity and vocation of the woman: *Mulieris Dignitatem*, long expected and much desired, appeared at the end of September 1988. Dated the Assumption, August 15, 1988, it was issued on the occasion of close of the Marian Year. The appropriateness of the occasion was no mere coincidence. For the purposes of that Year and the Marian themes particularly relevant to it have a direct and immediate bearing on the subject of what it means to be a man and to be a woman, in a word, what it means to be human and how that is effected. During the Synod of Bishops of 1987 this very point was made; indeed, it is underscored in the encyclical *Redemptoris Mater*, n. 46, as well. What it means to be a woman and what bearing that has on being human, both theoretically and practically, passes through the mystery of Mary to reach the mystery of the incarnation, in the light of which only does the eternal truth about man made in the image and likeness of God, male and female, find full understanding. The incarnation is the central event, the key to the history of salvation. At the heart of that event is the Woman, the Virgin Mary. Thus, at the fullness of time God sent his son to be born of the woman. (cf. Gal 4:4). According to the pope this is the fundamental fact and basic principle governing any reflection on the dignity and role of woman in the orders of creation and salvation. Seen in that light that dignity and role is indeed great, for in the fulness of time Mary attained as Virgin Mother of the Word Incarnate a union with God such as to exceed the expectations not only of the human spirit but of all Israel, in particular the daughters of the chosen people.

In this way the fulness of time reveals the extraordinary dignity of the woman in her capacity to be mother, even the mother of God. The annunciation at Nazareth sets in relief, via the Woman, the purpose of existence of every human being, male as well as female: elevation to the order of grace and supernatural life in God. But it also underscores a form of that union only possible to the woman, that of mother and child, one achieved when the Virgin became the Mother of God and the Son of God became her child. Mary, then, the Virgin full of grace, a fullness granted in order that she might become the "Theotokos" embodies in herself the fulness of perfection of that which is characteristic of the woman, namely of that which is feminine. That characteristic is crystallized in the Virgin's final response to the messenger of the Most High: Behold the handmaid of the Lord. Be it done to me according to your word. It is the love of the woman that is most profoundly capable of obedient, sacrificial love of God, because it is the woman who is capable of being mother. Mary's love, says the Holy Father, and therefore her service must be meditated both in terms of her being as creature, but also in terms of her dignity as Mother of her Son, thus in relation to that service and that consecration he lived as "Servant of the Lord," God though he was. The perfection of our Lady's consecration to her Son, namely her Immaculate Conception, involves her qua Mother most fully in the charity of that service her Son rendered the Father for the salvation of souls, for the redemption of the world. And it is this reality that determines the essential horizon for any reflection on the dignity and vocation of the woman.

This horizon is further elaborated and specified under four other considerations in the Letter where the mystery of Mary in Christ and in the church serves as the prism through which to understand both what it means to be a woman and why human nature, and the welfare of mankind at every level, is entrusted for better or worse to woman.

Thus, a meditation on the woman of Genesis, Eve, and the woman of the Annunciation, Mary, leads us to realize that the redemption of the human family from sin is the successful outcome of a struggle between the offspring of the Woman Mary and of the offspring of the Tempter, that the new covenant finds its beginning with a Woman, and that this Woman, Mary, embraces in herself the mystery of womanhood begun in Eve, "mother of all the living." In this way she assured that the Son of God in becoming her child would assume a human nature of the line of Adam, that is, ours. Not only is Eve redeemed in Mary as her "advocate," but transcended in her. Mary is the new principle of the dignity and vocation of the woman, of all and of each. In Mary Eve must find anew her true worth, a discovery to be shared by every woman as the form of her vocation and of her life.

That form is intimately related to the calling of mother and of virgin, both of which are perfectly realized in the Mother of God and both orientate the woman toward the paschal mystery. The task of the woman-mother, whether as she who bears (physical dimensions) or as she who teaches (the spiritual dimension of parenthood) entails sacrificial love, whose culmination is to be seen in the maternity of the Mother of God. The new covenant of God with mankind is accomplished in the flesh and blood of him who was born of the Virgin Mary. Her maternity brings her, and with her every woman, to the foot of the cross where a sword pierces her heart. The sufferings endured by the Woman constitute a unique contribution to the realization of the joy of the resurrection and of paradise.

The kingdom established by the Son of Mary in his victorious battle with the prince of this world is an everlasting kingdom. All consecrated life in the church is radically a witness to the eschatological character of Christ's work and of the church, viz., that a life of holiness, even when in this world, is not of it, but an anticipation of the world to come. But in a special way the ideal of virginity for the sake of the kingdom in a woman has unique value as a sign of eschatological hope. For the Savior was born of the Virgin Mother, who remains in heaven, as she was on earth, the great sign of hope a merciful God has given a sinful race.

In the encyclical *Redemptoris Mater* the Holy Father insists on the point that the Mother of God precedes the church in faith, in charity and in her union with God. The church in her relation to Christ has always been presented as bride, as spouse, because she is to believe, to love, to unite herself to Christ as the Woman who is his Mother. Hence, in the person of Mary is revealed the special contribution which every woman brings to the church and to the salvation of souls in seeking to be holy according to the mode appropriate to her femininity.

That mode is intimately linked to the order of love, where the groom is the one who loves and the spouse is she who is loved and returns that love. While it is true all the redeemed are loved by the Redeemer and are to return his love, the characteristic feature of supernatural charity is most clearly unveiled in woman, above all the Immaculate Virgin totally consecrated to her Son at the foot of the Cross, and to whom there her Son consecrated-entrusted the church and each of us. Here is the Woman, model of courage and strength, support of her beloved Son, mother and mistress of a new humanity whose fundamental law is charity and whose ultimate goal is not a temporal, but eternal one, not material well-being, but spiritual.

To those holy women who across the centuries have lived after the example of the Virgin Mary as mothers or as virgins or as widows, and who in every field of human endeavor have in so living left the stamp of their femininity, families, nations and the church are deeply indebted. For them and the great things wrought in them the church gives thanks to the Blessed Trinity. It is the continuing pursuit of this ideal of womanhood, not its replacement by and in the glorification of secular careers in science or politics which will ensure that mankind does not lose its essential humanity.

Promotion of this ideal is the work of "incorporating" the mystery of the Immaculate into life. That mystery of her unique, total consecration to Christ, her fullness of grace, in the encyclical *Redemptoris Mater*, is the point of departure for expounding the mystery of Mary in Christ and in the church, a mystery best described dynamically as her maternal mediation. Cultivation of devotion to the Virgin Immaculate qua mediatrix is but the development of a spirituality of total consecration to Jesus through Mary, whose center is the cross and the Eucharist.

In the Apostolic Letter *Mulieres Dignitatem* that same mystery of Mary's fullness of grace is the point of departure for an unfolding of the dignity and role of woman, of all and of each. For the same reasons that the Woman pre-served from all stain of sin through the merits of her Son is by that very fact involved in a struggle with the father of lies, so is every woman who seeks to realize her true femininity, who strives to find in the Immaculate Virgin Mother her advocate and ideal. That striving on the part of all women and every woman is crucial to the salvation of souls, to the welfare of the human family on earth and the final triumph of Christ's kingdom

At this juncture the relevance of the M.I. for women and of women for the M.I. is not difficult to see. The spirituality of the M.I. is one rooted in the mystery of the Immaculate Conception. Its apostolic dynamism is one predicated on the truth of Mary's maternal mediation in a context where the struggle between the Woman and the serpent has become particularly intense. Programs and policies favoring contraception, abortion, divorce, female ordination, and other forms of conduct and education undermining the Christian ideal of purity in thought, desire and work, are particularly vicious attacks on the dignity of woman. Their clear aim is the destruction of humanity by corrupting it in Eve, enslaving her again as the Serpent first did to the false spirituality and philosophy of secularism. Against the Im-maculate the Serpent cannot triumph. Where the presence of the Immacu-late constitutes the central reality in the lives of persons and communities, there these current attacks on the dignity of women and the true welfare of mankind cannot succeed. Promoting the M.I., incorporating the mystery of the Immaculate into life at every level we spread not only a devotion, but a spirituality. We make available not only an effective weapon for blunting a vicious attack, but contribute to the achievement of that dignity in every woman, intended originally by the Creator as a prolongation and reflection of the beauty of his Mother, the sign which he has given us on earth and in heaven guaranteeing his mercy and our everlasting bliss.

16

Marian Doctrine and Devotion

A Kolbean Perspective

Introduction

THE MARIAN MOVEMENT OF the nineteenth century and the first part of the twentieth century has often been accused of divorcing doctrine and devotion, or if not separating these at least not integrating them properly.[1] From the perspective of those making such criticisms the one or the other defect accounts for the arid "essentialism" and "intellectualism" of the doctrinal treatises of this period and the sentimental piety—fideism—of the devotion and apostolic zeal, even of saints of this period. The charges are not new; indeed, they have been current in the western world for many centuries. When leveled against the church as a whole, they reflect, as Cardinal Newman observed in an essay since become a classic of Marian literature,[2] not an accurate analysis of fact in the first instance, but an unfortunate prejudice against any recognition of the unique place of the Mother of God in the economy of salvation and a failure to understand the true basis for the marked devotion of the church toward the Virgin from its beginnings in every time and place as well as the sound balance of that devotion across the centuries. It is a prejudice that in those who indulge it leads naturally to a loss of faith in the person and work of the Savior.[3]

St. Maximilian Kolbe, surely one of the more outstanding and exceptional representatives of the Marian movement during the first part of our century, both during and after his life, was often accused of pietism and anti-intellectualism, but since his beatification and canonization (and the

---

1. Cf. De Fiores, "Mariologia / Marialogia.," 891–93.
2. Newman, "Letter to E. B. Pusey."
3. Newman, "Glories of Mary," 345–47.

effective refutation of such charges),[4] has been described oddly enough as indulging a kind of "essentialist," metaphysical-type Mariology.[5] Without doubt this saint did indeed insist on the primacy of charity; his heroic death as a martyr is but the crown of a life fully exemplifying that primacy, and the nature and source of true love. But the martyr of Auschwitz is just as insistent that the only love to be given such primacy is true love. Not all love is true for the same reason that not all love is divine (even if God is love), but only that love in accord with the truth, only that love coincident with that of the divine will, with that of the all-holy will of the Incarnate Savior with the sinless will of the Immaculate. The condition for this love in us is an unlimited love of the truth, an unconditional obedience to the word of God, viz., dogmatic faith. In the economy of salvation that dogmatic faith is mediated by the Immaculate. St. Maximilian saw clearly the implication: both human thought and human love tend as they are perfected to be Marianized.[6] The great work of this saint, then, the Militia of the Immaculate, is, via total consecration to the Immaculate, an implementation of the primacy of charity, the charity of the heart of the God-man, in the spiritual and apostolic life of the church and of her members.[7] The conversion and sanctification of all souls can have no other finality, nor can such sacerdotal, sacrificial love be effected except on the assumption that the Immaculate, is the mediatrix of all grace.[8] But that great work of his, the M.I, so often described by him as the cause of the Immaculate, he also described just as forcefully as a "global vision of Catholic life under a new form resting on our relation to the Immaculate, our universal mediatrix with Jesus."[9]

Evidently accusations of imbalance: affective or cognitive, can only be given a patina of plausibility by considering each of these poles of his work, viz., the primacy of charity and the global vision of life, in isolation. But it is just such isolation that is not verified in his life and work.[10]

4. For evidence of the theological-intellectual depths to be found in this saint cf. *Mariologia di S. Massimiliano Kolbe*.

5. Laurentin, *Dio mia tenerezza*, 144. It is fashionable to contrast existentialism and essentialism in favor of the first. Unfortunately, that use of the term essentialism can often misrepresent a kind of essentialism which is but a continuation of the ancient Augustinian-Franciscan metaphysics of exemplarism and illumination, as deeply concrete as it is human, precisely because it has so sharp a sense of the real "a parte rei."

6. *WK* 1246.

7. *WK* 1331.

8. *WK* 1029.

9. *WK* 1220.

10. On the intellectual formation of St. Maximilian cf. Domanski, "La genesi," and DiFonzo, "Le radici." His intellectual ability and theological competence are perfectly evident in his spiritual conferences, in the many apologetical dialogues to be found in

Quite the contrary of what his sharpest critics maintained, St. Maximilian intended to sanctify the intellect, not by abusing it nor by suppressing it, but by perfecting it "in the spirit of prayer and devotion" as St. Francis instructed St. Anthony when giving him leave to teach theology to the friars.[11] Of all the powers at our disposition the intellectual are the most precious. Their use or abuse is freighted with consequence. The failure to sanctify the intellect, in practice to perfect it in faith as the way to the clear vision of the truth, viz., God (thus recognizing that the intellect connaturally tends to faith) and so seek to "reduce" all intellectual disciplines to theology, is to leave the intellect prone to agnosticism and atheism, even if that unnatural condition first appears under the guise of false devotion. The program of the M.I. as its founder conceived it, is to incorporate the mystery of the Immaculate into life and into every dimension of human life, not least the intellectual and cultural.[12]

In this St. Maximilian is simply continuing in the footsteps of St. Bonaventure in cultivating the intellectual life and centering this work in the study of theology. His distinctive contribution is the "marianization" of this work; or one might also say the discovery of its latent or radically Marian character while probing the mystery of the Immaculate Conception. The "intellectus quaerens fidem" is an intellect seeking to be marianized, and thus *a parte rei* all the arts and sciences point to Mary Immaculate and through her to Christ. The "fides quaerens intellectum" is a faith seeking to understand ever more the mystery of the Immaculate so as to see and enjoy in charity the Word Incarnate.

The purpose of this study is neither to refute the critics of St. Maximilian, nor exemplify the insights of Cardinal Newman. It is rather to sketch in the words of the martyr of charity why and how Catholic doctrine and devotion find progressively greater integration and balance through their progressive marianization, why "our theology,"[13] and indeed our metaphysics, must not only be ecclesial, but Marian; why the "Sedes Sapientiae" is a central truth and a central actor in fundamental theology; why the "illuminatio mentis ac inflammatio cordis" so basic to the Christian intellectual tradition, has a Marian coefficient.

---

the volumes of his collected works, in his promotion of M.I. II groups for study and research at Niepokalanów, the desire for an Academy of the Immaculate, for a specialized library, the goal of placing the first fruits of science and technology at the service of the Immaculate.

11. *Opuscula Sancti Patris Francisci Assisiensis*, 94–95.

12. *WK* 486. Cf. Domanski, "Niepokalanów," 391–93. For an early statement of such a program cf. *WK* 92. For an indication of the balance in his assessments cf. *WK* 1180.

13. Scotus, *Ord.*, prol., p. 3, q. 3.

"Spiritus Orationis et Devotionis"

In one of the first chapters of the material he prepared for a book on the Immaculate Conception[14] St. Maximilian deals with the relation of study and piety in view of the mystery of the Immaculate. His exposition obviously recalls that of the same point in the Prologue of the *Itinerarium mentis in Deum* of St. Bonaventure.[15] Indeed the similarity is such as to postulate some influence of the Seraphic Doctor in the formulation and expression of St. Maximilian.

The essential point of St. Bonaventure is that prayer and grace must precede and conclude any effort to read and study about God. For the intellectual activity of the human intellect in this life properly theological is suspended between the "obedience of faith," what Bonaventure calls "symbolic theology" (roughly what might be called today credal or catechetical or, in the broad sense, sacramental theology) and the understanding of God which in this is bound up with the gift of infused contemplation (and in the life to come the beatific vision), what the Seraphic Doctor calls "mystical theology."[16] "Intellectual" theology, in so far as it entails an exercise of the native powers of the intellect rather than simple assent to the truth in faith and in living the sacramental life of the church, or repose in the truth in prayer, can only be fruitful in respect to the truth about God by reinforcing that submission and disposing for that repose to the extent it proceeds from an initial act of faith (and not private judgment) and disposes for an ardent love of the triune God and the Incarnate Savior. The more perfect the obedience of faith, the more intense the charity, the more fruitful will be that activity called "theology in the proper sense" in terms of the enlightenment and understanding which clarifies the faith professed and disposes for union with God and love of neighbor. The plan of meditative prayer in the *Itinerarium* as a progressive preparation for and initiation into the mystical life assumes the truth of this analysis of theology, an analysis whose philosophical counterpart is the Bonaventurian theory of exemplarism and illumination. Just as the primacy of charity in the Bonaventurian and Franciscan theological tradition far from being anti-intellectual postulates a radical respect for the intellect as the God-given power to assent and thus obey the truth, so that theological and philosophical speculation "contemplationis gratia ut boni

14. *WK* 1306; cf. also *WK* 634.

15. *Itin.*, prol., 4. For points of contact between Ss. Bonaventure and Maximilian, cf. Domanski, "La genesi," 261–62.

16. *Itin.*, c. 1, 7. The same concept of theology is easily discernible in *Brev.*, prologue, 16 (ortus, progressus et status of theology) and in the sermon "Christus unus omnium Magister" (knowledge of God, or theology, in so far as Christ is way, truth and life).

fiamus, et principaliter ut boni fiamus,"[17] sometimes described as "essential-ist," especially in its Scotistic version, in no way is an obstacle to, rather is the finest disposition for a charity authentically such, a spirituality "a parte rei," viz., realistic, not sentimental.

St. Maximilian in the passage of his writings under consideration has simply placed the study of the mystery of the Immaculate in this context as a privileged instance of theology. He gives four reasons why this is so:

(1) The study of the Immaculate is not the study of just something or just anyone, but of a creature who loves each of us ineffably, one who is all pure, without stain. Thus, a maximum of reverence is indispensable for that study.

(2) Not even the greatest minds among saintly doctors are able to give adequate expression; either interiorly or verbally, to the reality of her who is the masterpiece of God, who in virtue of her Immaculate Conception is the total possession of the three divine persons.[18] Thus a maximum of illumination from on high is necessary in undertaking any such study. In the preceding chapter of the material for a book[19] the saint also notes the essentially mysterious character of this truth, of this person, in herself a creature, yet so holy as to be the exclusive possession of the Trinity, so holy as to possess within herself as his Mother, God's own Son. If only up to a point we can grasp what it means to be a creature made in the image and likeness of God, and even less what it means to be an adopted child of God even with the help of faith, how much more beyond our native powers the understanding of what it means to be, not the adopted Mother of God, but his real Mother. Such is the Immaculate, the masterpiece of God, more per-fect than which he could not make in any possible world.[20]

(3) Without the purification of our minds and hearts via penance un-dertaken in a spirit of prayer the intellect will not enjoy that limpidity of thought indispensable for grasping the answer to the question: who are you, O Immaculate?

(4) The Immaculate is a person who in virtue of her unique relation to her Son, who has called himself the Truth and who is the source of all truth and light, also illumines and attracts. For that relation to her Son is the basis of her maternal mediation, one touching the intellectual as well as the affec-tive dimensions of the soul. Without her help, therefore, one is not capable of anything in the work of understanding and loving her. Hence without

17. *I Sent.*, proem., q. 3.
18. *WK* 1232, 1296.
19. *WK* 1305.
20. *WK* 1232.

prayer to her as a point of departure and without greater communion with her and confidence in her as a point of arrival in this work of study it will remain fruitless as a work of understanding.

Among the many profound insights contained in this passage these deserve particular attention in regard to the question of doctrine and devotion. The love of the Immaculate for us is the most perfect expression in any creature of the Savior's love for us. He could not love us more perfectly than loving us through his Mother. And that love we come to encounter and to understand through her "mediatory" action in him, an action therefore in some wise enlightening as well as inflaming. It is not difficult to discern here an adaptation of a classic Scotistic argument: Mary qua Immaculate is the most perfect fruit of a most perfect redemption accomplished by a most perfect Redeemer. Transferred to the order of practice that becomes the mystery of her divine and spiritual maternity. Its ultimate implication for our interior lives is the marianization of our thought, impossible apart from a progressively more thorough sanctification of our hearts.

But as soon as we observe the nature of the argument and its practical import, we grasp that in contemplating the perfection of Christ's salvific work in the person and mission of the Immaculate, we are contemplating the very focus or vertex of all those possibles God made or might have made. She stands at the point where divine and created love meet, the point where the *exemplatum* most perfectly matches the *exemplar*. She is the creature whose goodness most fully matches that of the Creator, the saint whose holiness most fully reflects that of the Savior. She is in a word the created Immaculate Conception, the "icon" of the Holy Spirit, the uncreated Immaculate Conception whose name she bears.[21] Thus, the metaphysical exemplarism and gnoselogical-ethical illuminationism of St. Bonaventure are shown to be not only Christic, but Marian at their heart, a heart however only clearly perceived through revelation.

Once, then, one realizes that there is no question here either of a Christic or of a Marian "itinerary" of the soul to God, as though one might with a single format substitute either Jesus or Mary in the role of mediator, but of a single itinerary, Christic because Marian and Marian because Christic—because the mediator and illuminator, the Word Incarnate, cannot in the order of salvation willed by God be separated from his mother and her active cooperation in the work of salvation—then it also becomes clear that the so-called "Christocentrism" of Bonaventure and "Mariocentrism" of Maximilian are but two views of "our theology": Christocentric because the Word Incarnate is the "medium" of the Trinity, the only way to the

21. *WK* 1318.

Father;[22] Mariocentric, because he neither comes to us nor we to him except through his Mother.[23] In the Franciscan theological tradition the doctrine of the Immaculate Conception and the absolute predestination of Mary to be the Mother of God in one and the same decree with the predestination of the Word to be the incarnate Savior is but the coefficient of the doctrine of the absolute primacy of Christ the King.[24] The Franciscan thesis in Maximilian is constantly formulated in terms of incorporating the mystery of the Immaculate into life, of becoming an instrument in her hands for the conversion and sanctification of all souls (for the sake of their itinerary to God), of conquering all souls for the Immaculate, so that the kingdom and the love of the sacred heart might triumph.[25] The mystery of the Immaculate in Christ and in the church is but the mystery of the most perfect fruit of a most perfect Redeemer and redemptive act of love, to which the life of the Immaculate is the connatural response or reaction, and to which our lives are more and more attuned to the extent we are consecrated to her totally and allow her maternal mediation to work fully in us.[26]

It is no surprise, then, to notice innumerable parallels between the thought patterns of Bonaventure and Maximilian touching points basic to Catholic theology and metaphysics. The theory of illumination, and the exemplarism which it presupposes, constitutes a dimension of that mediation of the Word, which when directly revealed is always revealed in a Marian key. Wisdom is not attainable apart from the Seat of Wisdom; thus the "reduction" of all the arts and sciences to theology[27] is not only Christic, but Marian. The manner in which St. Maximilian explains the development of the doctrine of the Immaculate Conception in[28] theology as an explicitation of the uninterrupted belief of the church in the unique and total sanctity of the Virgin Mother of God, first in view of the clarification of "symbolic theology" or our profession of faith, and then in view of its incorporation into life, viz., in relation to "mystical theology," shows plainly his notion of

22. Cf. for instance the formulation of such a criticism in Napiórkowski, "Le mariologie," 567–69.

23. Cf. Fehlner, "Immaculate . . . Trinity." This is a point of view not dissimilar to that taken by the Holy Father in his encyclical *Redemptoris Mater*, n. 26: the theological life of the church begins and ends in a contemplation of Jesus through Mary and Mary through Jesus.

24. Cf. Fehlner, "Mary in the Franciscan," *CE* 3, chapter 5.

25. *WK* 486, 1331.

26. Scotus, *Ord.* 3, d. 3, q. 1; *WK* 1284, 1286, 1326.

27. Cf. *Red. art.*

28. *WK* 1313.

theology, of the methodology characteristic of it and of the epistemology underlying it, coincide with the Bonaventurian.[29]

But what is of immediate import for this conference is that both share a single view of the relation between doctrine and devotion. Devotion is not a kind of love divorced from understanding and assent to the truth. Rather it is a spirituality that includes at its base a doctrine, and inevitably entails, not a suppression or neglect of intellectual activity, but its affirmation. That affirmation has two forms: of the "intellectus quaerens fidem," which in one way or another is verified in every art and science, even the humblest, because they are activities of a power whose ultimate goal is the truth; and of the "fides quaerens intellectum" or theology, the highest form of that activity in this life, known as theology, suspended as it were both as to its nature and finality between two poles, faith and contemplative prayer. That spirituality may be described as one of total conformity to the crucified with St. Francis (the explicit point of departure and arrival of St. Bonaventure in the *Itinerarium)* or as one of total consecration to the Immaculate (with St. Maximilian), but the reality is the same. It is the reality of our consecration to Christ through the hands of Mary Immaculate for the sake of the church. The more explicit the Marian coefficient becomes, the more fully is the mystery of our salvation in the church, or the greatest glory of God, not only understood, but shared.

Theology Marianized: A Global Vision of Catholic Life

In this perspective the spirituality of total consecration to the Immaculate is anything but devotionalism or fideism. Quite the contrary the founder of the M.I. rightly, and as it were spontaneously, described that work to which he gave his life as a global vision of Catholic life under a new form, that of our relation to the Immaculate, our universal mediatrix with Jesus.[30] The miraculous character both of his life, as well as his death, is a certification of that insight. This global vision is but the whole of theology, a knowledge

---

29. Cf. *Itin.,* c. 1, 7; *WK* 486. In St. Bonaventure theological reflection is suspended between the two poles of symbolic and mystical theology; in St. Maximilian theological reflection on the Immaculate is suspended between credal theology (profession of faith) and the incorporation of the mystery into life and serves to clarify the first and dispose for the second. The heart of that incorporation is contemplative prayer. Cf. the observations of Pyfferoen and Van Asseldonk, "Maria Santissima," 438, for a similar estimate of the relation between contemplative graces and theological reflection in St. Maximilian.

30. *WK* 1220.

of the truth about God and about his saving will, so that we might be good, viz., enjoy eternal life. It is under a new form, not in the sense of something either different from, much less contradicting the tradition once entrusted to the saints, but in the sense of a fuller expression and realization of what has already been realized in the Immaculate and through the Immaculate, and this for the sake of the church and every believer in a moment of their history when the struggle between the Woman and her seed (and the rest of his brethren) on the one hand and on the other the prince of this world and his legions has very much become a direct and open confrontation between truth and error, light and darkness, love and hate, goodness and sin, life and death for eternity. That is why such a spirituality of total conformity and total consecration with the doctrine and intellectual activity it includes take the form of a militia, one whose action is primarily offensive because aimed at the liberation of the erring from their error,[31] one seeking to offer to the Mother of God rather than to the father of lies the first fruits of every intellectual, artistic and scientific activity in the interest of the "intellectus quaerens fidem" and the "fides quaerens intellectum."[32]

The ontological foundation for this is to be found in the mystery of the Immaculate Conception. The Immaculate Conception of Mary is for the sake of her maternal mediation: in Christ and in the church.[33] That unique, universal mediation setting her apart from and yet in the midst of the rest of creation, as the vertex of love, the point where the most perfect creative love of God meets with the most perfect love of creation, is made possible by, finds its ultimate "ratio" in the mystery of the Immaculate Conception.[34] For Mary Immaculate is not only conceived immaculate, she is the Immaculate Conception, so perfectly conformed is her will to the divine as to be the icon of the Spirit of truth, the Spirit of the Father and of the Son: to be in the history of salvation the most perfect fruit of the love of Father and Word Incarnate as the Holy Spirit is in eternity, so perfect as to conceive the Son of God in her womb virginally by the power of the Holy Spirit.[35]

The mystery of the Immaculate Conception as the perfect conformity of a created will with the divine thus constitutes the dynamic basis as well

31. *WK* 1031, 1231, 1277.

32. *WK* 1218.

33. Kolbe. CK July 7, 1939: "Mary was Immaculate in order to be the mother [Mother] of God; she became the Mother of God because Immaculate." That mediation first realized in the divine maternity at the incarnation is consummated in Mary's spiritual maternity in the church. In the thought of St. Maximilian this is the basis of the Militia of the Immaculate. Cf. *WK* 1310.

34. *WK* 1318.

35. *WK* 1310, 1320.

for that perfect act of faith, that "fiat" culminating in the incarnation of
the Son of God. But that mystery transposed to the dynamic order also
constitutes the basis for a spiritual maternity, one whereby Christ is conceived in our minds and hearts, one by which intellect and will attain to
him who is the truth and the life, who is their ultimate objective. Crucial
to any discussion of the problem of Marian doctrine and devotion today is
the specific relation of the mystery of Mary to the intellectual life, of what
bearing that relation has on the balance of cognitive and affective factors
in human life, of why in practice the synthesis of doctrine and devotion
in the M.I. is a connatural, not an artificially or tyrannically imposed one,
precisely in virtue of that total consecration, or unconditional obedience, to
the Immaculate, of that perfect conforming of one's will to hers so as to be
more one with Jesus and through him with the Father.

For today intellectual activity, in particular what is reputed to be
mature intellectual life, and obedience are often conceived to be, if not
incompatible, at least not intrinsically related to one another. Piety is considered a matter of the will, of the affections alone, and obedience is an
aspect of piety. The intellect, then, is rendered radically a-pious or atheist. That assumption underlies what is sometimes called the autonomy of
intellectual life, i.e., to be genuinely free, I must be independent in my
thinking and judgment. At the very least this is a concept of personal life
in need of substantial qualification.

For if on the one hand thought is undoubtedly a personal activity to the
extent it is genuine, one indispensable for the attainment of freedom and a
mature dignity, one incompatible with the tyrannous, on the other hand the
nature of the created intellect is such that its central, radically simple act of
assent to the truth is a conforming of the intellect to the real, in so far as that is
real, either perfectly so in the divine being, or partially so in the creature in so
far as it reflects the divine exemplar. That conformation involves enlightenment from on high, what the ancient Christian doctors called illumination,
without which the created intellect would either constitute its own criterion
of truth or be uncertain of the truth itself, both unnatural conditions. Thus,
understanding and enlightenment in the created intellect cannot not be an
aspect of humility, of obedience, of dependence on the divine light, source of
all being and truth and good in the created order.

Thus, at its root the intellectual life of the creature, human and angelic,
is much affected by the degree of perfection in its personal life and corre-
spondingly impeded by the absence of obedience. The difference divides
what St. Maximilian calls love of truth from its opposite, hatred.[36] Without

36. *WK* 1246. The citation is taken from the final writing of the saint published

the love and spirit of truth in some degree the intellect will never in fact find its natural repose in the truth, will be blind in the scriptural sense, a blindness never completely inculpable because never absolutely inevitable. Philosophic and moral relativism, so fashionable today, is but a rationalization of a refusal to be humble intellectually. The autonomy which it makes possible is not genuine freedom, but in fact slavery, and leads not to true love and happiness, but to hatred and cruelty.[37] Recognition of the fact of a divine illumination in the intellectual life of a creature permits the differentiation of knowledge and wisdom and of the passage from one to the other; that is of attaining in the midst of many and varied cognitive activities possible to the created intellect the contemplation of the truth.

That attainment admits of degrees of perfection proportionate to the love of truth of which the creature is capable. The outer limits defining the native reach of the created intellect are indeed affected by the particular talents and moral state of the person and the human family; radically they are set by the degree of mediation—enlightenment—exercised by the Creator. The levels of understanding differentiated by the Creator are clearly described by St. Bonaventure in his *Itinerarium* in terms of the vestige, image and similitude of God, or levels of sense, intellectual (rational) and revealed (faith) knowledge. Attainment of a higher level of knowledge ultimately perfects rather than destroys the lower.[38] But the passage from one level to another always entails a purification, the fruit of a more perfect grace of illumination, until one passes from this world with Christ to the Father. In each instance that passage is effected, not by "industria" or effort on our part, but by a grace, to which on our part there corresponds primarily an acceptance and obedience, one initially resembling entrance into a "cloud," in contrast to what is a more familiar mode of understanding at a less perfect level of cognition.[39] There is nothing arbitrary in this, so long as the light to which we submit is truly divine. That light, only obscurely or indirectly recognized at the level of sense and reason, at the level of faith and later of vision in heaven is recognized as the Son of God, our one mediator with the Father.

Such recognition does not in fact occur apart from a recognition of the "Sedes Sapientiae," his mother, and for that reason she too directly affects the cultivation of the intellectual life, so much so that such a life fully mature is not only fully Christic, but fully Marian, and where this is not so such a life

---

before his martyrdom. Love for the truth is convertible with respect for the real, in the first instance God.

37. *WK* 1246.

38. *Itin.,* c. 1, 1–9.

39. *Itin.,* cc. 4, 7; *Hex.,* col. 2, nn. 29–34; col. 3, nn. 22–32.

is not fully itself. To think in this way is to think in the spirit of prayer and devotion of the Mother of God in thinking of her Son.

It is a merit of St. Maximilian, in discussing the relative perfection of each of these levels of cognition to have stressed the factor of obedience and the relative privation it entails at the lower level as a condition for passing to a higher. Perfection, he writes,[40] consists in the love of God, a love manifested in obedience, in doing the will of God certified by our legitimate superiors. That is also the case with the love of truth. The relative perfection of the life of reason over that of the senses is revealed precisely at that point where acknowledgment of the truth and its incorporation into life is preferred to the immediate pleasure of sense experience (or as St. Bonaventure says[41] at the point where the truth as well as a particular truth is acknowledged). So too, the superiority of faith as an intellectual light is made clear at just that point where assent is given not on the basis of reasoning or private judgment, but in deference to the judgment of God, in particular in those instances where "personal judgment" is simply incapable of providing the basis for any such assent, as in the case of the great mysteries of the Catholic religion. Far from being anti-intellectual then, the life of dogmatic faith is that on which the intellect of man naturally opens. Culture (for which intellect is the key) naturally opens on cult (obsequium), or it is an "unnatural," abusive culture. In each stage of advance toward a higher level of perfection the homage or obedience entailed at the crucial moment of cognition (assent to the truth) involves an absence: of sensation to which is preferred assent to the truth as such; of private or personal judgment to which is preferred deference to the divine authority of revelation as the ultimate ground of assent. And in each of these instances in the present state of human life after the fall and redemption the basic features of such an intellectual life as it is perfected are more and more closely intertwined with a total spiritual life, one whose course more and more runs toward the reality of sacrifice, of priestly sacrifice, of the consecration of Christ as victim for our salvation from sin. The "captivatio intellectus in obsequium Christi per fidem" and its counterpart the "captivatio affectus in obsequium Christi per charitatem" are distinct, but when consummated are inseparable "in the giving of one's life for another." In this regard both the stigmata of St. Francis conforming him even exteriorly to the crucified and the martyrdom of St. Maximilian as a priest giving his life for another complement each other as a single sign pointing at the heart of the intellectual life. That sign is a kind of extension of the sign which is the Immaculate, the most perfect of signs created by God

40. *WK* 51.

41. *Itin.*, c. 2, 6.

to indicate his existence and presence: most perfect because so one with the Holy Spirit in charity; so holy because the most perfect fruit of the perfect redemption. Because she is so one with the Holy Spirit as to bear his name: Immaculate Conception, she is his most perfect instrument, the Mother of God and Mother of the Church and of believers, viz., the instrument of the presence of Christ in the minds and hearts of men. We share in that spiritual maternity to the extent we share her consecration to the Blessed Trinity. That consecration is her Immaculate Conception.

In so far as the mediation of the Immaculate touches the intellectual life of believers, indeed is a factor making it possible, that mediation is particularly related to the mystery of the Immaculate Conception as the mystery of the most perfect consecration or obedience ever realized, or even conceivable, to the Word of God, so perfectly conformed to the divine will was Mary's will from her conception, so perfect therefore her practice of faith and charity throughout her life.[42] Thus, at every level and every stage of development the intellectual life of the Virgin enjoyed a perfection beyond compare. No created mind could reflect more perfectly than hers the divine Exemplar who is her Son, the Word of God. For that reason, her teaching, viz., her influence in and on the intellectual life of others, is utterly unique, both during her time of pilgrimage in faith and now in the glory of vision. That uniqueness consists in her unique association with him who enlightens every man coming into this world. "A parte rei" her unique influence in this order is the premise for any other teaching successfully leading to Christ, or successfully expounding the mystery of Christ. In this connection she is rightly called the "memory" of the church by Pope John Paul II. Her testimony is the gauge of all others, the measure of soundness or purity in the approach of any intellect in faith to the mystery of Christ. That soundness is the degree to which the believer's will is conformed to that of the Immaculate, according to St. Maximilian corresponding to the degree one responds or "reacts" to the love of the Father and of his Son for us in and through the Immaculate, the dynamic at the core of the spirituality resting on total consecration to the Immaculate and permeating every dimension of life, intellectual and affective, personal and social. That consecration issues, practically speaking, in a purification of our minds and hearts, so that we might know and love the heart of God as the Immaculate does, or better as she does with our minds and hearts. A genuine intellectual life reaches its apex only when fully marianized, i.e., integrated fully with devotion to the Immaculate.[43]

42. *WK* 1232, 1318.
43. *WK* 508, 616, 647, 1283, 1284, 1286, 1310, 1326.

Is this another version of "pious voluntarism," as inhuman and irrational as the impious version? Only if we suppose, a priori, that assent to the truth as such can be totally separated from the practice of true humility. It is not a supposition that can be demonstrated, for the simple reason no man can honestly pretend to be either the standard of truth or the norm of justice without exposing himself to becoming a liar and a disciple of him once called "father of lies." The nature of the intellect created by God is such that God cannot be effectively denied without annihilating the intellect as such. Any science apart from wisdom, theocentric and cultic by definition, is a-normal. Recognition of the mystery of divine illumination and exemplarism at the initial level of natural intellectual endowment is but the recognition of the nature of the created intellect in man and its ultimate finality. Once the theory of divine illumination as an aspect of that divine mediation whereby the interior life of men and angels is sustained and promoted, then the mediation of the Word Incarnate and that of his Mother in him no more renders our lives irrational than any other legitimate magisterium. Clearly there is a radical difference between the created will and the divine will as the final norm of conduct, including intellectual. Where the first is verified, conduct becomes radically arbitrary, even where it appears reasonable. In the second it is never so, for the divine will is identical with the truth of the divine essence. The choice which the M.I. of St. Maximilian confronts us is not that between the intellectual life of the independent thinker and that of the pious, uncritical believer (in practice "credulous"), but between the conduct of the intellectual life on one's own terms (radically unnatural and culpably blinding, as our Lord observed in the case of the Pharisees), or on those of the Creator-Savior, "unus omnium Magister," whose "cathedra" is the Blessed Virgin Mary. In the mystery of the Immaculate incorporated into our lives or not incorporated the difference can be read. With this background in mind, it is no surprise that a saint enjoying the gifts of mystical prayer such as St. Maximilian is thought with reason to have enjoyed[44] should have attained such "metaphysical depths" in his reflection on the mystery of the Immaculate Conception.

And since the perfecting of the intellect through the mediation of the Immaculate tends more and more to involve the one so perfected in a life of prayer consummated in the passage from this world to the Father with Christ, for the same ends for which he passed by way of the furnace of his passion and death on the cross,[45] such a life cannot but tend to find its connatural context in a community where the Immaculate is Queen and

44. Cf. Pyfferoen and Van Asseldonk, "Maria Santissima"; Beaini, "Le Mystère."
45. *Itin.*, c. 7.

fraternal charity is practiced in a heroic degree in the form of a "vita perfecte communis." A city of the Immaculate, a Niepokalanów, is the obvious
context for an Academy of the Immaculate, of the kind so much desired by
St. Maximilian where the finest efforts of scholarship would be fully at the
service of the Mother of God, but which circumstances never permitted
him to realize during his lifetime.[46] Rather his heroic death as a martyr
of charity, of the charity he learned from the Immaculate, the charity of
the great high priest of our confession, author and finisher of our faith, is
an even more effective guarantee of the validity of his insights, and of the
manner in which they can be implemented, in particular for the renewal of
theology and of the cultural life of mankind.

Conclusion

In connection with the problem of doctrine and devotion, one often raised
in relation to the Marian movement of the nineteenth and twentieth centuries one can begin to appreciate St. Maximilian's true worth as a thinker and
theologian who aspired "to reduce all the arts and sciences to theology" via
their marianization, and to deepen and perfect the knowledge of God, viz.,
theology, through and in the Mother of God.

This ambition, really a prolongation in this "age of the church and of
the Holy Spirit" of the classic Franciscan approach to the sanctification of
the intellect by cultivating it in the spirit of prayer and devotion—as St.
Francis prescribed and St. Bonaventure expounded—rests on the "Franciscan thesis" in theology: the Immaculate Conception as the masterpiece
of creative-redemptive love, the most perfect fruit of a perfect redemption
by a perfect Redeemer. Put dynamically that perfection is nothing more
than the maternal mediation of the Immaculate: as the Mother of God and
as Mother of the Church. It is this maternal mediation that is at the heart
of the Militia of the Immaculate, the great work of this great Franciscan,
"patron of our difficult age."

The harmonization of Marian doctrine and devotion within a balanced spirituality as this is realized in the Militia of the Immaculate is not
simply one of many contributions of this genial Franciscan to the Marian
movement. It is rather a key contribution to the whole of Catholic life. Marian doctrine and devotion are not simply particular aspects of the intellectual and affective life of Catholics to be developed in accord with certain
norms. At a far deeper level, that where uncreated and created meet and
are united, where the powers of the soul to know and to love are perfectly

46. WK 508, 647.

integrated in the contemplation and love of him who is, viz., the level our saint calls the "vertex of love," that doctrine and devotion in its perfected form of total consecration is the very key to an interior life, at once the glory of God and the salvation of souls. Her position as the Immaculate Conception, not merely one conceived immaculately, makes her in respect to the rest of creation, and in particular to a creation fallen in Adam, the universal mediatrix in Christ. The marianization of our theology, above all fundamental theology, and of all our culture and science, is but a corollary of that mystery when considered in relation to our interior life. In her the pursuit of being, the metaphysical, so often reputed to be a-personal and a-human, is perfectly integrated with the human-affective pole of life. The love of truth is no mere abstract, impersonal sentiment, as the knowledge of the good is no mere arbitrary, personal taste.

It is important to realize that for us direct, immediate access to God, to the divine persons, is only possible through a woman. As that access was once lost through the choice, viz., sin, of a woman, so it has been reestablished in far more wonderful fashion and through the obedience of another Woman. To recognize the difference between Eve and Mary is to recognize the difference between pride and humility. To identify with the one or the other choice is to choose to be blind or to see him who is the way, the truth and the life. Doctrine and devotion, the core of Catholic life, pass through the Woman who being the Immaculate is the Mother of God, for the same reason no child is related to his father except through and in his mother. Thus, we are neither brothers of Christ and children of the Father except in and through the Mother of God.[47] The mediation of a woman whereby our life is begun as human and personal is also the form of mediation whereby that life is rendered divine. This is why the Militia of the Immaculate is a global vision of Catholic life under a new form, that of our relation to the Immaculate, our universal mediatrix with Jesus.

Much, however, remains to be done before that vision becomes a commonplace under that form. Though numbering nearly three million members throughout the world and exerting an influence more unobserved than observed, the expansion of the M.I. is a far cry from what its founder desired, and its influence at present as well as the great good accomplished, especially for the interior life of so many, but a minuscule proportion of its true capacity. This is certainly the case with its potential for the renewal of theology and of the intellectual life. In this area it has hardly been tried. May these brief reflections inspire others to look more closely at the thought and work of the "patron of our difficult age" and discover in this "instrument of the

47. *WK* 1284. Cf. St. Bonaventure, *De don. Spir.*, col. 3, 13.

Immaculate," this "fool of our Lady," the same wisdom of the cross so many gifted intellectuals in the thirteenth century found in the little Poor Man of Assisi, who had so tremendous an impact not only on the piety, but on the intellectual life of the church. With the Seraphic Patriarch St. Francis may they burn with love for Christ, the one teacher of all, and with St. Maximilian salute her who is full of grace, the Seat of Wisdom: Ave Maria!

17

Martyr of Charity, Man of the Millennium

St. Maximilian Mary Kolbe

SINCE THE APPROACH OF the year 2000 *millennium* is a word on the lips of many. It is a subject fraught with many difficulties and no little danger, witness the constant recurrence of millenarism in the history of the church over the last two millennia, and without the church the continuing fascination of the multitudes with metempsychosis and reincarnation.

Notwithstanding the potential dangers inherent in the pursuit of this theme, and even more in the celebration of a new millennium, the subject is not only timely, but important. Timely, because it corresponds to an underlying need of the human heart to celebrate its fulfillment in conjunction with anniversaries responding to the providential rhythms of history. Important, because without a recognition of the day of visitation and time of fulfillment eternal disaster is inevitable. Indeed, so important that the Holy Father, Pope John Paul II, in his recent apostolic letter *Tertio millenio adveniente*, tells us that "preparing for the year 2000 has become as it were a hermeneutical key to my pontificate".[1] Hence, we are fortunate in having in this apostolic letter an authoritative guide for our reflections on the millennium: what it is and how to celebrate.

The starting point, then, for our reflections on St. Maximilian as man of the millennium, qua *martyr of charity*—not to be "reread" by revising (as do the cultural relativists),[2] but by discovering therein hitherto unrecognized depths of wisdom—quite naturally is that of the Holy Father in defining the celebration of the millennium as a form of jubilee.

In sacred writ, in the patristic-liturgical tradition of the church, indeed in great scholastic theologians, such as St. Bonaventure, jubilee connotes

---

1. John Paul II, *Tertio millenio adveniente*, 29.

2. See, for instance, in the case of St. Maximilian, the conferences of De Fiores, "Come presentare oggi," and Napiórkowski, "Esperienze," presented at the International Kolbean Congress in Poland (1994).

a privileged means of sanctifying time or history, and contains within it a twofold signification: one theoretical, or more exactly a theology of history, without which history is either unintelligible or misunderstood; and the other practical, viz., a mode of sanctifying history reflecting its rhythms or "recirculation" and what is called "the fullness of time" (Gal 4:4), or "recapitulation" in the classic exposition of St. Irenaeus.[3] These two considerations define precisely the two sections of this conference: the theory of the millennium, which in fact is a theology of history in brief; and how to sanctify it, precisely under the influence of St. Maximilian Mary Kolbe.

The Theology of the Millennium

The theology of the millennium rests on the premise that a dogmatic-metaphysical principle rather than an empirical-sociological one is primary for its interpretation, precisely because the origin of history, like time, is the Creator; the patterns and rhythms of history are determined in the first instance by the Creator in view of the ultimate purpose of time: holiness, not secular or temporal ends. With St. Bonaventure we may rightly find in the origin, patterns and end of history a Trinitarian appropriation: the *ratio originandi, exemplandi et finiendi.*[4]

---

3. In St. Bonaventure various dimensions of recirculation-recapitulation are often discussed under the heading *hierarchization*. Cf. Geiger, "Tending of God's Garden"; Fehlner, "Metaphysica mariana quaedam," *CE* 1, chapter 3.

4. Cf. *Brev.*, p. 1, c. 6, n. 4. The introduction of St. Bonaventure is not arbitrary, and this on two counts: because St. Maximilian clearly depends on him (cf. Domanski, "La genesi," 260–62), and one cannot correctly interpret (reread) the martyr of charity, except on the dogmatic-metaphysical-contemplative premises he shares with the Seraphic Doctor; and because his "essentialist" theology of history is a most useful vantage point for assessing many of the current "trends," none truly appreciative of the ancient wisdom so well articulated by St. Bonaventure. Stratford Caldecott, "In Search of a New Way," mentions four main intellectual and political movements in Europe and America at the present time: neo-conservatism (Novak, Neuhaus); postmodernism (Taylor, Milbank); praxis philosophy (Habermas); neo-patristic liberationism (Von Balthasar, DeLubac, Ratzinger). The first three in one or another way insist on the relative or absolute autonomy of the secular. The fourth places the accent on the primacy of faith and freedom. In some of the writers of this school (DeLubac, Ratzinger) there is undoubtedly a sympathy for and a discernible influence of St. Bonaventure, and with this, as is explicit in the article of Caldecott, of St. Maximilian (in relation to freedom) and St. Francis (in relation to poverty). But they tend to read the Seraphic Doctor "existentially," rather than "essentially" (as in this conference), in explaining his theology of history, and so find more links with Joachim of Fiore than I believe can be justified. The well-known work of Ratzinger, *The Theology of History in St. Bonaventure*, often cited in support of a primarily Joachimite Bonaventure should be read with these cautions in mind. Cf. also Fehlner, *Kolbe . . . Pneumatologist.*

The Holy Father puts it this way: the fulness of time, or end, on which like a great river the whole of human history from its beginning converges, is the incarnation. This mystery-fact is the basis for asserting as primary the obligation to sanctify time, of which all forms of secularism constitute a radical denial and for whose justification are proposed various forms of scientism, historicism, cultural relativism.

To be considered in this section are three contributions to an understanding of this crucial principle concerning the sanctification of time: that of the Holy Father as set forth in the apostolic letter *Tertio millenio adveniente*, one we may regard as an authoritative guide; and then that of St. Maximilian Mary Kolbe and that of St. Bonaventure of Bagnoregio as representative witnesses to the great tradition underlying the theory and practice of jubilees: the first because it will help us understand better someone whose example and influence is especially significant for the preparation and celebration of the millennium; the second, because it is an ample exposition of that theology of history, biblical, liturgical, Franciscan, where the correlation between the metaphysical and cultural in historical knowledge is correctly stated, and from which St. Maximilian drew.

The Doctrine of Pope John Paul II

The Holy Father begins his exposition with a reference to St. Paul: In the fullness of time God sent his only-begotten Son, born of a woman, born under the law, so that he might redeem those under the law, that we might receive the adoption of sons. (Gal 4:4–6). For purposes of defining the millennium correctly (and so of avoiding the dual pitfalls of metempsychosis and millenarism),[5] the following are to be noted with the pope.

5. Cf. the interesting comments in *Inside the Vatican* (April, 1994), 13–15, on an Augustinian versus Joachimite definition of the millennium. That of the Holy Father evidently is Augustinian, which gives priority to the unchanging over the changing, the fixed over that which develops or unfolds in historical stages, the last stage always superseding the earlier, an age of the spirit or millennium superseding the age of Christ and the church. This is what stands at the heart of all heretical millenarism. As we shall point out, it is St. Bonaventure as faithful interpreter of Augustine, who shows how the priority of exemplaristic metaphysics, or incarnation, enables us to account for the intelligibility of historical succession in terms of the permanent and unchanging at the very center of history, precisely in virtue of the principle of recirculation and recapitulation (cf. *Hex.*, col. 1, nn. 13–17). Hence, it is not an either-or question: metaphysics or history, being or becoming, but the priority of metaphysics and contemplation (wisdom) over the empirical process, whether the becoming is physical or psychological. From the start the mind is primarily metaphysical in orientation, which means it is also contemplative in orientation: *anima naturaliter contemplativa*. That orientation is only fully actualized by grace, and so in the Franciscan school at least the supernatural life of faith

a. The fullness of time occurs with the incarnation and constitutes the point on which all periods and moments, both of the human family and of every human person, converge and in which all find their fulfillment, or never find it.[6] That moment reflects the mystery of the Trinity, the unity and distinction of persons, of which the Virgin Mother is the privileged sign, the *complementum* in history.

b. From this fact arises the obligation of "sanctifying the time," viz., of ordering both personal lives and the common good of all toward this transcendent salvation, fully attainable only after death in the life to come, but now accessible by virtue of the incarnation [indeed, for time is fulfilled definitively when God enters history] through the life of grace in the church; and to the extent that this is possible in the conditions proper to a time of pilgrimage, it is given visible form also in what the Holy Father calls a "civilization of love," so much opposed and thwarted by a "civilization of violence and death" based on hatred. This has been rightly described by Jean Borella as the key mark of this last century, a "profanation of charity": either in the form of sentimental lust or violent cruelty.[7]

c. A privileged means of fulfilling this obligation is the jubilee year, originally every seventh year or sabbatical year (cf. Exod 23:10–11; Lev 25:1–28; Deut 15:1–6), and every fiftieth year or the greater jubilee celebrated with more solemnity (Lev 25:10). The Old Testament jubilees

---

is compared not only with reason (*fides et ratio*) but also with love (*fides et amor*). According to Léthel, "Verità e Amore," any adequate discussion of faith and reason requires also a discussion of the relations between faith and charity. What Léthel calls a pluralism of theological forms without relativism corresponds to the three modes of theology of St. Bonaventure, the highest or contemplative often dubbed the *orthopraxis* of the saints revealing the truth of faith. Cf. Fehlner, "Knowledge and Piety," *CE* 1, chapter 4.

6. This affirmation rests on the patristic thesis that in becoming incarnate the Son of God assumed the entire human race. This is misunderstood by the current crop of crypto-Pelagians as meaning everyone merely by being born is saved (the old "universalist" heresy in the USA) without need to believe and be baptized and enter the church. The true meaning becomes clear when we apply the principle of recirculation and recapitulation. We are all in the first, individual Adam, not in the sense that we can dispense with conception and birth, but in the sense that Adam is a public person, without descent from whom no one can become human. So too, Christ is a public person, new Head of the human family, without incorporation into whom by baptism no one can claim to be christian or find salvation.

7. Borella, *La charité profanée*. That profanation has roots intellectually in various aspects of nominalism, such as the sensism of John Locke and the sensualism of J. J. Rousseau, and affectively, not only in sensualism, but above all in various forms of pragmatism which divorce the decisions of the created will from any relation to truth, such as the autonomous ethics of Kant with its categorical imperative, and the utilitarianism of J. Bentham. In this regard one may usefully consult the recent encyclical of Pope John Paul II, *Veritatis Splendor*.

recall the typology of the Exodus, the freeing from bondage in Egypt and passage to fulfillment in the promised land, but they also typify a greater fulfillment in Christ and in the church ultimately in paradise. To this time of fulfillment, says our Holy Father, Christ himself refers during his public ministry when he said, quoting Isaiah 61:2, that he was sent to proclaim the year of the Lord's favor, and that this saying was fulfilled in the presence of those who heard him (cf. Luke 4:16–30).

The content of that fulfillment must not be referred only to the seventh day of rest with God, but to the "50th year," which is a sevenfold septenaria of years ($7\times7 = 49$) plus one ($= 50$), namely the eighth day or year, which begins, but does not end. This is the day or year of the resurrection, viz., eternal life, which Jesus makes available, on which all history converges for better or for worse, for the rise or fall of many, a sign to be contradicted (cf. Luke 2:34), the day which dawns, but does not set.

d. In this notion of jubilee year is included a correlation between liturgical time (history sanctified) and solar, viz., the rhythms of the universe established by God himself, so that via the various measures of time, we might have a means of celebrating or symbolically sanctifying our history. Whence the importance of anniversaries: both of persons (birthdays, marriages, ordinations, professions) and of communities (anniversaries of events). The millennium has always been regarded as a major anniversary, and especially is this the case with the celebration of the 2000th anniversary of the birth of the Savior and of the foundation of the church, whose influence on the preceding two millennia has been so great and on which history, both Christian and non-Christian, is converging.

e. For this major jubilee which is the initiation of the third Christian millennium there has been a systematic preparation, primarily guided by divine Providence: the recent Second Vatican Council, the synods of Bishops, the work of the Popes since Leo XIII, various anniversaries of local churches, such as the millennial celebrations of the baptism of Rus, of Poland, of Hungary, the 500th of the evangelization of America, the millennium and a half of the conversion of Clovis, etc.[8]

One particular preparatory event the Holy Father singles out as especially revelatory of the place this celebration of the new millennium has in the divine counsels guiding history and of the Marian coefficient of those counsels, namely, the Marian Year of 1987–88. By 1989 what had been considered by many as an impregnable obstacle to the triumph of a civilization of love, the political and military might of Russian communism, had begun

---

8. John Paul II, *Tertio millenio adveniente*, 31ff.

to collapse, and by 1991, the centenary of *Rerum novarum*, the fall of the totalitarian political systems in Eastern Europe was complete.

Their fall is not the triumph of a Christian culture; nonetheless it creates an opportunity, hitherto lacking for practically a century, since Leo XIII accurately predicted the meaning of the rise of socialism (and, though the Holy Father does not mention this, Leo XIII reportedly had been privy to a private revelation indicating Satan would be permitted one hundred years to attempt the overthrow of the church). The creation of this new opportunity for evangelization, for the introduction of a new era of peace (reminiscent of the promises of our Lady at Fatima, and of Rev 20:3–6) the Holy Father attributes exclusively to the intervention of Mary Immaculate.[9]

Here we encounter an initial, and indeed striking convergence of the teaching of the pope with that of St. Maximilian: that the approaching age will be one in which history will converge on its fulfillment in the church so as to reveal the fulness of Christ therein and the riches of his mercy, an age therefore singularly Marian and pneumatological,[10] or as St. Maximilian would explain: because Mary Immaculate is Spouse of the Holy Spirit, the uncreated Immaculate Conception.[11]

The Views of St. Maximilian

St. Maximilian does not ever make use of the word millennium, at least as far as I can determine, and only incidentally does he mention jubilees, e.g., the 1600th anniversary of the edict of Milan in 1913, and that of the redemption in 1933.[12] He speaks of our theme rather under the heading of a new epoch or new age in the life of the church.[13] Without doubt this new age closely resembles that described by St. John as the "millennium" (Rev 20:3–6), particularly as an era of paradisiacal peace and justice, the genuine one, only possible to the degree such is possible short of heaven, in a civilization based on the charity of Christ the High Priest, whose basic features he understood as exemplified in the City of the Immaculate (Niepokalanów) founded in 1927, a contemporary realization of St. Francis' proto-community at the Portiuncula.[14] Echoing an ancient patristic tradition, the martyr of charity considered Niepokalanów the direct opposite of the fraudulent

9. John Paul II, *Tertio millenio adveniente*, 33.

10. John Paul II, *Tertio millenio adveniente*, 53.

11. Cf. Fehlner, *Kolbe . . . Pneumatologist*.

12. *WK* 6, 7, 515.

13. *WK* 1242.

14. *WK* 1222.

paradise offered both by the Freemasons and by the totalitarians, a profanation of charity. Whence this epoch has two distinctive characteristics in the thought and practice of St. Maximilian: it is Marian and Seraphic.

a. The Marian coefficient. This coming era, like every major era in the history of the church is initiated with an intervention of the Virgin Mother of the Church, the body of Christ, in that history.[15] But in this case, that intervention, signaling the beginning of a new era for the church, long prepared for in the preceding age, is precisely that of the Virgin Mother qua Immaculate Conception. And the hour of intervention: December 8, 1854, with the solemn proclamation of the dogma of the Immaculate Conception, the foundation of her universal mediation.[16]

Nor should we be surprised that this hour should be one of dire tribulation for the church, for precisely in that way is the power and the mercy of the Most High manifested through the maternal love of the Immaculate: "Can a woman forget her infant" (Isa 49:15), as the pope remarks apropos the fall of totalitarian political systems.[17] For the mystery of the Immaculate, initially revealed at the beginning of human history (Gen 3:15) takes account of the struggle between the Offspring of the Woman and his brethren and the brood of the serpent and until all is consummated. The more the Woman intervenes clearly as the Immaculate, the more violent and frantic the opposition of the dragon (cf. Rev 12:1–17), but also the closer is the church to the desired consummation, the fulfillment of all history.

Hence the Marian coefficient of this new era involves the founding of her Militia,[18] not as some recent commentators on Kolbean spirituality mistakenly opine,[19] mainly in relation to cultural circumstances already dated, but directly in relation to those forces whose object has always been the secularization of time in direct opposition to its sanctification.[20] The choice of date for the founding of the M.I.: just before the devil made a key move to destroy the church and the fruits of the redemption via the Bolshevik revolution in Russia (November 1917; October, according to the Julian Calendar) and on the fourth centenary of the Lutheran revolt that divided Christendom and the second centenary of the re-founding of gnostic freemasonry, head of the enemies of the church, the most effective

---

15. *WK* 647, 1277, 1278, 1313, 1314, 1315.

16. *WK* 486.

17. John Paul II, *Tertio millenio adveniente*, 33.

18. *WK* 1328.

19. As De Fiores, Napiórkowski, and others at the (1994) International Kolbean Congress in Poland: cf. *San Massimiliano Kolbe e la Nuova Evangelizzazione*.

20. *WK* 1277, 1278.

tool for secularizing the intellect and offering a pseudo-unity in place of the Christian civilization of life.

The entire structure of the M.I. and of the spirituality of total consecration and "transubstantiation"[21] into the Immaculate is predicated on the mystery of the Immaculate Conception and the implications of her universal mediation for the theology of history. In a word there is nothing dated about it, for it is the practical coefficient of the basic dogmatic-metaphysical principle governing the theology of history. At the heart of that principle is the charity of Christ, whose noblest fruit is the Immaculate.

We see clearly, then, how the views of the Holy Father about our Lady's hand in ending the hundred-year terror of Marxism in Eastern Europe, the fruit of prayer and penance, is confirmed by the saint of Auschwitz, and further illustrated. For according to St. Maximilian, the Immaculate had already decisively intervened prior to the initiation of the hundred-year challenge in 1891, and during the course of that challenge at a crucial moment, 1917, so dark for the church, yet in reality so impossible for Satan to win.

Further, with St. Maximilian, we see that the singularly supernatural elements preparing for the coming celebration are not merely proximate, they reach back to the very beginnings of the execution of God's counsels in the fullness of time when the Son of God was born of the Woman, but in an especial way to the era of Church history immediately preceding the coming one, sometimes known as the age of faith, whose unity was first disrupted by laicism, then by the reformation, then by the revolutions, American, French and Russian,[22] and so described by Pope John Paul II as the millennium of

---

21. *WK* 508. The use of the term transubstantiation evidently recalls the close connection between Marian mysticism and the mystery of the Eucharist whose dogmatic foundation is so well expressed in the first line of an ancient hymn: *Ave verum corpus natum de Maria Virgine.* Cf. Fehlner, *Kolbe . . . Pneumatologist.* As to the further implications for a transformation into the crucified Savior via consecration to the Immaculate in the life of St. Maximilian cf. *WK* 509 (with notes) and in the lives of members of the M.I. cf. *WK* 579. Put dynamically the mystery of the Immaculate Conception in the Franciscan tradition is the basis of the coredemption: Mary's preservation from original sin is the means Christ the mediator uses to effect our liberation from sin.

22. St. Maximilian perceived a Masonic inspiration permeating each of these revolutions leading to an ever-greater secularization of culture and of the intellect and religious indifferentism. This is particularly the case with the American experiment (cf. *WK* 865), which is often denied or overlooked in discussions of the compatibility of modern freemasonry with post-Vatican II Catholicism. American culture, as it presently exists, where public education and public conduct is officially divorced from any moral authority higher than the American Supreme Court, is essentially secular and is the direct fruit of the masonic or gnostic deism which inspired in large part their revolution. So long as it remains such, the premises of Catholic belief and moral conduct will not be understood by such a culture, because secularized culture excludes *a priori* the metaphysical-dogmatic premises of Catholicism. Recent efforts (e.g., Woodward,

division. The thoughts of St. Maximilian on this aspect of the preparation we may conveniently call the seraphic coefficient.

b. The Seraphic coefficient.[23] St. Maximilian often referred to the relation between these two periods, whose dividing line in the nineteenth and twentieth centuries is marked by violent struggle, as two pages of Franciscan history,[24] the first having as its immediate object the theological and dogmatic elaboration of the mystery of the Immaculate Conception in relation to the primacy of Christ and his triumph on the cross and its popularization as a fundamental component of Christian spirituality and devotion, and the second having as its object the incorporation of this same mystery into the life of the church and of civilization, in such wise that the perfect charity of the heart of the great high priest of our confession might be everywhere triumphant.

In the view of St. Maximilian, it was in a very special way the essential vocation of St. Francis to be the saint of the crucified and of the Immaculate, and hence it was to his Order, in each of these two eras, but in a different way, that the promotion, first of the understanding and love of the mystery, and then of its incorporation into life so as to transform an entire age into one of Mary and of the Holy Spirit, was entrusted. For that indeed is how the penance and poverty of St. Francis have always been seen by the church herself: as a divinely inspired way to be conformed to Christ crucified and so repair the church through Mary.

Every saint is Marian in some way, St. Bonaventure tells us.[25] There are excellent reasons for saying that the distinctively Marian character of St. Francis is defined by the Immaculate Conception. This is the "hermeneutical"

Making Saints) to substitute for the traditional concept of dogmatic sanctity one of the "secular saint," whose love is philanthropic rather than sacerdotal, illustrate the point. Curiously, the promoters of "secular sanctity" and "dogma-free" virtue (always a masonic ideal) often cite the martyr of charity at Auschwitz in their favor, but only in so far as they can forget that his testimony to charity is not to any kind of love, but to that of a priest-martyr of dogmatic faith, and divorce his manner of death from the mystery of total consecration to the Immaculate.

23. *WK* 21, 485, 486, 991R, 1081, 1313.

24. Cf. Fehlner, "Other Page," *CE* 6, chapter 13.

25. "Numquam legi aliquem Sanctorum, qui non haberet specialem devotionem ad Virginem gloriosam" (*Sermo II in Purificationem*). The basis for this assertion is to be found in the mystery of the presentation-purification: "Et non sine causa voluit Christus offerri et Virgo Mater purificari—licet ad hoc non tenerentur—et hoc, ut ostenderet Christus, quod erat oblationum legalium finis; et Virgo, ut ostenderet, quod ipsa esset sanctificationum spiritualium exemplar et forma" (*Sermo II in Purificationem*). This is a very precise statement of what St. Maximilian will call "transubstantiation into the Immaculate," the final term of her mediation and of total consecration to her qua Immaculate. Cf. Fehlner, *Kolbe . . . Pneumatologist*.

key to the Kolbean interpretation of the Poverello, and without this key it is not possible to understand why St. Francis is not merely a saint of the Middle Ages, but above all a saint for the new millennium.

Without defining the point as exactly as St. Maximilian (who after all enjoyed the benefit of some hindsight in this) St. Bonaventure alludes to the same point when he describes St. Francis as founder of a contemplative order of mendicants corresponding to the cherubim, whose contemplative task is speculative, the study and preaching of penance, whereas St. Francis' own form of contemplative life is seraphic, corresponding to the choir of Seraphim, whose contemplative task is the "sursumactio" of charity, a form, however, which in the thirteenth century had not perhaps yet been given concrete expression as a religious order.[26] Could this seraphic, rather than cherubic, form of contemplative life correspond to that which St. Maximilian cultivated, based on total consecration, the primary (or fourth) Marian vow and "transubstantiation" into the Immaculate as the highest form of perfect conformity to the Crucified?

St. Maximilian nowhere provides a systematic analysis of the theology of history obviously implied here. Nonetheless, it is a well-known fact that in his last years he was an assiduous student of the Seraphic Doctor, particularly of the contents of volume V of the critical edition of St. Bonaventure's works, which contain such masterpieces as the *Breviloquium*, the *Itinerarium*, the Disputed Questions *de Mysterio Ss. Trinitatis* and *de*

---

26. "In ordine contemplantium sunt tres ordines respondentes supremae hierarchiae, quorum est divinis vacare. Intendunt autem divinis tripliciter: quidam per modum supplicatorium, quidam per modum speculatorium, quidam per modum sursumactivum . . . Tertius ordo est vacantium Deo secundum modum sursumactivum, scilicet ecstaticum seu excessivum . . . Quis enim iste est? Iste est ordo seraphicus. De isto videtur fuisse Franciscus . . . et in his consummabitur Ecclesia. Quis autem ordo iste futurus sit, vel iam sit, non est facile scire. Primus ordo respondet Thronis; secundus Cherubim; tertius Seraphim, et isti sunt propinqui Ierusalem et non habet nisi evolare. Iste ordo non florebit, nisi Christus appareat et patiatur in corpore suo mystico . . . illa apparitio Seraph beato Francisco, quae fuit expressiva et impressiva, ostendebat, quod iste ordo illi respondere debeat, sed tamen pervenire ad hoc per tribulationem." (*Hex.* 22, 20–23). In the course of his commentary in this collation the Seraphic Doctor remarks that not only the Dominican, but the Franciscan Order belongs, not to the seraphic, but to the cherubinic or speculative type of contemplation, an observation confirmed by Sixtus V (*Triumphantis Hierusalem*) where he describes Ss. Bonaventure and Thomas as "duo candelabra in domo Dei lucentia," the two complementary forms of speculation corresponding to the two complementary forms of mendicant spirituality. Is it possible to see in the Marian observance of the Franciscan Rule at Niepokalanów by St. Maximilian an "order" or form of common life corresponding to the seraphic mode of contemplation?

Scientia Christi, the conferences *de Decem Mandatis, de Donis Spiritus Sancti,* and *in Hexaemeron.*[27]

With St. Bonaventure he saw clearly that no resolution of the problems of human history could be offered, much less achieved, so long as the problem of history and culture was formulated in terms of a simple choice between dogma (metaphysics) or progress, as though the option for dogma renders cultural progression meaningless, or the option for cultural relevance gives event priority over being, "fieri" over "esse" a la Hegel. Rather in the dogmatic principle rather than from within the event, that we discover the source of intelligibility of the event. It is the mystery of the Immaculate Conception where the unchanging "esse" of the uncreated touches the "fieri" of historic love: the "vertex of love".[28]

Let us see if a more detailed outline of the patterns of church history in his mind can be proposed by consulting this last work of St. Bonaventure, well known as a classic statement of the theology of history in a dogmatic-metaphysical key.

The Testimony of St. Bonaventure

An initial point of contact between the Martyr of charity and the Seraphic Doctor is that based on the typology of contemplative forms of life, just mentioned, specifically what St. Maximilian understood by a thoroughly marianized observance of the Rule of St. Francis.

But this initial consideration acquires a greater systematic value when we consider where the two pages of Franciscan history fit in the general scheme of church history provided by St. Bonaventure, namely, in the sixth and seventh ages of the church.

a. The fundamental principle of a theology of history could not be put more clearly than St. Bonaventure puts it: all history is about Christ and his body, the church, and the antichrist or devil and his body. The struggle between the two cities is perfectly evident in the story of Cain and Abel. And the struggle reaches its final, glorious consummation in the fulness of time, first in the head of the church, and then in the church. "In paradiso fuit lignum vitae, et fuit lignum scientiae boni et mali, et sic in omnibus Scripturae mysteriis explicatur Christus cum corpore suo, et antichristus et diabolus cum corpore suo. Et hoc modo Augustinus fecit librum De Civitate Dei, ubi incipit a Cain et Abel".[29]

27. Domanski, "La genesi."

28. *WK* 1318.

29. *Hex.* col. 14, n. 17. This further clarifies the metaphor of the river of history

b. The rhythms, patterns, and parameters of history are determined not by the opposition to Christ, but by the divine counsels in view of what St. Bonaventure, like our present Holy Father, calls the fullness of time. In these terms the dogmatic-metaphysical principle rendering intelligible, i.e., *plene resolvens*, historical fact is that more familiarly known as recirculation and recapitulation associated with the name of St. Irenaeus. And that principle so formulated involves a correspondence between, a) on the one hand the patterns and rhythms of the original creation and structuring of the universe in a period of six days followed by a seventh of divine rest from such work (*tempora originalia*), which are exclusively the work of God,[30] and b) on the other hand the ages of human history, sacred in character and ordered to the incarnation and redemption, which involve actors other than God, but never beyond the limits set by the divine counsels. There is a clear parallel here with the remark of the Holy Father about the correlation between solar and liturgical-historical time.[31]

----

flowing into the fullness of time. It is perfectly possible to be a part of the devil's brood as well as of the Woman's offspring, and so go to hell rather than heaven.

30. St. Bonaventure takes the literal sense of day in Genesis to be that of a twenty-four-hour period, and the spiritual sense of those *tempora originalia* to be that of the ages of human history. Cf. Fehlner, "In the Beginning," *CE* 7, chapter 1. His views, like those of St. Maximilian (cf. Fehlner, "Vertex Creationis"), are quite incompatible with evolution, theistic as well as atheistic. A recent historian of the exegesis of Genesis, Fr. S. Jaki, *Genesis 1 Through the Ages*, 133–36, hardly does justice to the views of St. Bonaventure when he dismisses the Seraphic Doctor's reflections on the hexaemeron as merely an exercise in pious meditation: "what Bonaventure offers is not so much a food for the intellect as nourishment for the soul" (135). Fr. Jaki obviously thinks Bonaventure is a pietist with joachimite leanings who regards the rational and scientific as a threat to the spiritual: "The real world fares very badly throughout the Collations" (134). "The Collations represent his final major effort to oppose emphasis on a purely rational approach to God whose existential presence should be grasped in all things at all times . . . The true Christian, Bonaventure argues, must aim at a wisdom to be obtained by a six-fold understanding, implied in the six days of creation" (134). Fr. Jaki does not appreciate the traditional approach of St. Bonaventure, which understands the inspired literal sense of "day" in Genesis to be the basis of a twofold, inspired spiritual sense: one bearing on the six illuminations of the mind in the process of its sanctification and the attainment of an understanding *plene resolvens* in the light of the necessary, unchanging *rationes* (and in this he follows St. Augustine); the other bearing on the interpretation of human history on the basis of revealed patterns in the *tempora originalia* determined by God, not by the unfolding of events (and in this he "corrects" Augustine, opting not for total creation and structuring in an instant, but in steps, which enable us to understand history as it unfolds via recirculation and recapitulation). Bonaventure does not "range freely through a wild-variety of arguments," as Fr. Jaki thinks (134), but provides a very concise and carefully thought-out response to all forms of historicism: pious as well as secular.

31. John Paul II, *Tertio millenio adveniente*, 18.

The historical ages of the family of Adam are of two kinds: the figurative (*tempora figuralia*), which are none other than the continuance of the sixth day after God had completed his work in the formation of Adam from the slime of the earth and Eve from the side of Adam, with which the seventh day of divine rest runs concurrently, until the fullness of time at the incarnation, in the sixth figurative age. In turn, with the consummation of Christ's work at the end of this "sixth figurative day" and with his entrance into the rest of the tomb on the seventh day of holy week, the time of the church begins (*tempora gratiosa*), which are a continuance of the "sixth figurative day." With this runs concurrently the seventh day, that is, the presence of the church and each member of the church in the tomb with Christ, until the fulfillment of time for the church at the general resurrection. Thus, the outer form of the church, apparently of this world, veils a continuous dying with Christ, but also a rising with him, for concurrently with the sixth and seventh ages of the time of grace, runs the eighth day of the resurrection. Thus in the time of fulfillment it is not the number seven, but eight (7+1) which represents the final sanctification of time, that is, the jubilee number of 50, which for Bonaventure signals Pentecost of eternity, our sharing in the resurrection jubilee.

Schematically, we may illustrate St. Bonaventure's thought thus:

Tempora originalia: Days of Creation
Historical Ages
Tempora figuralia: Sixth Day continued as history after the first 24 hours:
Tempora gratiosa: Sixth Age of Incarnation continued as age of grace in Church to end of world:

T. originalia (days)
1 2 3 4 5 6 CREATION OF MAN⟶ AGES OF HUMAN HISTORY
                7 DIVINE REST⟶

T. figuralia (ages of human history)
1 2 3 4 5 6 INCARNATION⟶ AGE OF THE CHURCH
                7 REST IN TOMB
                  8 RESURRECTION OF CHRIST

T. gratiosa (ages of the Church)
1 2 3 4 5 6
                7 MILLENNIUM

7 . . . .   END OF TIME
                  8 GENERAL RESURRECTION

8 ASSUMPTION OF MARY
  RESURRECTION OF CHRIST . . . .

For our purposes we may note the correlation between fulfillment and the number six: on the sixth day God fulfills his work in creating and structuring the world as a home for Adam, a place to prepare for heaven and so enters his rest. The fulfillment is merely relative, because it is not the real fullness of time to occur at the incarnation, but only its prefigurement. At this point only God is "in his rest."

There is a second sense in which the fulfillment is merely relative, that is, from Adam's point of view, for neither naturally nor after sin and the loss of grace can he enter into rest. The sixth day is the fullness of time for man only when he can indeed enter the seventh day of rest (cf. Heb 3–4).

Next, in the sixth age occurs the incarnation, or the fullness of time absolutely, when as it were the "image of God" becomes fully his "similitude," when by dying in the evening of the sixth day, the New Adam, the Word Incarnate, enters his rest in the tomb on the seventh and rises on the eighth, so that the fullness of time of the sixth and seventh "figurative" days can continue for the church in the age of grace and make possible her final fulfillment in the eighth day of the general resurrection.

On the sixth day, whether original day of creation, or historical age of Adam and of Christ, there is a sign or coefficient exquisitely Marian. In the case of the sixth day of the Hexaemeron it is the *terra virgo* from which the body of the first Adam is miraculously formed by God and into which he breathes his spirit. The *terra virgo*, St. Bonaventure tells us, is a type of the Virgin Mother (which can easily indicate the Immaculate Conception),[32] in whose womb the body of the Son of God was virginally conceived from which the Incarnate Word was born virginally. "Homo conditus de terra virginea, quae nondum sanguinem susceperat, significat Christum de virgine natum, sicut etiam Eva de latere Adae formatae, sic Ecclesia de Christo latere".[33]

That virginal womb in turn is a sign of the newly hewn tomb in which the dead Savior rested "three days," and into which in baptism the believer enters so as to rise with Christ unto newness of life, first in the soul, and finally on the last day definitively in the body as well, if he perseveres unto the end.

Finally, the Virgin assumed gloriously into heaven after her death is the exemplar of all those perfections which will one day render the entire Church glorious as the new Eve, the bride of Christ without spot or wrinkle, viz., immaculate like the Immaculate.[34]

---

32. Cf. Testa, *Maria Terra Vergine*; Fehlner, review of *Maria Terra Vergine*.

33. *Hex.* col. 16, n. 21. Cf. Fehlner, "Mystery of Coredemption," *CE* 4, chapter 2.

34. Cf. Bonaventure, *Sermo V in Assumptione*: IX, 692b: "Quidquid enim dignitatis

Thus, it is not difficult to see that St. Maximilian's first page of Franciscan history falls in the sixth age of Church history according to St. Bonaventure, with its "praeclaritas victoriae, doctrinae et vitae propheticae," obscured at the time of transition by a humiliation of the church, a crisis of faith and of prophetic life.[35] His Marian era coincides with the seventh or last period of the church, marked by a restoration of worship of the Father, a reintegration of the city, viz., a civilization of love, and peace, in so far as this is possible in the conditions of pilgrimage.[36] Dying and rising with Christ concretely is effected to the degree the soul is "transubstantiated" into the Immaculate as She is transubstantiated into the Holy Spirit.[37] The more perfectly this is accomplished in each soul, throughout the church and in the entire culture, the more evident will be the conditions of the millennium described prophetically by the Apostle entrusted by the Savior to his Mother when dying (cf. John 19: 25–27). All this is a reflection, necessarily, of the glories of the Immaculate assumed into heaven and there crowned queen.

This seventh age begins with the end of the sixth day of the incarnation and runs concurrently with all the periods of the time of grace, but as it were veiled, whereas in the "millennium" mentioned by St. John, an era of great and long peace when Christ truly reigns in the hearts of all, the dying and rising of Christ in the life of the church will be more evident in the appearances, precisely in the three aspects mentioned by the Seraphic Doctor.

Thus, in his analysis there is no millenarism or Joachimitism, which places the seventh age of the church merely after the sixth. St. Bonaventure, instead, makes the seventh age run concurrently with the sixth, and the eighth with both. The seventh age is before all else the age of Mary, universal mediatrix of all those graces by which those who have gone down by baptism into the tomb of Christ are brought to newness of life and ultimately to the eight day themselves. Thus the millennium is the "rest" of the believer becoming more and more evident at the end of the sixth and final period of Church

---

et gloriae istis [sanctis] partialiter est collatum, sacrae Virginis integraliter est concessum"; *Sermo I in Assumptione.*: IX, 688b" "In horum omnium [sanctorum] vertice beata Virgo mons praeparatus dicitur, quia quidquid illis est promissum et revelatum, hoc est in ea impletum; et quidquid gratiae in istos influxit, ab ipsa et per ipsam derivavit."

35. *Hex.* col. 16, n. 29.

36. *Hex.* col. 16, n. 30.

37. The six illuminations and ages of the Hexaemeron may be compared with the six steps of acquired contemplation in the *Itinerarium*, apparently followed by the seventh of infused contempation and ultimately passage (*transitus*) from this world to the Father. Though no express mention is made of our Lady in this work outside the prologue, the themes of the seventh chapter, in particular dying and rising with Christ crucified, are substantially identical with the exposition in the *Collationes in Hexaemeron*. Cf. also Fehlner, *Kolbe . . . Pneumatologist.*

history precisely when through the purgative, illuminative and unitive action of Christ and Mary the sixth age tends to merge into the seventh and at the coming of Christ the latter into the eighth day of the Resurrection.

St. Bonaventure is a faithful disciple of St. Augustine, not of Joachim of Fiore and all historicists after him, who succumb to the great intellectual confidence trick of the prince of this world, viz., that change always enjoys priority over the unchanging. But he is the disciple of Augustine who has rendered explicit the basis for understanding the significance of events and of their progression without sacrificing the priority of the unchanging over the changing, the fixed over the unfolding in the history of the image as well as the time of the vestige via his metaphysics *plene resolvens*, viz., the dogmatic metaphysics of the hypostatic union.[38]

Nor does he make any attempt to discover the day or the hour in terms of mathematical measurements (the intellectual short circuit of all sensists and pious nominalists a la John Locke), because St. Bonaventure's is an interpretation of the phenomena in terms of a dogmatic-metaphysical principle, one which does not exclude becoming, but finds in being and the unchanging the prior basis for understanding change: not only change in the vestige, but history in the image. Thus, what is often cited today as a basis for an anti-metaphysical and anti-dogmatic theory of history becomes in the hands of the Seraphic Doctor the only viable foundation for the intelligibility of history.

And so the theology of history in the *Conferences on the Hexaemeron* is not only a refutation of millenarism, but of that even more subversive secularism, which would attempt a theory of history in purely secular, immanent terms and so seek to desacralize it, the aim of all gnosticism, the most virulent current form (viz., according to St. Maximilian, the head of the enemies of the church, but not the only gnostic enemy) being freemasonry.

Conclusion

1. The greater jubilee of the year 2000, the millennium, a celebration of the fullness of time, the preparation for which is a hermeneutical key to the

---

38. This is a main theme of the *Collationes in Hexaemeron*: there can be no complete "philosophy," except via an "intellectus plene resolvens," utilizing the native light of reason, the infused light of faith, and the gift of contemplative prayer. His approach necessarily collides or at least differs from any which posits the autonomy of the created intellect as starting and end point of a body of knowledge (implicitly denying the doctrine of the divine illumination). St. Bonaventure gives good reasons to show that his position is that of our Savior, St. Paul, St. Augustine, but not that of Plato or Aristotle. Cf. *Chr. mag.*, 16.

present pontificate, is indeed the Marian epoch, the age of the Holy Spirit of St. Maximilian, the seventh or final age of the church of St. Bonaventure, matching as far as possible before the end of the world and the coming of the Savior-Judge the perfection of the Queen of Angels gloriously assumed and crowned in heaven.

2. Evidently *millennium* as a term to describe this final age does not exclude subsequent fourth and fifth millennia in the chronological sense, but merely indicates that long period of time characteristic of the inner and outer life of the church just prior to the final coming of Christ as indicated in the Apocalypse of St. John.

3. The perfection of this age is that of charity, the love of God above all else, even to the contempt of self, the charity of the city of God, opposed consistently throughout history by another love characteristic of the body of the antichrist: the love of self, even to the contempt of God, or profanation of charity.[39]

Man of the Millennium: St. Maximilian, Martyr of Charity

The preparation for the millennium involved primarily the Blessed Trinity and the Virgin Mother, secondarily ourselves in so far as we are sufficiently disposed to be the servants of God through the mediation of the Immaculate. Some aspects of the preparation are the work of God and of the Virgin Mother alone, such as the fullness of time itself and the opportunity to share in it. For the Holy Father this is plainly the case with the opportunity the recent fall of totalitarian political systems in Eastern Europe provide.

But with their fall, he noted, there remain many problems to be resolved and obstacles to overcome, for whose resolution God wisely wills and awaits our cooperation. The Holy Father notes a number of these: the widespread need for personal conversion, penance and sanctification; the resolution of the divisions among Christians arising mostly during the second millennium; the continuing increase of ethnic conflict and exacerbated nationalism, religious indifferentism and cultural secularism, failure to implement Vatican II Council properly.

Resolving these problems and overcoming these obstacles requires, according to the pope, two things: the support of our Lady—the Marian Year was an anticipation of the Jubilee[40]—and a willingness to be martyrs of charity—*sanguis martyrum semen christianorum.*

39. Cf. Borella, *La Charité profanée*; Léthel, "Verità e Amore."
40. John Paul II, *Tertio millenio adveniente*, 33.

Without doubt, Pope John Paul deserves to be known as Pontiff of the Millennium, when we attend to that guidance that directs each of these rivulets to that great stream that meets the ocean of divine fullness in Christ Jesus. But if we look to one who by his example of devotion to Mary qua Immaculate, and by the influence of his life of purity and of his death as a martyr of charity for the sake of the age of Mary, then to those familiar with St. Maximilian Mary it seems only logical to name him man of the millennium. All the more so, because he sought to accomplish this precisely by giving to the Rule and life of contemplative prayer of St. Francis of Assisi a form appropriate to the era of seraphic love in the church.

Our reflections in this second section of the conference fall under two subheadings: (a) the abiding contribution of St. Maximilian, and (b) key, at once practical as well as theoretical, to overcoming the obstacles to a "civilization of love."

The Contribution of St. Maximilian

a. Total consecration to the Immaculate as mistress of history.[41] At the center of St. Maximilian's life and death is found ever the same distinguishing feature: the mystery of the Immaculate Conception. The inferences which the saint drew from that consecration for every level of human life: corporal, intellectual, spiritual; personal or communal, are at once historically and trans-historically valid, precisely because dogmatic-metaphysical in the sense of St. Bonaventure's intellect "plene resolvens." There is no sanctification of time in view of the incarnation and redemption, except on condition that the intellect be sanctified, just as there can be no desacralization of time except the intellect be secularized. The first is via the woman, as the second is via the serpent and his brood, the enemies of the church.

These inferences are such, because the mystery of the Immaculate Conception, at the beginning of history, throughout each of its periods, and at its end, lies at the juncture, the "vertex of love,"[42] between being and becoming, time and the fullness of time. This is how St. Maximilian understood the protoevangelium, and why he understood total consecration of this kind to involve one in the Militia of the Immaculate, in a struggle whose negative pole is victory over the antichrist and his body and whose positive pole is total incorporation into the body of Christ via transubstantiation into the Immaculate.

41. *WK* 1329, 1330, 1331, 1334.
42. *WK* 1318.

He is indeed an essentialist,[43] but in the fashion of St. Bonaventure who unlike the Platonists[44] does not ignore the empirical, but who finds the intelligibility of the phenomenon and of the historical in the being which does not change and cannot change,[45] rather than in the "cultural mediation" postulated by certain recent Kolbean commentators, who in the name of something called "personalism" make process and the vital experience the final criterion of relevance.[46] In such a system the person loses any semblance of real independence and retains value only in terms of his cultural relevance. Hence, the witness of the martyr of charity cries out: inculturation is without further qualification and explanation a very treacherous term, an explanation only possible and adequate if one begins with that "Augustinian-Bonaventurian" metaphysics whose profoundest realization is the incorporation of the mystery of the Immaculate into life.

Such a starting point touches both our understanding of the intellect and the relation of our free wills to the truth.

1. Language and concepts (the *veritas vocum*) in the Augustinian-Bonaventurian tradition are not linked for their meaning primarily, much less exclusively to the changeable element in culture, viz., the element of *fieri* in history, but to the constant. Hence, though the linguistic and conceptual are key aspects of the phenomenal, they primarily express being rather than becoming, because at the heart of all culture, whether at the level of vestige, e.g., *agricultura* (the mind and art); or at the level of the image, e.g., culture (the mind and science), or at the level of similitude, e.g., cult-worship (the mind and wisdom), as at the heart of all finite being (*veritas rerum*), is a fontal illumination of the light of truth from above.[47]

43. Cf. Laurentin, *Dio mia tenerezza*; Fehlner, review of *Dio mia tenerezza*.

44. Cf. *Chr.mag.*, 16.

45. *WK* 1246.

46. This is very evident in the conferences of De Fiores and Napiórkowski at the recent International Congress on Kolbean Mariology in Poland to celebrate the centenary of the saint's birth in 1894. In the conferences given by the aforementioned professors spiritual experience rather than doctrine is assumed to be the primary criterion of truth, and without "inculturation" the proclamation of the Gospel (and the message of the M.I.) is irrelevant, fossilized. The potential for subverting faith in a modernistic direction is unlimited here. Distinguendum: the "irruption" of the Spirit of St. Paul, to whom Fr. De Fiores appeals, is not something to be contrasted with doctrine (metaphysics), but the presence before all else of a more perfect doctrine, the only full "metaphysics," as St. Bonaventure notes. Nor should being and event be contrasted; rather the "event" of the incarnation entails a truth and a doctrine that is unchanging. So also St. Maximilian and the M.I. Adaptations for purposes of proclamation are of a technical kind not aiming at the "inculturation" of the metaphysics and moral teaching accompanying it, but at the purification of the "culture and morals" in view of the truth.

47. Cf. Geiger, "Tending of God's Garden."

And at the heart of every act of the intellect there is an irreducible and inescapable simple act of assent to the truth, even in revolting against it, just as that unjust revolt can never fail to include some recognition of the difference between just and unjust.

This is another way of saying the unity of culture and history is prior to its diversity and whatever clearly expresses a principle of unity, such as the Immaculate Conception, has no need of cultural mediation. This is an aspect of the miracle of faith, viz., of the intellect "plene resolvens" which can be understood despite differences of language and culture. Misunderstandings which de facto occur stem not from cultural limitations in the concepts and terminology of the saint, but from defects of a secularized culture which radically rejects the dogmatic-metaphysical in favor of the empirical as the ultimate norm of cultural validity and subordinates doctrine to life experiences.

2. Charity is not to be divorced from truth. There can be no enjoyment of the good, i.e., sanctification of time in such wise as to arrive at the fullness of time, without a prior sanctification of the intellect and of the culture which depends on it (civilization of love), that is to say, a proper formation of conscience.[48] There is no way a secularized culture (scientism and evolutionism) while remaining secularized can serve the interests of true love. It will always remain historicist in orientation and will not admit the finality of the incarnation and divine maternity as eternally normative for all generations. And so it will *natura sua* promote religious indifferentism rather than genuine sanctity.

Those who require a reformulation of St. Maximilian's assertions concerning the eternity and oneness of truth, of the need to enter the church and acknowledge the primacy of the pope because not sufficiently "ecumenical" and "open-minded," or of his use of such terms as possession, instrument, annihilation of self as not sufficiently "personalist,"[49] have in fact capitulated to the anti-metaphysical bias, the desire of a dogma-free Christianity which is the postulate of all western secularism since Ockham (nominalism, voluntarism) as it was of all ancient gnosticism and contemporary freemasonry.

---

48. These and related themes have been the subject of the recent encyclical, *Veritatis Splendor*.

49. Cf. De Fiores, "Come presentare oggi," and Napiórkowski, "Esperienze." In addition one may consider the regrettable apology for the outdated theology of a saint in the editorial note appended to *WK* 1246 in the first Italian edition of the works of St. Maximilian (*Gli scritti di Massimiliano*, vol. III, 563), the last article of the saint published during his lifetime (Dec. 1940), dealing with the eternal character of truth and the crisis of civilization during World War II.

All this St. Maximilian lumps under the rubric: head of the enemies of the church, because head of the enemies of the Immaculate.[50]

b. Niepokalanów.[51] The city of the Immaculate, or city of God fully wrapped in the mantle of the Immaculate, is the finest exemplification of the foregoing, precisely in view of the religious (love and life, or wisdom), cultural (knowledge and science) and technological demands of the fullness of time in the coming millennium. It is an effective bulwark at once of the fideist and rationalist version of a secularized culture. For at the level of the similitude there is a recognition that our worship of God the Father through the Son cannot be perfect until it has been fully marianized, that is, transubstantiated into that adoration of the Immaculate Heart. At the level of the image there is a recognition there can be no intellectual life *plene resolvens* unless it be centered on a dogmatic-metaphysics also marianized, one which recognizes the place of the Immaculate Conception and universal mediatrix in our theology and metaphysics. Finally it is a recognition that there can be no authentic civilization of love except that it breathe the spirit of poverty and obedience of the Virgin Mother and give expression to the mystery of communion in the church (cf. John 17) even in matters of technology and economics. In Bonaventurian terms Niepokalanów reveals how in the conditions of pilgrimage the sixth age passes to the seventh via a "transubstantiation" into the Immaculate.[52]

St. Maximilian clearly intended this metaphysical-contemplative dimension to take precedence over the merely pragmatic value of Niepokalanów as a particular apostolic publishing venture, and so to enjoy permanent, unchanging validity for the age to come.[53] In the light of this, without

---

50. Cf. the remarks of Cardinal John H. Newman in his famous 1879 *"Biglietto" Address*, on receiving in Rome official notification of his cardinalate. In this he clearly indicates the root feature of all modern history: the opposition between the dogmatic principle of Catholicism and the anti-dogmatic liberalism, which appeals always to the possibility and advantages of a secular culture, viz., virtue and good works without dogma. Never, says the Cardinal, has the devil perfected so clever an instrument against Christ's Church. Since only a divine remedy could prevail against the allure of "secular sanctity," the Cardinal was confident Christ would provide. Could it not be possible that this root remedy is to be found in total consecration to the Immaculate?

51. *WK* 1222, 1284. Cf. Fehlner, "Niepokalanów," *CE* 6, chapter 5; "Two Testaments," *CE* 6, chapter 18.

52. On the primacy of charity entailed in this Marian Franciscan spirituality, in particular the Bonaventurian analysis of similitude of God with the accent on charity, cf. Fehlner, "Knowledge and Piety," *CE* 1, chapter 4.

53. *WK* 336, 687, 773, 836, 1246. With St. Bonaventure St. Maximilian clearly differentiates between the freedom essential to the will as such which bears on the supreme good and its fruition in contemplation and that freedom of choice which bears on contingents, and which is perfected to the degree it is perfectly one via obedience with that

depending on some process of "cultural mediation," one can easily discern the secondary, transitory features of Niepokalanów as the primary implementation and exemplification of what total consecration is all about without recourse to complex systems of "inculturation" and "cultural mediation," only nominally distinct from historicism and evolutionism.

Plainly, the contrast between Niepokalanów as a preview of the heavenly paradise and the ersatz gardens of pleasure that the prince of this world can offer, whether in capitalist or socialist forms, is basic to the saint's thought and enables us to grasp the implications of a choice of the one or the other: the city of God or the city of the prince of this world.

c. The mission of the Immaculate.[54] Nonetheless, as St. Bonaventure notes and St. Maximilian affirms, the missionary thrust is an intrinsic element of this form of contemplative life, not only in view of preaching (and the study or sanctification of the intellect which must precede and accompany it), but above all in view of that witness to charity (and the study or sanctification of the intellect which must precede and accompany it), culminating in the desire for and grace of martyrdom,[55] in an age of infidelity, whose primary agent is the secularization of the intellect, above all via an evolutionary scientism which denies (a) the truth about the *tempora originalia* and the formation of Adam from the virgin earth and of the second Adam from the Immaculate Virgin; and (b) that the proper name of the first person of the Trinity is Father only.

Infidelity is of two kinds: negative, today in particular in a secular, scientific culture, where however the truth about the Immaculate and her Son and Savior has not yet been heard; and positive where it has been heard, accepted, but subsequently repudiated. The first was the object of St. Maximilian's witness to charity in his missionary efforts in Asia, hardly to be restricted merely to Japan; the second of his missionary witness to charity on his return to Poland and a Europe living the curse of a civilization devoid of its essence: the love of God and of neighbor as defined by the cross of Christ.

d. The fourth or Marian vow of total consecration and the Rule of St. Francis.[56] It is well known that St. Maximilian wished to add a fourth vow of total consecration to the Immaculate to the three normally professed by all Franciscans. During his lifetime, only he and friars destined for the foreign missions were allowed to make this vow, and only as a private vow. Nonetheless, the point is essential to his contribution to the preparation

---

of the will of God. Cf. *Myst. Trin.*, q. 7, a. 2, in corpore, for a summary statement.

54. *WK* 199, 419, 603, 1086.

55. *WK* 46, 1336.

56. *WK* 395, 398, 399, 409, 419, 492, 653.

for the millennium. The fourth vow is not so much another vow as a perfection of the observance of the Rule of St. Francis and of the three vows
on which it rests. It is a definitive expression of seraphic charity and of
perfect conformity to the crucified in communal form, by making over all
possessions and property rights to the Immaculate,[57] by making oneself
unconditionally available through obedience[58] to be involved in the mission of the Immaculate re charity in the face of violent infidelity and secularization of time, by willing to be transubstantiated into the Immaculate
in making one's own heart, mind and will identical with hers as Spouse of
the Holy Spirit, the uncreated Immaculate Conception. Is it possible to see
in this what St. Bonaventure meant by the seraphic form of contemplative
life as distinct from that of the cherubinic mode of observing the Rule in
common? *Judicet benevolus lector!*

Problems and Obstacles

These are many. Three, however, seem particularly significant in the light
of the foregoing remarks about St. Maximilian as man of the millennium.
In the first instance he is that because he is an effective channel for that
grace, both illuminating and inflaming, necessary for the inauguration of
the Marian era par excellence; and in the second instance because his witness to charity introduces criteria[59] which when accepted will bring about
profound transformations at the three primary levels of human existence,
both personal and social, so as to initiate concretely what the Holy Father
calls a civilization of love.

　　a. Ethnic violence, exacerbated nationalism and anti-family policy, or
the culture of lust and death. There is no doubt that the increase of violence
of all forms is linked to the breakdown of family life and the right order between the private (the personal and familial) and public spheres of human
existence. In short there is a direct correlation between the culture of death
and the promotion of lust: contraception, abortion, infanticide, euthanasia,
genetic experimentation. Greed is the vice that best characterizes the mentality and motivation at the root of the tragedy of our century of satanic
challenge to the kingship of Christ. It means that desire for the goods of

57. WK 137, 140, 150, 299, 300, 313, 314, 382, 395, 414, 436, 605.

58. WK 343, 419.

59. The criteria in question reflect the unchanging element uniquely present in the
fullness of time, not in the sense that change is necessary (as is sometimes affirmed),
but in the sense that before there can be any change, or any assessment of change as
desirable or not, good or bad, there must be something unchanging.

this world takes absolute precedence over any other consideration. And it is best described in the words of old prayer in honor of St. Francis: "frigescente mundo"—"when the world was growing cold."[60] The saint anticipates the opposition between the two cities, the two bodies in practical terms: between true charity which is warm, and its profanation which rests on the coldness of greed, a pragmatism without limit, aptly described by G. K. Chesterton as a "Utopia of Usurers."[61]

For that there is no remedy other than that holy poverty which warms the heart to the love of God, the blessed poverty of Christ, of Mary, of Francis. Why is it blessed, why does it make blessed, why is it at the heart of the civilization of love? Because it makes persons, societies, cultures the possession and property of the Immaculate, as she is the exclusive property of Christ and of the Father, for she is the Spouse of the Holy Spirit, the Spirit of Father and Son, of truth and of love. That is why the expressly Marian mode of observing poverty at Niepokalanów is such an effective sign for the celebration of the millennium It restrains an unbridled freedom of choice and execution in all areas: knowledge, expression, experimentation, indulgence, and sets it in relation to the truth so as to transform it from license into justice and so initiate peace in place of violence, life in place of death.

b. The secularization of life. This has many facets. The most important, however, is the secularization of the intellect, of science, of the arts, because the denial, theoretical and practical, of the essentially religious character of the mind, of its fundamental orientation toward wisdom and God is the indispensable means for attaining that liberation or unrestricted freedom (academic above all today) without which, according to the prince of this world, we cannot become gods. St. Bonaventure saw this clearly as the modern scientific world was beginning; hence his little masterpieces: *Christus unus omnium Magister*, and *De reductione artium ad theologiam*, and his unfinished masterpiece, the *Collationes in Hexaemeron*.

---

60. The full text of the prayer: "Domine Jesu Christi, qui frigescente mundo, ad inflammandum corda nostra tui amoris igne, in carne Beatissimi Patris nostri Francisci passionis tuae sacra Stigmata renovasti: concede propitius; ut eius meritis et precibus crucem iugiter feramus, et dignos fructus poenitentiae faciamus. Qui vivis . . . "

61. Chesterton, *Collected Works*, vol. 5. Chesterton's classic analysis of capitalism and socialism as essentially the same materialism which would deprive families of their property and make of them mere economic units of the private corporation or state. In either case the same persons control matters, as private persons in capitalist, or as public officials in socialist systems, because they have cornered control over the means of exchange. Both deny the dignity and freedom of the person. Analogous is the root identity of pietism and fideism on the one hand and secular humanism, liberation theology, etc., on the other which agree in their anti-metaphysical, anti-dogmatic view of the intellect as radically secular and agnostic.

As the centuries passed his warnings were not heeded. Nominalism leads to scientism, and this to evolutionism. The first says our mind exists only to sort out sense experience, not to know being itself; the second says the only way to know material things is the scientific in view of a higher "quality of life"; and the third says in virtue of human science secularized we can control the course of evolution until we reach the plane of gods. All this is directly opposed to the sanctification of the intellect, described in the *Collationes in Hexaemeron* in great detail. Here we merely wish to note the significance of Niepokalanów for the reversal of this disastrous reduction of the arts and sciences to the secular rather than to Christ. It is by way of a believing intellect, "plene resolvens," one identical with that of the Immaculate via obedience. Hence the place of study, of preaching, of offering the first fruits of science to the cause of the Immaculate, of marianizing every aspect of culture.

c. The third problem is that of indifferentism, particularly acute in the formerly Christian society of the western world.[62] One may be secular-minded, but still "pious." The piety is superficial, nonetheless real. But the "indifferentist" lives beyond piety and impiety alike: he is bored by the spiritual. From the Christian point of view, this is spiritual death. It is the greatest obstacle to the new evangelization and the construction of a civilization of love, for the indifferentist systematically lives only for ends immanent in this world. His is the vision of the historicist. No mere theoretical analysis by itself will ever convert the indifferentist. Only the answer of the cross, the answer Christ gave both to the mocking scribes and priests and to the skeptical Pilate, to Jew and gentile alike, can effectively counter the forces represented by contemporary indifferentism.

And this is what the witness of the Martyr of charity at Auschwitz is about: the witness of priestly, not philanthropic, love, a witness resting not on subjective considerations, even those of personal piety and holiness, but on that of divine authority and truth, permeating every fiber of one's being via a "transubstantiation" into the Immaculate. It is the Immaculate who formed the body of the priest which once hung on the cross, the instrument of our salvation; and it was the Immaculate who formed the slave of love who offered his life not only for another, but for all others in the concentration camp of the prince of this world. Whence the importance of cities of the Immaculate founded on total consecration and "transubstantiation" into the Immaculate for the conversion and sanctification of souls and for the building of a civilization of love based on the Gospel.

---

62. Cf. St. Maximilian's observation in 1919 about the plague of indifferentism overtaking the Western world, Christians as well as infidels, clergy and religious as well as laity: *WK* 25.

If we have insisted that the underlying principle governing the celebration of a jubilee-millennium is dogmatic-metaphysical, or better contemplative, so as to include memory, understanding and love, because it
is that of the person "plene resolvens," we can see from this brief review of
the Holy Father how the key problems of our troubled century are rooted
in options taken long ago: options to repudiate the dogmatic-metaphysical, the priority of contemplation and wisdom. Chesterton in his critique
of Bernard Shaw[63] at the beginning of our century, without realizing it,
repeated the point of the Seraphic Doctor: first one must begin with the
Word in eternity, viz., with the dogmatic-metaphysical; then one can begin
to grasp the empirical fact of history.

Concretely, the dogmatic and contemplative is "Immaculatist," for
Mary Immaculate is the key to the mystery of recirculation and recapitulation governing the economy of salvation. And the repudiation, concretely,
is anti-immaculatist. And there we meet the basic pattern of history foretold in the protoevangelium: the struggle between the Woman and the
serpent-dragon (Rev 12:1–17).

Hence, it is no accident that the three basic errors of the secularist
mind-set identified by St. Bonaventure are those of the anti-immaculatist
mind-set: the eternity of the world, the unicity of the agent intellect, the
denial of rewards and punishments after this life.

The pragmatist or greedy man—*homo modernus*—always takes the
world for granted: it always was, evolution assures him, and so he can be
confident it will always be. Genesis is but a myth, a symbol of some moral-
ism that will keep the rabble in check.

The secular intellectual, whose name is legion, does not admit any
higher standard of truth than his culture. Those who do not measure up to
his particular version of personalism are outdated and so without rights of
citizenship in the coming civilization. The person is relative to the culture,
even the saint. Behold in "big brother," or better "big sister," the sole "agent
intellect" so much castigated by the Seraphic Doctor. *Nil novi sub sole.*

Finally, the indifferentist does not believe in rewards and punishments. His is the autonomous conscience, which will never accept dictation from the heavenly legislator. He will form his own evaluation of events
based on the fruit of the tree of the knowledge of good and evil, viz., of

63. Chesterton, *George Bernard Shaw, Collected Works*, vol. 11, 363: "The philosophy of facts is anterior to the facts themselves. In due time we come to the fact; but in
the beginning was the Word." The answer to Pilate's question: "What is truth?" is always
metaphysical, "the philosophy of facts"; and the final form of that answer, as it touches
science dealing with the phenomenal and wisdom with the eternal, is the "wisdom of
the cross," always mediated by the Spouse of the Holy Spirit, the Immaculate.

experience versus metaphysics-dogma. Of this more in *Veritatis Splendor*. It is enough here to note with St. Bonaventure an option governing all history: eating from the tree of life, or from the other forbidden tree. One leads to blessedness, the other to eternal damnation.

Conclusion: Man of the Millennium

Eve succumbed to the tempter, because she was curious, and sinned; she induced her husband, Adam, to eat of the forbidden fruit and in consequence of their sin, both were subject to the concupiscence of the eyes, and of the flesh and to the pride of life. Mary Immaculate lived by faith, and so prudently discerning the message of the Angel consented to be the Mother of God and lived by the fruit of the tree of life, of the life of the Son she bore, and was made blessed in living the counsels of poverty, chastity and obedience.

That is because she is the Immaculate Virgin, the Spouse of the Holy Spirit, the "uncreated Immaculate Conception,"[64] the "ratio finiendi seu complementi," as the Son is the "ratio exemplandi" and the Father the "ratio originandi" in the Blessed Trinity. The structure of the economy of salvation, the pattern of time and history, the duration of finite being reflects the mystery of the Trinity and is so organized as to introduce the children of Adam into the company of the divine persons.

The element of conflict between two bodies: that of the Christ and that of the antichrist, which in fact marks that history from beginning to end, revolves about the mystery of the "created Immaculate Conception," the "ratio finiendi" in creation, and that of the antichrist. Only one who understands, and even more lives the mystery of the Immaculate Conception can realize in a definitive way in himself the "ratio exemplandi" and so give honor and glory and adoration to the Father from whom all things come and to whom all must return.

St. Maximilian Kolbe above all is the saint who has most clearly and forcefully promoted, both in his personal form of life and in his apostolic endeavors, the mystery of the Immaculate Conception: uncreated and created, in his life and by his death as the Martyr of charity for a troubled time when charity has been profaned. That is why he is the "man of the millennium," not because there could not be a fourth and a fifth millennium, but because history is now entering that period when until the final coming its most prominent feature will be the Marian, the Immaculatist, that of total consecration to and total possession by the Immaculate of all who belong to the body of Christ. As the Virgin Mother is the great

---

64. *WK* 1318. Cf. Fehlner, "Immaculate . . . Trinity," *CE* 6, chapter 3.

sign of the fullness of time, the incarnation, so the city of the Immaculate, "Niepokalanów" is the great sign of that fullness for the church, a fullness which is that of the paradise of the Blessed Trinity, of whom the Immaculate is the "Complementum."[65]

Hence, in the second phase of preparation for the year 2000 the Holy Father insisted very much on its Trinitarian character, because centered on Christ, the Son of God made man, it is necessarily theological, and so inevitably Marian. The first year focused on the Word of God, with the objective of strengthening "dogmatic faith" and of a longing for true holiness, which match the faith of Peter in the Son of God and in the Eucharist. Precisely as the Mother of God Mary is the model of faith for all believers.

In the second year the focus was to be the Holy Spirit, by whom the Virgin conceived and brought forth her child, with the objective of strengthening the appreciation of the faithful for the mystery of the Holy Spirit and of the "created Immaculate Conception," and of stimulating that hope in salvation which will spur all to promote the new evangelization, a continuance of the spiritual maternity of the Immaculate, and the true basis for a "civilization of love" in these last times, understood neither in the millenarist nor in the secularist sense, but in that of Augustine and Bonaventure.

Finally, the focus of the third year of preparation was the Father, with the objective of making the jubilee a great act of praise for the Father: "Blessed be the God and Father of our Lord Jesus Christ, who has blessed us in Christ with every spiritual blessing" (Eph 1:3-4). The worship of the Father, through the Son in the Holy Spirit: this is the authentic culture, which the culture of death: greed, secularism and indifference, seeks to oppose, nowhere more so than in radical feminism which would deny the very name of Father as the proper name of the "fontal plenitude of all goodness." This has two aspects: one negative of penance and conversion, the other positive of charity, of choosing the good. In this way, the principal challenge of this period of transition can be met: that of the crisis of civilization via penance; that of dialogue with authentic charity.

However, many the activities involved in meeting this double challenge, our rereading of St. Maximilian in the context of the millennium and on the premises of St. Bonaventure shows him to stand as a beacon lightening the mystery that stands at the heart of the consummation of charity in the fullness of time: the Immaculate Conception, the "ratio finiendi" in eternity and in history, the sign which God gives us of victory over sin and death, over the "culture of death."

---

65. Cf. Fehlner, "Complementum Ss. Trinitatis," *CE* 6, chapter 4.

Guided and inspired and supported by his priestly witness to the perfect love of God and neighbor on the cross let our response be that of total consecration to the Immaculate, by whose preservation from original sin we are freed from slavery to sin and to the prince of this world; let it be one of unconditional longing for the heavenly "Niepokalanów" and of unrestricted service in promoting the kingdom of the sacred heart of Jesus to the glory of God the Father.

Two prayers of St. Francis of Assisi, the *Absorbeat* (not composed by him, but his because used by him) and the Marian Antiphon for his *Office of the Passion*,[66] dear to St. Maximilian, may fittingly end our reflections on the millennium:

"Please, O Lord, let the fiery, honeyed force of your love lap up my spirit from everything there is under heaven: so that I may die for love of love for you, who deigned to die for love of love for me."

"Holy Virgin Mary, there was never anyone like you born into the world among women: daughter and handmaid of the most high King, our Father in heaven; mother of our most holy Lord Jesus Christ; Spouse of the Holy Spirit! With the archangel St. Michael and all the Virtues of heaven and all the saints pray for us at the throne of your beloved most holy Son, our Lord and Master."

66. Cf. Schneider, *Virgo Ecclesia Facta.*

——— 18 ———

Two Testaments[1]

IT IS A COMMONPLACE in communities, in particular religious, to speak of their traditions as a kind of heritage left them by their founder. This has been particularly true of the Franciscan Order, where the custom is linked to a particular writing of St. Francis known as his *Testament.* Almost from the death of the saint that *Testament* has been the focus of a series of disagreements, quarrels and divisions among the friars over the nature of their heritage and the correct manner of using and developing it. And however much it is generally acknowledged[2] that this *Testament* is not to be read in the narrow sense of a legal document, a kind of final rule superseding all previous rules, it still retains and must retain a permanent role in identifying the characteristic features of the Franciscan charism not subject to change, against which the fidelity of subsequent generations to their tradition must be measured, and whose recurrence according to type make any community professing St. Francis as its father authentically Franciscan. In a word, that *Testament,* a kind of valedictory, or farewell address, enjoys the finality associated with the last words intended by a father of a family to serve as a reminder of essentials and as an exhortation to fidelity, so as to enjoy the blessings of that family.

And if it is true that this semantic usage entails an analogy, it is not merely a literary convention, much less an arbitrary metaphor. There is a certain connaturality in the choice of analogy worth noting, because in modern times questions of inheritance are very much tilted toward considerations of a materialistic and individualistic character, namely, what

---

1. This essay was written in 1985 and, in terms of chronology, should appear after chapter 5. However, it was only discovered as the volume was going to press and placing it its proper chronological place would have entailed major editorial adjustments. Hence, I have decided to include it as final chapter of this volume. —Ed.

2. Conti, "Testamento di San Francesco," cc. 1815–18. For the writings of St. Francis used in this study, cf. Esser, *Die Opuscula*; for the English translation Armstrong, ed., *Francis and Clare.*

is inherited is a good of a material or temporal kind, and that inheritance is primarily a matter of private right or possession. On the contrary, in a Christian and Catholic perspective it is the spiritual, eternal good that enjoys pride of place, an inheritance not simply a matter of individual right, but one belonging to the entire community, constituting as it were the commonwealth, the patrimony of all, and hence is very much a constituent of the public domain, for better or for worse. The individual shares this heritage, precisely by membership in the community that is heir to this tradition. It is the failure to appreciate this point that forms a major obstacle for the modern mind in comprehending the traditional Catholic notion of solidarity: in sin with the first Adam who by his disobedience lost our original spiritual patrimony; and with the second Adam who by his obedience regained it, and more.

This, of course, suggests another aspect observed in the use of the Testament analogy in reference to the Franciscan tradition: its relation to the formation of the covenant through the work of a mediator whose last will or testament, made operative by his death, forms the grounds on which the community and its members, namely, the church, inherit. That covenant was foreshadowed in the establishment of the human family, and more so in the formation of the chosen people of old. But it is in relation to the church that the Testament, stigmatization and death of St. Francis attain a deeper, mystic significance in assessing the traditional and on-going role of the Franciscan Order in the church.[3] Thus, every discussion of that heritage is not merely a discussion of rules and regulations, virtues and vices, but bound up in those practicalities a discussion of the profoundest mysteries of salvation, i.e., of our cooperation with the Savior in the work of conversion and sanctification of souls—our own and others.

To the extent that each friar lives this tradition in observing the Rule and the vows he has professed, to that extent he contributes as well to the final realization of all that the crucified Christ desired in inspiring St. Francis to establish this form of life, thus enriching the heritage St. Francis himself indicated, and in this he is echoed by St. Maximilian, that his personal sanctity was not the equivalent of that sanctity to be achieved by the Order as a whole. "Let us begin, brothers, to serve the Lord our God for up to now we have made little or no progress."[4]

But there are certain among the Franciscan saints whose contributions to the heritage are exceptional in the sense that they directly affect that heritage as a part of the public domain, not in changing or adding to

3. Conti, "Testamento di San Francesco," cc. 1812–13.
4. *1 Cel.* 103; *WK* (I, 895).

it, as the archetype of Franciscanism, but in perfecting its comprehension and implementation among the heirs of Francis. Every genuine development in spiritual as well as in doctrinal matters is of this kind; others rather are corruptions or adulterations of the tradition, a dissipation or squandering of the inheritance.[5] Such saints are quite rare, but St. Bonaventure's reputation as "second founder" of the Order, and St. Bernardine's as "reformer of the Order" surely are examples of this kind, whose work is on a level with that of the Patriarch himself, as that of no other saint is, and whose work like that of the founder enjoys a normative value not only for individual friars, but for the community as a whole, and hence in one way or another for each and every friar.

In our own times it is claimed more and more that the heritage of St. Maximilian Kolbe affects the Order in the same way, not merely individual and small groups within it, but as a whole. This is not only the claim of his disciples; it also represents his own estimate of the impact his whole work—he would say rather the whole work of the Immaculate—should and would have on the entire Order, renewing, reuniting and bringing it to unheard of heights of sanctity and missionary fruitfulness. Such would be achieved via the eventual marianization of the institutions, in a word in making the entire Order a Niepokalanów, the property and possession of the Immaculate in fact as well as in theory, in deed as well as in word.[6] His work is but the incorporation of the mystery of the Immaculate into life, above all else the life of the Order.[7] For, in the belief of St. Maximilian the Immaculate Conception is the Franciscan thesis par excellence, the heart of the Franciscan heritage, the measure of that distinctive sanctity for whose attainment the Order was founded and continues to exist, the object of "our part" to which we are exhorted by St. Francis. Given the character of the claim it is hardly surprising that St. Maximilian also employed the *Testament* genre as a means of crystalizing that heritage for his successors and of encouraging them to be faithful and steadfast to it, and this after a mystical experience in Japan in some ways comparable to the stigmatization of St. Francis[8] in his life, and like

---

5. Newman, *Development of Christian Doctrine*, 171–206.

6. *WK* 485 (I 891); 991 R (II 899).

7. *WK* 486 (I 895); 1168 (III 360).

8. The first recorded occasion on which St. Maximilian spoke of his Testament is that of a conference given in Rome in 1933 and preserved in the *Cronaca della Sede Primaria*, 27, and published in Villepelée, *La Milizia dell'Immacolata*, 15. The second, on which he made reference to a special grace assuring him of heaven, is contained in the testimony of Br. Taddeo M. Maj, in *Beatificationis et Canonizationis*, 857–61. In his testimony, *Beatificationis et Canonizationis*, 171, Br. Cyprian Grodzki describes this as a Testament.

St. Francis accompanied by an assurance that what he was doing was indeed the will of God and that heaven was assured him.

The claim is surely an extraordinary one, and were Saint Maximilian not the great saint the church recognizes and proclaims him to be, would be difficult, if not impossible to sustain. He is in fact a great saint, and that sanctity, in particular the testimony of his death, cannot be divorced from the claim. It is too prominent a feature of his life and work, consciously perceived both by the saint, his sympathizers and critics, during and after his life, as having a direct bearing on the Franciscan heritage as a whole. St. Maximilian understood his work, i.e., the work of the Immaculate in him, particularly as it came to be concentrated and crystalized in that singular institution known as Niepokalanów, the garden, the paradise of the Immaculate, not as a change of or even as a supplement appended to the work of St. Francis, but as its natural development and fulfillment, in particular as regards the manner of practicing poverty and obedience. His reason: the Franciscan thesis, namely, the cause of the Immaculate, the golden thread running throughout the Franciscan heritage from beginning to end.[9]

His critics, quite obviously, neither then nor now agree. From their point of view the mode of observing poverty and obedience at Niepokalanów entails a kind of uniformity incompatible with the unity of the Order, a reform bound either to change the Order (making it something other than Conventual) or split it anew.[10] The disciplinary criticisms, however, are closely linked to a doctrinal one: the *Testament* of St. Francis is Christocentric and his spirituality a kind of Christ-centered affectivity; whereas the spirituality and doctrine of St. Maximilian are Mario-centric, with a corresponding affectivity. The organization of the spiritual and apostolic life of the Order about the Immaculate as mediatrix of all graces in the form of a Niepokalanów whose tenor of life is determined by a strict and "rigid" interpretation of poverty cannot but unbalance the tradition and spirituality of the Order as determined by Saint Francis.[11] Hence, the critics concluded, Niepokalanów

---

9. *WK* 21 (I 35); 486 (I 895).

10. The criticisms in their objective, viz., elimination of that total consecration to the cause of the Immaculate which differentiated Niepokalanów from the other friaries of the Order, are reflected in *WK* 325 (I 512) and implicit in his response, the utter fidelity of Niepokalanów in obeying the successor of St. Francis: *WK* 487 (I 900–901). Cf. also the testimony of Br. Luke Kuzba, *Beatificationis et Canonizationis*, 153.

11. This basic difficulty, with his reply, is reflected in *WK* 643 (II 202). The problem of a choice between a Christocentric or Mariocentric spirituality is reflected in the remarks of Fr. Felix Wilk, *Beatificationis et Canonizationis*, 162, and those of Br. Cyprian Grodzki concerning the visitation and criticisms of Fr. Peregrine Haczela in 1933, *Beatificationis et Canonizationis*, 175. Recently alleged opposition between the Christocentric and Mariocentric orientations within Franciscan spirituality has been

must undergo a "leveling", an adjustment to the form of observance of the other friaries, or become an independent community, with its distinctive spirituality, but one other than Franciscan.

St. Maximilian, in assessing the relation of his charism to that of St. Francis and to the history of the Order, saw the alternatives somewhat differently. Either the entire Order would become, as it were, a Niepokalanów in practice and thus there would be no "difference" in observance within the Order, or Niepokalanów would cease to exist as an institution within the Franciscan Order (a tragedy), or would continue to exist faithful to its nature with a relative autonomy vis-a-vis the Provinces within the Order until the Niepokalanów of the Order became sufficiently numerous and strong to effect the total marianization of the Constitutions of the Order in the spirit of total consecration to the Immaculate.[12]

The existence of the testaments of St. Francis and St. Maximilian provides a convenient basis for assessing these claims and counterclaims, serving by way of comparison as a kind of objective test of the compatibility or opposition of the heritage of each to the other. Is it presumptuous to place the work of St. Maximilian in some way on a level with that of Saint Francis? Or does in fact a careful study of the *Testament* of St. Francis not only permit, but point toward a reading which the Testament of St. Maximilian must give it, if the Kolbean position is indeed the correct one? If this is so, then demurrals from and requests to modify and adapt Niepokalanów in essentials entail a serious misinterpretation of the Christocentrism of St. Francis. But more importantly, the testament of Saint Maximilian becomes a guide to the renewal of the Order at every level, whose importance for this "second page" of Franciscan history cannot be underestimated.

The Testament of St. Francis

In the study of the *Testament* of St. Francis contemporary scholars are agreed that a recognition of its peculiar literary genre is an important condition for a correct interpretation of its contents. Thus the *Testament* is not to be confused with the *Rule* (and *Constitutions*). It is not a legal document binding consciences, in the same way as the *Rule* (and *Constitutions*), much less an application and/or interpretation of these in specific cases, as though it were a kind of court of appeal from the legitimate decisions of the superiors of the Order and of the church. Thus a certain kind of "literalism" confusing or identifying examples with principles, the first

suggested by Napiórkowski, "Die Theologie Angesichts," 40–41, 43.

12. *WK* 485 (I 891).

admitting of a certain variation, the second not so admitting, over the matter of poverty in the *Testament,* is to be avoided, because the church has so interpreted the *Testament* as not binding in this way, and because in fact St. Francis did not so intend it as another Rule.[13]

But it would be equally, and in some ways even more disastrous, to subject the *Testament* to a kind of interpretation that can only be described as totally relativizing its contents as the expression of an ideal valid for a thirteenth-century culture, one from which something can be learned, but with no immediate bearing on the realization of that ideal in another culture. Such a view effectively denies to the *Testament* any permanent, public role in the future life of the Order. It is a position quite in accord with cultural relativism and process philosophy; it is one which in fact logically leads to the progressive "secularization" of the Franciscan tradition, in theory and in practice via a constant adaptation to new situations without reference to any criteria other than those inherent within that situation, and which divorces the unity of the Order from any objective uniformity in doctrinal, devotional and disciplinary forms. Such an approach is quite clearly not compatible with the "sine glossa" of St. Francis, a stance supposing the existence of objective forms, of the "essence" or "reality" of the Franciscan way objectively given, considered "a parte rei", prior to any interpretation and experience of that way by the community and friars, and valid whatever the generation and culture. It is this "essence", inherited by the Order via the *Testament* of St. Francis, some of whose key features are described therein.

The fact that only some of these features, i.e., those in particular at the time of composition seeming especially important to St. Francis and particularly revelatory of that unchanging "essence," are given and in a way not always clear to subsequent generations of friars, either unaware of the complete background, or not enjoying that depth of understanding and charity of a St. Francis, does not render these any less accurate or necessary in assessing the nature of the Franciscan heritage or the care with which it is being preserved or developed in any given time or place. The problem is not their lack of relevance, but of discovering what it is they revealed so clearly to St. Francis, yet even to a great many of his contemporaries was merely implicit, and for whose appreciation the passage of time, experience and development would be necessary. Without that *Testament,* to be read "sine glossa", that development would hardly be distinguishable from an arbitrary identification of Franciscanism with whatever innovations an individual or group chose to designate by that term.

---

13. The classic example is that of not seeking any dispensation from the Holy See or from the pope in regard to the interpretation and application of the Rule.

Thus, as a literary genre within the Franciscan tradition distinct from the *Rule* and other legal documents the *Testament* in fact functions as a reminder of the origin of that life and as an exhortation and encouragement to pursue it faithfully for the same purposes for which it was given, so as to share the blessings which are its reward. But whether one examines those points of the *Testament* serving as a reminder of origin, or those pointing to its goal, the same mystery, at the heart of the Franciscan charism, is implicit in the intentions of Saint Francis. It is this mystery, to use the metaphor of St. Maximilian, which is the "golden thread"[14] running throughout Franciscan history and constituting the source of its distinctiveness in every dimension of its existence. The consideration of the genre leads next to a study of the contents of the *Testament,* viz., a recognition of the "golden thread".

The first section of the *Testament* nn. 1–23 contains a series of reminders recalling the origins of the Franciscan form of life and which are especially indicative of its nature. Undoubtedly the most important of these is the repeated statement: the Lord showed me what to do; no man showed me what to do, but the Lord; and the Lord Pope confirmed this for me. The divine origin of the ideal, of the tradition-heritage, its confirmation by the pope, places it beyond tinkering by men. Only a few years ago Pope Paul VI, contrary to the desires of many friars, reserved the interpretation of the *Rule* to himself as pope. If there are points of the *Rule* subject to change, it is clear that the essence of that life of which the *Rule* is the norm is not subject to change, and the differentiation of these two is not a matter of private judgment of the friars or of the Order.[15]

In essence that form of life is one of penance. The Lord Christ showed Francis how to do penance, first by learning to love lepers, by learning how to find sweetness in sacrifice, in what is naturally repugnant, by learning to love and practice poverty and humility. Then he gave him such faith in churches as to adore Christ there in the mystery of the cross, and then in priests endowed with the power to consecrate the Eucharist. Finally, he showed Francis how to live this life of penance, the "life of the gospel" in common with other brothers, viz., by living strict poverty, living content with the barest necessities, the form of life in common without property (*vita perfecte communis*), by praying the office of the clerics of the Roman Church or of the "Our Father", by doing manual work, not however for gain, but for "example" and by not being ashamed to beg where the absolute necessities were not provided by work.

14. *WK* 486 (I 895).

15. Cf. McDonagh, "History and Background," 62–63.

The character of such a life seen in its origins quite logically explains the exhortation stressing poverty and obedience:[16] a poverty that is content with the minimum material necessities, a poverty orientated toward total abnegation of one's own will in favor of the Lord's as revealed through his vicars in the church and in the Order, which never manipulates a superior to one's own advantage by seeking special dispensations or personal privilege, and which seeks always to be totally loyal to the church and pope.

Taken as a whole the *Testament* affirms the ideal of Saint Francis, an ideal at once the root of every norm and goal within the Order. Even the most summary study of the *Testament* of St. Francis leaves no doubt that his spiritual ideal is doctrinally Christocentric in form and that ascetically speaking its characteristic virtue coloring the exercise of love for God and neighbor is poverty. Equally obvious is the relation of this Christocentrism and gospel poverty to the finality of Francis' vocation: conformity to the Crucified Savior via a life of penance and poverty, as lesser brethren, for the sake of the conversion and sanctification of souls for whom Christ gave his life on the cross, and as he gave it with the same love. As such a love gave origin to the church, such a love would sustain and repair it, above all through the conversion of sinners.

But when that analysis is pressed more in depth, questions are raised concerning the "essence" of that spiritual tradition, the mystery implicit in the description of Francis, and which questions have not always received the same answer, either in theory or in practice.[17] The saints of the Order, whatever their family, knew the answer; and the church has corrected aberrations and exaggerations. But between the "scientia sanctorum Franciscanorum" and the guidance of the Lord Pope there has remained over the centuries an area whose study and clarification is undoubtedly an aid to the better understanding and observance of the *Rule*.

It is, for instance, true that Franciscan spirituality is Christocentric, but so as a matter of fact is every other Catholic spirituality. To affirm that it is enough to distinguish Franciscan spirituality in describing it as Christocentric is in fact to say nothing at all specific, or to identify being Catholic, or observing the gospel life with being Franciscan, a position neither in accord with the truth nor the virtue of humility. To ascribe that distinctiveness to the degree of conformity to the crucified is to state a fact, but hardly to explain the why and the how of this distinctive conformity.

Similarly, difficulties are encountered when poverty, the other distinctive feature of the *Testament* is pondered as the central, distinctive

---

16. *Test.*, nn. 24–39.

17. For examples cf. *Franciscan Educational Conference* 29 (1948) 142.

characteristic of Franciscanism. And indeed, poverty in common is undoubtedly a uniquely Franciscan contribution to religious life in the church, but its interpretation and application in practice has been the occasion of innumerable disagreements and divisions among Franciscans, not excluding a number of interpretations in the fourteenth century condemned as heretical. The root of the error was a conception of poverty as an end in itself rather than a means to an end, namely, perfect charity for God and for neighbor after the example of Christ and Francis. But so conceived, there still remains a considerable range of opinion between a stress on poverty in view of the contemplative aspects of Franciscan life, tending toward a very strict interpretation, and a stress in view of the apostolic inclined to a considerably broader interpretation to favor a more effective apostolate. Historically it has not always been easy to strike a happy balance in practice between the two essential dimensions of Franciscan life, with the consequence that extremes of pious self-righteousness or worldly laxity are often met in the course of that history. The theory of the mixed life is one thing; the achievement of a proper balance in practice quite another. Perhaps this lack of clarity surrounding the interpretation of poverty in practice has over the centuries inclined spiritual writers to place that poverty in relation to one or another of the virtues honored by Saint Francis in his *Salutation to the Virtues* as a key to placing that poverty in correct perspective.

Curiously, no other commentator before St. Maximilian has suggested the mystery or cause of the Immaculate as the key to understanding the distinctive character of Franciscan spirituality, and to the harmonious integration of the contemplative and apostolic in practice. Of course, it has been noted that in no place in his *Testament* does St. Francis mention Mary, much less her Immaculate Conception. At first glance this might appear to militate against the position of St. Maximilian, and confirm the contrast alleged by some to exist between the Christocentrism of St. Francis and the Mariocentrism of Saint Maximilian. Nonetheless, on several counts, the case of Saint Maximilian is, historically speaking, a strong one.

First, the *Testament* of St. Francis can only be regarded as not including Mary if it is considered a kind of taxative description of the Franciscan heritage—which it is not. A comparison with the *Form of Life Given to St. Clare and Her Sisters* clearly indicates the implicit presence of Mary in the *Testament*. In the *Form of Life* St. Francis says that to choose to live according to the Gospel is to choose the Holy Spirit as one's spouse and to make oneself daughter and servant of the most high king and heavenly Father. In the Magnificat antiphon of the *Office of the Passion* it is the Mother of God whom Saint Francis calls par excellence Spouse of the Holy Spirit and daughter of the Father, a title subsequently to be especially associated with the mystery of the Immaculate Conception.[18] In the *Last Will for St. Clare* St. Francis reaffirms his desire to follow the life and poverty of our most high Lord Jesus Christ and his most holy Mother until the end, and exhorts the Poor Clares to do the same. The profession of Franciscan life, viz., as a distinctive way of living the gospel, is a sharing in the life and poverty not only of Christ, but of his Mother as well. In the mind of Francis there is no question of a choice of one or the other, but of both together, exactly what Saint Maximilian says in *WK* 643. Thus, there exist in the mind of St. Francis evident grounds for discovering in the mystery of Mary the root of that Christocentrism and poverty distinctively Franciscan, a root St. Maximilian affirms is the Franciscan thesis, viz., the Immaculate Conception. Thus, it is no accident that the Virgin Mary addressed as full of grace in the *Salutation to the Virgin* is for Francis the epitome (for St. Maximilian the vertex) of a holy life, and that the synthesis of virtues praised at the end of this *Salutation* and its companion piece, the *Salutation to the Virtues,* so similar in style and form, should in fact coincide with the fulness of grace in the Virgin.

One might rephrase this by saying that the ideal of Saint Francis was to love, to adore Jesus as Mary qua Immaculate did and does as the most perfect fruit of that Redemption, with a love that matches as perfectly as possible the love of the divine heart pierced for us on the cross, and to translate that love into a form of life, to "incorporate" it into every fiber of his being by sharing the poverty and humility of Christ as Mary Immaculate did. In view of this our Lord's remark to Saint Margaret Mary Alacoque takes on its true significance: Saint Francis is the saint closest to his heart, precisely because as St. Maximilian saw so clearly it is the Immaculate who loves the Savior and responds to his love in Francis.

In granting St. Francis the grace of this particular vocation, Christ willed de facto the Immaculate *qua talis* to be loved by Francis as Christ loved her and for the same reason, that he might be loved by Francis as she loves him, and that Francis and his followers might love those for whom Christ died as his Mother, the mediatrix of all graces, to whom he entrusted these souls, loves them and seeks their conversion, and sanctification. It is this love that is the source of the greatest of blessings, conversion and perseverance; it is this love that is the "personification" of divine mercy, an espousing of the Holy Spirit. It is in the conversion of sinners above all that the repair of the church is effected, not in some presumptuous attempt to change its divinely appointed structures. It is this love of the Immaculate, penitential in form, because an initial link with the cross, which effects the "cure" of the spiritual leper.

18. Fehlner, "Saint Francis and the Immaculate Conception," *CE* 3, chapter 3.

Quite logically, the contemplative and apostolic aspects of this love can be integrated in a single form of life because both are already so integrated in the single mystery of the Immaculate, mediatrix of all graces and Advocate of the Order. To the extent Franciscan life is led under her aegis, viz., poverty making the community as well as individual friars her possession and obedience without conditions making the community and its members the instrument of her mercy for sinners, to that extent the Franciscan community will faithfully preserve and realize the type set forth in the *Testament*.

From this spring two other considerations undergirding the Kolbean version of Franciscan history, as comprising two great eras, the two "pages", the first recording the elaboration of a plan of apostolic-missionary action on behalf of the church, the second the actual implementation of the plan. The first effectively is focused on the articulation of the Franciscan thesis: the devotion and cultus of Mary qua Immaculate, initiated by St. Francis, and the elaboration of its doctrinal basis, particularly associated with the name of Duns Scotus; and the second still to be completed, the full incorporation of that mystery into life. The dividing line between those two eras is the dogmatic definition of the Immaculate Conception, the formal recognition by the church of that mystery to provide the grounds for the final sanctification of the church, "without wrinkle or spot" (Eph 5:27), in preparation for the consummation of Christ's kingdom.

The mystery of the Immaculate formulated in the dogma of 1854, understood practically, is the cause of the Immaculate, that which is the "golden thread" providing the internal logic of Franciscan history, so much so that without the first step, i.e., the recognition of that mystery as a truth of salvation and its acceptance as the basis of the pastoral-missionary thrust of a new age, and not merely as a matter of private devotion or personal opinion, the second step, i.e., the full realization of that potential for sanctity and sanctification inherent in the Franciscan form of life, is not possible. The question of poverty, of fidelity to the mind of Francis, of the unity and consequent strengthening of the Order would be resolved, according to St. Maximilian, when in fact the cause of the Immaculate was recognized as the heart of Franciscan spirituality and further incorporated into every aspect of its life. In such a perspective Niepokalanów becomes the typical realization of the form of life set forth by St. Francis in his *Testament*. For this reason, the testament of St. Maximilian is not another "testament", but as it were the exegesis of that of St. Francis. The heritage of St. Maximilian is but that of St. Francis, preserved according to type and brought to that degree of perfection appropriate to the needs of the church and of souls at this hour, foreseen by Christ and his Mother in calling Francis to found his Order.

The Testament of St. Maximilian

Two documents, both "reportationes", deserve to be called a kind of testament of St. Maximilian. Indeed, in the first he himself employs the term to describe his talk, and in both he was concerned with the faithful preservation and continuation of a way of life and work, not devised by humankind, but of divine origin, mediated by the Immaculate, and who, in the second he affirms, has given and will continue to give assurance of the worth of this work and the final blessing of eternal life for those who give themselves entirely to this cause. This second "reportatio" bears a conscious relation to our Lord's conversation at the Last Supper on the night before he died. Further, it makes explicit reference to a prior mystical experience, which like the stigmatization of St. Francis brought him a "confirmation in grace", an assurance of everlasting bliss, and the presage of a glorious death, that of a martyr, the highest privilege of those who serve Christ, in the case of Saint Maximilian to witness the manner of love exercised by the Son of God and of Mary in dying for sinners. That mystery, witnessed by his martyrdom, is the mystery of the love of the mediatrix of all graces, the Immaculate. Like the glory of our Lord in his transfiguration, and the stigmata of St. Francis, this grace of St. Maximilian was revealed only to a select few, for their consolation and strengthening, and not to be made public until after his death.

The first of these "reportationes" (from 1933) has immediate antecedents clearly demonstrating the connection in St. Maximilian's thought between the heritage of St. Francis and that which he was handing on to his followers. The evidence for this link is found in two sets of writings of the saint, immediately preceding the 1933 conference in Rome.

1. WK 485, 486, 487 & 1168

These three letters: to his Provincial, to the clerics of the Order and to his Minister General, and an article—in fact an address to all the friars of the Order—originally published in the *Bulletin* of his Province, were all written within the space of a single week, between February 25, 1933 and March 1, 1933. If not exhaustively, nonetheless with sufficient accuracy and detail he sets forth his theory of Franciscan history with its roots in the devotion and belief of St. Francis in the Immaculate Conception. The proximate occasion of these writings was the controversy surrounding the activities and projects of St. Maximilian, centered on Niepokalanów, its missions and formation system, and the proposal on the part of some to "level" these to the form of observance found in other friaries. But the roots of the ideas expressed by the saint considerably antedate this controversy.[19] In these writings, however, they form a genuine synthesis which may be summarized as follows: the cause of the Immaculate has always been at the very heart of the Franciscan tradition, starting with St. Francis. That cause is so linked to the very nature of the "Order of Penance" and apostolate of "penitential preaching" as to be both its source and its goal and norm, its ideal. The growth of the Order and the value of its history turn on this cause: in an initial period on the recognition of that mystery by the church as a dogma of faith, a truth of salvation, and in a second period on the incorporation of that mystery into life. It is in the pursuit of this cause in this second period that the Order will find its ultimate reason for existence, the touchstone of its reform and renewal, the resolution of the question of poverty and of the unity of the Order in achieving unheard of levels of sanctity and apostolic effectiveness under the aegis of the Immaculate. To this end the Immaculate has entrusted to the Order a precious instrument, her Militia (M.I.), and which when applied without limit within the Order itself, takes the form of Niepokalanów—the M.I. in the form of a friary.[20]

Niepokalanów, its style of life, the heroic practice of poverty and obedience, its total and exclusive commitment to the conquest of all souls, particularly those most inimical to the church and to the Immaculate[21] far from being alien or merely incidental to the Franciscan tradition, potentially divisive of the Order, is its purest expression. The reason for this is very simple: the cause of the Immaculate is that of the Order, and that cause the Immaculate has always advanced via the strictest poverty and most perfect supernatural obedience centered on the pope. That cause is the incorporation of the mystery of the Immaculate into life.

What that means has best been stated as follows:

> During her appearance at Lourdes the Immaculate proclaimed in the language of our Order: Penance, Penance, Penance, and thus refreshes the memory of the "Order of Penance," for she wishes, in it and through it, to restrain souls from the road of self-indulgence, to enter into their hearts, to take possession of them, to direct them toward true happiness, toward God, along the way of self-denial, to prepare in them the throne of divine love, of the divine heart, to teach them to love him, to inflame them with love. She wishes to love this very heart in them and

19. For example, a 1918 letter to his brother, friar Alphonse, *WK* 21 (I 35); on the problems of the Order *WK* 1278 (III 668); on proposals for reform *WK* 1342 (III 813–14).

20. *WK* 1380 (III 867).

21. *WK* 300 (I 459); 336 (I 536); 1328 (III 772).

through them, to be them herself and to make them herself. This
is a sketch of the incorporation (into life) of the truth (mystery)
of the Immaculate Conception—merely a sketch, simple and
incomplete, but true.[22]

This, he continues in the same article, is the second page of our history,
beginning now in which all of the Order must belong totally to her—the
souls of the religious, and . . . Niepokalanów. How this is to be realized, how
the Order is to become entirely hers and the entire world and every soul
conquered for her is a question to be put to her.

And the answer, indeed, has been given in the form of the M.I., whose
essence is total, unrestricted consecration to the Immaculate as such, so as
to be her instrument in the conversion of souls, especially those farthest
from the church, and whose emblem is the miraculous medal, i.e., of the
Immaculate, mediatrix of all graces, above all the grace of conversion in the
most difficult of cases. From the moment that the M.I. statute, i.e., M.I. 3,
pervades the Constitutions of the Order, as it pervades Niepokalanów, from
that moment the spirit of St. Francis will be deepened in the Order, as it
is at Niepokalanów, and there will arise within the whole Order a renewed
growth comparable to that experienced at Niepokalanów.[23] For the scope of
Niepokalanów is that of the Immaculate: the conversion and sanctification
of sinners; that is also the scope of the Franciscan Order. It is why Christ
showed Francis how to do penance, viz., with the love of the Immaculate
for his heart, with a love capable of seeking out even the worst sinner. It
is why such a form of life as it develops must tend to a holiness without
limit, and why as it develops it becomes more and more the property of the
Immaculate. Once that occurs, the Order will begin to realize the ultimate
purpose of its existence: to foster a global vision of Catholic life under a new
form, consisting in its links with the Immaculate, our universal mediatrix
with Jesus.[24] This is nothing more or less than the essence of the M.I., in view
of which all its organizational forms are but the subordinate means.

2. The Meditations on the Conte Rosso

Such an analysis places in intimate relation the speculative and practical, the mysteries of faith and the conduct of life, a procedure typical of
Franciscan theology across the centuries, in a very real way evident in the

22. *WK* 1168 (III 361).
23. *WK* 485 (I 891–92).
24. *WK* 1220 (III 491).

Testament of St. Francis. The contemplative side of Franciscanism centers on the mystery of Christ, the practical on the exercise of poverty, or if one wishes the perfect common life modelled on the life of the poor Christ and his Mother. The purpose of Franciscanism is the repair of the church through the conversion of sinners. This style of theological reflection on the mysteries of salvation is calculated to foster just that kind of love and devotion whose ultimate aspiration is to be a victim with Christ, and to enjoy the grace and privilege of martyrdom in the cause of his mission. It is the genius of St. Maximilian to have seen clearly that Franciscan Christocentrism in thought and Franciscan poverty in practice for the sake of Christ's kingdom both converge on a single distinctive factor: the mystery of the Immaculate, which as the "golden thread" of the Franciscan tradition in practical terms is her cause. This is what Christ willed in willing the Franciscan Order, because this is what the Immaculate, the mediatrix of all graces, the advocate of the Order and mother of mercy, requested of her Son for the sake of sinners. The miraculous medal is the badge of the M.I., crystalizing its essence and purpose in the same way as the Portiuncula indulgence crystalizes the entire tenor of Francis' life with the Queen of the Angels: mercy for mankind and love for Jesus crucified. For this reason the three meditations[25] made on the Conte Rosso in 1933 during his return to Poland for a provincial chapter and recorded in his diary, are particularly important for appreciating the "testament" of 1933.

The first meditation on the mystery of the Immaculate Conception begins with a reflection on the Angelic Salutation. Being full of grace the Immaculate as such in a certain, but real way, is a part of the Trinity, inseparable and unthinkable apart from the divine persons in the economy of salvation, as they are from each other in eternity.[26] All that occurs in the universe occurs "in the name of the Father, and of the Son and of the Holy Spirit through the Immaculate." "The divinity in some way from eternity flows from the Father to the Son and from Father and Son unto the Holy Spirit; in time from the Trinity there flows into the Mother of God, of Jesus, the prototype of the perfect, holy man, the God-man. According to this model saints are formed, i.e., through Mary Immaculate." "Without her neither God nor Jesus is present; wherever she is present, there is present the Trinity, Jesus. To be guided always by her is to return evermore to the serenity of love."

---

25. *WK* 991 O (II 888–89); 991 Q (II 894–97); 991 R (II 898–900).
26. *WK* 643 (II 202).

The practical import: the Immaculate as such is the universal mediatrix,[27] the personification of God's redemptive mercy,[28] as the perfect fruit of a perfect redemption, whose central aim is the conversion and salvation of every soul by means of that mercy, to the praise of the glory of the mercy of him who has done great things for her. The Immaculate is the perfect fruit of a perfect redemption as the fruit of the mutual love of Father and Word Incarnate in the Holy Spirit. It is above all her first privilege of Immaculate Conception, the first fruit of a perfect redemption, so stressed by St. Maximilian,[29] which links the Virgin Mother uniquely to the cross, viz., associates her in a special and definitive and active way with the bases of the economy of salvation, making her coredemptrix-mediatrix, and thus a part of the economic Trinity. The mystery of the Immaculate Conception is the basis, then, of the mystery of the cooperation of creation in general and mankind in particular with the Redeemer in bringing glory to the Father and the entire Trinity, and centers on the perfection of her "fiat," the perfect reaction to the "fiat" of the Creator.

The second meditation concerns the M.I., the mystery as it were of the extension of that cooperation with the Savior to the rest of his brethren. In practical terms the mystery of the Immaculate Conception is the sanctity of a cause, the scope of her existence: love and mercy for souls, a mercy to be exercised not in isolation, but through and with those reborn of water and the Holy Spirit, viz., her spiritual children.[30] The scope of the M.I. is the formation of such a communion of souls in which the Immaculate acts in and through its members, loves Jesus in converting others through them who in turn love Jesus, especially in the mystery of the Eucharist, with her heart, her love, i.e., with a love truly pure and free from defect. To this end the M.I. is constructed, its essence consisting in total consecration and its "sacramental" the miraculous medal. Its scope is nothing less than the conquest of the world for the Immaculate,[31] and the promotion of a deeper and more global vision of Catholic life, and consequently the cultivation in particular of every aspect of the interior life in view of the mystery of the Immaculate.[32] As in theology, so in spirituality and in the apostolate the mystery of the Immaculate is the key, the "foundational treatise". And because it is a question of salvation and the

27. *WK* 339 (I 541–2); 1331 (III 787).
28. *WK* 339 (I 541–2); 1331 (III 787).
29. *WK* 1331 (III 786); 1292 (III 691).
30. *WK* 1326 (III 769).
31. *WK* 1330 (III 782).
32. *WK* 1220 (III 491).

enemy of Christ has increased his efforts to snatch souls from the Savior, the work of the M.I. is that much more pressing.

The third meditation concerns the Order, in particular the poverty and obedience proper to it. To bring the M.I. and the Franciscan Order into relation with one another, to make of this relation not merely a conjunction, or juxtapositioning, as at Grodno where the M.I. was attached to a friary, but rather a living symbiosis as at Niepokalanów where the M.I. took the form of a friary,[33] is to provide the M.I. with its dynamic center and the Order with its source of renewal. Not only the problem of money and its proper use by Franciscans, but the more basic questions of poverty and obedience (linked also in the *Testament* of St. Francis), how they are to be conceived and practiced, will be resolved in making the entire community and each of its members the total possession and property of the Immaculate, when in fact community and members are devoted totally to one cause, hers, under her direction, without limit, because out of love for her, and when because of her love in them poverty in common, the reduction of all personal needs to a bare minimum and the exercise of heroic, supernatural obedience are no longer a chore, but a joy and a privilege. For where such is the case, viz., at Niepokalanów, the ideal is not a vision to be realized or recalled, but a person already present: the Immaculate.[34] The Franciscan community life so lived marks the turning point from the first page of Franciscan history with all its accomplishments to the second page.

With this in mind one can understand why the Testament St. Maximilian spoke of at the end of this voyage can be summarized in one word: Niepokalanów—to be of the Immaculate. This is his heritage, and it is a heritage no different from that of St. Francis.

3. *The Testaments*

In the "testament" of 1933 St. Maximilian speaks of his approaching death and of the obligation of his confreres, his heirs, to continue to dedicate themselves to the work of the M.I., without restriction, without limits. In the face of every sacrifice they are to promote the M.I. to the farthest corners of the world, because this is a holy cause, the will of the Mother of God that the Order which once promoted the knowledge of her Immaculate Conception for her, should also diffuse her cult under that title (viz., the incorporation of this mystery into life).

33. *WK* 1376 (III 857–58); 1380 (III 867).
34. *WK* 1210 (III 474–76).

Two points deserve attention. St. Maximilian places his work in line with that of St. Francis in founding the Order, a work not to cease with his death, or to be considered appropriate only to certain times and places, not because it is his choice of work, but that of the Immaculate, who asked for the Order for this very purpose. It is her will, so perfectly one with that of the three divine persons, which makes of the M.I. as of the Order a single holy cause, and merits for St. Maximilian a special place alongside St. Francis.

Second, St. Maximilian's heirs are obliged to heroism in their manner of observing the Rule, particularly in respect to poverty and obedience.[35] Only such heroism can meet the desires of St. Francis that his sons do "their part," aim at a sanctity without limit, a height of perfection the Immaculate will accomplish in those totally consecrated to her, because her Immaculate Conception is the ideal of virtue which brought Francis so close to the sacred heart. That ideal postulates the gospel life of penance, of poverty, obedience and humility as its connatural form in this time of pilgrimage, a form pleasing to God, who looked kindly on the humility of his handmaid, and attractive to sinners drawing them to the love of Jesus.

The "testament" of 1937 clearly serves a similar purpose. Recorded in writing only many years after the occasion taken by St. Maximilian to reveal a very special grace, the account recalls the setting, even the phraseology of our Lord at the Last Supper, and the preoccupation that his heirs, those especially chosen by the Immaculate for this and to whom the Holy Spirit had granted the special privilege of a deep understanding of the mystery of his spouse should enjoy some special assurance of the holiness of the cause to which they were totally consecrated, and an encouragement to persevere in loving the Immaculate. That mark of encouragement is the confidence, not to be revealed until after his death, that the Immaculate had assured him, their Father Guardian, of his salvation, a private revelation clearly confirming the sanctity of the cause promoted in her name, as the subsequent beatification and canonization in their own way serve as a public confirmation.

If, then, it is fair to say with Fr. Bede Hess, a Minister General of the Order,[36] that no friary so perfectly exemplified what St. Francis intended to achieve by the observance of his Rule as Niepokalanów, it is also fair to say that the "testament" of St. Maximilian makes explicit what is implicit in that of St. Francis: the Immaculate, or better the cause of the Immaculate, that which is dearest to her heart because it is the will of her Son, which when realized within the Order can be expressed in one word: Niepokalanów, where contemplative love for the crucified Savior and

---

35. *WK* 299 (I 454); 300 (I 459); 1190 (III 415–17).

36. *Beatificationis et Canonizationis*, 204–5.

apostolic-missionary zeal for the conversion of sinners and non-believers
are perfectly integrated in the love of the Immaculate.

At the end of his *Testament* St. Francis wrote:

> Whoever shall have observed these things may he be filled in
> heaven with the blessing of the most high Father and on earth
> with the blessing of his beloved Son with the most Holy Spirit
> the Paraclete and with all the powers of heaven and all the
> saints. And I, little brother Francis, your servant, in as much
> as I can, confirm for you this most holy blessing both within
> and without.[37]

That blessing came upon Niepokalanów, already within the lifetime
of St. Maximilian, and on each and every Niepokalanów subsequently
founded and conducted according to the same spirit and norms, flourishing amidst trials and opposition, truly a foretaste of paradise, the garden
of the Immaculate.

Conclusion

Why, to what purpose Niepokalanów, all this effort?[38] To a fair question, a
fair answer. St. Maximilian believed the fair answer was to be sought from
the Immaculate, and that her answer had been given with sufficient clarity
in the history of the Order read against that Immaculatist tradition, that
"golden thread" whose origin was none other than St. Francis, and whose
meaning was becoming clearer and clearer in the Marian events since the
apparitions in the Rue du Bac in 1830, the dogmatic definition of 1854 and
the apparitions at Lourdes in 1858.

Past generations of Franciscans have done their work. It remains to
complete the work building on those solid foundations of penance, an
effort confirmed as it were by the church in proclaiming the dogma of
the Immaculate Conception. The completion of that work is none other
than the incorporation of the dogma into life, first of all into Franciscan
life. How is that to be done? Ask our Lady, he repeats. In fact, the method
of the Immaculate is the M.I.: total consecration. When the M.I. exists
not merely aside a friary, or province, but takes the form of a friary or
province, there will be found the meaning of incorporation in practice
and the dynamic center for its realization throughout the world, i.e., for

37 Francis, *Test.*, n. 40.
38. *WK* 1168 (III 359, 361).

the conquest of the world for the Immaculate, so that it might truly be worthy of the love of the Savior.

Hence, Niepokalanów, far from being a dated or dubious project of the past, is a postulate of authentic Franciscanism in the age of the Holy Spirit, of the church, of the Immaculate, to be preserved and fostered as St. Maximilian conceived it: res et proprietas Immaculatae, with the right and duty to expand throughout the world by establishing other Niepokalanów, wherever the cause of the Immaculate requires this in order that she be known and loved. For a Niepokalanów is the natural center of that cause, wherever it flourishes. All this in fidelity to St. Francis, to the Advocate of the Order and her Spouse whom St. Francis once called General of the Order.[39]

For this, two things viewed by St. Maximilian as necessary[40] are still so. First the Niepokalanów must have the right and ability to conduct their own formation program, for the demands of heroism normally require a special preparation. Until the mystery of the Immaculate should be completely incorporated into every fiber of the Order, such a preparation can only be available if offered at a Niepokalanów. Second, the various Niepokalanów should be united so as to form within the Order a Province or Provinces, so as to increase their influence as well as strengthen their spirit, within and without, until as St. Maximilian foresaw, the spirit of the Immaculate would have transformed the entire Order, not merely the Conventual family, but all Franciscan families, providing about the standard of the Immaculate a new and profounder unity among brothers all working for the same goal, all inspired by the same love and all governed by the same ideal: the Immaculate, the measure of their love for the divine heart and for his triumph in the hearts of all. This is the wonder of Niepokalanów: not a place of miracles, but the miracle itself.[41]

39. 2 Cel. 193. Cf. Fehlner, "A Thesis," CE 6, chapter 2.

40. WK 336 (I 536); 485 (I 891).

41. Cf. the testimony of Br. Cyprian Grodzki, Beatificationis et Canonizationis, 177, where St. Maximilian is reported as saying during a meditation in common that God does not will Niepokalanów to become a place of miracles.

Bibliography

Alastruey, Gregorio. *Tratado de la Virgen Santísima*. Madrid: Editorial Católica, 1956.

Alimondi, Gaetano. *Il dogma dell'Immacolata: Ragionamenti*. Genova: Tipografia di Gaetano Schenone successore Frugoni, 1856.

Alonso, Joaquín María. "Hacia una Mariología Trinitaria: Dos Escuelas," *Estudios Marianos* 10 (1950) 141–91.

Amato, Angelo. "Lo Spirito Santo e Maria nella ricerca teologica odierna delle varie confessioni cristiane in occidente." In *Maria e lo Spirito Santo. Atti del 4° Simposio Mariologico Internazionale (Roma, ottobre 1982)*, 9–103. Rome: Marianum, 1984.

Anasagasti, Pedro de. "Principios teologicos de la piedad mariana de San Francisco de Asis." *Estudios Marianos* 48 (1983) 391–441.

Antonelli, Ferdinando. *La Madonna nella Spiritualità Francescana. Quaderni di Spiritualità Francescana* 5. Assisi: Santa Maria degli Angeli, 1963.

Armstrong, Regis J. *Clare of Assisi: Early Documents—The Lady*. Hyde Park, NY: New City Press, 2006.

Armstrong, Regis J., and Ignatius C. Brady, editors. *Francis and Clare: The Complete Works*. New York: Paulist, 1982.

Armstrong, Regis J., J.A. Wayne Hellmann, and William J. Short, eds. *Francis of Assisi: Early Documents—Volume II: The Founder*. New York: New City Press, 2001.

Balić, Charles, ed. *Virgo Immaculata*, vol. 7: *De Immaculata Conceptione in Ordine S. Francisci*. Rome: Academia Mariana Internationalis, 1957.

Balthasar, Hans Urs von. *First Glance at Adrienne von Speyr*. San Francisco: Ignatius Press, 1981.

Beaini, Pierre. "Le Mystère de l'Immaculée Conception dans les écrits du Père Maximilien Kolbe." *Miles Immaculatae* 22 (1986) 346–58.

Beatificationis et Canonizationis Servi Dei Maximiliani M. Kolbe, Sacerdotis Professi Ordinis Fratrum Minorum Conventualium: Positio Super Virtutibus, vol. 2. Ecclesia Catholica, Sacra Rituum Congregatio. Rome: Typis Guerra et Belli, 1966.

Bengoechea, Ismael. "María, Esposa o Sagrario del Espíritu Santo?" *Ephemerides Mariologicae* 28 (1978) 339–51.

Benoit, Ignace-M., and Ephrem Longpré. *Le Chevalier de Notre-Dame-des-Anges*. Montreal: Editions Franciscaines, 1952.

Bethell, Tom. "Agnostic Evolutionists: The Taxonomic Case Against Darwin," *Harper's*, February 1985, 49–61.

Bierbaum, Athanasius. *Der hl. Franziskus von Assisi und die Gottesmutter*. Paderborn: Junfermann, 1904.

Bittremieux, Joseph. "Relationes Beatissimae Virginis ad personas Ss. Trinitatis." *Divus Thomas* 38 (1935) 6–41.

Blasucci, Antonio. "Francesco d'Assisi." In *Dizionario Enciclopedico di Spiritualità*, vol. 2, edited by Ermanno Ancilli, 793–4. Rome: Studium, 1975.

———. *Il Celeste Pegno della Madonna: La Medaglia Miracolosa.* Padua: Centro Nazionale M. I. Basilica Del Santo, 1944.

———. "Note caratteristiche della pietà mariana nella ascetica francescana." In *La Madonna nella Spiritualità Francescana. Quaderni di Spiritualità Francescana* 5, 76–87. Assisi: Santa Maria degli Angeli, 1963.

Bonaventure. *Breviloquium.* In vol. 5 of Opera Omnia, 201–91. Florence: Ad Claras Aquas, 1891.

———. *Christus unus omnium magister.* In vol. 5 of Opera Omnia, 567–79. Florence: Ad Claras Aquas, 1891.

———. *Collations on the Seven Gifts of the Holy Spirit.* St. Bonaventure: Franciscan Institute, 2008.

———. *Collationes de septem donis Spiritus Sancti.* In vol. 5 of Opera Omnia, 457–503. Florence: Ad Claras Aquas, 1891.

———. *Collationes in Hexaëmeron.* In vol. 5 of Opera Omnia, 329–454. Florence: Ad Claras Aquas, 1891.

———. *Commentarius in evangelium S. Lucae.* Vol. 7 of Opera Omnia. Florence: Ad Claras Aquas, 1895.

———. *Commentarius in IV libros Sententiarum.* In vols. 1–4 of Opera Omnia. Florence: Ad Claras Aquas, 1882–89.

———. *Itinerarium mentis in Deum.* In vol. 5 of Opera Omnia, 295–313. Florence: Ad Claras Aquas, 1891.

———. *Legenda maior.* In vol. 8 of Opera Omnia, 504–564. Florence: Ad Claras Aquas, 1898.

Borella, Jean. *La charité profanée: subversion de l'âme chrétienne.* Paris: Cèdre, 1979.

Brlek, Mijo. "Legislatio Ordinis Fratrum Minorum de Immaculata Conceptione B.V.M." *Antonianum* 29 (1954) 3–44.

Brown, Raphael. *Our Lady and St. Francis. All the Earliest Texts Compiled and Translated.* Chicago: Franciscan Herald Press, 1954.

Caldecott, Stratford. "In Search of a New Way." *Inside the Vatican*, October 1994, 49–55.

Calkins, Arthur B. *Totus Tuus: Pope Saint John Paul II's Program of Marian Consecration and Entrustment.* New Bedford: Academy of the Immaculate, 2017.

Calvo Moralejo, Gaspar. "La Piedad Mariana en San Francisco de Asis y la exhortación apostólica 'Marialis Cultus.'" *Estudios Marianos* 43 (1978) 301–31.

Campana, Emilio. *Maria nel culto cattolico*, 2 vols. Turin: Marietti, 1933.

———. *Maria nel Dogma Cattolico*, 2nd ed., revised. Turin: Marietti, 1923.

Carreyre, Jean. "Jean-Jacques-Auguste Nicolas." In *Dictionnaire de Théologie Catholique*, edited by Vacant, Alfred, vol. 11, pt. 1, coll. 548–55. Paris: Letouzey et Ané, 1931.

Carroll, Warren H. *1917: Red Banners, White Mantle.* Front Royal, VA: Christendom, 1981.

Chesterton, G. K. *Collected Works*, vol. 5. *The Outline of Sanity.* San Francisco: Ignatius Press, 1987.

———. *St. Thomas Aquinas-St. Francis of Assisi.* San Francisco: Ignatius, 2002.

Christian, Eugène. *Our Lady. Devotion to Mary in the Franciscan Tradition.* Chicago: Franciscan Herald Press, 1954.

Congar, Yves Marie-Joseph. *Je Crois en l'Esprit Saint*. Paris: Éditions du Cerf, 1981–83.

Conrad of Saxony. *Speculum Beatae Mariae Virginis Fr. Conradi a Saxonia*. Ad Claras Aquas: Collegii S. Bonaventurae, 1904.

Conrad of Saxony and Pedro de Alcántara Martínez. *Speculum seu Salutatio Beatae Mariae Virginis ac Sermones Mariani*. Grottaferrata: Collegii S. Bonaventura ad Claras Aquas, 1975.

Contenson, Vincent. *Theologia Mentis et Cordis*. Augustae Taurinorum: Guibert & Orgeas, 1769.

Conti, Martino. "Testamento di San Francesco." In *Dizionario Francescano spiritualità*, edited by Ernesto Caroli and Ginepro Zoppetti, cc. 1805–26. Padua: Messeggero, 1983.

Dante, Henrico. *Patavina seu Cracovien: beatificationis et canonizationis servi Dei Maximiliani M. Kolbe sacredotis professi ordinis fratrum minorum conventualium: positio super virtutibus*, vol. 2. Rome: Guerra e Belli, 1966.

Darricau, Raymond. "Nicolas." In *Catholicisme*, edited by Gérard Mathon and Gérard-Henry Baudry, vol. 9, coll. 1247–9. Paris: Letouzey et Ané, 1980.

d'Argentan, Louis-François. *Conférences théologiques et spirituelles sur les grandeurs de la Très-Sainte-Vierge Marie, Mère de Dieu*. Paris: Albanel, 1842.

de la Cerda, José. *Maria Effigies, Revelatioque Trinitatis, et Attributorum Dei*. Almeriae: Ex Typographia Episcopali, 1640.

de Provin, Clovis. "Notre-Dame de la Trinité," *Études Franciscaines* 44 (1932) 385–400.

———. *Notre-Dame de la Trinité: d'après la Théologie, l'Art et la Mystique avec citations des Pères et des Docteurs de l'Eglise*. Blois: Grande Imprimerie de Blois, 1932.

de Vega, Cristoval. *Theologia Mariana*. Neapoli: Bibliopola Bibliothecae Catholicae, 1866.

Di Caccia, Francesco. "Il 'Saluto alla Vergine' e la pietà mariana di Francesco d'Assisi." *Studi Francescani* 79 (1982) 55–64.

———. "Il senso dell'Immacolata' nella Madre di Dio di Francesco d'Assisi." *L'Italia Francescana* 58 (1983) 529–34.

DiFiores, Stefano. "Come presentare la spiritualità di S. Massimiliano Kolbe." In *San Massimiliano Kolbe e la nuova evangelizzazione: atti del Congresso internazionale, Niepokalanów, Polonia, 19–25 settembre 1994*, 407–27. Rome: Centro Internazionale Milizia dell'Immacolata, 1999.

———. "Mariologia / Marialogia." In *Nuovo Dizionario di Mariologia*, edited by Stefano di Fiores and Salvatore Meo, 891–920. Cinisello Balsamo: Edizioni Paoline, 1985.

DiFonzo, Lorenzo. *Doctrina S. Bonaventurae de universali mediatione B. Virginis Mariae*. Romae: Pontificia Facultas Theologica O.F.M. Conv., 1938.

———. *La formazione romana del Padre Kolbe*. Roma: Miscellanea Francescana, 1985.

———. *L'immagine di S. Francesco nei Sermoni e nell vita del Fasani: con selezione del testo originale latino dell'intero Sermonario del Fasani*. Bari: Comitato Esecutivo Regionale, 1986.

———. "Le radici storiche e dottrinali del pensiero kolbiano." In *La Mariologia di S. Massimiliano Kolbe: Atti del Congresso Internazionale Roma, 8–12 ottobre 1984*, 11–205. Rome: Miscellanea Francescana, 1985.

Domanski, Giorgio (Jerzy). *Il Pensiero Mariano di P. Massimiliano M. Kolbe*. Rome: Centro Nazionale M. I., 1971.

———. "La genesi del pensiero mariano di S. Massimiliano Kolbe." *Miles Immaculatae* 20 (1984) 246–76.

————. "Lo Spirito e la forma nella M.I." *Collegamento e d'Informazione M.I.* 15 (1983) 50–58.

————. "Lourdes et le Père Maximilien Kolbe. Esquisse de sa mariologie." *Miscellanea Francescana* 58 (1958) 195–224.

————. "Milizia dell'Immacolata del primo grado." *Collegamento e d'Informazione M.I.* 16 (1984) 7–20.

————. "Niepokalanów nella visione e realizzazione di S. Massimiliano M. Kolbe." *Miles Immaculatae* 20 (1984) 378–96.

————. *Per la Vita del Mondo: San Massimiliano M. Kolbe e l'Eucarestia.* Roma: Centro Internazionale M. I., 1982. [English: *For the Life of the World: Saint Maximilian and the Eucharist.* New Bedford: Academy of the Immaculate, 1999.]

Dominguez, Olegario. "La acción común del Espíritu Santo y María en la obra de santificación y en la vida de la Iglesia." *Ephemerides Mariologicae* 28 (1978) 215–37.

Esser, Kajetan. *Die opuscula des hl. Franziskus von Assisi.* Grottaferrata: Editiones Collegii S. Bonaventurae ad Claras Aquas, 1976.

————. "Franziskus von Assisi und die Kattarer seiner Zeit." *Archivum Franciscanum Historicum* 51 (1958) 225–64.

————. "Die Marien Frommigkeit des hl. Franziskus von Assisi." *Wissenschaft und Weisheit* 17 (1954) 176–90. English Translation: "Mary in the Spirituality of St. Francis." In Esser, Kajetan, *Repair My House,* 131–54. Chicago: Franciscan Herald Press, 1963.

————. "Sancta Mater Ecclesia Romana: Die Kirchenfrommigkeit des hl. Franziskus von Assisi." *Wissenschaft und Weisheit* 24 (1961) 1–26.

————. *Temi Spirituali.* Milan: Biblioteca Francescana, 1973.

Feckes, Carl. "Die Gottesmutterschaft." In Sträter, Paul, *Katholische Marienkunde.* II. *Maria in der Glaubenswissenschaft,* 13–100. Paderborn: Schöningh, 1947.

Fehlner, Peter Damian. "Complementum Ss. Trinitatis," in *Miles Immaculatae* 21 (1985) 177–203. Appears in the present volume.

————. The Conventual Charism: A Historical and Contemporary View, 1987. Unpublished Manuscript, Collected Papers of Peter Damian Fehlner. Appears in volume five of the *Collected Essays of Peter Damian Fehlner, OFM Conv: Ecclesiology and the Franciscan Charism.*

————. "De metaphysica mariana quaedam." *Immaculata Mediatrix* 1/2 (2001) 13–42. Appears in volume one of the *Collected Essays of Peter Damian Fehlner, OFM Conv: Marian Metaphysics.*

————. "The Immaculate and the Mystery of the Trinity in the Thought of St. Maximilian Kolbe," *Miscellanea Francescana* 85 (1985) 382–416. Appears in the present volume.

————. "Il Mistero della Corredenzione secondo il Dottore Serafico San Bonaventura." In *Maria Corredentrice. Storia e Teologia II,* 11–91. Frigento: Casa Mariana Editrice, 1999. Appears in volume four of *Collected Essays of Peter Damian Fehlner, OFM Conv: Bonaventure, Johns Duns Scotus, and the Franciscan Tradition.*

————. "In the Beginning." *Christ to the World* 33 (1988), 56–72; 150–64; 237–48. Appears in volume seven of the *Collected Essays of Peter Damian Fehlner, OFM Conv: Theology of Creation.*

————. Introduction to Bonaventure, *The Triple Way.* New Bedford: Academy of the Immaculate, 2012.

———. "La mariologia di San Francesco Antonio Fasani nel 'Mariale' e nelle '7 Novene Mariane.'" In Francis Anthony Fasani, St., *Le 7 Novene Mariane*, 265–304. Padova: Messaggero, 1986. Appears in volume three of the *Collected Essays of Peter Damian Fehlner, OFM Conv: Franciscan Mariology—Francis, Clare, and Bonaventure*.

———. "Maria nella tradizione francescana: 'la Vergine fatta Chiesa.'" *Miles Immaculatae* 17 (1981) 180–98. Appears as "Mary in the Franciscan Tradition: "The Virgin Made Church," in volume three of the *Collected Essays of Peter Damian Fehlner, OFM Conv: Franciscan Mariology—Francis, Clare, and Bonaventure*.

———. "The Marian Issue in the Church." *Missio Immaculatae International* 16/1 (2020) 24–31.

———. "Mary and Theology: Scotus Revisited." In *The Newman-Scotus Reader: Contexts and Commonalities*, edited by Edward J. Ondrako. New Bedford: Academy of the Immaculate, 2015. Appears in volume one of the *Collected Essays of Peter Damian Fehlner, OFM Conv: Marian Metaphysics*.

———. "Scotus and Newman in Dialogue." In *The Newman-Scotus Reader: Contexts and Commonalities*, edited by Edward J. Ondrako, 111–80. New Bedford: Academy of the Immaculate, 2015. Appears in volume eight of the *Collected Essays of Peter Damian Fehlner, OFM Conv: Studies Systematic and Critical*.

———. "Niepokalanów in the Counsels of the Immaculate." *Miles Immaculatae* 21 (1985) 309–52. Appears in the present volume.

———. Opening Address. In *Bl. John Duns Scotus and His Mariology Commemoration of the Seventh Centenary of His Death, Acts of the Symposium on Scotus' Mariology, Grey College, Durham-England*, edited by Peter D. Fehlner, 13–17. New Bedford: Academy of the Immaculate, 2008. Appears in volume four of the *Collected Essays of Peter Damian Fehlner, OFM Conv: Bonaventure, John Duns Scotus, and the Franciscan Tradition*.

———. "The Other Page." *Miles Immaculatae* 24 (1988) 512–30. Appears in the present volume.

———. "Redemption, Metaphysics and the Immaculate Conception." In *Mary at the Foot of the Cross-V*, edited by Peter Damian Fehlner, 186–262. New Bedford: Academy of the Immaculate, 2005. Appears in volume one of the *Collected Essays of Peter Damian Fehlner, OFM Conv: Marian Metaphysics*.

———. Review of *Dio mia tenerezza*, by René Laurentin. *Miles Immaculatae* 24 (1988) 535–37.

———. Review of *First Glance at Adrienne von Speyr*, by Hans Urs von Balthasar. *Faith and Reason* 9 (1983) 69–75.

———. Review of *Maria Terra Vergine*, by Emmanuele Testa. *Miles Immaculatae* 22 (1986) 402–7.

———. *The Role of Charity in the Ecclesiology of St. Bonaventure*. Rome: Miscellanea Francescana, 1965. Appears in volume three of the *Collected Essays of Peter Damian Fehlner, OFM Conv: Franciscan Mariology—Francis, Clare, and Bonaventure*.

———. "Scientia et Pietas." *Immaculata Mediatrix* 1/3 (2001) 11–48. Appears in volume one of the *Collected Essays of Peter Damian Fehlner, OFM Conv: Marian Metaphysics*.

———. "St. Francis and Mary Immaculate." *Miscellanea Francescana* 82 (1982) 502–19. Appears in volume three of the *Collected Essays of Peter Damian Fehlner, OFM Conv: Franciscan Mariology—Francis, Clare, and Bonaventure*.

————. *St. Maximilian Ma. Kolbe, Martyr of Charity – Pneumatologist: His Theology of the Holy Spirit.* New Bedford: Academy of the Immaculate, 2004.

————. *The Theologian of Auschwitz: St. Maximilian M. Kolbe on the Immaculate Conception in the Life of the Church.* Hobe Sound, FL: Lectio, 2019.

————. "The Two Testaments," *Miles Immaculatae* 21 (1985) 354–80. Appears in the present volume.

————. "Una tesi di S. Massimiliano su S Francesco e l'Immacolata alla luce della ricerca recente." *Miles Immaculatae* 20 (1984) 165–86. Appears in the present volume as "A Thesis of St. Maximilian Concerning St. Francis and the Immaculate in the Light of the Recent Research."

————. "Vertex Creationis: St. Maximilian and Evolution." *Miles Immaculatae* 21 (1985) 236–58. Appears in the present volume.

Fernandez, Domiciano. "El Espiritu Santo y María. Algunos Ensayos de Explicación." *Ephemerides Mariologicae* 28 (1978) 137–50.

————. "El Espíritu Santo y María en la obra de L. Boff." In *Maria e lo Spirito Santo. Atti del 4° Simposio Mariologico Internazionale (Roma, ottobre 1982),* 303–23. Rome: Marianum, 1984.

Fasani, Francis Anthony. *Le 7 Novene Mariane.* Padua: Messaggero, 1986.

————. *Mariale. Interpretazione allegorico-spirituale del Cantico dei Cantici: con appendice di altri testi biblici.* Padua: Messaggero, 1986.

Gagnan, Dominique. "Le symbole de la femme chez saint Francois d'Assisi." *Laurentianum* 18 (1977) 256–91.

————. "Typologie de la Pauvreté chez Saint François d'Assise: l'Epouse, la Dame, la Mère." *Laurentianum* 18 (1977) 469–522.

García Garcés, Narciso. *Títulos y grandezas de María o éplicación teológico-popular de los misterios y prerrogativas de la celestial señora.* Madrid: Coculsa, 1940

Garriguet, Louis. *La Vierge Marie: sa prédestination, sa dignité, ses privilèges, son rôle, ses vertus, ses mérites, sa gloire, son intercession, son culte.* Paris: Pierre Téqui, 1933.

Gay, Peter. *The Enlightenment.* 2 volumes. New York: Knopf, 1966–69.

Geiger, Angelo. "A Tribute to Fr. Peter Damian Fehlner." *Missio Immaculatae International* 15/3 (2019) 21–25.

————. "'In the Counsels of the Immaculate': Peter Damian Fehlner's Contribution to the Renewal of Franciscan Immaculatism." In *The Spirit and the Church: Peter Damian Fehlner's Development of Vatican II on the Themes of the Holy Spirit, Mary and the Church: Festschrift,* edited by J. Isaac Goff, Christiaan W. Kappes, and Edward J. Ondrako, 58–76. Eugene: Pickwick, 2018.

————. *St. Maximilian Kolbe's Marian Vow.* Unpublished Manuscript.

————. "The Tending of God's Garden: The Coredemption and the Culture of Life." In *Mary at the Foot of the Cross,* vol. 1, 119–53. New Bedford: Academy of the Immaculate, 2000.

Ghinato, Alberto. "La Madonna nella pietà e nella vita di San Francesco." In *La Madonna nella Spiritualità Francescana. Quaderni di Spiritualità Francescana* 5, 41–56. Assisi: Santa Maria degli Angeli, 1963.

Godts, François-Xavier. *Marie Complément de Toute la T. S. Trinité.* Esschen: S. Alphonse, 1926.

Goff, J. Isaac. *Caritas in Primo: A Study of Bonaventure's Disputed Questions on the Mystery of the Trinity.* New Bedford: Academy of the Immaculate, 2015.

Goretti-Miniati, Cesare. *Elementi di Fisica.* Rome: Cuggiani, 1907–9.

Grignion de Montfort, Louis Marie. *True Devotion to the Blessed Virgin*. Translated by Frederick W. Faber. New York: P. J. Kennedy, 1909.

Guitton, Jean. "Convergenze Mariane di due Testimoni del nostro tempo." *Miles Immaculatae* 18 (1982) 2–4.

Hebblethwaite, Peter. "St. Maximilian Kolbe's Doubtful Spirituality," *National Catholic Reporter*, October 1, 1982, 7–8.

Hopkins, Gerard Manley. *Duns Scotus's Oxford*. In *Poems of Gerard Manley Hopkins*. Oxford: Oxford University Press, 1952

Jaki, Stanley. *Genesis 1 Through the Ages*. London: Thomas More Press, 1992.

Janssens, Aloïs. *De Heilige Maagd en Moeder Gods Maria*. III, *De Heerligkheden van het Goddelijk Moederschap*. Antwerp: Standaard-Boekhandel, 1928.

Janssens, Laurentius. *Tractatus de Deo-Homine sive De Verbo Incarnato; Pars II: Mariologia, Soteriologia*. Freiburg im Breisgau: Herder, 1902.

Jean de Dieu. "La Vierge e l'Ordre des Frères Mineurs." In *Études sur le sainte Vierge*, vol. 2, edited by Hubert du Manoir, 785–831. Paris: Beauchesne et ses Fils, 1952.

Jérome de Paris. *La Doctrine Mariale de Saint Laurent de Brindes: Étude théologique*. Rome: Curie Généralice des Frères Mineurs Capucins, 1933.

John Duns Scotus. *Doctoris Subtilis et Mariani Ioannis Duns Scoti Ordinis Fratrum Minorum opera omnia*, 14 vols. Edited by Charles Balic, Barnaba Hechich, et al. Rome: Typis Vaticanis, 1950–2013.

John Paul. II. *Tertio millenia adveniente*. Boston: Pauline, 1994.

Johnson, J. W. G. *The Crumbling Theory of Evolution*. Brisbane: Queensland Binding Service, 1982.

Joseph de Sainte Marie. *La Vierge du Mont-Carmel. Mystère et Prophétie: Élie, Thérèse d'Avila, Fatima*. Paris: Lethielleux, 1985.

Kalvelage, Francis Mary. *Kolbe, Saint of the Immaculata*. New Bedford: Academy of the Immaculate, 2001.

Kleinschmidt, Beda. *Maria und Franziskus von Assisi in Kunst und Geschichte*. Düsseldorf: Schwann, 1926.

Klotz, John W. "The Philosophy of Science in Relation to Concepts of Creation vs. the Evolution Theory." In *Why not Creation?*, edited by Walter Lammerts, 5–24. Grand Rapids, MI: Baker, 1970.

Kolbe, Maximilian. *Gli Scritti di Massimiliano Kolbe*. Florence: Città di vita, 1975–78.

———. *Roman Conferences of St. Maximilian M. Kolbe*. Translated by Peter Damian Fehlner. New Bedford: Academy of the Immaculate, 2004.

———. *The Writings of St. Maximilian Maria Kolbe*, 2 vols. Florence: Nerbini International, 2016.

Koźmiński, Honorat. *Święty Franciszek Seraficki: jego życie, wielkie dzieła, duch, dary, pisma i nauki i ich odbicie w naśladowcach jego*, vols. 1–3. Warsaw: Druk Piotra Laskauera i Spółki, 1901–5.

Lainati, Chiara Augusta. "Introduzione." In *Fonti Francescane*, 2211–40. Assisi: Movimento Francescano, 1977.

Lammerts, Walter, ed. *Why not Creation?* Grand Rapids, MI: Baker, 1970.

Lampen, Willibrord. "De S.P.N. Francisci cultu Angelorum et Sanctorum." *Archivum Franciscanum Historicum* 20 (1927) 3–23.

———. "S. Franciscus cultor sanctissimae Trinitatis." *Archivum Franciscanum Historicum* 21 (1928) 449–67.

Laurentin, René. *Dio mia tenerezza: Esperienza spirituale e mariana, attualità teologica di s. Luigi Maria da Montfort*. Rome: Edizioni Monfortane, 1985.

Leclercq, Jean. "Maria Christianorum Philosophia." *Melanges de Sciences Religieuses* 14 (1956) 103–6.

Lemaitre, Henri. *Saint Francois d'Assise: son oeuvre, son influence, 1226–1926*. Paris: E. Droz, 1927.

Leo XIII. *Divinum Illud Munus*. Acta Sanctae Sedis 29 (1896–97) 644–58.

Lépicier, Alexis Henri Marie. *Tractatus de Beatissima Virgine Maria Matre Dei*. Rome: Ex Officina Typographica, 1926.

Léthel, François-Marie. "Verità e Amore di Cristo nella teologia dei santi: L'orientamento teologico della Lettera Apostolica 'Novo Millennio Ineunte.'" *Pontificia Academia Theologica* 1 (2002/2) 281–314.

Longpré, Ephrem. "L'Assomption et L'Ecole Franciscaine." In *Vers le dogme de l'Assomption: journées d'études mariales, Montréal, 12–15 août, 1948*, 203–30. Montréal: Fides, 1948.

———. "La Sainte Vierge." *Revue de l'Université d'Ottawa* 36 (1966) 551–63.

———. "Saint François d'Assise," in the entry "Frères Mineurs." In *Dictionnaire de spiritualité ascétique et mystique, doctrine et histoire*, vol. 5, edited by Viller, Marcel, Charles et al., col. 1271–1303. Paris: Beauchesne, 1964.

Manteau-Bonamy, Henri-Marie. *La Doctrine mariale du père Kolbe: Esprit-Saint et Conception Immaculée*. Paris: P. Lethielleux Dessain et Tolra, 1975.

Maria e lo Spirito Santo. Atti del 4° Simposio Mariologico Internazionale (Roma, ottobre 1982). Rome: Marianum, 1984.

La Mariologia di S. Massimiliano Kolbe: Atti del Congresso Internazionale Roma, 8–12 ottobre 1984. Rome: Miscellanea Francescana, 1985.

Martinez, Pedro de Alcántara. "El culto a María según Conrado de Saxonia." In *De Cultu Mariano Saeculis XII–XV*, 583–603. Rome: Pontificia Academia Mariana Internationalis, 1980.

Mazzucco, Ippolito. "Note su arte e culto dell'Immacolata nella basilica romana dei Santi XII Apostoli." *Miles Immaculatae* 24 (1988) 178–88.

McCurry, James. "Homage to Fr. Peter Damian Fehlner." In *The Spirit and the Church: Peter Damian Fehlner's Development of Vatican II on the Themes of the Holy Spirit, Mary, and the Church: Festschrift*, xi–xv. Eugene: Pickwick, 2018.

———. "Maximilian Kolbe and the Franciscan Tradition." *The Cord* 33 (1983), 227–38.

McDonagh, Jarlath. "History and Background to the Constitutions, O.F.M. Conv." *Inter-Province Conference of the Order of Friars Minor Conventual* 27 (1976) np.

Merkelbach, Benedictus Henricus. *Mariologia: Tractatus de Beatissima Virgine Maria Matre Dei atque Deum inter et Homines Mediatrice*. Paris: Desclée, De Brouwer, 1939.

Miravalle, John-Mark L. "Mary and Divinization: Peter Damian Fehlner on Our Lady and the Holy Spirit." In *The Spirit and the Church: Peter Damian Fehlner's Development of Vatican II on the Themes of the Holy Spirit, Mary and the Church: Festschrift*, edited by J. Isaac Goff, Christiaan W. Kappes, and Edward J. Ondrako, 88–96. Eugene: Pickwick, 2018.

Miravalle, Mark. "In Continued Dialogue with the Czestachowa Commission." In *Mary at the Foot of the Cross III: Mater Unitatis—Acts of the International Symposium on Marian Coredemption*, 359–97. New Bedford: Academy of the Immaculate, 2003.

Molari, Carlo. "Riflessioni sul X congresso." *Rassegna di Teologia* 24 (1983) 552–55.

Molien, André. *Les Grandeurs de Marie d'aprés les Écrivains de l'École Française*. Paris: Desclée, De Brouwer, 1936.

Morris, Henry M. *Scientific Creationism*. San Diego: Creation Life Publishers, 1974.

Müller, Joseph. *De Sanctissima Dei Matre sive Mariologia*. Innsbruck, 1918.

Napiórkowski, Stanisław Celestyn. "Die Theologie Angesichts der Marienverehrung in Polen." *Collectanea Theologica* 53 (1983) 31–44.

———. "Esperienze delle persone e delle comunità cristiane come fonte di teologia." In *San Massimiliano Kolbe e la nuova evangelizzazione: atti del Congresso internazionale, Niepokalanów, Polonia, 19–25 settembre 1994*, 333–47. Rome: Centro Internazionale Milizia dell'Immacolata, 1999.

———. "Le mariologie et ses problèmes dans notre siècle." In *La Mariologia di S. Massimiliano Kolbe: Atti del Congresso Internazionale Roma, 8–12 ottobre 1984*, 564–75. Rome: Miscellanea Francescana, 1985.

Nicolas, Jean-Jacques Auguste. *La Vierge Marie et le Plan Divin: Nouvelles Études Philosophiques sur le Christianisme*, vol. 1. Paris: Poussielgue Frères, 1875.

Newman, John Henry. *An Essay on the Development of Christian Doctrine*. London: Longmans, Green, and Co., 1903.

———. "A Letter Addressed to the Rev. E. B. Pusey, D.D. On the Occasion of his Eirenicon of 1864." In *Certain Difficulties Felt by Anglicans in Catholic Teaching*, vol. 2, 1–170. London: Longmans, Green, and Co., 1900.

———. *Addresses to Cardinal Newman with His Replies, etc. 1879–81*. London: Longmans, Green, and Co., 1905.

———. *An Essay in Aid of a Grammar of Assent*. London: Longmans, Green and Co., 1903.

———. "The Glories of Mary for the Sake of Her Son." In *Discourses Addressed to Mixed Congregations*, 342–59. London: Longmans, Green, and Co., 1902.

O'Carroll, Michael. *Theotokos: A Theological Encyclopedia of the Blessed Virgin Mary*. Wilmington, DE: Glazier, 1983.

O'Connell, Patrick. *Original Sin in the Light of Modern Science*. Houston: Lumen Christi Press, 1973.

———. *Science of Today and the Problems of Genesis*. Hawthorne, CA: Christian Book Club of America, 1969.

Olier, Jean-Jacques. *Vie intérieure de la Très-Sainte Vierge: ouvrage recueilli des écrits de M. Olier*. Rome: Salviucci, 1866.

Omaecheverria, Ignacio. "El 'Espiritu' en la regla y vida de los hermanos menores." *Selecciones de Franciscanesimo* 3 (1974) 192–211.

Ondrako, Edward J., ed. *Newman-Scotus Reader: Contexts and Commonalities*. New Bedford: Academy of the Immaculate, 2015.

Pancheri, Francesco Saverio. "Cristocentrismo e pneumatologia nella marioiogia di San Massimiliano Kolbe." *Nuova Umanità* 7 (1985) 113–22.

———. "L'eredità Kolbiana e la vita dell'Ordine oggi." *Commentarium Ordinis Fratrum Minorum Conventualium* 83 (1986) 86–109.

———. "Nuances et Problèmes." *La Mission de l'Immaculée* 72 (March 1985) 3–5.

———. "S. Massimiliano Kolbe e il Francescanesimo." *Miles Immaculatae* 18 (1982) 131–55.

Philippe, Marie-Dominique. "Il Mistero dello Spirito Santo e di Maria secondo il Padre Kolbe." *Miles Immaculatae* 18 (1982) 37–59.

Piacentini, Ernesto. "Analisi degli scritti di p. Kolbe e loro valorizzazione teologica." *Miscellanea Francescana* 85 (1985) 327–81.

———. *Dottrina mariologica del P. Massimiliano Kolbe: Ricostruzione e valutazione critico-comparativa con la mariologia prima e dopo il Vaticano II.* Rome: Herder, 1971.

Plessis, Armand. *Manuale Mariologiae Dogmaticae.* Pontchateau: Librairie mariale, 1942.

Poiré, François. *La triple couronne de la bienheureuse Vierge Mère de Dieu.* Tournai: Casterman, 1849.

Pompei, Alfonso. "Maria, Madonna, Madre, Immacolata." In *Dizionario Francescano*, edited by Ernesto Caroli, coll. 931–52. Padua: Edizioni Messsaggero, 1983.

Poulenc, Jérôme. "Conformità." In *Dizionario Francescano*, edited by Ernesto Caroli, coll. 219–26. Padua: Edizioni Messsaggero, 1983.

Pyfferoen, Hilarius. "Ave . . . Dei Genetrix Maria. 'Quae es Virgo Ecclesia Facta (S. Francisci).'" *Laurentianum* 12 (1971) 412–34.

———. "Fuditne S. Franciscus suas duas preces mariales ad S. Mariam de Angelis ad Portiunculam?" *Laurentianum* 11 (1970) 267–307.

———. "S. Maria de Angelis ad Portiunculam." *Laurentianum* 10 (1969) 329–52.

Pyfferoen, Hilarius, and Optatus van Asseldonk. "Maria Santissima e lo Spirito Santo in S. Francesco d'Assisi." In *De Cultu Mariano Saeculis XII–XV*, 413–45. Rome: Pontificia Academia Mariana Internationalis, 1980.

Ragazzini, Severino. *La Spiritualità Mariana di S. Massimiliano Maria Kolbe dei Frati Minori Conventuali.* Ravenna: Centro Dantesco, 1982.

———. *Maria, Vita dell'Anima. Itinerario Mariano alla SS. Trinità.* 2nd ed. Frigento, Italy: Casa Mariana Maria SS. del Buon Consiglio, 1984.

Ratzinger, Josef. *Die Geschichtstheologie des heiligen Bonaventura.* Munich: Schnell and Steiner, 1959. English translation: *The Theology of History in St. Bonaventure*, trans. Zachary Hayes. Chicago: Franciscan Herald Press, 1971.

———. *The Ratzinger Report: An Exclusive Interview on the State of the Church.* San Francisco: Ignatius, 1985.

Rezette, Jean-Pierre. "Similitudo." In *Lexique Saint Bonaventure*, edited by Jacques-Guy Bougerol, 119. Paris: Editions Franciscaines, 1969.

Rivellini, Bernardino. "Elementi di pietà mariana in San Francesco nella 'Legenda Maior' di S. Bonaventura." *Incontri Bonaventuriani* 1 (1965) 97–110.

Rivera de Ventosa, Enrique (Feliciano). "La devoción a María en la espiritualidad de San Francisco. Fundamentación dogmática." *Estudios Franciscanos* 62 (1961) 249–74; 63 (1962) 5–21; 277–96.

Roschini, Gabriele Maria. *Il Tuttosanto e la Tuttasanta: Relazioni tra Maria SS. e lo Spirito Santo.* Rome: Edizioni "Marianum," 1976–7.

———. *Mariologia. Tome 2, 1: Summa mariologiae. De beate Maria Virgine considerata in sua singulari missione.* Rome: Belardetti, 1947.

Rossi, Filippo. *L'Immacolata Concezione di Maria e i Francescani Minori Conventuali dal 1210 al 1854: cenni vari per un sacerdote umbro.* Rome: Salviucci, 1854.

San Massimiliano Kolbe e la nuova evangelizzazione: atti del Congresso internazionale, Niepokalanów, Polonia, 19–25 settembre 1994. Rome: Centro Internazionale Milizia dell'Immacolata, 1999.

Scarfia, Gabriel. "The Role of the Church's Faith within the Sacramental Theology of Bonaventure." *Franciscan Studies* 39 (1979) 206–29.

Scheeben, Matthias Joseph. *Mariology*. St. Louis: Herder, 1946–48.

Schmucki, Octavian. "De Seraphici Patris Francisci habitudine erga beatissima Virginem Mariam." In *Regina Immaculata: Studia a sodalibus capuccinis scripta occasione primi centenarii a proclamatione dogmatica immaculatae conceptionis B.M.V.*, edited by Melchior a Pobladura, O.F.M. Cap., 15–47. Rome: Institutum historicum Ordinis Fratrum minorum capuccinorum, 1955.

———. "Franziskus von Assisi erfährt die Kirche in seiner Brüderschaft." *Franziskanische Studien* 58 (1976) 1–26.

———. *Linee Fondamentali della "Forma Vitae" nell'esperienza di San Francesco: Lettura Biblico-teologica delle fonti francescane*. Rome: Pontificium Athenaeum Antonianum, 1979.

Scneider, Johannes. *Virgo Ecclesia Facta: The Presence of Mary in the Crucifix of San Damiano and in the* Office of the Passion *of St. Francis of Assisi*. Translated by Peter Damian Fehlner. New Bedford, Academy of the Immaculate, 2004.

Scordato, Cosimo. "Il X Congresso." *Rassegna di Teologia* 24 (1983) 546–52.

Sparacio, Domenico. *Frammenti Bibliografici di Scrittori ed Autori Minori Conventuali dagli ultimi anni del 600 al 1930*. Assisi: Casa Editrice Francescana Assisi, 1931.

Swiecicki, Jozef Marian. "Prospettive Mariologiche del Beato Massimiliano Kolbe." *Miles Immaculatae* 15 (1979) 315–27.

Szabó, Tito. "Chiesa." In *Dizionario Francescano*, edited by Ernesto Caroli, coll. 185–218. Padua: Edizioni Messsaggero, 1983.

Teetaert a Zedelgem, Amadeus. Review of *Maria nel culto cattolico*, by Emilio Campana. *Collectanea Franciscana* 6 (1936) 298–99.

Terrien, Jean-Baptiste. *La Mère de Dieu et la Mère des hommes d'après les Pères et la théologie*. Premier partie: *La Mère de Dieu*. Paris: Lethielleux, 1900.

Testa, Emmanuele. *Maria Terra Vergine*, vol. 1, book 5. Jerusalem: Franciscan Printing Press, 1985.

Thomas Aquinas. *Summa Theologiae*. Opera Omnia. Vols. 4–12. Rome: Typographia Polyglotta S.C. de Propaganda Fide, 1888–1903.

van Asseldonk, Optatus. "De Traditione Vitae Orationis in Ordine Nostro." *Analecta Capuccinorum* 89 (1973) 55–87.

———. "Maria Sposa dello Spirito Santo, secondo S. Francesco d'Assisi." *Laurentanium* 23 (1982) 414–23.

———. "Madre." In *Dizionario Francescano*, edited by Ernesto Caroli, coll. 1707–38. Padua: Edizioni Messaggero, 1983.

———. "Spirito Santo." In *Dizionario Francescano*, edited by Ernesto Caroli, coll. 919–30. Padua: Edizioni Messsaggero, 1983.

van Corstanje, Auspicius. "Dit zeg ik je als Moeder." *Franciscus van Assisi* 14 (1977) 162–80.

van Dijk, Stephen J. P. *Sources of the Modern Roman Liturgy*. 2 volumes. Leiden: Brill, 1963.

Villepelée, Jean-François, et al. *La Milizia dell'Immacolata*. Rome: Centro Internazionale M.I., 1982.

Wittkemper, Karl. "Dreifaltigkeit. I. Dogmatik." In *Lexikon der Marienkunde*, edited by Konrad Algermissen, et. al., vol. 7, coll. 1444–53. Regensburg: Verlag Friedrich Pustet, 1967.

Woodward. Kenneth. *Making Saints: How the Catholic Church Determines Who Becomes a Saint, Who Doesn't, and Why*. New York: Simon and Schuster, 1990.

Index

Printed in Great Britain
by Amazon

32059805R00215